Pan's Script

Pan's Script

Astronumerology

ELKIE WHITE

BALBOA
PRESS

A DIVISION OF HAY HOUSE

Balboa Press books may be ordered through booksellers or by contacting:

Balboa Press
A Division of Hay House
1663 Liberty Drive
Bloomington, IN 47403
www.balboapress.com.au
1 (877) 407-4847

ISBN: 978-1-4525-2904-2 (sc)
ISBN: 978-1-4525-2905-9 (e)

Print information available on the last page.

Balboa Press rev. date: 09/21/2017

Dedication

This book is dedicated to everyone who cherishes life and who wants to understand.

Contents

How to calculate your date path and interpret the significance of your date of birth
- why it's called the date path
- a 2-part process for calculating the date path to minimize errors
- the distinction between the primary, secondary, tertiary, heart, and quintessential date path
- how to interpret a number that is missing in a run of date paths
- the echo effect: beyond the highest date path
- numbers zero to 71
- ways to apply each number in your daily life
- people who exemplify the first twelve date paths

Understanding vowels and consonants: their difference and respective meanings

Part A: The Vowel Number
- the significance of the vowel number
- how to calculate the vowel number
- the table of correspondences
- example: P!nk
- interpreting the vowel numbers as inherent qualities of the soul
- vowel numbers 1-12, plus 22

Part B: The Consonant Number
- ♦ the distinction between vowels and consonants
- ♦ how to calculate the consonant number
- ♦ interpreting the consonant numbers as modes of survival
- ♦ consonant numbers 1-12, plus 22
- ♦ vowel-consonant combinations: a guide to your inner resources

Vowels 1-9 with consonants 1-9 plus 11

Vowel 11 with consonants 1-9 plus 11

Vowel 22 with consonants 1-9 plus 11

With over 300 examples of successful people

The significance of your name and its components: the power behind your ideals
- ♦ interpreting the name number as the driving force behind the date path
- ♦ how to calculate the name number
- ♦ name numbers 1-12, plus master numbers 11 - 99 with examples
- ♦ the leading letter of your name
- ♦ the key to your inner growth and development
- ♦ the name table
- ♦ the intensity number

Opening acts on the stage of life: using your birthday number to make headway in daily life
- ♦ how the birthday number differs from the other core numbers
- ♦ an overview of the birthday numbers
- ♦ the birthday numbers in greater detail with examples

Birthday-date path combinations:

Birthday numbers 1-9 with date paths 1- 9 plus 11 and 22

Birthday number 11 with date paths 1- 9

Birthday number 22 with date paths 1 – 9

When the master numbers double up: birthdays 11 and 22 with date paths 11, 22, 33, 44 and 55

Including over 800 examples of successful people
- ♦ the core numbers and a handy summary of their spheres of influence
- ♦ relationships

Understanding your true personality
- ♦ the maturity number as an indicator of your authentic personality
- ♦ how to calculate your maturity number
- ♦ interpreting the maturity number
- ♦ the twelve archetypal patterns
- ♦ numbers 72 to 180 as archetypal personalities, with examples

Types of intelligence
- ♦ the concept of multiple intelligences: people are intelligent in different ways
- ♦ the Pythagorean cross and the date chart: the geometry of your date of birth
- ♦ introversion and extraversion
- ♦ Clusterings of numbers and types of intelligence chart
- ♦ the 3 vertical bands:
- - 1, 2, 3: linguistic intelligence
- - 4, 5, 6: kinesthetic intelligence
- - 7, 8, 9: logical-mathematical intelligence
- ♦ the 3 horizontal bands:
- - 1-4-7: survival intelligence
- - 2-5-8: interpersonal or people intelligence
- - 3-6-9: spatial intelligence
- ♦ the 2 diagonal bands:
- - 1, 5, 9: self-intelligence (worldly)
- - 3, 5, 7: self-intelligence (cultural)
- ♦ the 8 introverted bands: missing clusters
- - missing 1, 2, 3: linguistic intelligence (introverted)
- - missing 4, 5, 6: kinesthetic intelligence (introverted)
- - missing 7, 8, 9: logical-mathematical intelligence (introverted)
- - missing 1-4-7: survival intelligence (introverted)
- - missing 2-5-8: interpersonal intelligence (introverted)
- - missing 3-6-9: spatial intelligence (introverted)
- - missing 1, 5, 9: self-intelligence (introverted/other worldly)
- - missing 3, 5, 7: self-intelligence (introverted/existential)
- ♦ unlined charts
- ♦ multiple examples throughout
- ♦ interpreting number by number
- ♦ concluding comments

Identifying the forces that are shaping your life
- ♦ how to calculate your challenges:
- - subtraction reveals the challenge-pattern
- - the 4 challenges in the date path: 1st, 2nd, whole life and polarity
- - challenges great and small
- - timing the date path challenges
- - the 3 challenges within your name
- - locating missing numbers by comparing the date chart with the name chart

- ◆ karmic challenges as collective issues
- ◆ repeated numbers as representing an energy crisis, with examples
- ◆ prioritizing the challenges
- ◆ interpreting the challenges:
- - interpreting the karmic challenges: a clue from the date chart
- - interpreting the challenge of repeated core numbers
- - challenging master numbers
- - interpreting the whole life challenge: 0 – 9, with examples
- - interpreting the polarity challenge: 0 - 9
- - interpreting the challenge of missing numbers: 1 – 9 with examples
- - a run of missing numbers with an example
- - challenged core numbers
- - interpreting the vowel, consonant and name challenges: 0 - 9 with examples
- ◆ every step in action: Jeannette Walls

How to set out your base and attainment cycles and interpret them
- ◆ a structure for understanding the unfoldment of your life story
- ◆ calculating the attainments
- ◆ example: Daniel Radcliffe
- ◆ the life cycles: first base, birthday base, home base
- ◆ timing the bases
- ◆ timing the attainments
- ◆ interpreting bases and attainments 1 - 9
- ◆ first bases 10, 11, and 12

How to calculate and interpret your personal years
- ◆ A model, a metaphor, and personal experience
- ◆ calculating your personal year cycle:
- - the importance of the world year
- - the significance of your achievement number
- ◆ interpreting the personal years
- ◆ one year at a time: personal years 1- 9 including research findings

Correlating numerology and astrology
- ◆ placing the personal years into the wheel of the zodiac
- ◆ the signs of the zodiac and their rulers
- ◆ colouring the wheel
- ◆ how the planets and the signs of the zodiac interact with the personal years

A diagram of the personal years within the wheel of the zodiac
- ◆ potent partnerships
- ◆ the days of the week
- ◆ the undulation of yin and yang
- ◆ the astrological houses
- ◆ the age cycle
- ◆ the phases of the moon
- ◆ the progressed lunation cycle
- ◆ archetypal space-time reality
- ◆ the counter-clockwise seasonal cycle
- ◆ combining the solar and lunar influences on the cycle

Your first name, as it cycles through your life
- ◆ the complementary nature of the personal years and the growth cycle
- ◆ calculating the growth cycle
- ◆ interpreting the letters as a part of a progressive cycle
- ◆ the a-z of personal growth and development
- ◆ the personal years and the growth cycle in action: example: Richard Branson

Uniting your numbers and your horoscope
- ◆ how to calculate your astro-number signature
- ◆ checklist
- ◆ elemental composition and dominant modality
- ◆ the formula
- ◆ when there are multiple signatures
- ◆ a description of each astro-number signature from Aries-1 to Pisces-12
- ◆ twin signatures
- ◆ career profiles
- ◆ about wealth
- ◆ LGBTQ: the findings
- ◆ The New Millennium Children
- ◆ Dementia: a preliminary study

Acknowledgements

To esteemed numerologists, past and present, thank you. This work builds on yours. I may not agree with you on every point but in many cases your work catalysed the inspiration that created this book. I have analyzed your work carefully, trialled your various systems and documented my findings. My aim is to add to the body of knowledge that we have on this vital subject and my prayer is that it be truthful.

I also thank the friends and family members whose belief in me held firm throughout the lengthy process of bringing this book to birth. Your positive thoughts kept the wheels turning. To my husband I owe special thanks for his love and support.

Integrated into all of the above, I thank the Guiding Light that taught me as we went along. May that Self-Same Spirit continue to inspire every reader!

To understand the Numbers is to understand Life

Preface

The reason for writing this book could not have been simpler: to allow the numbers to speak for themselves. And speak they did but oh how difficult it was to stay out of their way! Only gradually did the personal give way to the universal, but when it did the numbers revealed an evolutionary current operating behind all aspects of life. I would come to realize that to understand the Numbers is to understand life itself.

From start to finish I wanted a beginner to the subject be able to read and comprehend it, yet I also wanted to contribute to the body of knowledge already available in this subject. In 1999 I had been studying numerology for eleven years yet vital questions remained unanswered. Why the chasm between the Chaldean and Pythagorean systems of numerology - they must surely have come from a common source? And they both seemed to work in their own way. The intriguing thing was that *all* of the systems proposed by numerologists worked to some degree. Why? Why is it that numerology works at all? And how do the various facets of it knit together? There was no book that adequately answered these questions, and so I sat down and began writing and observing, meditating and modifying until some preliminary answers emerged. The first draft was a whirl of inspiration, the second stabilized the theoretical base that had formulated through a steady process of research and insight, and the third integrated the case studies. Through these I could see how the Numbers were actually influencing people and I adjusted my words accordingly. The hypothesis was providing the framework while real people fleshed it out. Beyond this stage the formulae emerged and the theoretical structure gained strength. The initial process took seven years and birthed a system both ancient and modern: a timeless, precise, ingenious, universal script.

Apart from my stipulation that a beginner should be able to start working with the ideas presented, I was also determined that I was not going to touch astrology! It was not that I did not like astrology. On the contrary, it was because I had so much respect for this ancient science that I felt that it should be left to the experts, those who have studied it for at least a couple of decades. Yet I was equally determined to let the book lead me. Therefore when what I came to know as *Pan's Script* was revealed to me, I had no choice but to begin an intensive study of astrology in order to comprehend it. I was naturally delighted to find that whichever way I turned the model held firm. I soon realized that astrology and numerology are interdependent, and that one is not complete without the other. However it was not until the manuscript was in its third year of writing that the Astro was added to Numerology. By the end of the fourth year, I realized that these two are actually conjoined twins. United within every vital organ of the universal body, astrology and numerology are two facets of one science.

The time has come for such science to be recognized and reinstated as an academic study. After a fallow period of four centuries, astrology is gradually returning to our universities. A scholarly approach to the ancient texts is now available and accredited. The model of astronumerology advanced in this book represents the child of this ancient parent, a child that had to wait for its time. The model here presented is thus based on mathematics known to the builders of the pyramid yet with equal precision, tailored to our current world context.

They may be twins but it should not be assumed that numerology and astrology are identical. One of the errors that I became aware of as I did the research for this book was that of interpreting numerology as if it were astrology. Adding astrology to my studies forced me to address the question: 'What is the difference between an astrology reading and a reading of the numbers?' Borrowing a traditional way of categorizing planetary expressions, I realized that the numbers are 'dignified' in the conceptual realm. In other words, the world of concepts is their natural place of abode. Furthermore, the numbers are 'exalted' in the symbolic realm, which means that they are at their best when an interpretation of them includes their existential, philosophical and mystical implications. The numbers are in 'detriment' in the astral realm because that is where one could be tempted to interpret them as if they were sun signs. And finally, the numbers are in their 'fall' in the physical realm where they are sublimated to material concerns. Because of the insight that the study of astrology has given me, I am now certain that the numbers encode prototypes and should be interpreted as such. The emotive expressions that we occasionally witness are actually coming from the astral realm and the way that individuals react to their life's circumstances. The numbers themselves are not emotional or reactive. Indeed the reason why they are vital in the quest for truth is because of their constancy.

The following analogy may help to clarify the above. If we think of a number as a geometric form, such as a tetrahedron, and we place this pure crystalline form into a pure, transparent glass and add pure, transparent water, we would see it for what it actually is. Then if we were to colour the water blue, it would *appear* that the tetrahedron is blue, but in fact it is not. Despite the colour of the water, it remains a transparent, crystalline form. The water is akin to the astral realm and describing the condition of the water is the task of astrology. Furthermore, if we were to also alter the glass holding the water, the geometric form might appear to change as well. If the water represents the astral body then the container represents the physical body, in which the pristine geometric form is housed. The numbers cannot be other than what they are - ideal forms – however their vibration does impact on the astral and physical membranes. And that's the key to interpretation: we must firstly gauge the influence of each Number, and then we can consider the likely effect on the astral body, as reflected in the horoscope, and the physical body, as registered on the palms of the hands. This is PAN's Script: Palmistry, Astrology and Numerology. You won't find any palmistry in this book but what you will find is a detailed account of numerology and the building blocks of astrology united as a single study.

Pan also refers to the Greek god of nature. This 'Pan' dwells in the liminal place between light and dark, where 'he' regulates the harmony of the spheres through 'his' syrinx. Pan as a prefix to words such as panorama and Pangaea, means 'All'.

Pan is also an old Chinese word. Spelled P'an, it is the first part of the word P'an-Ku, a Taoist Creation Being, who chiselled the world from the rocks of eternity. Similar to the Nordic Giant Ymir, and the Babylonian Tiamat, P'an-Ku's bones transformed into rocks, flesh into earth, marrow, teeth and nails into metals, hair into herbs, veins into rivers, and breath into wind. The four limbs of P'an-Ku became pillars that marked the four corners of the world. And so the concept of Pan belongs to several of our most ancient cultures. With its multiple layers of meaning, the title of this book symbolizes the subtle, sacred dance between the ordinary and the extra-ordinary, the spirit of nature and the quest to comprehend the nature of spirit.

What is distinct about *Pan's Script* is its comprehensiveness: it is a complete system. Even the chapters follow the basic paradigm, each one reflecting the theme of its number. To a numerologist the headings will look familiar, but don't be deceived, the slight changes are not cosmetic. Similar words and formats are used to avoid unnecessary complexity but *Pan's Script* knits into the framework that practitioners are already familiar with, a whole new perspective; one that is consistent across three disciplines. Much that has previously been confused has been unravelled and rewoven, providing astronumerology with a distinct set of definitions and methodology.

You will find that *Pan's Script* provides a theoretical framework upon which you can base your own research projects however personal or impersonal these may be. Whether you want to understand what makes someone tick or how the world evolves, it will support your efforts. You will learn a lot about yourself as you progress through the chapters of this book and the learning will continue long after you complete them. Please read the book as it was written – joyfully and organically – it was such a pleasure to write! If you keep an open mind and heart, the numbers will speak to you as they did to me, and then you will see for yourself that they encode the entire order of existence.

E. W. Summer 2014

A Musical Instrument

By Elizabeth Barrett Browning (1860) with one slight but significant change in the final verse *

1.
What was he doing, the great god Pan?
Down in the reeds by the river?
Spreading ruin and scattering ban,
Splashing and paddling with hoofs of a goat,
And breaking the golden lilies afloat
With the dragon-fly on the river.

2.
He tore out a reed, the great god Pan,
From the deep cool bed of the river:
The limpid water turbidly ran,
And the broken lilies a-dying lay,
And the dragon-fly had fled away,
Ere he brought it out of the river.

3.

High on the shore sat the great god Pan
While turbidly flowed the river;
And hacked and hewed as a great god can,
With his hard bleak steel at the patient reed,
Till there was not a sign of the leaf indeed
To prove it fresh from the river.

4.

He cut it short, did the great god Pan,
(How tall it stood in the river!)
Then drew the pith, like the heart of a man,
Steadily from the outside ring,
And notched the poor dry empty thing
In holes, as he sat by the river.

5.

'This is the way', laughed the great god Pan
(Laughed while he sat by the river),
'The only way, since gods began
To make sweet music, they could succeed'.
Then, dropping his mouth to a hole in the reed,
He blew in power by the river.

6.

Sweet, sweet, sweet, O Pan!
Piercing sweet by the river!
Blinding sweet, O great god Pan!
The sun on the hill forgot to die,
And the lilies revived, and the dragon-fly
Came back to dream on the river.

7.

Yet half a beast is the great god Pan,
To laugh as he sits by the river,
Making a poet out of a man:
Creation* sighs for the cost and pain,
For the reed which grows nevermore again
As a reed with the reeds in the river.

Chapter 1

The Date Path

The date path encodes what you had in mind to work on when you incarnated. This set of numbers specifies the ideals that you strive to realize (subconsciously perhaps). As such, they weave their way through your life as reoccurring themes. Consequently you can never feel totally at peace until their calling has been responded to. Conversely, when you commit to them, you sense being subtly supported. This is because the soul already resonates with this pattern of ideals. To understand your date path you must appreciate that it is mental in nature, and therefore your attitude to it is the key to your success in making it happen. Unlike the life path and birth path written about by other numerologists, the date path acknowledges the *full* potential encoded in the date of birth.

How to Calculate

To calculate the date path number, write out the date of birth in full placing the month first. The months of the year are assigned their sequential numbers: January = 1, February = 2, March = 3, April = 4, May = 5, June = 6, July = 7, August = 8, September = 9, October = 10, November = 11, December = 12.

If you were born on January 1, 2000, you would calculate your date path thus:

January 1 2000
= 1. 1. 2 = 4. This is the horizontal method of calculation. The vertical method follows:

January = 1
$\quad$ 1 = 1
$\quad$ 2000
$\quad$ 2002 = 4. There is no other possibility.

However, if you were born on January 10, 2000, your horizontal calculation would show:

January 10 2000
= 1. 10. 2 = 13 (the highest possible number; this will spearhead the other ideals)
=1. 1. 2 = 4 (i.e., 1 +1 + 0 + 2 + 0 + 0 + 0 = each single number of the date added together)

The primary date path is still 4, but we now have a secondary date path: 13.

Vertically:

January = 1
    10 = 10
      2000
      2011 = 4

Continuing the sequence, if you were born on January 19, 2000, your horizontal calculation would specify three variations:

January 19 2000
= 1. 19. 2 = 22 (the highest possible number, spearheading the other ideals)
= 1. 10. 2 = 13 (i.e., 1 +1 + 9 + 2 + 0 + 0 + 0 = each single number of the date added together)
= 1. 1. 2 = 4 (i.e., each number reduced to its lowest digit)

Vertically:

January = 1
    19 = 19
    2000
    2020 = 4

The primary date path is 4, the secondary is 13, and the tertiary date path is 22. By running across horizontally and then down vertically, the calculations can be checked and all of the potentials revealed.

Returning to the above sequence of examples:

January 28, 2000
= 1. 28. 2 = 31 (the highest possible number, spearheading the other ideals)
= 1. 10. 2 = 13 (i.e., 1 +2 + 8 + 2 + 0 + 0 + 0 = each single number of the date added together)
= 1. 1. 2 = 4 (each number reduced to its lowest digit)

Vertically:

January = 1
     = 28
    2000
    2029 = 13; and 1 + 3 = 4.

The primary date path is 4; the secondary is 13, but the tertiary date path is now 31.

Turning back the clock to 1999 reveals a remarkably different set of numbers:

December 31 1999
= 12. 31. 28 = 71 (the highest possible number, spearheading the other ideals)

= 3. 4. 28 = 35 (i.e., 1 +2 + 3 + 1 + 9 + 9 + 9 = each single number of the date added together)
= 3. 4. 1 = 8 (each number reduced to its lowest digit)

Vertically:

December = 12
　　　　= 31
　　　　1999
　　　　2042 = 8

The primary date path is 8, the secondary is 35, and the tertiary is 71.

Finally an example that reveals all possible gradations of the Date Path:

August 17 1963
= 8. 17. 19 = 44 (the highest possible number, spearheading the other ideals)
= 8. 8. 19 = 35 (i.e., 8 +1 + 7 + 1 + 9 + 6 + 3 = each digit in the date added together)
= 8. 8. 1 = 17 (each number reduced to its lowest digit)

And 1 + 7 = 8

Vertically:

August = 8
　　　　17
　　　　1963
　　　　1988 = 26; and 2 + 6 = 8.

The primary date path is 8, the secondary is 17, and the tertiary is 26 (revealed only via the vertical method); 35 is the heart date path and 44 is the quintessential. The order is precise and significant.

Calculation Summary:

1. Calculate the highest possible number.
2. Add each single digit in the date.
3. Reduce each number to its lowest digit and then add them all together.
4. Calculate vertically.
5. If necessary, reduce to the primary date path.

Interpreting the primary, secondary, tertiary, heart, and quintessential date paths:

Primary Date Path: The primary date path is the most reduced form of the number. This single digit delineates the broad band within which the variations of the date path lie. It represents the ideal that inspired your life in the broadest possible way, and it will be apparent in every aspect of your life.

Secondary Date Path: This number specifies the ego's task in bringing the ideal of the primary date path into being.

Tertiary Date Path: This number symbolizes the contribution that your personality will make to the fulfillment of your primary date path. This is generally a social ideal that can be readily expressed and shared with others.

Heart Date Path: This ideal can take the form of a heartfelt specialization. It is the ideal that is most likely to become a subconscious habit in your life.

Quintessential Date Path: Few people have one of these, and it seldom becomes relevant until the senior years for those who do. It may then become the spiritual epicentre of your life.

Latent Potential

Because much of our potential is dormant, you may initially find it difficult to recognize all of your date path numbers. People claim the power and responsibility of each date path at exactly the time that is right for them. The primary date path is the most familiar and definitely the one you should become acquainted with first. Once the broad band of vibration that is influencing your psyche is understood, the ego's task encoded in the secondary date path can be more easily grasped. All numerologists acknowledge the primary date path although by different names. Several accept the other numbers as a background influence or specific mission, up to a point. However, the claim made in *Pan's Script* is that the highest possible number can become the most significant in your life, as you become more interested in exploring your potential. None-the-less, it is an error to think of the date paths as increments in terms of spiritual ascendance. Rather, as the numbers become increasingly complex, think of progressive layers of depth.

Missing Date Paths

You will notice that in the fourth example above, one of the date path numbers did not turn up in the calculation. January 28 2000: The primary date path is 4 and the secondary is 13, but the tertiary date path is 31 (not 22). When they are all present, the number 4 series of date paths runs like this: 4, 13 (1 + 3 = 4), 22 (2 + 2 = 4), 31 (3 + 1 = 4), etc. In this case, number 22 has not turned up in the calculation. When interpreting what this might mean, you need to first be aware that the number is not really missing. The date paths can be thought of as the circular rings that result when a stone is dropped gently into a lake; there are no missing rings. Every number is present on the mental plane of existence, but some are more directly accessible than others. When a date path does not turn up in the calculation, it is significant because it tells us that one or more components of the series is less accessible than the others and that we must adopt a certain attitude in order to draw out its potential. Think of the calculable impulses as rippling across the surface of the conscious mind, whilst the ones that do not appear in the calculations bubble away in the subconscious. When a date path is 'missing,' the link it provides from the one before it to the one after it is below conscious awareness (until, maybe, later in life). In the case of our example, the ideal symbolized by number 22 may be difficult for the person to get his or her head around.

Number Sequences:

1, 10, 19, 28, 37, 46, 55, 64
2, 11, 20, 29, 38, 47, 56, 65
3, 12, 21, 30, 39, 48, 57, 66
4, 13, 22, 31, 40, 49, 58, 67
5, 14, 23, 32, 41, 50, 59, 68
6, 15, 24, 33, 42, 51, 60, 69
7, 16, 25, 34, 43, 52, 61, 70
8, 17, 26, 35, 44, 53, 62, 71
9, 18, 27, 36, 45, 54, 63, 72

Echo Effect

Occasionally, all of the numbers are missing except the primary date path. The first calculation example demonstrated this: a person born on January 1, 2000 has only primary date path 4; no secondary, tertiary, heart, or quintessential date path. What does this mean for them? Similar to missing date paths, explained above, the full sequence is there but subconscious. It may be only with hindsight that a person can see the impact of these numbers on his or her life. They then become very important to that person.

The remainder of this chapter is devoted to an explanation of the numbers from zero to seventy-one, including some examples.

Zero

Zero is the abode of all possible realities; it perpetually anticipates birth from within itself. It is unscientific to think of zero as 'empty' because modern physicists have discovered that space is actually teaming with life. In like manner, zero represents the phenomenal ability to suddenly materialize and equally as suddenly, to dematerialize. As the poet, Thomas Traherne, put it: *"No brims nor borders in my self I see, / My essence is Capacity"*

Primary Date Path Number One

Power of Self

From the place of apparent chaos where all things begin, number 1 gives 'potential' a focal point. Think of the digit as a shaft of light and you are close to understanding number 1.

An example of a person with primary date path 1 is Maya Angelou. Famous for her pioneering work in the autobiographical genre, she was born on April 4, 1928.

April 4 1928
4. 4. 20 = 28 (the highest possible number)
4 + 4 + 1 + 9 + 2 + 8 = 28 (each single number of the date added together in this case revealing the same Number as the highest date path)
4. 4. 2 = 10 (each number reduced to its lowest digit)

Vertically:

April = 4
      4
<u>1928</u>
<u>1936</u> = 19 = 10 = 1

The primary date path is 1, the secondary is 10, the tertiary is 19, and the heart date path is 28.

What Maya had in common with other number 1's was self-determination. She was a versatile writer but the genre that most clearly reflects number 1 is autobiography. Over a period of forty-four years and in seven books, she wrote about herself and her life, and by so doing she set a precedent for others. She once said that all of her work was about survival and not just raw survival but surviving with grace: "While one may encounter many defeats, one must not be defeated." The emphasis on survival and the creed to never be defeated is pure number 1. Maya's life is legendary and her son described her as a 'warrior for equality, tolerance and peace'. And 'warrior' is number 1's archetype. Willpower, self-determination, seminal works, courage, and strong sense of personal identity, define primary date path 1.

Having number 1 as your primary date path means becoming aware of what you can offer that no-one else can. To fully appreciate the value of your number 1, you need to grasp the difference between the ego and the Ego. The Ego is the unique expression of the individual soul: a spark of the creative consciousness. It grants us the ability to know ourselves and consequently, to know others. Through the Ego we can trust our activity in the world as being aligned with the common good. However when the ego assumes an existence independent of the soul it develops a casement around itself, which obstructs the natural flow of energy from the source. Whenever you are unsure of whether your activity is based on the ego or the Ego, there is a simple question that you can ask: "Upon what intention do I base my actions?" Once the issue of motivation is placed on higher ground, effective action soon follows.

Primary Date Path Number Two

Power of Duality

As number 1 symbolizes the spark within the seed that catalyzes a new life, so number 2 provides the environment that the seed needs for growth. Number 2 represents the energy that receives, retains, and embraces, which means that people with date path number 2 are highly impressionable.

An example of a person with primary date path 2 is Belinda Giblin. Born on March 2, 1950, she has been selected because she had not only primary date path 2 but also birthday 2 and a name that begins with the second letter of the alphabet: a rare find. She should therefore provide us with a clear example of the number.

March 2 1950

3. 2. 15 = 20 (the highest possible number)
3 + 2 + 1 + 9 + 5 + 0 = 20 (each single number of the date added together)

3. 2. 6 = 11 (each number reduced to its lowest digit)

Vertically:

March = 3

$$\begin{array}{l} 3 \\ 2 \\ \underline{1950} \\ \underline{1955} = 20 = 2 \end{array}$$

The primary date path is 2, the secondary is 11, and the tertiary is 20.

While number 1 represents knowing yourself through your actions on your environment, in number 2 people learn about themselves by comparing and contrasting themselves with another person. In the case of acting they actually become someone else for a while and whilst not necessarily making acting their profession, most people with '2' in their numbers experiment with being someone else at some time; occasionally losing sight of their personal identity altogether. As well as actor, teacher, director and producer, Belinda exemplifies date path 2 as a freelance contractor. She provides training in role-play, coaching, negotiation, facilitation, mentoring, interviewing and partnering and each of those words belong in the realm of number 2.

Duality is fundamental to understanding number 2 - life is based on it – especially the duality of male and female. Duality, or being in two minds about things, can lead to indecision and projection. Intense likes and dislikes come with number 2, yet its qualities include tact and diplomacy to offset this.

In tandem with the concept of duality, choice is a core aspect of 2 and it is your choice as to how you will react to other people. You can take your pick from opponent, assistant, and companion, all of which accompany number 2. You could also learn how to become an exceptional team-player and a bridge between worlds.

It is vital for all of us to understand Number 2 because we live in a millennium that is fronted by that number. It is the nature of number 2 to polarize and we could therefore see the division between men and women, rich and poor, widening. Number 2 also stands for the principles of co-creation, co-operation and interdependence. Let us hope these latter qualities prevail!

Primary Date Path Number Three

Power of Image

Wherever it appears, number 3 encourages us to enjoy the creative process of which we are all a part. Being the third, this millennium will be strongly influenced by number 3, especially during the twenty-first century. This is already evident in the explosion of fast communication systems such as mobile phones, the internet, email and e-commerce. Numbers 1, 2, and 3 constitute the essential trinity of father, mother and child, which have been clothed in many guises. '3' invigorates the powers in the mind that give shape to imaginings.

Born on September 26, 1948, Olivia Newton-John provides a perfect example of date path 3.

September 26 1948

9. 26. 22 = 57 (the highest possible number)
9 + 2 + 6 + 1 + 9 + 4 + = 39
9. 8. 4 = 21 (each number reduced to its lowest digit)

Vertically:

September = 9
26
1948
1983 = 21 = 3

The primary date path is 3, the secondary is 21, the tertiary is 39, and the heart date path is 57.

Olivia's perennial youthfulness, singing, performing, and activism all resonate with number 3. 21, her secondary, catalyzes social consciousness and verbal intelligence. 39, Olivia's tertiary, would further help her to appreciate her role in the greater scheme of life. Despite the trials that life brings, '39' would help Olivia to believe in the essential goodness of humanity. Number 57 is Olivia's heart date path and whether she realizes it or not, it is strengthening her will to create a shift in perspective on a large scale. Her interest in promoting environmental awareness is, in part, an expression of this date path. Number 3 celebrates creativity, self-expression, and personal ideals.

Date Path 3 will encourage you to participate in the creative process of which you are a part. It continually sparks your curiosity and provided nothing goes seriously wrong, you will always love learning new things. Indeed you will be a perennial student throughout your life. You tend to ask lots of questions and think about people's response to them, just as a journalist would. You then express your own ideas about the subject matter, in the way that suits you best. Number 3 stimulates imagination and will make you conscious of the image that you present to the world. Unless there are other influences to off-set it, you may find that you excel at 'moving on' but that you are not so good at reflecting on your actions.

Primary Date Path Number Four

Power of Form

Number 4 encodes the fashioning of form. In humans, animals, plants and minerals, a physical encasement provides a reservoir through which life flows. Within each of these 4 kingdoms are the 4 components of physical creation: light, sound, shape and depth (or volume) and the laws of 4 elements govern their specifications. Furthermore, the spherical shape of our beautiful planet has 4 aspects: a central point, diameter, circumference and area. Thus the number 4 symbolizes the foundation upon which the material world is built. It defines space and resonates with the heartbeat of the earth. In the Hindu tradition, number 4 can be correlated with karma yoga and the belief that the soul cloaks itself in a physical body because it is only through a material form that certain states of consciousness can be experienced. However every action we make whilst in this body has its effect on every other living thing.

Karma monitors action and reaction, cause and effect. If we do our work to the best of our ability but do not attach its outcome to our own back, then our work does not become a burden to us. Karma is neither good nor bad but simply natural consequence.

The 'householder guru', Lahiri Mahasaya, born on September 30, 1828, provides an example.

September 30 1828
9. 30. 19 = 58 (the highest possible number)
9 + 3 + 0 + 1 + 8 + 2 + 8 = 31
9. 3. 1 = 13 (each number reduced to its lowest digit)

Vertically:

September = 9
　　　　　　30
　　　　　1828
　　　　　1867 = 22 = 4

The primary date path is 4, secondary 13, tertiary 22, heart 31, and quintessential 58.

Lahiri Mahasaya provides an ideal example for people with this date path because although he was self-realized by 33 years of age, he continued to live and work as an ordinary householder and accountant until he was 58 when he was retired on a pension. Date Path 4 is evident in his integrity, dedication, and ability to work with steady concentration over a lengthy period of time. Number 13 suggests that his ego underwent a complete transformation, (which it did). Number 22 would have helped him to formulate a systematic method of spiritual attainment based on the ancient wisdom of his native land (which he did). Number 31 will always tend to structure ideas due to enter the mainstream of consciousness, in this case kriya yoga, while number 58 would have supported his efforts to transform others, through such ideas. The exemplary teacher died on September 26, 1895 = 58! Self-discipline, integrity, dedication and practicality are characteristics of number 4.

Primary date path 4 will encourage you to work for the love of it. It will help you to find your place in the material world, supporting your efforts to 'grow things' from the ground up, one step at a time. In the everyday story of your life, how do you give form to your ideas? That's the vital question here. To be successful, set your mind on a potentially productive idea and stick with it.

Primary Date Path Number Five

Power of Growth

Number 5 symbolizes the soul's bid to locate its centre within the body-mind-soul-ego complex it inhabits. This can spark off, quite literally, the adventure of a lifetime. Although sociable, this is essentially a solitary path, with the Number 5 encouraging the Traveller to become the Guide.

An example is James Twyman, musician and author of *Emissary of Light*, born on March 20, 1962.

March 20 1962
3. 20. 18 = 41 (the highest possible number)
3 + 2 + 0+ 1 + 9 + 6 + 2 = 23
3. 2. 9 = 14 (each number reduced to its lowest digit)

Vertically:

March = 3
        20
     1962
     1985 = 23 = 5

The primary date path is 5, the secondary 14, the tertiary 23 and the heart date path is 41.

Jimmy, as he is most often called, is a peace troubadour who advocates prayer as a viable method of non-violent activism. During the war in 1995, he visited Croatia to sing songs of peace in a troubled land and so began an adventure that would teach him to look beyond apparent change and uncertainty. He would realize that our choice is always fear or love, bondage or freedom, and that this choice is one that we make each and every moment. Such realization resonates with number 5; to release fear and allow love to take central place in one's life, fortifies the body of light. Number 14 would help Jimmy to break new ground in peaceful activism, while 23 would help him to perceive that overcoming confusion – the offspring of fear - is the single most important step towards freedom. Number 41 would support his efforts to formulate the practice of applying passion, with its inherent joy, contentment and enthusiasm, to open the door that mobilizes the flow of light into the world. In these ways, James Twyman demonstrates the power of number 5 to uplift and revitalize human consciousness. Number 5 sharpens sensory awareness, bringing a willingness to learn, grow, and expand one's consciousness. It is entrepreneurial; able to seize the moment and go with the flow.

'5' is the number of evolution and it will help you to evolve as a human being. You can thus expect constant change in your life – and yourself – as you learn and grow. However, once you are able to centre yourself and act from the core of your personal ingenuity, you will come to see change as an opportunity to evolve beyond what you thought possible. Your number 5 is encouraging you to explore your personal genius. This begins with acknowledging your talents and evolves into realizing your unique gift to society. Everyone has something they are good at, something that comes naturally to them and which gives them pleasure. Date Path 5 facilitates the location of one's particular genius: where you 'shine' and have something to give.

Primary Date Path Number Six

Power of Cohesion

Number 6 symbolizes the magic of integrating one idea with another. The word cohesive comes from a Latin word meaning 'to stick'. It means being able to unite separate parts so that they form a harmonious or credible whole. Consider our example …

Doctor Elisabeth Kubler-Ross, psychiatrist and pioneer researcher into the stages of coping with trauma, death and life beyond that transition, was born on July 8, 1926.

July 8 1926
7. 8. 18 = 33 (the highest possible number and also 7 + 8 + 1 + 9 + 2 + 6)
7. 8. 9 = 24 (each number reduced to its lowest digit)

Vertically

July = 7
     8
  1926
   1941 = 15 = 6

The primary date path is 6, the secondary is 15, the tertiary is 24, and the heart date path is 33.

Everything that one could say about number 6 was embodied in this compassionate woman. Before beginning her formal training as a doctor she was actively involved in the international voluntary service for peace and would describe their heroic undertakings following the war in Europe, as music to her soul. She was grateful to be able to help those in need. Elisabeth loved her home and family but had a heart that sought to embrace the whole world. She believed that the only thing that truly heals people is unconditional love. Number 15 resonates through her advice that the gift of free will places on our shoulders the responsibility of choice. "You can choose to blame or heal and grow", she would say. This vibration also gave her the ability to perceive adversity as the recipe for increased strength. Number 24 would help her to learn that when you accept a situation, the pain eases. Also pertinent to this number, she taught that care and companionship are the best medicine and that a loving heart can heal almost anything. Number 33 adds the spice of inspiration to the mix. It would spark her imagination with a way to formulate and communicate the stages of grief and trauma and later, the states of immediate post-death experience as well. The characteristics of number 6 include the ability to think methodically, and the ability to orchestrate – musically in some cases – but more typically events and ideas.

Date Path 6 will help you to integrate the various facets of who you are: the so-called 'good bits', the so-called 'bad bits', and everything in between. You are a critical thinker who can spot inconsistencies and yet you are also idealistic. Number 6 is especially active in the social arena of life and this is where you will want to apply your ideals. Number 6 would have you evolve within the parameters of your community. Date Path 6 grants you the ability to craft the substance of our collective hopes and fears into acts of compassion.

Primary Date Path Number Seven

Power of Truth

Whereas number 6 heightens the perceptive powers of the third eye, number 7 intensifies the ability to *reflect* on what we see. It encourages us to analyze, research, and think things through until eventually we arrive at our personal truth. Number 7 promotes discretion and reveals its gifts through self-honesty. And through honesty, life on earth is sanctified.

Rabbi Zalman Schachter-Shalomi, born on August 28, 1924, provides an example.

August 28 1924
8. 28. 16 = 52 (the highest possible number)
8 + 2 + 8 + 1 +9 + 2 + 4 = 34
8. 1. 7 = 16 (each number reduced to its lowest digit)

Vertically:

August = 8
     28
   1924
   1960 = 16 = 7

The primary date path is 7, the secondary is 16, the tertiary is 34, and the heart date path is 52.

Approaching 60, with a successful life behind him, a gnawing depression prompted Reb Zalman to embark on a forty-day retreat. Wandering off on one's own and surrendering to the soul is characteristic of date path 7. Author of *From Aging to Saging,* the famous Rabbi gave voice to the decree of all spiritual elders with the words, "I want to work on myself, even if it means facing past and present anxieties. I want to be generous, pure and clean in the face of Spirit. I want to live the truth as I see it". Although written about older humanity, this declaration is made at least subconsciously by everyone with date path 7 regardless of age. Secondary 16 facilitates the shift from 'victim consciousness' to 'healing consciousness'. And in Reb Zalman's case this vibration acted as midwife to his 'elder-self'. It awakened him to a profounder sense of reality and beauty. Tertiary 34 is evident in his ability to structure and express this awakening through storytelling and scholarly writing. Heart date path 52 champions the freedom that comes from reclaiming those parts of Self that were compromised in order to please others and to feel safe. It fulfills itself through the promotion of spiritual awareness. Just so, through song, prayer, meditation and counseling, Reb Zelman encourages people to discover *their* truth based on *their* experience of the world.

Genesis embraces several layers of meaning, but one thing is clear: day seven is different to the preceding six days. From early childhood, you may have perceived this difference between you and other people and it probably left you feeling frustrated and misunderstood. Yet number 7 comes with its own antidote: a potent mixture of introspection and insight. In regular doses it will help you to make peace with yourself. Primary date path 7 urges you to reflect on your life and discern what is important and what is not. It will encourage you to research, compare and contrast, and to weigh up divergent points of view until you arrive at your personal truth. There may come a time in your life when you want to go on a 'vision quest', sit quietly with your creator, and ask what you are here to do. This is not as easy as it sounds because it involves honest introspection. Until you have confronted your denial, apathy, grief, fear and pain and transmuted them all to love, your inner work – and it is work – is not complete.

Primary Date Path Number Eight

Power of Integration

The figure 8 reminds us of the connection between 'above' and 'below' and the eternal dance between them. There is no chance of denial here; everyone has a shadow-self and we must each decide what to do with it. Number 8 encourages people to descend into their personal 'hell' and reclaim all parts of self, in the name of love.

The first democratically elected State President of South Africa, Nelson Rolihlahla Mandela, born on July 18, 1918, provides an example.

July 18 1918

7. 18. 19 = 44 (the highest possible number)
7 + 1 + 8 + 1 +9 + 1 + 8 = 35
7. 9. 1 = 17 (each number reduced to its lowest digit)

Vertically:

July = 7
    18
   <u>1918</u>
   <u>1943</u> = 17 = 8

The Primary date path is 8, the secondary 17, the tertiary 35 and the heart date path is 44.

Nelson Mandela is the epitome of a human being who has been to hell and re-emerged triumphant over himself. His personal struggle was interwoven with the struggle of a nation. Number 17 can be witnessed as his tendency to listen carefully, and then to read and research, before reaching a decision. 17 is introspective in nature and throughout his autobiography we evidence Mandela's honest, even ruthless self-assessment. He would intuit the number 17 as his more introverted side that loved solitude. Within the deep recesses of his mind the search for truth would quietly distill experience into conviction. Number 35, on the other hand, would support the more flamboyant and gregarious Nelson Mandela and being his tertiary date path, would be the most visible. It would aid him in the courtroom and his public speaking engagements, promoting optimism when things were grave. Heart Date Path 44 kept Nelson focused on the task at hand and stabilized the groundwork for the future. When it comes to devotion to duty, nothing can rival a 44; heart and soul go into whatever they are committed to. Like Rolihlahla, the branch bender, the unstinting work done by those with date path 8 becomes their legacy to humanity. To understand people with date path 8, you must understand what motivates them.

If number 8 is your date path, you are probably talented at networking and organizing (or would like to be). At a subtle level, it is the various parts of yourself that you are trying to unite. As you integrate the various parts of yourself, your organizational skills are likely to improve. Furthermore, you are learning that although you would like to do the right thing by everyone, you need not compromise your personal integrity in the process. You are loyal, stubborn, and a potentially brilliant tactician. You probably have your own code of honour. How will you fight the just cause in the name of love, is the key question here?

Primary Date Path Number Nine

Power of Faith

Like 3 and 6, number 9 stimulates the imagination, specifically mythic imagination. It gives people the power to think big and create meaning.

No one embodies the energy of the 9 more than Mata Amritanandamayi does. Born on September 27, 1953, her primary date path is 9 and her birthday, month and year also reduce to 9 and so nowhere are we going to find a better example of this number.

September 27 1953
9. 27. 18 = 54 (the highest possible number)
9 + 2 + 7 + 1 +9 + 5 + 3 = 36
9. 9. 9 = 27 (each number reduced to its lowest digit)

Vertically:

September = 9
27
1953
1989 = 27 = 9

The primary date path is 9, the secondary 27, the tertiary 36, and the heart date path is 54.

Amma, as she is affectionately known, embodies the mother principle of creation: raw maternal energy converted into vitality within the human form. Through her extraordinary humanitarian achievements, Amma demonstrates the power of such unconditional love. She embraces everyone and everything – quite literally! And through her selfless service, she is bringing out the best in others, encouraging them to abandon selfishness. Date path 27 brings the insight that the love of the creator manifests through human love. Number 36 engages the mind in a multi-layered, creative and artistic attitude to life. Songs of devotion have been literally pouring forth from Amma's mind and heart since she was a small child. Number 54 belongs to 'survivors' who overcome obstacles, despite their personal sensitivity. When such hard-wrought wisdom becomes public, it seeks to liberate others from pain and suffering. In Amma, '9' reaches outwards by healing, teaching and counselling from a global and futuristic perspective. That wise saying that 'to know all is to forgive all' applies here.

The ability to generalize comes with date path 9. This enables you to make sweeping statements and that's a problem when it degenerates into over-generalization. But it can also help you to understand the universality of humanity, and that regardless of race, age, creed or gender, we all have common needs. With 9 as your date path you can very generous in your thinking. Such expansiveness will help you to create your own mythology from the wealth of your life's experience. '9' is inclusive. It embraces all philosophies, religions and faiths including atheism. It will help you to tolerate, respect, and ultimately appreciate other people's beliefs. A mythology wrought of love is its premier expression.

At the end of the sequence of single digits, '9' represents the wisdom learned from life. It embraces all thoughts, feelings, emotions and ideals, and that's a big call! '9' enables surrender through unconditional love, which means loving the Earth and all of her children.

Date Path Number Ten

Stabilizing the Ego's Potential

Building on Number 1, 10 is about illuminating the potential of the Ego - not the yappy little ego - but the true and everlasting Self.

Augusta Ada Byron was born on December 10, 1815, date path 37/19/10/1. Not only are her birth day and secondary date path both 10 but also the first letter of her name resonates with number 1, which means that both qualities were strong in her. Her pioneering work in the field of computers exemplifies number 1 while the fact that such work was foundational to future developments exemplifies number 10. Lots of people initiate things but only a few such initiatives lay a foundation for the future. That takes effort, persistence, and tenacity: all '10' words. Ada, as she was known, was a gifted mathematician. She met Charles Babbage in her 19th year (her tertiary date path being 19). At 28 (her missing date path) she supplemented his notes on the analytical engine. These notes contain what is now considered to be the first computer program. Ada's contribution paved the way for the modern computer. She died just before her 37th birthday (37 being her heart date path).

'10' will encourage you to be decisive and to take responsibility for your Self. This number governs the steady but sure development of the Ego, which is the source of your inner authority and unique contribution to humanity. With number 10 as your date path you are learning to stand on your own two feet and develop a strong, straight spine. Do not expect someone else to be your 'authority figure'; you are your own such person. Because 10 is 2 x 5, it has an innovative quality that you can put to good use in the process. 5 times 2 means shining the light of your personal 'genius' within a team situation. 'One' might be a solo number but 'ten' is not.

Date Path Number Eleven

Scintillating the Mind with Fresh Inspiration

All prime numbers are a law unto themselves and none more than this one; indeed its double-1 makes mavericks of otherwise easygoing folks. Being the fifth prime, number 11 is excitable, adventurous and highly sensitive.

Baruch Spinoza was the most radical and controversial philosopher of his time and his ideas can still spark intense intellectual probing and spiritual soul searching. In this way he typifies number 11. He was born on November 24, 1632, Date Path 47/20/11/2. An independent thinker, his unorthodox opinions caused an uproar in his day. Spinoza realized quite early in life that he would have to abandon all hopes of wealth and security in order to be true to his conscience. Yet he was cautious about publishing his views, for those were dangerous times. Cautiousness is an aspect of number 2 but Spinoza's emphasis on the importance of the inner light, and independence in interpreting the 'word of god', is pure number 11, and so was his antiauthoritarian approach to worship. Spinoza and others of like mind were branded atheists but actually theirs was a commitment to religious reform. A person, who writes that true piety consists only in the love of god and one's neighbours, is hardly an atheist. It was because he believed that the outward expression of that love (the form it takes in public religious practice), is irrelevant that Spinoza was vilified. However he also attracted like-minded individuals who analyzed his unorthodox views carefully. Spinoza had that mixture of traits peculiar to number 11: he was outspoken, yet in dread of quarrelling, and peace-loving yet provocative. A charismatic personality, somewhat stoic, he led an exemplary life because, despite the opinions of others, his was a moral and ethical stand, taken from the urge to enlighten people and dispel superstition. Through his works he aimed at demonstrating that happiness depends on reasoning, and that through this channel we can come to love god with a free spirit. Inadvertently, this tells us much about number 11.

Number 11 as your date path will catalyze upheavals in your mind and propel you into realms beyond your initial understanding. Because '11' stimulates the intuitive faculties of the mind, you will need to learn how to listen to that quiet voice within you. The extra-ordinary level of mental stimulation that comes with 11 has a tendency to strain the nervous system. As the inspiration floods in, your unprepared ego might revert to the less positive behaviours of number 2 such as dependence, but you will find little satisfaction there. The way forward is to strengthen your nervous system through yoga (or something similar). When you steady your nerves and realize that you are as adequate as anyone else is, you will discover that you are a natural group facilitator who excels at inspiring and encouraging other people.

Date Path Number Twelve

Believing In Your Ability to Create a Change of Consciousness by Exercising Your Imagination and Expressing Your Ideas

Number 12 resonates with the social reformer with high ideals: a crusader, perhaps, who almost instinctively replaces "Why me?" with "Why not me?" Choice is the perennial issue that accompanies 'number 12' and essentially involves choosing between an impulse emanating from the ego and one that is coming from the soul. Ultimately it is a choice of perspective. People with secondary date path 12 are typically called on to make choices that create a world of difference not only to them but also to the people around them.

William Butler Yeats was born on June 13, 1865, Date Path 39/30/21/12/3. The fact that he was a poet and playwright exemplifies date path 3, and the fact that he explored the potential of such gifts, becoming one of the foremost figures of twentieth century literature, exemplifies 30. Becoming a pillar of the Irish and British literary establishments further exemplifies 30, specifically as 3 x 10. Yeats had a life-long interest in mysticism, spiritualism, occultism, and astrology, all of which resonate with number 12. His involvement in politics exemplifies

39/12 in particular. As a Senator and Nobel Prize Winner in Literature, Yeats promoted Irish nationalism. People with date path 12 often become involved in a 'movement' of some kind, as Yeats did. Social activism is typically one of their 'job descriptions', and they sometimes serve as midwives of social regeneration. There's usually evidence of a major turning point in their lives when they suddenly 'see' things differently. For Yeats such a major turning point happened when he realized that the national revolutionary movement came mostly from the lower-middle and working classes rather than the so-called upper echelons of society.

If 12 is one of your numbers and your ego is running roughshod over your soul, you may need to pacify your defense system and pay attention to your inner partner. Conversely, if your ego is not strong enough to bring your vision to fruition, you may need to work on any issues you have about self worth. You can enhance the development of your soul-life by setting aside time daily to contemplate your actions as if it were someone else who had done them. This will enable you to confront yourself as a stranger and to see yourself from someone else's point of view. In the human realm, the power of number 12 lies in facing our vulnerability and acting in accordance with our deepest feelings. Because number 3 is intrinsic to number 12, you will quickly realize that the way you present yourself and your ideas is crucial to your success. It's the way that you look at things that lies at the crux of date path 12.

Date Path Number 13

Undergoing Transformation

The function of number 13 is to instigate a complete transformation to the status quo. People who fear change fear the number 13, but those who are willing to take the plunge into the depths of their soul will ultimately re-emerge fearless. 13/4 symbolizes the natural process of a caterpillar transforming into a butterfly.

If 13 is one of your numbers, the important thing to remember is that transformation begins in the mind with the dissolution of fear. The steps that lead to such a transformation are: realizing your potential (that's 10); listening to the intelligence of your soul (11), and being willing to adjust your perspective on life (12).

Date Path Number 14

Reshaping Thought Patterns

Inside every '14' a rebel must dwell because there is something belonging to the past from which they must break free. When outer circumstances are tempered by personal integrity, the opportunities that this vibration magnetizes will be experienced as fortunate synchronizations.

With 14 as one of your numbers, you are progressive in your thinking but you do not totally disregard society's conventions. '14' breaks new ground through presence of mind, common sense, and attunement to the inner voice. In the process, continual change is something that you will need to get used to. It will help you to appreciate the moment; a profoundly spiritual experience if you are open to it.

Date Path Number 15

Perceiving the Harmony within the Chaos

Number 15 is an extension of number 6 and thus represents a specific type of coherence. It is uniquely 5 x 3 and 3 x 5 and as such combines the powers of imagination and evolution. Following on from 14/5, people with date path 15 are freedom-loving individuals who need to select a focus for their profuse creativity.

With 15 as one of your numbers, you will find that perceptiveness and magnetism accompany you throughout life, the latter tending to attract people in need. '15' will help you to spot inconsistency in other people and thereby equip you to confront it within yourself. The ability to take advice is crucial, because this resonance attracts the full gamut of human experience. If you let it, number 15 will bring you to the realization that even the most mundane tasks and chaotic events stand in connection with the cosmos as a whole. But firstly you must learn to accept the so-called 'imperfections' within yourself and within others. In '15', faith in yourself and faith in the process of life join forces. The possibilities are endless and it may be difficult to focus your energy on one exciting project at a time.

Date Path Number 16

Appreciating the Subtleties Going On Around You and Within You

This vibration tends to catalyze sudden and significant shifts in perspective. Number 16 seeks truth by negating non-truth, thereby arriving at the essential. It is when everything else falls away that reality is revealed. This dropping away of illusion in order to unveil the truth is the power and purpose of number 16.

Date Path 16 will test your problem-solving skills – and strengthen them. With '16' as one of your Numbers, you are likely to experience a sudden and significant shift in perspective at some point in your life. This is likely to be grossly unwelcome at the time yet ultimately this shock to the system will open you up to a more sublime sense of reality. Spiritually this might be termed a crisis of faith. If you stay true to the process, your former self-centered ways that served to protect your ego will, in a flash of insight, yield to a more honest perception of the world in which you live. Faith in yourself and your ability to solve problems will increase accordingly.

Date Path Number 17

Forging Insight through Contemplation, Education, Organization and Networking

17 is the 7th prime number, which emphasizes the number 7 and its quest for truth. 17 and 7 are equally enigmatic. They must be expressed in a uniquely personal way.

In '17', the ego's task is honest self-appraisal as a basis for action. With 17 as one of your numbers, you probably use education, more or less consciously, as a means of empowerment. You tend to be both philosophical and combative, because of the ego's inclination to project its issues. Typically these issues are reflected in the social arena of life, which means that as you work through your personal issues, you also accomplish much on behalf of others. Case studies reveal that number 17 typically accompanies a profound and personal victory over heart-breaking circumstances. Ultimately this transmutes into wisdom and compassion. In this way, your personal story can bring hope to other people. But to achieve this, the shadow side of yourself must be acknowledged and appreciated or it will sabotage the heroic part of who you are. Once your ego unifies its team there is little that can stop you. Faith in yourself, and faith in your organizational skills, offer you the power to accomplish a great deal, but don't forget to balance busyness with quiet, introspective time.

Date Path Number 18

Exercising the Power of Your Ego for the Common Good

With Number 18 comes the commitment to an ideal, typically a social ideal that has been taken personally. The choice of ideal lies entirely with the individual, yet whatever it is, the commitment will be far from superficial. This number stimulates courage, resoluteness, and organizational skill, but also warns of the need for honesty.

This is a powerful and extreme vibration and so you will need to temper any tendency that you may have to imagine that the only way to get things done is by forcing the issue. If you don't, you are likely to be labelled a firebrand or hothead. Commitment to an ideal is what lies behind this force, which is admirable, but you must learn how to express it in an appropriate way. Numbers 1 and 8 relate to the planet Mars and as such represent willpower in top gear. Number 1 can be assertive or aggressive, depending on your motive, and likewise, number 8 can be resourceful or revengeful or anything in between as it relates to achieving results. Occasionally we meet a person who turns this energy against themselves, immobilizing their power to act on all levels: physically, emotionally, socially and even spiritually. Such people feel as if they are working hard and getting nowhere, and cannot understand why. The trick is to decide where to focus your energy without trampling over other people. You are learning how to harness your willpower to a just cause and to act from your authentic Self rather that your defensive ego. Once you conquer your impatience, with yourself as much as with others, you will find yourself mobilizing activities that are of enormous benefit to the world around you.

Date Path Number 19

Reconciling Your Personal Ego with the Rest of Humanity

The fact that 19 is a prime accentuates the individualism of number 1 up-front, leaving the universality of Number 9 in the background. However '19' reduces to 10 and so there's plenty of potential here for exploring the greater Self as well as the personal self. The ordinal factor is 7 (it's the 7th Prime Number), which helps people to reflect on their actions and reconcile the contractions within themselves. '19' comprises the extremities of the digits – first and last – and the difference between them is 8, which indicates that the way that personal power and authority are applied, is critical to the successful fulfillment of this date path.

19

Number 19 is about reconciling your personal ego with the rest of humanity. You are typically concerned with principles, which naturally have an impersonal touch, and so you will need to watch the tendency to love humanity (in your ideal world) but dislike humans (as they really are). Date Path 19 is about realizing that you are the world and the world is you. Therefore to the extent that you change yourself, you change the world. Make this your standard and your achievements will be legendary.

Date Path Number 20

Illuminating the Potential of the Soul through Team-Work

Number 20 marks a shift in consciousness. No longer is the ego, represented by number 1, at the forefront. With the 20's comes the focus on others and all manner of reactions to them. $20 = 4 \times 5$, the 4 stabilizing the energy-field while the 5 encourages movement, evolution and change. Balance is imperative.

Date Path 20 will encourage you to explore your potential within a team setting. Keep in mind that you are sensitive to discord and vulnerable to taking things personally. Your feeling life is very intense and you will need to learn how to ride with your feelings, despite what other people are doing or saying. This is akin to riding through the storm of other people's reactions. Rather than stubbornly standing in opposition, number 20 asks you to lift yourself above the pull of random emotions and focus on your true feelings. Some philosophers believe that feelings are opposed to intelligence but in fact it is our feeling-life that aids the development of rational principles. When you demonstrate compassion for another person because you know it's the right thing to do, you are demonstrating rational principles. With date path 20 comes the opportunity to become a valued member of a team of people who care about each other as they work towards a common goal.

Date Path Number 21

Expressing Imagination and Insight

'21' is uniquely 3 times 7 and within this number the imagination that comes with number 3 and the insight that is inherent to number 7 combine. With 7 as a part of the equation, number 21 includes the ability to reflect on your actions, which is not typically a strongpoint for number 3. If number 1 represents the ego and number 2 the soul, it is when the ego yields to the wisdom of the soul that the magic of date path 21 begins.

Date Path 12 can only evolve to date path 21 when you realize that the changes, which you believe are necessary in the world around you, are preceded by change within you. As you regulate your inner life and assume responsibility for your thoughts and feelings, your imagination becomes increasingly rich and bountiful and you realize the significance of the fact that thoughts and feelings are as real as physical objects. With the above in mind, know that date path 21 stimulates the urge to participate in a campaign. Which campaign is up to you but the advice here is to choose just one rather than scattering your energy all over the place.

Date Path Number 22

Demonstrating That Co-Operation, Inspiration and Sensitivity Are Practical Tools of Great Benefit

Whilst the double-1 (11) prompts us to live an inspired life in co-operation with others, the double-2 takes this a step further, challenging us to create something tangible with our inspiration. '22' is called the mastermind number because it enables people to orchestrate large-scale projects. Typically these require tact and a profound understanding of human nature.

With 22 as one of your numbers you will become adept at applying cooperation, inspiration, and sensitivity to practical projects. This number will encourage you to acknowledge your fears, let life transform you, and act for the greater good despite your concerns. You have the ability to create win-win solutions to intractable problems. You can think in broad terms and yet come up with workable solutions (i.e., think globally and act locally as the expression goes).

Date Path Number 23

Extending the Boundaries of Perception

Number 23 encodes the soul's ability to come up with creative new ideas that quicken the consciousness of the people and facilitate evolution.

In company with date path 14, 23 will help you to blaze your own trail through conflicting ideas. Work with it and you will find that opposition ceases to throw you off-centre. Rather, it will fuel your enthusiasm. Having no factors, number 23 is individualistic, yet it tends to reconcile opposing opinions. It will help you to see their commonality and that they are actually a part of one story. Your task is to blend sensitivity (2) and imagination (3) with your personal life-experience (5). You can make the most of the inner freedom and outer opportunities that accompany 23/5, by focusing on something that allows you to express your personal ingenuity. As you shift your perception of reality you may notice that others shift theirs too.

Date Path Number 24

Enabling Connections for Practical and Cohesive Outcomes

Numbers 2, 4, and their sum, represent the first three even digits and the sense of balance and proportion that comes from that. 24 has multiple factors: 2 x 12, 3 x 8, and 4 x 6, most of which are also even numbers.

With date path 24 a variety of skills is available to you: the ability to see both sides of a given situation and a knack for social networking to name just two. You take your duties and responsibilities seriously. You like to work in a team setting and you are naturally dependable, hardworking and systematic. Plain common sense comes with 24/6, as does compassion and a fertile imagination. Such qualities and skills are yours to use however you choose.

Date Path Number 25

Empathizing With an Increasing Range Of People

Date Path 25 stimulates an appreciation of life through the active expression of love. The soul is quite capable of holding its own amidst the swirling waters of life, even the unpredictable currents that typically surface with this vibration, if the ego is willing to listen to and act upon the advice offered from that deep place within the heart and mind.

With '25' as one of your Numbers, you will discover that introspection alone will not do; you must be willing to put your awareness to the test in the material world, translating the love that you feel for other people into acts that support their development. The factors 5 x 5 suggest that you like to be on the move, exploring the world around you. The '7' part of the equation will have you exploring inwardly as well. 25/7 can give you the insight that you need to understand other people and work with them in a mutually beneficial way.

Date Path Number 26

Weaving a Web of Love from Your Life's Experiences

The soul reigns supreme here yet must learn to dance with other souls and not lose sight of other people's realities. Through the awakened ego, the soul seeks a way to express its passion.

With '26' as one of your Numbers, you tend to drive yourself because you want to make a contribution to the creation of a more beautiful world. Life may feel meaningless to you unless you are able contribute to weaving of a web of love around the globe. Yet you must allow the collective to press against the personal and give it form; it's a two-way process. Number 26 as 2 x 13 portends that at some point in your life you will undergo a transformation so profound that it will not only change your values but your whole perspective on life. Once you have integrated whatever has happened, you will strive to disseminate the wisdom that you have learned from it.

Date Path Number 27

Recognizing Immortal Love within Mortal Love

Number 27 represents the marriage of love and truth. The shadow side of this vibration is the restless search for something to believe in (such as a religion or a philosophy), which is big enough to contain this marriage.

In '27' the balance between generalization and truth is dependent upon your ability to reconcile polarities and acknowledge diversity. It takes substantial maturity to turn fantastic ideas into ones that work in the everyday world. For your own peace of mind, you must journey inwardly to resolve your personal dilemmas, sort out your values, and find your personal truth. If you are able to return from such intense inner work with awareness that divine love resonates through human love, then you will know peace. Number 27 is never an easy pattern to live with because there's something quite dramatic about the way it manifests.

Date Path Number 28

Stabilizing Your Most Promising Initiative through Teamwork

Number 28 is both social and solitary. The even numbers are companionable and stabilizing yet four times seven is distinctly individualistic.

28 is an immensely constructive Number – great works can be instigated here – but you absolutely must hone your people skills. '28' represents the dual urge to be self-reliant and also part of a team; you want both. This is a success-orientated Number that offers business acumen. As 2 x 14 you can break new ground with it. As 4 x 7 you can reconcile differences through insight, and improve the likelihood of practical solutions being found. This goal-setting, goal-achieving number will make a clever problem-solver of you. 28/10 likes to steer the ship, but with it, you can also empower others to take the lead too. It offers you diplomacy (2), resourcefulness (8), and a cast iron will (10).

Date Path Number 29

Visioning a Brighter Future for Humanity

29 is the tenth prime number and thus people with this date path tend to be mavericks with very strong principles.

To work productively with number 29 you will firstly need to overcome any resistance you may have to listening to your intuition: that subtle prompt within your own mind. Once you begin to exercise it, you will discover that the intuitive faculties of your mind work most effectively when principles temper emotions. However these principles cannot be arbitrary; they must be personally meaningful and ring true in your soul. Nowhere is there more need for self-honesty than here; without it you may fall prey to delusions. Contemplate what life means to you, sort out your values accordingly, and then team-work with others who have reached similar conclusions. Date Path 29 is about visioning a brighter future for humanity. Doing your bit to make the world a better place is a vital step in that direction.

Date Path Number 30

Realizing the Power and Potential of Your Imagination

Number 30 has multiple factors just as the imagination has multiple modes of expression. From imagination arises thought, speech, and action, all of which impact on other people and the environment. And this is the realm of number 30

Date Path 30 would have you choose your role models wisely. You need people who stimulate your thinking. You are advised to cultivate the art of creating significant conversation with all types of people, even those you may initially dislike, because everyone has something to teach you. The flipside of this is your potential to inspire others. Choose what gives you the most joy and then polish your powers of expression so that other people can benefit from it too.

Date Path Number 31

Formulating an Idea Due To Enter the Mainstream of Human Consciousness

Both 13 and 31 are prime numbers and are thus individualistic in nature. 13 is the sixth prime number and as such restores harmony by transforming something. 31 on the other hand is the eleventh, which gives it a maverick quality. And with '3' up-front, you can expect some creative conflict here.

With 31 as one of your numbers, you will probably show an interest, at some time in your life, in formulating a new idea. There are both 'looking-back' and 'looking-forward' qualities to this Number. In other words something from the past, which still has value, will catch your attention and you will want to interest others in it. You will see the intrinsic worth of the old and that it needs to be preserved and continued in an updated form. Ideally you will match up past, present and future. For example, you may want people to notice something from their cultural heritage that is relevant to them and beneficial to future generations as well. Allow others to help you shape this idea and bring it forth. The shadow quality attached to 31 is patience.

Date Path Number 32

Shifting and Structuring Perceptions

A key difference between 23 and 32 is the factors: 23 is a prime number and therefore emphasizes the personal whereas 32 has factors and is thus more interpersonal. 2 up-front places the qualities of 2 up-front such as teamwork whereas 3 up-front places personal imagination in the foreground. Usually people with date path 23 also have 32 and so it's like splitting straws and it's probably more useful to consider how they might work together. '23' is concerned with extending perceptions and 32 as 4 x 8 with organizing such perceptions. Having explored your personal ingenuity (5), broken new ground (14) and shifted a few perceptions (23), '32' is where you formulate your most promising ideas and turn them into something productive.

Date Path 32 will help you to formulate your ideas in a way that other people can relate to and benefit from. 3 up-front will stimulate your imagination and help you to create the image that you want to project. Choice is where number 2 comes in, keeping in mind that the finer qualities of that number include cooperation, diplomacy, sensitivity, and empathy.

Date Path Number 33

Gathering and Sorting Information from Diverse Sources for the Purposes of a Grand Synthesis

As 3 times 11, number 33 constantly stimulates the mind with fresh ideas. This can be very exciting but also hard on the nervous system.

The word 'teacher' adds up to 33, and as a component of your date path, it will test your capacity to care and share within the light of self-knowledge. By sharing not only your strengths but also your vulnerability with others, you indirectly teach that all of the pain and joy of life are meaningful. Most apparent when you are able to view your experiences through the 'bigger picture lens', number 33 stimulates your mind to care about the welfare of the world and contribute to its healing. Undoubtedly the most inquisitive of all the numbers, '33' will prod you to find solutions to the big questions. It would have you remain open to criticism, as your ideas gel and become increasingly consistent.

Date Path Number 34

Applying Imagination to the Quest for Truth

As two times 17, Number 34/7 aids self-appraisal and applies it to appraising others. There's a distinctly introspective quality to this number that helps people to assess the value of their ideas.

Date Path 34 offers you the ability to inject new life into ideas from the past. It will encourage you, through contemplation and education, to reject falseness in your quest for truth. Aim to learn as much as you can from your life so as to gather a rich store of experience. From this you can create a reliable and useful framework for your ideas. Success hinges on acting courageously regardless of what others might think of you.

Date Path Number 35

Catalyzing Fresh and Productive Ideas

The factors of 35 are 5 times 7, which highlights the '5' part of the number. Thus the qualities of ingenuity and enterprise unite with the expressiveness of number 3 and the seriousness of number 8. Numbers 3 and 5 are naturally social, and 8 is about networking and so 35/8 is characterized by social networking. 7 in the background will insist on keeping everything honest.

Your date path 35 will help you to create connections, link people up, and get things happening. Your task is to unify the powers of your mind with the powers of your heart, so that they can operate as one great passion. You are never short of a bright and profound idea and you thrive on the pursuit of diverse ideas that can be hung on one peg. People with date path 35 tend to turn their passion inward to the source of their creativity during the second half of life, becoming increasingly focused on the point where the 'above' and 'below' parts of the symbol for 8 intersect.

Date Path Number 36

Bringing Together the Creative Forces within Your Mind

36/9 has multiple factors and is thus a versatile Number; its conglomeration of factors targeting the extraction of meaning from multiple perspectives. 36/9 has the power to shape outcomes through measured expression. '3' looks forward with the eagerness of a child, '9' looks back and tries to make sense of life, while '6' integrates these two impulses in the present moment.

Because 36 has multiple factors, you are likely to develop multiple skills over your lifetime. You may try your hand at many different things and discover that you can do some of them really well. You will ponder the meaning of life and you may be able to formulate your ideas into a coherent theory. 36/9 will help you to become aware of the power of your thoughts. Although unseen, they are as real as physical objects especially when they are shaped into a hypothesis. With 3 you can imagine wonderful things for yourself, and with 9 you will extract meaning from actual experience. Standing between them, number 6 will attempt to merge the imaginary and the actual. 36/9 thus catalyzes self-expression. If some of your ideas are at odds with other peoples, '36' will encourage you to transport yourself into other points of view to broaden your perspective.

Date Path Number 37

Breathing New Life into Timeless Truths

Prime Numbers are a law unto themselves and this one is inherently paradoxical as well. '3' cares little for reflection but reflection is core to number 7. The difference between 7 and 3 is 4, which makes structure, form and heritage important to the person with date path 37. Add 3 and 7 and you arrive at 10, which supports the ideal of an ordered set of principles. '3' is social while '7' is solitary and such principles must therefore allow for both needs.

Number 37 facilitates the ability to observe yourself and the consequence of your actions. An inquiring mind accompanies this date path, but also the fear of being misunderstood. The concept of truth fascinates you although you may not always adhere to it. You like to test the strength of other people's ideas. Number 37 prods you to act as 'devil's advocate' and to ask the questions that others would prefer to ignore. It challenges you to seek the truth and speak the truth – i.e., your truth – not clichés borrowed from someone else. Your imagination, your truth, and your principles need to line up because date path 37 involves harnessing restless and ambivalent energy to a just cause.

Date Path Number 38

Bridging Contemporary and Ancient Wisdom

Number 38 demands versatility in handling the imagination that comes with number 3, the seriousness that comes with number 8, and the charisma, inspiration, and extremities than accompany numbers 2 and 11; the greater the flexibility in moving between these qualities, the greater the likelihood of using them productively. 2 x 19 equaling 38 implies that although this number brings a tendency to go it alone, the reaction of other people is actively sought.

As one of your numbers, 38 will help you learn how to turn obstacles into opportunities. Polarities are likely to crop up everywhere and you will probably make a profound effort to reconcile them. This number will encourage you to turn those flashes of inspiration that course through your mind into achievements that inspire others. 38/11/2 would have you become an inspiration by demonstrating that opposing tendencies can be reconciled. To maximize the potential of date path 38, learn to value the images that arise from the subtle planes of consciousness. From these come revelations, which may be 'heard' as ideas and metaphors, music, poetry or song. When respected, these perceptive faculties gain reliability.

Date Path Number 39

Believing In the Essential Goodness of Humanity

In 39/12/3 the number 3 is first and last highlighting the significance of imagination and communication. Number 12 uses such powers to help people to see things from a variety of viewpoints. To this Number 9 adds the ability to see the bigger picture and create meaning. 39 = 13 x 3, and so we must also expect transformation to be a part of the process.

'39' encourages a shift from a purely personal perspective to one that embraces the thoughts, opinions, and feelings of the whole gamut of humankind. With number 6 representing its shadow quality, watch any tendency you may have to criticize; seek resolution instead. Date Path 39 refuses nothing and accepts everything. Your task is to look at things from as many angles as you can think of, allow other people's points of view to spark your imagination, and reverse your thinking when necessary.

Date Path Number 40

Applying the Power and Potential of the Physical World to Whatever You Set Your Mind To

The 40's bring a change of emphasis from imagination to integrity. '40' as 2 x 20 and 4 x 10 embodies stability, the potential to reconcile polarities, and become an authority in a chosen field of interest. 5 x 8 offers further stability but also the ability to integrate everything that one learns from life on Earth, in which change is the one constant.

As one of your numbers, 40 will encourage you to develop moral fibre so you can cope with whatever life brings to you. By all means stay within the realm of your personal experience but never assume that what you see is all there is to what you can experience. Number 40 will help you to progress beyond what you initially thought possible while keeping you firmly anchored in the material world. Similarly, it would encourage you to explore your past and learn from it in order to live more fully in the present.

Date Path Number 41

Enhancing Evolution by Stabilizing Initiatives

We are experiencing 41 when we realize that the groundbreaking work of number 14 is not simply about righting the wrongs of the past but also about laying a foundation for the future.

Number 41 supports the effort made by 14 to break new ground, 23 to juggle opposing forces, and 32 to communicate what you have learned. Like the other 5's, '41' is resourceful and ingenious but this one will help you to face the unexpected with composure. 41 is the thirteenth prime number and so you must expect transformation to be an important part of your life. It will keep your feet on the ground as life presents you with one challenge after another. Date Path 41 facilitates change and excels under pressure.

Date Path Number 42

Perceiving the Order of the Universe

Number 42 is distinctly 7 x 6 and 6 x 7 and as such integrity and sensitivity combine with insight and coherence. '42' also equates with 3 x 14 and so there's plenty of groundbreaking action here as well.

With 42 as one of your numbers, you can formulate a more cohesive view of reality; one that takes into account the paradoxes of the world in which we live. At another level, 42/6 brings insight into human nature and thus insight into yourself. It will heighten your awareness of both the sufferings and blessings of life on earth. Social idealism is strong here alongside practical activity. You want to be 'a part of the solution' and teach people what you have learned.

Date Path Number 43

Using a Cultural Framework to Express Your Truth

43/7 elicits the tendency to research and review the past before initiating plans for the future. It encourages prudence rather than speed; the tortoise rather than the hare. Yet as the fourteenth prime number it also chips away at making necessary changes.

In date path 43 integrity and imagination must combine. Blending them will nurture and develop your insight. This process and its outcome will be uniquely your own because 43 is a prime number. 43/7 will help you to break new ground within an existing cultural framework. It will encourage you to adopt or create a paradigm that can contain your personal truth.

Date Path Number 44

Fulfilling Lives Past and Paving the Way for Lives to Come

Whilst the single 4 is steady and methodical, the double 4 specializes in 'soaring productivity'. As 4 times 11 and 2 times 22, number 44 catalyzes inspired ideas that seek practical outcomes.

Your date path 44 gravitates towards laying down a foundation for something that might prove useful in the future. You are thus motivated by the vision of a legacy to humanity; you want to make a tangible and an enduring contribution. You will build on what has been and thus pave the way for what could be. You will work towards this one step at a time, patiently overcoming each obstacle along the way. Honour, dedication, and passion are your passwords.

Date Path Number 45

Reconciling Universal Law and Free Will

9 x 5 = 45, emphasizing both the 9 and the 5 aspects of this number. Yet 4 is up-front and so there's no freedom without integrity and no satisfactory mythology without form here. 3 x 15

brings numbers 3 and 1 (imagination and initiative) into the mix along with the impulse to find harmony and consistency within law of eternal change.

If you think of 4 as the moon and 5 as the sun and 45 as the interaction between the two of them through every nuance of light and dark, you can appreciate why it is that you seem destined to experience 'life with the lot'. You want to be free of the *conditioning* of the past and help to build a better world, but in order to do so; you must deal *with* the past, both collectively and personally. Coping with the contradictory behaviour of other people will factor into this. When you realize that the multitude of humanity lies within you, as Walt Whitman said, you will begin to understand that these apparent contradictions also lie within yourself. Number 45 will help you to appreciate that you are attracting certain experiences in order to explore the breadth of who you are. Neither by constructing castles in the air, nor by wrangling over dichotomies, will you acquire this knowledge. It comes by immersing yourself in life. Number 45 sparks a keen interest in other people because it is by participating in the lives and struggles of others that we come to understand ourselves and feel whole. It leads to accepting every part of who you are. Date Path 45 will help you to understand the dynamics of free will operating within the mechanics of the physical world.

Date Path Number 46

Establishing Principles upon Which Other People Can Depend

Within '46' integrity (4) and coherence (6) coalesce into perennial wisdom (10) but there's more to this number than rock-solid reliability. '46' = 2 x 23 and as such can generate ideas that will stretch your thinking and encourage you to cooperate with other people.

As you travelled through numbers 1, 10, 19, 28, and 37, you probably flaunted your ego, exercised your potential, brought your deepest desires to fruition, and impressed others with your version of the truth, but to enter this domain you must take your personal story into the lives of other people and lay it at their service. Number 46 will test the principles that you live by in the arena of work and practical activism. To do this successfully, you will need to assume responsibility for the myth upon which you base your life and keep in mind that you have the opportunity to be a part of an evolutionary process that is helping all forms of life attain a higher level of potential.

Date Path Number 47

Discerning the Value of Your Insight and Inspiration

The higher the 11 family goes, the more they prompt us to protect our intuition from the egos of other people and to exercise discrimination in our decision-making processes. As a prime number, 47 is one of a kind and potentially a maverick. As the fifteenth prime, it is orientated towards freedom, growth and evolution. A vision of a saner world accompanies this date path.

With 47/11 as one of your numbers, you lead best by example. And the implications of being true to yourself is bigger than you think. '47' will help you to see your inner self reflected in the outer world, which means that you can expect to see your inner world mirrored in those around you. This can be quite daunting, and until you learn to manage this situation, you may feel overwhelmed by other people. Number 47 will help you to stand in the light of your own truth and to articulate that truth as clearly as you can. It's a sophisticated number and so don't expect to master it until you are at least 47 years old.

Date Path Number 48

Applying Your Most Innovative Ideas to Practical Situations

'48' is a complex number pattern with multiple factors: 2 x 24, 3 x 16, 4 x 12, and 6 x 8. Likewise it expresses itself in diverse ways through human beings – yet always such ways have a practical orientation.

As one of your numbers, 48 will help you to combine common sense and imagination. It grants you the ability to see things from multiple points of view. Date Path 48 enables you to focus on one idea at a time, plumb its depths, and shape it into something of practical benefit to you and to others. What you can achieve with this number is limited only by your imagination.

Date Path Number 49

Structuring Thoughts Transformed through Experience

49/13/4: front and back this number is a 4, and in 49, all of the other 4's and the entire sequence of 40's, strive for fulfillment. '49' is also 7 x 7 and as such emphasizes the quest for truth. Date Path 49 necessitates making peace with the story of your life.

Date Path 49 can only be fulfilled once a transformation has occurred within your mind, i.e., 49 must pass through 13. Transformation is here wrought by honest introspection (7 x 7). '49' will encourage you to formulate your personal truth and then apply it on daily basis. Doing so will enrich the substance of our collective experience and has subtle but far-reaching implications.

Date Path Number 50

Exploring the Impact of Sensory Experience on the Mind

The 50's provide the opportunity to realize that evolution is always a work in progress and that the source of this ingenious creativity is living and evolving through each one of us. As 2 x 25, '50' blends ingenuity with empathy. It would have us recognize our common humanity with people whose views may be polar to our own. As 5 x 10, 50 can keep us centered and stable as we explore the greater potential of who we are.

As you explore the potential of number 50, you will become aware that to evolve consciously is the freedom being sought by every living thing. Once this hits home, the realization that you are making an impact on the universe in each and every moment, is not far behind. Tapping the wellspring of this insight can resolve the most intractable problems. Date Path 50 will help you to feel more centered, more alive, and more aware of the potential of your life. It will draw out your personal ingenuity and encourage you to apply it within your community.

Date Path Number 51

Reconciling Inner Drive with External Expectation

As 3 x 17, '51' requires that insight forged through contemplation be expressed through education, organization and networking. Number 51 brings the dynamic relationship between the inner and outer worlds into focus.

Through '51' ingenuity and action unite for the benefit of the community: your internal community and your external community – both. If you have a tendency to blame others when things do not accord with your expectations, 51 would have you re-claim your personal power to evolve, and resume responsibility. Date Path 51 will help to reconcile your inner and outer worlds and the process of doing so will stimulate insight. From what you learn will emerge your personal truth. You can then share such experience with your community in your own unique way. Doing so could lead to healing and restoration, both personally and collectively.

Date Path Number 52

Promoting Love and Truth

Through number 52 the power of ingenuity helps people to radiate their personal truth regardless of what others may think of them. The factors 2 x 26 and 4 x 13 inform us that this is done by blending sensitivity, compassion, integrity, initiative, and imagination. And by letting the world transform us. We are in 7's domain, which means that all of the above will bring forth insight and shape our 'truth'. Date Path 52 can lead to the realization that the more subtle worlds of existence seek accord with the material ones, and vice versa.

In number 52 the task is to find a way through the controversies, complexities and ambiguities of life by anchoring yourself in the truth, for the love of it. In return your gifts will begin to unfold of their own accord. And as your gifts unfold, you will want to share them. By kindling a lamp within your own heart, you enable your higher self to harmonize with the physical body so that it can be used as an instrument for love. As you become a channel for inspired truth, your clairvoyance will increase in reliability and value. Then truth and illusion can be distinguished and fear dispelled. '52' is four times number 13 and so you can anticipate some real transformation in your life as you engage in the above process.

Date Path Number 53

Perceiving the Interconnection of All Life-Forms

It is the scientific approach that distinguishes number 53 from 35, the latter providing the speculative thinking behind the experimental inclination inherent in 53. As the sixteenth prime number, '53' is individualistic yet service-orientated. It blends initiative, ingenuity, and imagination with compassion.

With 53 as one of your numbers, you will wander around from one philosophy to the next until you find one from which you can orientate your thinking. Once you have found a philosophy that feels right for you and upon which you can grow in understanding of other philosophies, you will feel a deep sense of peace and gratitude.

Date Path Number 54

Recognizing Your Impact on Evolution

Number 54 helps us to become aware of the impact we make on evolution at a global level. Through this vibration our personal stories become reconciled within the greater story. The factors of 54 - 6 x 9, 3 x 18, and 2 x 27 – facilitate the synthesis of art and science and can help you to create a wholistic philosophy of life.

Throughout the 9's you have been exploring the apparent conflict between the forces of dark and forces of light in many guises. Here at 54 you face the subtlest expression of this general theme: objectivity versus subjectivity. Whilst you must strive for objectivity, any meaning that you give to your findings is inherently subjective (yet you can still maintain objectivity as the goal). Integrating art and science is a vital part of the process.

Date Path Number 55

Re-Creating Oneself, Over and Over Again

Number 55, as '5 x 11', encodes the life-engendering process of perpetual re-creation. The journey through the double-5 takes people in spiral-fashion ever closer to the core of their existence. Along the way it can bring faith in the process of life and the existence of love in the universe.

As one of your Numbers, 55 will motivate you, time and again, to try new things and become a 'new' person. This is a life-affirming process that helps people discern the fundamental principles within a world of continual change. It can lead to a quantum leap in consciousness.

Date Path Number 56

Mobilizing the Collective

As the 7 x 8 and 8 x 7, number 56 is where we are invited to re-assess our values for the greater good. This can be experienced quite literally at age 56 when the things that we thought were important when we were younger gradually yield to a more universal set of values. A point of maturity is reached here that allows us to get things in perspective so that we can appreciate the significance of life. A deeper level of truth can then permeate all of our achievements.

Date Path 56 would have you undertake a pilgrimage and dialogue with your environment. Such pilgrimage may be simply a walk around your neighbourhood, along your nearest waterway, or up your closest peak. Done mindfully, your senses will become permeated with emotion as your mental faculties unite in the celebration of life. You may even come to see the whole of your life as a pilgrimage. As one of your numbers, 56 will steer you towards spiritual freedom. But like it or not, it could also make you stand out as a non-conformist.

Date Path Number 57

Shifting Perspective Collectively

We have already seen that number 12 can offer a fresh perspective on life and even the opportunity to see things in a way that is contrary to initial thinking. We have traced its development through number 39 where the personal becomes global, and 48, where the practical applications of such 'global' ideas are formulated. We have seen that the twin themes of 'peace of mind' and 'global peace' are ever present in this number family. The next one up - number 57 - encodes the expansion of the soul's intricate faculties within the body, a process that creates turbulence physically, emotionally and mentally. The reason for this is that in its movement towards complete cohabitation within the physical form, the soul perpetually regurgitates every moral issue that we encounter. As 3 times 19, '57' amalgamates imagination, ingenuity and personal initiative with universal truth.

Date Path 57 has a way of creating turbulence in the psyche but from such turbulence can emerge an organic form of creativity that is continually questioned and refined. If you allow it, '57' can reveal the limitations of your perception of life and encourage you to learn by exploring other people's 'truth' alongside your own.

Date Path Number 58

Transforming the 'Positive' and 'Negative' Aspects of Life into Works of Substance and Significance

58/13/4 brings together ingenuity and initiative, imagination and integrity, in a way that can transform a person and bring forth the hidden treasures and resources within the deeper recesses of their soul. The factors 2 x 29 highlight the need for teamwork based on an understanding of the broader scope of reality. As we change, the whole universe changes with us and we come to realize that the future is forever a work in progress, which we can influence. This is the type of awareness that can come with date path 58.

As one of your numbers, '58' is bound to transform you on every level. This will happen naturally as you take the reins of your life, give your imagination voice, and show integrity when you are challenged to do otherwise. As you express the ingenuity that arises from the deeper places within you, other people will take more notice of you. Date Path 58 would advise that instead of reacting to petty emotions, exemplify and encourage teamwork. Listen carefully to other people's thoughts on life and share your own accordingly.

Date Path Number 59

Blazing a Trail That Liberates Human Consciousness

59/14/5 is a prime number and as such behaves as a law unto itself. Add this to the fact that number 14 tends to break new ground while number 5 stimulates personal growth, and a person influenced by this number could be quite radical. 59 is the seventeenth prime and can thus be equally proactive and reactive. Behind the scenes, number 9 seeks to understand the bigger picture. Through number 59 we explore how the world *could* be.

This vibrant number will force you to break out of all forms of limited thinking in order to expand your imagination. If you can maintain the innocence of a child and keep faith in the process of life, no matter how many times you experience rebuff and rejection, people will begin to gravitate around you and your presence will help to unblock their pain and release their talents simultaneously with your own. You will evolve as you go along and you will never stop learning. Your perceptions will constantly expand. Rather than waiting for your 'sacred mission' to be revealed to you, simply make a move in the direction that feels right at the time. In other words, you need to set the wheels in motion. Once rolling, events will unfold of their own accord, with you engaged as one of several participants.

Date Path Number 60

Unifying the Potential of the Personal and the Potential of the Collective

As 10 times 6 and 6 times 10, number 60 takes the power and potential of cohesion to a whole new level. People of the corresponding age (emerging from their second Saturn Return) may actually feel this surge of power. As 2 times 30 it is imagination that facilitates such cohesion because imagination 'sees' ways of uniting people. As 4 times 15, '60' can apply integrity, initiative and ingenuity to conflict resolution. As 5 times 12, '60' helps people to experience and understand vastly different points of view. This versatile number aids groups of people with a compassionate goal.

'60' will give everything you do a wide-angled lens. It adds the archetypal to the personal and enables you to serve your community compassionately. It bestows the ability to bring people together and orchestrate events. Date Path 60 would have you recognize that it is only from the inner sanctuary of love that you can you truly respond to other people. Conflicts then become more easily resolved and creative synergy attained. That's the power and potential of number 60.

Date Path Number 61

Carving an Authentic Existence for Yourself Out Of the Collective Psyche

61 as a prime number is a law unto itself, and as the eighteenth prime, it harbours the power to create seminal works that of substantial benefit to one's community.

When number 61 is active, you will feel that the source of who you are is on the journey with you. When this realization comes to you, it will accompany the desire to carry the revelations that you receive from the supersensible worlds into this one. You will find yourself contemplating what the creator wants from you. Simultaneously you will want to do something that has lasting benefit to others. Self-honesty and discernment are critical to your success because the world is intolerant of faults in those it sets up as a 'standard'. Thus as you 'grow' into this level of consciousness, the world becomes your crucible: it will test the worth and consistency of your words and deeds. Date Path 61, as per all of those beyond number 42, is futuristically orientated; only fully accessible once your other date path numbers have been explored and integrated into daily life. This number might only become accessible when you are in your 60's.

Date Path Number 62

Restoring All Parts of Self to a State Of Love

As 2 times 31, '62' excels at breathing new life into timeless truths in a world forged from duality, paradox, and contradiction.

Like 26/8, 62/8 is conservative in nature but here you will seek to conserve the essential goodness within the collective consciousness in order to nourish future generations. To fulfill this number you must learn to love people wholeheartedly, just as they are, and temper the urge to 'modify' them.

Date Path Number 63

Perceiving one's Role as Co-Creator

63 as 7 x 9 enhances the ability to discern fact from fiction yet bring forth meaning from both.

The inversion of the numbers 3 and 6 in 63 implies a re-evaluation of your beliefs and the ideals that spring from them. As part of the process, 63 would cast you in the role of reviewer. Whilst aiming for as much objectivity as you can muster, this process is not merely criticism. It is a creative act. An essential part of such review involves acknowledging the wounds that you have suffered as the forces of dark and light battled on within you and around you. Where there is misunderstanding between yourself and another, there in particular, you can examine the hurt that awaits healing within you. Date Path 63/9 will help you to derive meaning from the struggle.

Date Path Number 64

Shaping the Collective Psyche

The Numbers 6, 4 and 10 suggest that 64 is a practically orientated ideal and its factors support this. As 4 x 4 x 4, there's a lot of integrity in this date path and as 8 x 8 it comes with organizational ability. To this 2 x 32 adds the ability to shift perceptions that have become polarized. 64/10 can help people to see that a completely different view of reality is possible.

Number 64/10 carries a responsibility not only to oneself but also to the collective of which you are a part, and only by integrating date paths 1, 10, 19, 28, 37, 46, and 55 can you do this successfully. Date Path 64 embraces a dynamic team of numbers that will help you to overcome the fear of becoming the guide to your own destiny, and a part of our collective evolution. Recognizing the sovereignty of the earth will help you to fulfill the creative potential inherent to number 64.

Date Path Number 65

Sharing the Delight of Fulfilling Our Collective Needs

As 5 times 13, there's plenty of evolutionary potential in 65. It could help a person to continually transform as they evolve to increasingly refined states of consciousness.

When 65/11 operates within the human domain, people have a tendency to become social barometers. As your heart opens to the needs of other people, inspired ideas for how to meet these needs will begin to flood into your mind. You may then be able to think of ways to act on your inspiration without compromising either your personal freedom or social responsibility. You can use your date path 65 to collaborate with your friends in projects that build a sense of community.

Date Path Number 66

Circulating Compassion

Several double-numbers come together in 66. Most importantly 6 x 11 tends to put the inspiration generated by 11 to practical use within one's community. In 2 x 33 there's plenty of gathering and sorting of information from radically different points of view. And in tandem with 3 x 22, come the skills to communicate all that one has learned in a way that 'speaks' to people. 66/12 helps people to 'see' the world more compassionately. We tap into this highly magnetic resonance when we realize that what we thought were simply our personal 'issues' are in fact collective ones. We are then in a position to consciously heal others as we consciously heal ourselves. This is where we realize the significance of finding a suitable wardrobe (or way to dress up our ideas) and to begin exploring the world of make-believe (i.e., the land where everything is possible).

Number 6 stimulates the perceptive faculties, with the double 6 highlighting the fact that perception is always a subtle two-way process. As your highest date path, you will find that '66' endorses the scientific hypothesis that the observer impacts on the observed and vice versa. Even our observances are projections that can harm or heal, and do so constantly. '66' is socially responsive; it will fill you with compassion for those who are suffering.

Date Path Number 67

Dancing Between Chaos and Harmony

67/13/4 combines cohesiveness and insight with initiative, imagination and integrity. As the nineteenth prime number, such qualities could manifest in rather extreme ways. 19 is a prime number itself, which doubles the likelihood of 67 living by its own rules.

Instead of craving pre-established order, date path 67 will help you to realize that harmony comes from appreciating difference. Once you accept what you cannot change, you can find ways to make it work for you. Run with it, then dance with it, and eventually learn to love it!

Date Path Number 68

Treasuring Life Such As It Is, and By So Doing, Unleashing Our Collective Ingenuity

68/14/5 is a number that supports 'movers and shakers'. It is an excellent number for people who want to change something that is unjust or limiting. Its factors temper extreme expressions with insight and integrity.

With 68 as your highest date path you may come to perceive that not only did the material world evolve from spiritual forces but that to evolve further, those forces must go deeper into the experience of life on earth. Past, present and future are seen in context when we realize that our collective light-body is formed through all of our sensory experiences, feelings, thoughts, and passions and that they are the substance of our collective future. There is nothing personal about 68, yet it can feel very personal, and earthy as well. You may find yourself involved in the formation of structures and organizations that secure rights, dignities, and relationships.

Date Path Number 69

Realizing the Inherent Beauty of Humanity

Number 6 targets integration, often bringing together ideas that appear impossible to reconcile. At 69, the culmination point of the 60's, we would therefore expect reconciliation at a global level. As 69/15/6, this date path must pass through '15' with its test of faith in oneself and faith in the process of life. Just so, 69/15 is focused on perceiving the perennial harmony within the chaos of temporal existence. As 3 x 23, the emphasis is on the application of imagination to this task. The '23' factor blends imagination with the magic of polarity, life experience, and personal ingenuity.

If this is one of your date paths or even a distant echo, you will eventually come to see the whole world as your family, connected by the power of love. And as you perceive your inter-dependence within the web of life, your sense of responsibility will simultaneously be heightened. You will realize that any power you have is due to a collective effort and is therefore not yours alone, yet it is yours to apply.

Date Path Number 70

Illuminating the Potential of Love Beyond The Personal

Outwardly simple inwardly rich, summarizes the essence of this vibration.

There are only two date paths in the 70's but we will study these numbers further in chapter 5. Within the 70's people become fully engaged in the activity of extra-sensory thinking, which unites the soul with the spiritual reality of the physical world. This does not mean divorcing yourself from the physical world. On the contrary, it means stretching your thinking beyond its most obvious revelations so that you can comprehend its purpose – past, present and future. The sense-world is not an illusion as some have said, but we turn it into one when we allow the illusions to act in the place of authenticity.

Not even a handful of birthdays have this actual date path. It began on December 31, 1899; re emerged on December 31, 1989 and again in December 31, 1998, last appearing on December 30, 1999. And that's all; it will not appear again for hundreds of years and so if you have this one, you are in for a unique adventure!

With 70 as your highest date path or a distant echo of your natal pattern, you are on course to learning not only from insight but also from rapture. During rapture all of the faculties of the body are in a state of suspension, delusion is stripped away, and elevation comes naturally, even to the body on occasions. Rapture consumes selfishness and all that is faulty, miserly and tepid, and thus the soul emerges victorious over all of the issues that people with date path 7 typically grapple with. The potential of number 70 is this: a soul that resides in truth becomes truth, with neither end nor beginning. All other truths hinge on this truth as all other loves hinge on this love. The relationship with your soul sets the standard for all other relationships. Your interior peace and delight will be evident to one and all. Deep within all people with date path 7 resides the awareness that bliss is their natural state, and in 70, residue aloofness gives way to an appreciation of life that is unshakeable, because it comes from first-hand experience.

Date Path Number 71

Daring To Be Different

Like all of the prime numbers we have considered, '71' has a 'mind of its own', but as the twentieth prime, team work is as important as individualism. As people progress through the family of 8's, the courage to stand at the front line of an activity or organization considered 'different' by the mainstream, grows within them until they arrive here at 71/8, and probably quite late in life. For if we try to begin at the top, missed steps will turn up as projections. Conversely if we take one step at a time and allow the inner faculties to develop in tandem with outer experiences and skill development, we eventually arrive at a state of consciousness where we know that there is nothing to fear.

People with date path 8 are compelled from a very deep place within to spread their love everywhere, but firstly they must run the gauntlet of self-honesty, humility, and the willingness to admit error, all of which begins with date path 17 (if not before) and continues to develop through both the intimate and social arenas of number 26. Mental ingenuity develops through 35 as assumptions loosen sufficiently to allow speculation, but then decisions must be made and held onto with integrity if we are to progress into the realm of 44. When we begin to explore the paradigm we have adopted in a scientific manner, we know that we are in 53-consciousness. If it proves valid it will speak to the collective soul and endure through several generations (62). Finally there comes the sublime yet palpable peace that characterizes number 71. Yet having defined the sequence it must also be understood that at any one time there is a juxtaposition of all of these qualities. And just because 71 is the highest possible date path at this point in time does not mean that it is the end of the line. Our consciousness is ever developing and 71 represents merely the beginning of the 70's and a stepping stone towards the 80's wherein work, family life, and spiritual development operate as a single unit.

Just by having this date path your soul is daring to be different, for it was only available on a single day: December 31, 1999 and cannot be experienced again as a date path number, until December 31, 2998 and so you are different! Having date path 71 suggests that you can trust that you have all of the resources that you need to do whatever it is that you came here to do.

Chapter 2

Vowels and Consonants

Part A: The Vowel Number

In ancient times vowels were considered sacred and in some parts of the world, they still are. They encode the 'voice' of the soul. The original name represents the original impulse, whilst later names represent later developments. The vowels articulate the way that the soul will express itself if it is not repressed. In this way the vowel number (i.e., the aggregate number of all the vowels in the name) reveals the way that the soul works towards the fulfilment of the ideals encoded in the date path.

What Is A Vowel?

In English, A E I O and U are always vowels. Every syllable in a word must have a vowel and so if one of these five regular vowels is not present look for the letter y. Y can be a vowel, especially when preceded by one of the five regular vowels if *together* they sound like a vowel, as in ey and ay. The name C*ayce* provides an example.

Calculating the Vowel Number

The most popular method of calculation is the so-called Pythagorean system. Born around 580 BC, Pythagoras lived his formative years on the island of Samos off the coast of Asia Minor or Turkey as it is known today. Research suggests that his father was a merchant and that Pythagoras had contact with the belief systems of many different cultures. His early adult years were spent studying in Egypt and Babylon, the chief centres of learning at that time. The ideas he formulated represent a synthesis of the timeless wisdom of the Egyptians, Druids, Chaldeans, Phoenicians, Magi and Persians, whose knowledge bore a strong resemblance to the Hindu Vedas. Furthermore the Hebrew people were in Babylon at the time Pythagoras was there, and so he had access to their knowledge as well. At around fifty years of age, Pythagoras began a school in Crotona, Southern Italy. He taught that all things accord to number and that number encodes the secrets of the cosmos. Because one of Pythagoras' methods of analyzing a word was to reduce the word to a number value that fitted into the sacred decad, the number system we use today that reduces numbers to a single figure between 1 and 9 is called 'Pythagorean'. When the Ancient Greek, Hebrew and Phoenician alphabets are compared with modern English, 38 per cent are basically the same. This is quite remarkable but also indicates the limitations of correlating the older alphabets with our present one. I therefore prefer to call the system of English Language Correspondences just that.

Letter Correspondences:

1	2	3	4	5	6	7	8	9
A	B	C	D	E	F	G	H	I
J	K	L	M	N	O	P	Q	R
S	T	U	V	W	X	Y	Z	

Every language has its own structure and purpose in the evolution of humanity. Those people who think that English is inferior to the more ancient tongues may not have realized what an extraordinary tool of thought we currently have at our disposal. English is possibly the most adaptable language that there has ever been. The versatility of the English language enables it to embrace many viewpoints and alternate realities, to shape-shift and re-emerge metamorphisized. Its innovativeness has accelerated the spread and scope of knowledge throughout the world. Therefore its correspondences to the number system we currently use are important to us.

Worksheet and Example

A worksheet for calculating the vowel, consonant and name numbers is included in the worksheets section of the book and what follows is an example of how the worksheet can be used.

Original Name

					11				5					17	= 38/11 Vowel Number
1		5		9	1			5			6	6	5		
A	L	E	C	I	A		B	E	T	H	M	O	O	R	E

Although not a date path number, we can turn to chapter 1, date path 38, to interpret Alecia's vowel number. Rather than an attitude however, we must here interpret it as a soul longing. Vowel Number 38 indicates that Alecia's soul longs to unite the imagination that comes with number 3, the seriousness of number 8, and the charisma of number 11. Flexibility is needed to bring such qualities together. Alecia Beth Moore is better known as Pink (stylized as P!ink), nominated as one of the 100 greatest women in music. And she is definitely flexible!

Stage Name

				9	= 9 Vowel Number
	9				
P	I	N	K		

Vowel 11 and Vowel 9 are compatible. Both long to contribute to the welfare of humanity and the environment. Both numbers encourage broad mindedness. As vowels they both yearn to share their ideals and need an outlet for the desire to make a difference.

In 2006, Pink married Carey Hart and took the name Alecia Beth Moore Hart.

Married Name: Original Name plus 'Hart':

				1	= a total Vowel Number of 39/12
	1				
H	A	R	T		

The original vowel number of 11 will remain with Alecia regardless of future names but numbers 9 and 12 are now impacting on it and shaping it in a particular way. Numbers 9, 11 and 12 all tend to be idealistic and so it's not surprising that Pink uses the power of her voice to support organizations that care about the welfare of animals such as PETA, PAW, and the RSPCA.

Interpreting Vowel Numbers

Vowel Number 1

The longing encoded in vowel number 1 is to determine your own course of action. Just as 'one' is a common factor of all numbers, so is this quality common to all people. To be truly vowel number 1, the name would have to consist of a single 'a' and contain no other vowel. Therefore in most cases the vowel number is actually '10', which has been written about further into this chapter.

Vowel Number 2

The innate soul quality encoded in vowel number 2 is engagement with another person. Thus people with vowel number 2 find themselves continually drawn into intimate relationships. With '2' as your vowel number, building bridges with other people will support the development of your date path. By interacting personally with others you will learn how it feels to be dependent, and then by contrast independent. Should you remain true to your heart, you will eventually arrive at interdependence or 'win-win', which reconciles this apparent polarity. With vowel number 2 (or more likely 20), you have a deep longing to engage in personal and meaningful relationships with other people. If your vowel number is an 11, read also that section further into this chapter.

Vowel Number 3

The longing of the soul encoded in vowel 3 is to feel a part of a group of like-minded people. With 3 as your vowel number, you want to know the contentment that comes with being able to share your ideas without the fear of being personally criticized. Vowel 3 will encourage you to exercise your imagination and that could scatter your thoughts all over the place, especially if there are several other 3's in your astronumerology. What would give your soul the most satisfaction however is to focus on the one thing that gives you the most joy. Once you've chosen something to focus your imagination on, learn everything about it from books, observing people, asking questions etc. Don't get too serious about it though because vowel 3 brings with it the ability to see the funny side of life. If your vowel number is a 12, read also that section further into this chapter.

Vowel Number 4

Encoded as vowel number 4 is the soul's longing to feel secure in the material world. With 4 as your vowel number, your soul longs for stability. You need to feel secure before the ideals encoded in your date path can come to fruition. Your soul yearns to find a corner of the working world that allows it to express its integrity and commitment to quality. And you may have known from an early age that inner and outer work go hand in hand for you. Number 4 brings time into perspective. It will help you to appreciate the contribution of the past and thereby to know what needs to be done in the present. There's concern here with the preservation and protection of all that is good for future generations. Should your vowel number include 13 in the calculation, then there is also longing to transform yourself so that you can feel in complete harmony with your environment. Such soul-longings must factor into your date path, and if your vowel calculation includes number 22 there is more - read on to the end of this section.

Vowel Number 5

It is the soul's longing for liberation that is encoded in vowel number 5, making this is a restless vibration that does not tolerate limitation. With 5 as your vowel number, you will feel constantly restless until you locate that still place in the epicentre of your soul. In the meantime you need the freedom to investigate *everything!* You will want to be on the move and to feel like you are making progress. You want to evolve, and you will do this through sensory experience. Ideals, imagination and intent are important but they must engage the senses. You need to touch, taste, see, smell, and hear life in all of its facets. Some of the darker expressions of humanity can be experienced vicariously; you never need to go there personally but you *do* need to acknowledge them if you are to fully understand your human potential. Lived without undue fear, vowel 5 can set you on the path to true liberation.

Vowel Number 6

The innate soul quality encoded in vowel 6 is to cluster with other souls and experience belonging to a group that is working together for a common purpose. With 6 as your vowel number it is the way that you interact with other people that either supports or obstructs the development of your date path. Because 6 is a 'double 3', there is much thinking, imagining, worrying and excitement going on here, all of which can bring forth the soul's capacity to care. Vowel 6 can entrap you in other people's expectations, especially if you have a need to feel needed. Conversely it tends to project expectations onto others. It's an on-going balancing act to find a way to express the compassion you feel in your heart, without assuming responsibility for another person's soul-journey. Managed carefully, number 6 will help you to create a saner and more beautiful world wherein everyone feels valued.

Vowel Number 7

The innate soul quality seeking to radiate into the world here is the beauty of simplicity. Consequently, the longing encoded in vowel 7 is to know the truth. With 7 as your vowel number you need to comprehend the significance of the material world but it will probably take you a while to sort out what is useful information from what is simply weighing you down. It requires a tremendous amount of self-honesty to achieve this, and you must be willing to examine the way that you relate to other people as a part of the process. Frequent intervals of peace and quiet are necessary, because at such times the soul can shake off the shroud of self pre-occupation and posit a more universal viewpoint. You would benefit from spending as much time in the natural world as you can because in nature you will find the perennial truth that you seek. The inner work done, vowel 7 can grant you coolness under fire when it is most needed, emanating from a deep sense of peace.

Vowel Number 8

The innate soul quality being radiated here is resilience in the midst of apparently opposing forces, such as life and death. The figure 8 can be imaged as a double zero and thus encode the soul's desire to showcase its potential in the material world. Yet zealousness must be checked by the alignment of personal will with the greater will of humanity. If the ego is able to shake off self-importance, the outcome is the realization of the eternality of the cycle of giving and receiving, symbolized by the way that we draw the figure 8. As the double 4, vowel 8 extends the soul's integrity into the world at large through its essential goodness and awesome strength. In true '4' style this happens by the perpetual creation of goals that form steps of achievement. And each of these achievements, no matter how small, is significant because each demonstrates the soul's resourcefulness. Vowel Number 8 stimulates the desire to know and integrate all parts of you through effective action in the material world. It will lead you to the realization that you are limited only by the power to imagine the possibilities.

Vowel Number 9

Whereas vowel 8 plumbs the depths of the soul, vowel 9 explores its breadth. This tends to stir up the soul's desire to contribute to the betterment of humanity and the environment so that each and every soul's greatness can be fully realized. With 9 as your vowel number it is your response to the mass of contradictions that life presents to you that will determine how effectively you bring the ideals encoded in your date path to fruition. Number 9 catalyzes intense discussions about the meaning of life, and the yearning to share one's understanding of the human condition. Idealism runs strong here and will provide a major undercurrent behind your date path, especially if you have other 9's in your astronumerology. Your soul needs to feel that it can contribute to the betterment of the world and it will do so through your ego. Vowel 9 stimulates the desire make a difference. Your task is to find a way that works for you.

Vowel Number 10

There are two inherent and inseparable soul qualities seeking to radiate themselves here: authenticity and fearlessness. Authenticity means tossing aside the masks and being truly yourself and that takes a certain amount of fearlessness. It's not so much about bravado as about knowing that you have nothing to hide and therefore nothing to fear. Your soul is guiding you towards a position of leadership so that it can express its full potential. As a leader you have the opportunity to become a guiding light for others, even a pillar within your community. It is essential therefore that you find your own unique and authentic 'voice' and learn to express it.

Vowel Number 11

Generally speaking the odd numbers encode the soul's power to repel (i.e. individuate) whilst the even numbers symbolize its power of attraction (i.e. absorption in other souls). In number 11/2 the soul does both at once! In other words, vowel 11 longs to stand in its own light within the 'group soul'. This creates a charismatic light within the group, a focal point for other souls; ideally, an inspiration. When it is used wisely, '11' has the potential to create rapport between the members of a group. As a Vowel Number, the double-1 represents the longing to share your ideals with like-minded people. You need an outlet for your inspired ideas. Initially this will be a personal outlet: some form of creative self expression. At some time in your life however you will want to find a group of people who share your ideas. Or you may feel compelled to form a group of your own wherein you can explore your ideas with other people. If you are finding it difficult to cope with the unpredictable surges of energy that accompany number 11, the advice offered is to learn yoga because therein are the breathing exercises and physical postures that will stabilize your energy.

Vowel Number 12

Occasionally the vowel calculations reveal a 12 (rather than a 3, 21 or 30) and '12' holds a distinct place within the astral wheel, which will be discussed at length in later chapters. Here it suffices to say that vowel 12 represents the soul's urge to merge with an ideal. The numbers tell it this way: the ego up front (i.e. number 1) yearns to enlist the co-operation of the soul in a social ideal. In the process however, the soul is likely to turn the tables on the ego and seek its co-operation in a much broader concept than initially envisaged. If '12' appears in your vowel number, your soul wants to feel a part of a social 'movement' that is helping to create a more compassionate society. Vowel Number 12 indicates that at some time in your life you will want to merge with an ideal such as the ones described by your date path.

Vowel Number 22

People working positively with vowel 22 are like tall trees. Their feet (or roots), are planted squarely on the earth, whilst their head (or crown), dances in the breeze. They have vision, patience and integrity and they long to construct something tangible that will continue to be of benefit to the world after their passing. If '22' appears in your vowel number, you need to find a way to make your visions tangible so that we can all benefit from them. As a double 11, 22 can strain the nervous system. When it gets too much to bear, you will revert to vowel number 4 and opt for step by step progress rather than grand schemes and there's nothing wrong with that. Working steadily and in cooperation with other people is exactly what 22/4 is about; yet the bigger picture ideals will always lie in the back of your mind. A famous person with this soul desire was Iambilichus, the philosopher who created a unique branch of Neo-Platonism. Reworking the ideas of his predecessors, he fused mathematics and mysticism into a unique cosmology. He is an important source of information on Pythagoras, being one of only two people who had the foresight to write a biography on the famous philosopher – and 'foresight' is the hallmark of the master numbers.

Part B: The Consonant Number

While the vowel number resonates with an impulse from the soul, the consonant number indicates the instinctive survival mode of the body, which that soul inhabits. As such, the consonant number reveals the involuntary image that you present to strangers. It has a way of becoming what others expect from you. The consonant vibration can either block or assist the date path, depending on your level of awareness. It is therefore in your best interests to understand the meaning of this number so that you can work with it to achieve your goals.

Calculating Consonant Number

Calculation of the consonant is easy; the tricky bit was determining the vowels. Consonants are actually a subtle form of gesture and provide the essential shape of words. To determine the consonant number, add up all of the consonants in the name and reduce to a single digit. The exceptions are always 10, 11, and 12.

Continuing with our example:

Original Name

A	L	E	C	I	A		B	E	T	H		M	O	O	R	E			
	3		3				2		2	8		4			9				
					6					12						13	Consonant Number = 31/4		

As with the vowel number, we can look to chapter 1 for the interpretation of consonant number 31. Rather than an attitude or a soul longing however, we must here interpret it as an instinctual behaviour or habit. Number 31 resonates with the impulse to formulate an idea due to enter the mainstream of human consciousness. There's a maverick quality about this number. It looks back for inspiration just as Alecia drew inspiration from Janis Joplin. And it takes such inspiration forward, giving it a form that is relevant to the present generation.

Stage Name

P	I	N	K			
7		5	2			
				14	Consonant Number = 14/5	

Number 14 tends to break new ground just as Pink has done with her music. An interesting fact is that Alecia adopted the name 'Pink' when she was 14 years old. She was 14 when she auditioned to become a member of *Basic Instinct* and began performing in Philadelphia clubs. Vowel 9 with consonant 5 unites idealism and progressive ideas. Pink has changed the sound of modern pop music and paved the way for other female vocalists.

Married Name: as above plus

H	A	R	T		
8		9	2		
				19	= a total Consonant Number of 50

Number 50/5 extends the theme of Consonant 14/5. Although it's not the same as her original consonant number, or any other of her significant numbers for that matter, '5' is a congenial number that helps other numbers shine.

Interpreting the Consonant Numbers

The consonant number of the original name is valid throughout life but subsequent names also impact on the way that you appear to other people. It is therefore wise to consider both.

Consonant Number 1

The instinctual response encoded in consonant 1 is the one that we are most familiar with: fight. As a member of the animal kingdom, fight is humanity's most basic survival instinct. Yet although this instinct is as common to humans as number 1 is a factor common to all numbers, consonant 1 is actually more likely to be consonant 10, and so the reader should look there for further information.

Consonant Number 2

Consonant 2 encodes the instinct to role-play with another person. As a mental power, this extends to the ability to maintain engagement with a subject of interest and retain information about it. With 2 as your consonant number it is likely that you are proficient with data. You might also have an excellent memory for personal details. You are apt to be cautious, tactful and diplomatic, because you are responsive to other people's feelings. At times you might be inclined to act a little coy and understate yourself. Consonant 2 brings forth the team player, who knows how to listen to and support other people. There is scope here to explore your ability to accommodate and reconcile differences. If there is an 11 in the calculation, see also consonant 11.

Consonant Number 3

Consonant 3 encodes the instinct to befriend. This probably relates to the herd instinct and what we call 'safety in numbers'. Translated into a mental power it becomes the ability to make associations, imagine possible scenarios and speculate. With 3 as your consonant number, friends are vitally important to your sense of well being. You probably enjoy making all sorts of acquaintances and learning from them but you tend to choose your friends based on mutual interest such as a particular lifestyle or ideal that you have in common. Consonant 3 enhances the ability to make associations on all levels: socially, intellectually and spiritually. This number stimulates the imagination so that you can envisage possibilities – again on all levels. You are naturally curious and a perennial student; you will want to continue learning until the day you die. You are probably also innately optimistic. There is scope here to explore your ability to motivate other people. If there is a 12 in the calculation, see also consonant 12

Consonant Number 4

People with consonant 4 are naturally dependable because their survival strategy is to slot in with the way that things are done. The instinct encoded in consonant 4 is to fulfil your role within your family or social unit, which may be witnessed in a pride of lions or pack of wolves, for example. The fact that every member knows his or her place ensures stability and continuation. This translates into integrity, which is the hallmark of number 4. With 4 as your consonant number, you are naturally productive and conscientious. You have an intrinsic need to work harmoniously with other people and your health suffers if there is disharmony in your environment. Consonant 4 will help you to structure any project that you turn your hand to. There is scope here to explore your ability to create harmony from chaos. If there is a 22 in the calculation, see also consonant 22.

Consonant Number 5

People with consonant 5 tend to survive by exploring their options and opportunities. Instinctually they adapt and make the most of things, hence their obvious versatility. With 5 as your consonant number, you are naturally progressive and youthful. This number will grant you an abundance of energy and a vigorous personality. With consonant 5 comes the opportunity to realize that evolution is always a work in progress and that the source of this ingenious creativity is living and evolving through each one of us. Consonant 5 will help you to feel more alive. It will draw out your personal ingenuity and encourage you to apply it within your community. There is scope here to explore your ability to promote the talents of others as well as your own. The natural propensity of the entrepreneurial '5' is to seek progress and variety in a socially beneficial way. If there is a 14 in the calculation, breaking new ground comes instinctively to you.

Consonant Number 6

An instinct displayed by the bird kingdom is to peck at another bird that is weak or out of place. Transmuted into a mental power granted to human beings, this would seem to be our critical faculty. It gives us the ability to destroy a defective point of view. As a mental power, this relates to the quest for consistency. With 6 as your consonant number, you are naturally dutiful, loaded with common sense, and have high expectations of yourself. You are also naturally affectionate and performing acts of kindness gives you real pleasure. Unifying the destruction of weakness and the performing of compassionate acts is your tendency to restore whatever is discordant to harmony. Consonant number 6 grants you a well-developed critical faculty. You can spot a defective point of view a mile off because you instinctively look for consistency. You will find that consonant number 6 inclines you towards watching over other people and attempting to improve their well being and state of mind. Your survival strategy is to adjust whatever needs adjusting (from your perspective). There is scope here to explore your ability to heal by meeting the everyday trails of life with love. If there is a 33 in the calculation, as in Clive Staples Lewis or Julian Paul Assange, you also have a strong urge to gather information and express your opinions.

Consonant Number 7

The instinct encoded in consonant 7 is to hibernate. Within the human being this translates into the ability to go into the cavern of the mind, on a periodical basis, and experience the peace and sustenance therein. With 7 as your consonant number, you are naturally reserved and quite difficult to get to know on a personal level. You might come across as aloof, but you would prefer other people to think of you as simply 'holding your own counsel'. Your survival strategy is to withdraw from conflict. You enjoy time alone to analyze, contemplate and develop theories that explain such things as conflict (rather than actually experiencing it). There is scope here to explore your ability to discern of fact from fiction, and to impart an understanding of natural law.

Consonant Number 8

The instinct behind number 8 relates to what is commonly called flight but instead of the withdrawal that characterizes 7, this is the instinct to keep on running until the pursuer gives up. It may accompany an irrational but persistent feeling of being hounded (perhaps by one's own daemon) yet it transmutes into the ability to pursue. With 8 as your consonant number, you are naturally goal-orientated. You are also naturally tenacious and resourceful, once you set your mind to a task. You come across to other people as serious and efficient. Your self-motivation accompanies the need for independence so that you can get on with the job at hand. Consonant 8 grants you the ability to 'go the long haul' and do whatever needs to be done to accomplish something that you feel passionate about. There is scope here to explore your ability to *enjoy* tackling problems with lasting benefits. If there is a 44 in the calculation, as in John Maynard Keynes, it offers the innate ability to create a work of substance, building it up from scratch into something durable and worthwhile.

Consonant Number 9

The instinct encoded in consonant 9 is to surrender. Cognitively this implies being able to suspend judgment while you consider something that cannot be understood at the time. With 9 as your consonant number, you are naturally idealistic. Consonant 9 catalyzes an understanding of the bigger picture, as the associations characteristic of Number 3 develop into generalizations. '9' generates a generous attitude, granting you the ability to forfeit the personal and make room for the universal. There is scope here to explore your ability to overlook the faults of others, and embrace widely divergent points of view.

Consonant Number 10

In Consonant 10 our innate fighting instinct is extended into the ability to 'hold one's ground', which is a sophisticated form of 'fighting', at any level. With 10 as your consonant number, you are naturally self-motivated. Even in your early years, you might also be the tower of strength upon which others depend. Mostly you come across to other people as confident, self-reliant, and decisive. There is scope here to explore your ability to initiate projects and assume the lead role in their fulfilment. When 10 is a reduced form of number 55, as in Michael Francis Moore, versatility enters the equation and you have the ability to re-create yourself time and again without losing your authenticity.

Consonant Number 11

Consonant 11 encodes the instinct to defend one's young, evident in higher animals. Translated into a mental power it becomes the ability to defend a point of view that is in danger of being quashed, ignored or overlooked. With 11 as your consonant number, you are naturally intuitive and far-sighted. You are probably also charismatic and slightly ahead of your time. Beware of any tendency you may have to want to 'clone' other people so that they behave just like you. With consonant 11/2, you are learning to appreciate other people such as they are. Consonant 2 is relatively easy to work with, and so some people with consonant 11/2 decide (probably subconsciously) to stick with the characteristics of number 2 and deny number 11 an existence. It takes courage to work with number 11 and a hefty dose of self-honesty. To those who can handle 'the heat', consonant 11 bestows the ability to stand firm in the face of opposition and to bring your attackers around to your way of thinking. There is scope here to explore social reform based on authentic vision.

Consonant Number 12

Building on the instinct encoded in number 11 to defend those who cannot defend themselves, 12 becomes the remarkable instinct to rescue. This instinct has been witnessed in several higher animals including dogs, wolves and dolphins. Each of these species is known to have rescued at least one human being at some time. Number symbolism suggests that this is a sophisticated form of the herd instinct (3). As 4 x 3, consonant 12 relates to the instinct to ensure the survival of the herd. With 12 as your consonant number, you are naturally idealistic and probably a crusader for peace and justice. You are learning to see things from multiple points of view and to present your ideas in a way that other people can understand. Consonant 12 attracts companionship. There is scope here to explore your ability to apply friendship to healing the rift within people and between people.

Consonant Number 22

Building on what has already been written regarding consonant 4, 22 would seem to be the instinct to formulate a routine that ensures the survival of whatever group one is a part of. With 22 as your consonant number, you are naturally sensitive and sensible. You may appear to some people as super-human because you want to right the wrongs in the world and will not stint in your effort to accomplish whatever you can. With consonant 22/4 you are learning to apply your sensitivity to practical projects that benefit other people. Consonant 4 is relatively easy to work with, and so some people with consonant 22/4 decide (probably subconsciously) to stick with the characteristics of number 4 and deny number 22 an existence. It takes humility and integrity to work with number 22. There is scope here to explore your ability create systems, structures and methodologies that have broad implications.

Part C: Vowel-Consonant Combinations: A Guide To Your Inner Resources

Combining the longing of the soul and the survival instinct of the body

People with vowel number 1 are likely to find themselves propelled into positions of leadership because in some way, large or small, they are pioneers and trailblazers.

<u>Vowel 1 with consonant 1</u> intensifies individualism. You may harbour a compelling urge to do things your own way, but if you give your best, you might also find partnerships rewarding. Examples include: *Aldous Leonard Huxley and Bertrand Arthur William Russell: pioneering philosophers, *Alphonse Louis Constant, Maria Ellen Mackillop, and Narendranath Datta (Swami Vivekananda): spiritual pioneers, *Archibald William Roach ("Archie Roach") and Kathryn Dawn Lang (k. d. lang): pioneering singer/songwriters.

<u>Vowel 1 with consonant 2</u> unites the longing to pioneer something with the need for social engagement. This pair catalyzes a healthy drive to communicate. Examples include: *Thomas Cook: travel agent pioneer.

<u>Vowel 1 with consonant 3</u> unites initiative and imagination, catalyzing fresh ideas. Examples include: *John Varley: astrologer & watercolorist, *Joseph Chilton Pearce: educator, *Joseph Priestley: chemist and *Williamina Paton Stevens: astronomer.

<u>Vowel 1 with consonant 4</u> offers initiative, integrity and enthusiasm. Examples include: *Bryan Gaenster, Gregor Johann Mendel, Mary Fairfax (Somerville) and Robert Heinrich Herman Koch: scientists, *William Brugh Joy: doctor, *Edmund Spenser: poet (the name 'Kabir' also has this pattern), and *Robert Allan Monroe: author: *Journeys Out of the Body*.

<u>Vowel 1 with consonant 5</u>, unites vitality, courage, and compassion. Examples include: *Arthur Francis Grimble: administrator, anthropologist and writer, *John Ronald Reuel Tolkien, John Griffith Chaney ("Jack London"), and William Horwood: writers, and *Maria Francesca Cabrini: nun and social worker.

<u>Vowel 1 with consonant 6</u> ignites social activism. Examples include: *Albert Camus and Anna Laetitia Aiken: writers, *Carole Anne Millwater (Kudu): PNG politician, Charles Augustus Tulk: social reformer, and Neville Thomas Bonner: first indigenous Australian to become a member of Parliament and *Kuppuswamy Iyer (later known as Swami Sivananda): medical doctor, hospital director and author of over 100 books.

<u>Vowel 1 with consonant 7</u> catalyzes the drive to accomplish something worthwhile in one's own unique way. Examples include: *David Glynne Ross: one of the first Concorde pilots, *Gladys Maria Knight and Henry John Deutschendorf Jr ("Denver"): singers.

<u>Vowel 1 with consonant 8</u> unites willpower and organizational ability. Together they can throw their considerable force behind an ideal. Examples include: *Alexander Graham Bell: inventor & teacher, *Edgar Cayce: photographer & psychic, *Margaret ("Peggy") van Praagh: ballet dancer, choreographer, teacher, advocate, *Mikhail Sergeyevich Gorbachev and William Pitt: statesmen.

<u>Vowel 1 with consonant 9</u> yokes idealism to an abiding belief in the potential of humanity. This pair can set in motion some wonderful creativity. Examples include: *Muriel Sarah Spark (novelist) and Samuel Barclay Beckett (playwright), *Timothy Allen Dick ("Tim Allen"): actor & comedian, and *William Wynn Westcott: co-founder of 'The Golden Dawn', doctor & freemason.

<u>Vowel 1 with consonant 11</u> unites vision and determination. This pair fuels social activism. You may want other people to see things in a whole new way. Examples include: *Alan Alexander Milne, Ernest Miller Hemingway, Patrick Victor Martindale White: writers, *Gustav Mahler: composer & conductor and *Stefani Joanne Angelina Germanotta ("Lady Gaga": singer & songwriter: vowel 55 with date path 55), and *John Stuart Mill: philosopher, political economist & writer. See also vowel 1, consonant 2.

<u>Special case</u>: Mary Adams: astrologer and numerologist, her vowel 1, consonant 22 matching her birthday 1 and missing date path 22.

People with vowel number 2 yearn to be 'bridge-builders'.

Most of these combinations are uncommon, some quite rare, hence some professional names have been included. The earthy quality of number 2 is evident in several examples.

<u>Vowel 2 with consonant 1</u> unites the longing for intimacy with the courage of one's personal convictions. Examples include: *Francis Arthur Fox: metallurgist, and *Joan Chandos Baez: singer.

<u>Vowel 2 with consonant 2</u> intensifies the urge to engage in meaningful relationships with other people, and sparks the drive for integrity within such relationships. Examples include: *Hans Last (better known as James Last, musician, composer, and arranger), and *Epicurus: Greek philosopher (not his real name yet he bears the earthiness of number 2).

<u>Vowel 2 with consonant 3</u> unites the longing for intimacy with imagination. Together they catalyze social ingenuity. Examples include: *Juno Belle Kapp: (better known as Juno Jordan, numerologist), *John Russell Waters and Walter Stacy Keach: actors.

<u>Vowel 2 with consonant 4</u> unites the longing for intimacy with integrity. Together they catalyze compassion. Examples include: *John Galsworthy: novelist and playwright, *Marc Edmund Jones: astrologer, and *William Sharp: an artist born in 1749 and a poet, born in 1855 who wrote under the pseudonym Fiona MacLeod.

<u>Special case</u>: Marian Wright resonates with this pattern while her married name - Marian Wright Edelman - resonates with its inverse: vowel 4, consonant 2 (11). She was a lawyer and activist for civil rights in general and children's rights in particular.

<u>Vowel 2 with consonant 5</u> unites the longing for intimacy with ingenuity. Together they can stimulate real insight into the nature of life and people. Examples include *Joseph Smith: founder of the Church of the Latter Day Saints, *Michael Hugh Lavarch: Attorney-General of Australia 1993-6, lawyer, educator, and *William Schaw: one of the founders of Freemasonry.

<u>Vowel 2 with consonant 6</u> unites the longing for intimacy with compassion, fuelling the drive to achieve something within your community. Examples include: *John Linnell: artist (vowel 20, consonant 33), *Karl Marx: co-author of the *Communist Manifesto*, and *Margaret Mary Tew: better known as Mary Douglas, anthropologist.

Vowel 2 with consonant 7 unites the longing for intimacy with insight. A healthy mixture of idealism and enterprise can emerge from this combination. Examples include *Baruch Spinoza: optician & philosopher, and *Yitzhak Rabin: 1st native-born PM of Israel, who shared the Nobel Peace Prize with his former adversaries.

Vowel 2 with consonant 8 unites the longing for intimacy with persistence. Together they fuel the drive to create something of lasting value. Examples include: *Franz Joseph Haydn: composer and *William Beckett: musician-singer-songwriter, *Max Karl Ernst Ludwig Planck (vowel 20, consonant 80): theoretical physicist, and *Steven Paul Jobs: co-founder of Apple Computer Corporation.

Vowel 2 with consonant 9 unites the longing for intimacy with the meaning that you attribute to life. Shared dreams that benefit the world can be realized but self-honesty must be maintained. Examples include: *Jonathan Coleman: larger-than-life radio funnyman, *Glenn Singleman: physician, adventurer, film-maker, motivational speaker, *Suzanne Malherbe: artist, and *Wystan Hugh Auden: poet and dramatist.

Vowel 2 with consonant 11 unifies inspiration and team-work. This combination will help you to transform something that is not working into something of great value. Examples include: *Andrew Fisher and Winston Leonard Spencer Churchill: politicians, *Edith Joy Scovell, poet who wrote "our love... was all that the Earth needs" (a theme that resonates with this combination), and *Robin McLaurin Williams: actor. See also vowel 2, consonant 2.

People with vowel number 3 need to channel their creative potential into projects that they can enjoy.

Vowel 3 with consonant 1 unifies imagination and initiative. This combination will help you to create things of tangible benefit. If you want to stretch your personal development try working within a team setting. Examples include: *Andrew Marvell, John Keats, John Milton, Samuel Johnson: writers, *Norbert Wiener: mathematician and founder of cybernetics, *Wilhelm Richard Wagner: composer and *Taylor Alison Swift: singer/songwriter.

Vowel 3 with consonant 2 yokes imagination and intimacy with the drive to evolve. Examples include *Simone Lucie Ernestine Marie Bertrand de Beauvoir: writer and companion of Satre.

Vowel 3 with consonant 3 intensifies imagination. This combination would have you exercise your imagination in the service of your community. Examples include: *Hillary Diane Rodham/ Hillary Rodham Clinton (both names have the same pattern) senator, *Melanie Richards Griffiths (vowel 48/12, consonant 84/12, with date path 39/12): actor and model, *Paul Leroy Robeson (vowel 39, consonant 39): singer, actor, activist, *Samuel Taylor Coleridge (vowel 48, consonant 48) and William Cowper: poets.

Vowel 3 with consonant 4 brings imagination and integrity together. This combination stimulates insight that can be put to practical use. Don't be afraid to take the lead sometimes! Examples include: *Burnum Burnum: activist & storyteller, (Harry Penrith, his other name, is vowel 4, consonant 3), *Irmgard Charlotte Keun: author, and *Lester Bowie: composer.

<u>Vowel 3 with consonant 5</u> unifies imagination and personal ingenuity. Together they stimulate the drive to achieve something worthwhile, but don't overlook teamwork. Examples include: *Elizabeth Jane Coatsworth: poet & Newbery Medal writer, *Paul Foster Case: musician & teacher of the occult, and *Robert Peel: founder of the London Police Force.

<u>Vowel 3 with consonant 6</u> unites imagination and compassion. Together they spur the drive to make the world a better place in which to live. Examples include: *Jacques Yves Cousteau: marine biologist & inventor of the aqualung, *Arnold Alois Schwarzenegger and Katharine Houghton Hepburn: actors, *Marie-Joseph-Pierre Teilhard De Chardin: archaeologist, palaeontologist, philosopher & priest, and *Rudolfus Josephus Laurentius Steiner: philosopher & teacher.

<u>Vowel 3 with consonant 7</u> blends imagination and insight. Together they fuel the drive to stand tall and do something worthwhile. Examples include: *James Young Simpson and John Snow: medical pioneers, *Judith Arundell Wright: poet, conservationist & campaigner for aboriginal rights, *Kathleen Kenyon: archaeologist, and *Michael Mansell: lawyer & land rights activist.

<u>Vowel 3 with consonant 8</u> blends imagination with persistence. This combination can lead to exceptional achievement; but you must remain flexible! Examples include: *Alan Lloyd Hodgkin: physiologist, *Edwin Arnold and Paul-Marie Verlaine: poets, and *John Napier: mathematician who invented logarithms.

<u>Vowel 3 with consonant 9</u> unifies imagination and idealism. The scene is set for social activism but always remember to factor in compassion. Examples include: *Robert-Victor-Felix Delaunay Sydney Robert Nolan and William Dobell: artists, *Mohandas Karamchand Gandhi: politician (former PM of India), *Richard Charles Nicholas Branson, and Poppy Cybele King: entrepreneurs.

<u>Vowel 3 with consonant 11</u> unites imagination and inspiration, and together they can lead to ground-breaking achievements. Examples include: *George Herbert Walker Bush, Harry S Truman, Ralph Johnson Bunche: statesmen, *Igor Fyodorovich Stravinsky: composer, *Jean Nicolas Arthur Rimbaud, and Peter Bradford Blazey: writers.

People with vowel number 4 must find a corner in the working world that allows them to express their integrity and commitment to quality.

<u>Vowel 4 with consonant 1</u> unites integrity and initiative. Together they fuel the drive to evolve beyond current limitations. Examples include: *Alice Hamilton: physician & leading scientist in industrial medicine, health & safety, *Charles Babbage: mathematician & inventor, whose mechanical and calculating devices are now considered forerunners of the computer, and *John Harrison: pioneer clock maker.

<u>Vowel 4 with consonant 2</u> unifies integrity and intimacy. Together they support the drive to do something worthwhile within one's community. No examples of consonant 20 have yet been found; see consonant 11.

<u>Vowel 4 with consonant 3</u> brings integrity and imagination together. There is a strong drive within you to understand the nature of truth. Examples include: *Drew Blyth Barrymore: actor, and *Dwight David Eisenhower: 34th US President, * Hugo Philipp Jakob Wolf, Louis Hector Berlioz, Quincey Delight Jones Jr. ("Quincy Jones"), William Martin Joel ("Billy Joel"): musicians, and *Mary Catherine Bateson: anthropologist and author.

<u>Vowel 4 with consonant 4</u> intensifies the qualities of integrity and dedication. This pair amplifies the drive to create something of lasting value. Examples include: *David Herbert Lawrence, Charles Pierre Baudelaire, William Wordsworth: writers, *Howard Carter: archaeologist & Egyptologist, *Marsilio Ficino: astrologer, physician, priest, translator of ancient texts, and *Rita Levi-Montalcini: neurologist, awarded a National Medal of Science.

<u>Vowel 4 with consonant 5</u> blends integrity and enterprise. This could result in something of real benefit to humanity or the environment. Examples include: *Fred Alan Wolf: author of *The Eagle's Quest: A Physicist's Search for Truth*, *Miriam Frances Gow (Mimi Macpherson): entrepreneur, environmentalist, TV celeb, *James Dixon Swan ("Jimmy Barnes") and Neil Leslie Diamond: singer/songwriters.

<u>Vowel 4 with consonant 6</u> unties integrity and compassion. This combination stimulates the drive to stand tall and do something worthwhile but teamwork could be a challenge for you. Examples include: *Colleen Shirley Perry and Rosa Louise McCauley (Parks): civil rights leaders, *Helen Adams Keller and Matthew Arnold (with birthday 6, date path 4): writers, and *Roger Tory Peterson: ornithologist, artist & educator (vowel 40, consonant 60, name 100).

<u>Vowel 4 with consonant 7</u> blends integrity and insight, and could lead to inspiration of practical value. Examples include: *Paula Lexine Masselos: human rights activist, *Thomas Woodrow Wilson: President, *Samuel Langhorne Clemens: better known as the writer, Mark Twain, and *Steven Allan Spielberg: film director and producer.

<u>Vowel 4 with consonant 8</u> intensifies the drive to create something useful. Organization, networking and persistence, are needed to make dreams a reality. Examples include: *Daniel Louis Armstrong and Johannes Brahms: musicians, *John Philip Holland: pioneer of the modern submarine, *Nettie Maria Stevens: pioneer geneticist, *William Thomson (Lord Kelvin): pioneer in thermodynamics, and *Mirka Madelaine Zelik (Mora): artist.

<u>Vowel 4 with consonant 9</u> blends integrity and broadmindedness. This combination could lead to the transformation of the status quo but you will need to exercise versatility. Examples include: *Eugene Henri Paul Gaugin: artist, *Florence Nightingale: nurse, *Svante August Arrhenius: chemist, and *William Booth: founder of Salvation Army.

<u>Vowel 4 with consonant 11</u> brings integrity and inspiration together. For this pair to work successfully, you will need to constantly monitor your level of self-honesty. Examples include: *Herbert George Wells: novelist, *Philip Peter Ross Nichols: founder of the Order of Bards, Ovates and Druids, *Robert Peter Williams ("Robbie"): entertainer, singer/songwriter, and *William Lawrence Bragg: physicist. See also vowel 4, consonant 2.

People with vowel number 5 seek to experience all that life has to offer and then express what they have learned in their own congenial way.

<u>Vowel 5 with consonant 1</u> unifies ingenuity and initiative. Together they fuel the drive to initiate something within one's community. Integrity is essential to success. Examples include: *Alfred North Whitehead, who made significant contributions in the areas of maths, logic and the philosophy of science and education (*Adventures in Ideas*), *Anna Eleanor Roosevelt: civil rights campaigner, diplomat, philosopher & writer, *Helen Patricia Sharman: pioneering astronaut, *Carl Heinrich Maria Orff, Cherilyn Sarkisian, and George Harrison: musicians.

<u>Vowel 5 with consonant 2</u> brings personal ingenuity and the need for intimacy together, behind the drive to live one's truth. The only example found was *Jacob Boehme: cobbler and mystic.

<u>Vowel 5 with consonant 3</u> unifies ingenuity and imagination. Together they fuel the drive to achieve, but team-work is vital to success. Examples include: *Andrew Warhola and Henri Emile Benoit Matisse: artists, *Bernard Jean Etienne Arnault: business executive & civil engineer, and *Nova Maree Peris: athlete, hockey player and personal development coach.

<u>Vowel 5 with consonant 4</u> unites ingenuity and integrity. Together they catalyze big ideas with far-reaching consequences. Examples include: *Alexander Mackenzie, a stonemason who became Canada's second Prime Minister, *George Denis Patrick Carlin, Greta Lovisa Gustafsson (Garbo) and Shirley MacLaine Beaty: actors, and *James Jesse Lynn: businessman and second President of the Self-Realization Fellowship.

<u>Vowel 5 with consonant 5</u> intensifies the need to express your personal ingenuity. Progressive ideas and enterprise come with number 5 and foster leadership potential. Examples include: *Marie-Rosalie Bonheur (Rosa Bonheur): artist (vowel 50, consonant 50), *John Dewey: psychologist, philosopher, educator, social critic and political activist, who travelled extensively supporting women's suffrage, progressive education, educator's rights and world peace (vowel 23, consonant 23), and *John Winston Lennon: singer and songwriter.

<u>Vowel 5 with consonant 6</u> unites ingenuity and compassion. Together they inspire the drive to initiate something of benefit to one's community. Examples include: *Antonio Lucio Vivaldi: composer, *Geoffrey Chaucer: poet, *Jerome David Salinger: novelist, *James Abbott McNeill Whistler, Leonard Lloyd Annois and Paul Klee: artists.

<u>Vowel 5 with consonant 7</u> unifies ingenuity and insight. Progressive ideas catalyze social idealism but you may need to work on your team-building skills. Examples include: *Angela Bridget Lansbury and Charles Eugene Boone ("Pat"): actors, *Jonathan Edwards and Norman Vincent Peale: ministers & theologians, and *Thomas Jefferson: statesman and third US President.

<u>Vowel 5 with consonant 8</u> brings ingenuity and resourcefulness together. This combination fuels the drive to create change. Examples include: *Daniel Gabriel Fahrenheit and William Henry Bragg: physicists, *Jonas Edward Salk: physician, *Jeremy Bentham: chief architect of modern government, *John Maynard Keynes: theorist in the realm of economics, and *Jonathan Dean Swift: clergyman & leading satirist of his time.

<u>Vowel 5 with consonant 9</u> unifies ingenuity and idealism. Progressive thinking will enable you to break new ground but your integrity should never be compromised. Examples include: *Anders Celsius and Georg Simon Ohm: physicists and mathematicians, *Lillian Florence Hellman: playwright, Suzanne Arundhati Roy: author & activist, and *William Harvey: physician who discovered the circulation of the blood.

<u>Vowel 5 with consonant 11</u> unites ingenuity and inspiration. You are probably an inspired and progressive thinker who is motivated to improve your community. The outcome could be far-reaching but something may have to 'give' first. Examples include: *George Washington: 1st US President, *James Tyler Kent: physician & forefather of modern homeopathy, *Mary Louise Carr (Moore), Niccolo Paganini, Richard Starkey (Ringo): musicians, and *Rose Hawthorne: nun and social worker (Mother Alphonsa Lanthrop).

People with vowel number 6 need to find a way to express their compassion.

<u>Vowel 6 with consonant 1</u> combines compassion with initiative, and together they stimulate the urge to live one's truth. Flexibility is necessary to bring out the best in this combination. Examples include: *Johann Heinrich Pestalozzi: pioneer educator, *Marchette Gaylord Chute: historical writer, Vera Mary Brittain: author/poet, and *Robert James Lee Hawke: politician.

<u>Vowel 6 with consonant 2</u> unites compassion and intimacy. Together they fuel the drive to achieve something of lasting value. No examples of consonant 20 have yet been found.

<u>Vowel 6 with consonant 3</u> unifies compassion and imagination. This combination catalyzes big ideas with far-reaching consequences. Examples include: *Anne Inez McCaffrey: sci-fi writer and Vincent Noel Serventy: natural history writer, *Emanuel Kant, Jean Jacques Rousseau and Johann Heinrich Schulz: philosophers, and *Louis Braille: educator, who adapted his 6-dot Braille system to maths and music.

<u>Vowel 6 with consonant 4</u> unites compassion and integrity. Together they fuel the drive to accomplish something that will stand the test of time. Examples include: *Alberta Hunter and Frances Theresa Densmore: musicians, *Alfred Tennyson: poet and *Ralph Waldo Emerson: writer, *Angelina Emily Grimke and Catherine Wilson Malcolm (Kate Sheppard): suffragettes.

<u>Vowel 6 with consonant 5</u> brings compassion and ingenuity together. Progressive thinking is the keynote here. You have the ability to 'see' what needs to happen next but you must find the courage to act on such hunches. Examples include: *Hilaire Germain Edgar Degas and Yoko Ono: artists, *Frederick Matthias Alexander: physiotherapist, *William Penn: lawyer & reformer, and *William Butler Yeats: poet.

<u>Vowel 6 with consonant 6</u> intensifies the urge to unite people so that they are working towards a common, humanitarian goal. This combination spearheads social activism. Examples include: *Alfred Bernhard Nobel: chemist and instigator of the Nobel Peace Prize, *Lise Meitner: physicist, *Loren Corey Eiseley: anthropologist, and *Lloyd Frederic Rees: artist and conservationist.

<u>Vowel 6 with consonant 7</u> unites compassion and insight. There is potential here to instigate something that transforms the status quo. Examples include: *Ingrid Bergman: actor, *Johann Sebastian Bach and Joscelyn Godwin: musicians.

<u>Vowel 6 with consonant 8</u> unites compassion and resourcefulness. The relentless pursuit of a goal could result in something ground-breaking and progressive; but team-work is vital. Examples include: *Elliot Lovegood Grant Watson: biologist & prolific writer, *Jean Henri Dunant: founder of the International Red Cross, and *Jules Gabriel Verne: popular science fiction writer.

<u>Vowel 6 with consonant 9</u> unifies compassion, idealism and imagination. Together they stimulate the drive to create something harmonious or beautiful. Examples include: *Dylan Thomas: author/poet and Thomas Hardy: novelist/poet, *David Hilbert: mathematician, *Juan Colell: pharmacist, and *Victor Cousin: educator & philosopher.

<u>Vowel 6 with consonant 11</u> brings compassion and inspiration together. Progressive thinking, versatility and enterprise are necessary to fulfil the potential of this combination. Far-sightedness fuels the drive to achieve something honest and original. Examples include: *Benazir Bhutto: *11*th Prime Minister of Pakistan, *Edwin Eugene Aldrin: astronaut, *Edwin Powell Hubble: astronomer, *James Gregory: first person to design a reflecting telescope, *Joseph Rudyard Kipling, Thomas Stearns Eliot: writers and poets, *Michael Joseph Jackson (with birthday 11, date path 6), Olivia Newton-John, and Wolfgang Amadeus Mozart: musicians. See also vowel 6, consonant 2.

People with vowel number 7 yearn to know 'the truth' and typically look to the natural world for clues.

<u>Vowel 7 with consonant 1</u> unites insight and initiative. You have leadership potential and you will never feel completely at peace until you use it to achieve something for your community. Examples include: *Eugene Curran Kelly: choreographer, *William Turner Walton: composer, *Francis Scott Key Fitzgerald: writer, *Thomas Birch: historian, *Michael Faraday: chemist & physicist who discovered the laws of electrolysis, and *Mustafa Kemal Ataturk: first President of Turkey.

<u>Vowel 7 with consonant 2</u> unites insight and intimacy. There's a part of you that longs for solitude and another part that wants to engage in meaningful relationships with other people. This potent pair of numbers works best when placed on 'higher ground', such as thinking globally and acting locally. Your personal ingenuity and willingness to teamwork, can pave the way for actions of long-lasting benefit to the environment. For examples see consonant 11.

<u>Vowel 7 with consonant 3</u> brings insight and imagination together. Together they stimulate the drive to create something of lasting value. Examples include: *Giambattista Della Porta: physician, ophthalmologist, scholar/writer of works on architecture, geometry, hydraulics & magic, and *James Braid: physician who coined the word hypnosis, *Harriet Martineau: journalist, philanthropist & writer, and *Norman Kingsley Mailer: novelist, journalist, poet, playwright, film maker and philosopher, *Robert Frederick Zenon Geldof ("Bob"): musician and activist.

<u>Vowel 7 with consonant 4</u> unites insight and integrity. Inspiration and imagination light the way for developments that can change the future; theory and practice can come together here. Examples include: *Annie Jump Cannon: scientific theorist, *Alfred Rupert Sheldrake: biologist, *Calvin Richard Klein: fashion designer, *Ludwig van Beethoven, Norman Luboff, and Reginald Kenneth Dwight ("Elton John"): musicians.

<u>Vowel 7 with consonant 5</u> unites insight and ingenuity. Together they catalyze imaginative ideas with social outcomes. Be sure to work on your team-building skills. Examples include: *Hermann Hesse and Muriel Sarah Camberg (Spark): novelists & poets, *Nadia Elena Comaneci: Olympic gold medal gymnast, *Paul David Hewson ("Bono"): singer and social activist.

<u>Vowel 7 with consonant 6</u> brings insight and compassion together, and fuels the drive to transform something personally and collectively. Examples include: *Norman Cousins: political journalist, professor & world peace advocate, and *Robert Edward Turner: global benefactor, television network executive & visionary.

<u>Vowel 7 with consonant 7</u> intensifies the quest for truth. There is huge potential here to create change and break new ground. Examples include: *Albert Schweitzer: musicologist, Emma Lee Bunton: singer, *Peter Joshua Sculthorpe and Richard Georg Strauss: composers, *Henry Wadsworth Longfellow: educator, linguist and poet, *Lawrence Percival Coombes: aeronautical engineer, *Pierre Gassendi: philosopher, priest, scientist, astronomer and mathematician.

<u>Vowel 7 with consonant 8</u> brings insight and resourcefulness together. This combination fuels the drive to create peace, healing, or harmony, within one's community. Initiative is necessary and so is persistence. Examples include: *David Spangler and Mark Allen: philosophers & writers, *Edward Bach: physician, and *Frederick Cossom Hollows, international eye surgeon, and *John Franklin: Arctic explorer.

<u>Vowel 7 with consonant 9</u> unites insight and idealism. Together they stimulate the drive to dispel illusion and share what you know with others. Examples include: *Ernest Henry Shackleton: explorer & sailor, *Stephen Rodger Waugh: cricketer, *Louisa May Alcott and Penelope Ruth Fletcher (Mortimer): writers, *William Lyon Mackenzie: advocate of democratic reform, journalist and mayor.

<u>Vowel 7 with consonant 11</u> unifies insight and inspiration. This pair fuels visions of a more idealistic society. Honesty and integrity are essential. Examples include: *Albert Einstein and Tyge Ottesen Brahe ("Tycho Brahe"): scientists; *Peter Charles Doherty: Nobel Prize winner in Medicine, *Matthew Manning: author & healer, *Benjamin Franklin: inventor, printer, public benefactor & writer, *Florence Evylinn Campbell: astrologer & numerologist, *William Morris: artist, poet and social activist. Read also vowel 7, consonant 2.

People with vowel number 8 have a desire to integrate all parts of themselves through effective action in the material world.

Vowel 8 with consonant 1 unites resourcefulness and initiative. This powerful partnership fuels far-reaching ideals making significant achievements possible. Self-honesty is vital if actions are to yield positive results. Examples include: *Aaron Ronald Castan: lawyer & champion of human rights, *Linus Carl Pauling, who won two Nobel prizes: one for Chemistry & one for Peace, *Niels Henrik David Bohr: physicist, and *Richard Buckminster Fuller: scientist, engineer and inventor.

Vowel 8 with consonant 2 brings resourcefulness and intimacy together. Together they fuel the drive to create something of lasting value within one's community. All of the examples have consonant 11 as no examples of consonant 2 were found: *Peter Michael Falk: actor, *John Flaxman: artist, and *Werner Karl Heisenberg: physicist.

Vowel 8 with consonant 3 unites resourcefulness and imagination, which can catalyze genuine inspiration. Flexibility and versatility are needed to pioneer something that has not been done before. Examples include: *Amalie Emmy Noether: creative mathematician, *Charles Lutwidge Dodgson: writer, geometrician & photographer (better known as Lewis Carroll), and *Joseph Campbell: author of several books on mythology.

Vowel 8 with consonant 4 unifies resourcefulness and integrity. Together they stimulate the drive to create something of real and practical value that impacts on one's culture and heritage. Examples include: *Gloria Steinem and Vida Jane Mary Goldstein: activists for women's rights, *John Mc Connell: initiator of Earth Day, the Earth Flag & the Earth Magna Charta, *John Locke: physician & philosopher, and *Philip Richard Carr-Gomm: psychotherapist.

Vowel 8 with consonant 5 brings resourcefulness and progressive thinking together. Together they fuel the drive to transform something that needs a complete overhaul. Imagination is vital to success. Examples include: *Cornelia Frances Zulver: actor, *Graham Cyril Kennedy: television personality, *James Esdiale: medical doctor, and *Victor Peter Chang: cardiothoracic surgeon, and *Leslie Lynch King Jr ("Gerald Ford"): US President (with date path 8/birthday 5).

Vowel 8 with consonant 6 unites resourcefulness and compassion. This pair stimulates the drive to break new ground. Team-work is essential. Examples include: *Carl Gustav Jung: psychotherapist, *William Lilly: astrologer & doctor, *John Singer Sargent: artist, *Sigrid Undset: writer, and *Theodore Roosevelt: statesman and 26th US President.

Vowel 8 with consonant 7 combines resourcefulness and research. Together they catalyze the drive to initiate something that causes change and improves one's community. Examples include: *Alexander Fleming: microbiologist who discovered penicillin, *Catheryn Antionette Tennille (Toni), Loretta Webb (Lynn), and Kiri Te Kanawa: singers, *Elizabeth Garrett and Josephine Diaz: pioneering doctors, *Francis Bacon: attorney general, Lord Chancellor, philosopher and writer.

Vowel 8 with consonant 8 intensifies the drive to dispel misconceptions and initiate change within one's community. Examples include: *Austin Osman Spare: artist and occultist,

*Gretchen Michaela Young ("Loretta") and Jessica Claire Biel: actors, the latter being nominated for the 'Do Something Award' which is characteristic of number 8, and *Elizabeth Blackwell, the first female doctor in the US.

<u>Special mention</u>: Meg Heather Frances (Lees): vowel 26/8, consonant 62/8, name 88: politician, and Wayne Douglas Gretzky: vowel 35/8, consonant 53/8, name 88 with birthday and date path 8: hockey star.

<u>Vowel 8 with consonant 9</u> combines resourcefulness with broad-minded idealism. This pair fuels the drive to initiate action that leads to a new level of understanding among people. Examples include: *Jean Francois Champollion: Egyptologist who deciphered the Rosetta Stone, *Julian Rossi Ashton: artist, founding teacher of an art school & writer, *Laura Elizabeth Ingalls, Nigel Godwin Tranter, and Raymond Douglas Bradbury: writers.

<u>Vowel 8 with consonant 11</u> unites resourcefulness and inspiration. This combination sparks the drive to create something of lasting value to humanity and the environment. Team-work is vital. Examples include: *Gordon Matthew Sumner (Sting) and Roger Robert Woodward: musicians, *Eleanore Marie Sarton, Henry Fielding, and Thorton Wilder: novelists, *Samuel Leonard Lewis and Vittal Rao (Ramdas): spiritual leaders. See further examples under vowel 8, consonant 2.

People with vowel number 9 need to feel that they can contribute to the betterment of the world.

<u>Vowel 9 with consonant 1</u> unites idealism and self-reliance. Together they foster the drive to achieve something of lasting benefit. Organization is essential. Examples include: *Colette Besson and Herbert James Elliott: athletes, *Helen Beatrix Potter: writer of stories for children, and *Thomas Hobbes, who wrote *Leviathan*, a book about the history of political thought.

<u>Vowel 9 with consonant 2</u> unites idealism with the need for social engagement. This combination fuels the drive to do something that hasn't been done before; to set in motion an idea that has come into its time. Research increases the likelihood of success. Examples include: *Alice MacLeod (Coltrane): jazz pianist and composer.

<u>Vowel 9 with consonant 3</u> combines idealism and imagination. Social activism tempered by compassion will result in the best outcomes. Examples include: *Aung San Suu Kyi: human rights activist who won the Nobel Peace Prize in 1991 for establishing Burma's National League for Democracy Party, *Norman Mc Alister Gregg: ophthalmologist, *Ronald David Laing: psychiatrist, *Agatha Mary Clarissa Miller (Christie), Harry Heine, and Thomas Traherne: writers.

<u>Vowel 9 with consonant 4</u> brings idealism and integrity together. This combination fuels the drive to transform something. Flexibility is essential to success. Examples include: *Deepak Chopra and Franz Anton Mesmer: physicians, *John Middleton Murry and Kathleen Mansfield Beauchamp: husband and wife writers, *Georges Eugene Sorel: philosopher, and *Joseph Addison: essayist and politician.

<u>Vowel 9 with consonant 5</u> unites idealism and progressive ideas. This pair fuels the drive to undertake ground-breaking work. Integrity is essential. Examples include: *Carol Ann Duffy: poet, playwright, and professor, *Catherine-Marie-Agnes Fal de Saint Phalle (Niki): sculptor, painter and film maker, and *Henry Ford: pioneer in the automobile industry.

<u>Vowel 9 with consonant 6</u> combines idealism, compassion, and imagination. These compatible numbers stimulate the drive to create health and harmony within one's community. Examples include: *Abraham Lincoln: statesman (16th US President), *Charles Robert Darwin: natural scientist, *Coretta Scott (King) and Natasha Jessica Stott Despoja: political activists, *Peter Robert Garrett: conservationist, politician, and singer, and *Richard Charles Rodgers: composer of musical theatre.

<u>Vowel 9 with consonant 7</u> unites idealism and insight. Together they fuel the drive to dispel misconceptions and initiate change within one's community. Team-work is essential. Examples include: *Carmen di Barrazza: healer, Dorothy Jane Roberts: mystic, *Charles James Fox: statesman, *David Joseph Bohm: theoretical physicist, and *Charles Stewart Parnell: political leader, whose vowel 9, consonant 7 was matched with birthday 9, date path 7.

<u>Vowel 9 with consonant 8</u> brings idealism and resourcefulness together. Together they stimulate the drive to educate and create change. Don't be afraid to step up and get the ball rolling! Examples include: *Gottfried Wilhelm von Leibniz: mathematician, *Johannes Eckhart, Stuart Wilde and Thomas Merton: mystical thinkers, *Roger Bacon: friar, philosopher, scholar and writer (somewhat prophet).

<u>Vowel 9 with consonant 9</u> intensifies idealism. People with vowel 9, consonant 9, name 9, tend to create their own opportunities. Triple-9 fuels global activism. Examples include: *Emily Dickinson, Gustave Flaubert and John Dryden: writers, *Benjamin McLane Spock: paediatrician, and *Morgan Scott Peck: psychiatrist, *Rachel Louise Carson: biologist, ecologist, and writer.

<u>Vowel 9 with consonant 11</u> combines broad-mindedness with far-reaching idealism. The expression 'think globally, act locally' belongs here, and teamwork is essential. Examples include: *Carl Friedrich Stumpf: philosopher & psychologist who declared that "the whole is greater than the sum of the parts", *Caroline Chisholm: humanitarian, *James Francis Thorpe: professional athlete, *Celine Marie Claudette Dion, Robyn Rihanna Fenty ("Rihanna"), Roy Kelton Orbison, Zubin Mehta: musicians, and *Wilfred Eade Agar: zoologist. See also vowel 9, consonant 2.

People with vowel number 11 need an outlet for their inspired ideas.

<u>Vowel 11 with consonant 1</u> unites inspiration and initiative. This tends to fuel social activism, but it must rest on solid principles to be effective. Examples include: *Evelyn Sybil Mary Eaton: pioneer author, *Henry Ross Perot: founder of Electronic Data Systems, *Jacob Ludwig Carl Grimm: one of the founders of comparative philology, *Phineas Parkhurst Quimby: pioneer in mental healing, *Louis ("Leonard") Bernstein, Robindro Shaunkor Chowdhury ("Ravi Shankar"), and Steveland Judkins Morris ("Stevie Wonder"): musicians. See also vowel 2, consonant 1.

Vowel 11 with consonant 2 combines inspiration with the need for social engagement. Together they fuel the drive to transform something within society. No examples of vowel 11, consonant 20 were found and so the following examples have vowel 11, consonant 11: *Edith Joy Scovell: poet and Jacqueline Lee Bouvier: editor & journalist, *George Henry Martin: record producer and *Simone Young: conductor & musician, *Michael Donald Kirby: High Court Judge, human rights activist and law reformer. See also vowel 2, consonant 2 and vowel 11, consonant 11.

Vowel 11 with consonant 3 unites inspiration and imagination. This combination fuels the drive to break new ground. Resourcefulness and tenacity are essential to success. Examples include: *Edvard Hagerup Grieg: pianist/composer and Kathleen Mary Ferrier: singer, and *John Joseph Nicholson Jr ("Jack"), actor: vowel 38/11, consonant 66/12. See also vowel 2, consonant 3.

Special case: *Nicole Mary Kidman (actor) and husband Keith Lionel Urban (musician), both have exactly the same pattern: vowel 38/11, consonant 39/12, name 77/5.

Vowel 11 with consonant 4 unites inspiration and integrity. Together they can spark progressive and community-minded initiatives. Examples include: *Alecia Beth Moore ("Pink"): singer, *Nicholas Culpeper: medical astrologer and herbalist, *Paul Ambrose Toussaint Jules Valery: philosopher, critic and poet. See also vowel 2, consonant 4.

Vowel 11 with consonant 5 combines inspiration and ingenuity. Together they can dispel misconceptions and initiate change within one's community. Examples include: *Adam Smith: economist and philosopher, *Cynthia Morris Sherman and Raffaello Sanzio: artists, *Orpah Gail Winfrey ("Oprah"): talk show host, actor and business executive, *Karl Friedrich Benz and Thomas Alva Edison: inventors. See also vowel 2, consonant 5.

Vowel 11 with consonant 6 combines inspiration with compassion. This pair fuels the drive to reform one's community. Progressive thinking is essential to success, as is flexibility. Examples include: *Elizabeth Ann Bloomer (Betty Ford): author & founder of the Betty Ford Center, *Andrew Lloyd Webber, and Eunice Kathleen Waymon ("Nina Simone"): musicians, *John Fitzgerald Kennedy: author and statesman (35th US President). See also vowel 2, consonant 6.

Vowel 11 with consonant 7 unites inspiration and insight. This pair brings forth visions of a more idealistic society. Integrity and practicality are needed for such visions to become real. Examples include: *Edward Warrigal Anderson, who received the David Unaipon Award for his writing, *Heinz Rudolf Pagels: physicist and author of *Cosmic Code*, *Robert Edwin Peary: admiral, engineer, scientist & first man to reach the North Pole, *Russell Charles Hitchcock and Vincent Damon Furnier (Alice Cooper): musicians. See also vowel 2, consonant 7.

Vowel 11 with consonant 8 combines inspiration and resourcefulness. This pair sparks the drive to create something of lasting value but communication skills must keep pace with the formulation of ideas. As well as several actors the examples include: *Arthur William Fadden: *11th* Prime Minister of Australia, *Edward Osborne Wilson: biologist and proponent of biodiversity and socio-biology, *Phillip Calvin McGraw ("Dr. Phil"): psychologist, TV personality & author, and *Yehudi Mnuchin (Menuhin from age 3): violinist (vowel 11, consonant 44). See also vowel 2, consonant 8.

Vowel 11 with consonant 9 unifies inspiration and idealism. Together they stimulate the drive to team up with other people and do something of global significance. Examples include: *Annette Marie Sarah Kellerman: professional swimmer and vaudeville star, *Jakob Ludwig Karl Grimm: folklorist and founder of comparative philology, *Robert Boyle: physicist, chemist, inventor and author. See also vowel 2, consonant 9.

Vowel 11 with consonant 11 catalyzes the drive to construct something of benefit to current and future generations. Reconciling the practical and the theoretical is essential. Examples include: *Amerigo Vespucci: explorer, financier, cartographer (vowel 38, consonant 38), *David Unaipon: inventor, preacher and writer (vowel 29, consonant 29).

Special case: the famous singer Nathaniel Adams Coles had the name pattern vowel 29/11, consonant 40, while his daughter, also a singer, Natalie Maria Cole, has the name pattern vowel 38/11, consonant 29/11. Natalie found it difficult to handle the fame that can come with the 11's.

People with vowel number 22 need to find a way to make their visions tangible.

Vowel 22 with consonant 1 combines inspiration and initiative. Together this pair fuels the drive to facilitate the evolution of human consciousness. All examples were profoundly spiritual people, including:*Faye Wright: author of *Finding the Joy within You*, and *Ralph Waldo Trine: author of *In Tune with the Infinite*. See also vowel 4, consonant 1.

Vowel 22 with consonant 2 unifies inspiration and social engagement. Together they fuel the drive to find practical solutions to social problems. Examples include: *Isabella Ross: MD, who helped to establish baby health centres in early Melbourne, Australia,*Joan Paige: army nurse, and *Masaru Emoto: author of *The Hidden Messages in Water*. See also vowel 4, consonant 2.

Vowel 22 with consonant 3 unites inspiration and imagination. Together they fuel the drive to work with other people in a mutually beneficial way. You want the whole world to benefit you're your endeavours. Examples include: *Roger Godel: medical genius, *Rudyard Kipling: poet, writer, and a Nobel Prize Winner for Literature. See also vowel 4, consonant 3.

Vowel 22 with consonant 4 yokes inspiration to integrity. You may feel driven to find workable solutions to problems. You might also enjoy weaving a web of love around you. Examples include: *Dorothy Rudd: poet, singer, & founder of the Society for Black Composers, and *Uri Geller: inventor and psychokinesist (vowel 22, consonant 22). See also vowel 4, consonant 4.

Vowel 22 with consonant 5 brings inspiration and ingenuity together. This pair quickens the drive to investigate the significance of life and do something with the knowledge gained. Examples include: *James Earl Carter: 39th US President, *Johannes Kepler: astronomer/ astrologer, *John Carew Eccles: neurophysicist, *Paul Leonard Newman: actor, business manager, humanitarian, and racing enthusiast. See also vowel 4, consonant 5.

<u>Vowel 22 with consonant 6</u> combines inspiration and compassion. Together they stimulate the drive to initiate something that can endure the test of time. Examples include: *Francis Thompson: poet (*The Hound of Heaven*), *Hazel Henderson: independent futurist, author of *Building a Win-Win World,* advocate for ecologically sustainable human development & socially responsible business investment, *Susana Eger Valadez: of the Huichol Center for Cultural Survival and Traditional Arts. See also vowel 4, consonant 6.

*Special case: Helen Reddy, singer of lyrics that changed the world: vowel 22, consonant 33, name 55.

<u>Vowel 22 with consonant 7</u> combines inspiration and insight. Yoked to compassion, this pair can spark the drive to contribute to the well-being of other people and their environment. Examples include: *John Aubrey: antiquary & biographer (*Brief Lives*), *Nikola Tesla: engineer & inventor, *Rafael Alberti Merello: painter and poet. See also vowel 4, consonant 7.

<u>Vowel 22 with consonant 8</u> unites inspiration and resourcefulness. Together they fuel the drive to create something that makes a difference. Ground-breaking ideas are possible here, but not without imagination, integrity, and initiative. Examples include: *Avram Noam Chomsky: linguist, *George Fox: religious leader who founded 'Friends', later known as Quakers, *John Paul Getty: business man and public benefactor. See also vowel 4, consonant 8.

<u>Vowel 22 with consonant 9</u> unifies inspiration and idealism. This pair stimulates the drive to formulate plans and ideas that can transform the world in which you live. Examples include: *Peter Paul Rubens: diplomat & painter, *Thomas Paine: philosopher and writer. See also vowel 4, consonant 9.

<u>Vowel 22 with consonant 11</u> heightens the drive to gather and sort information for the purposes of synthesis. Examples include: *Éduoard Schuré: philosopher, poet, playwright, novelist, music critic, and author of *Pythagoras and the Delphic Mysteries*, *Helen Frankenthaler: artist, and *Mark William Latham: politician and author of *The Latham Diaries.* If you are having trouble working with the intensity of this combination, work with vowel 22, consonant 2, or vowel 4, consonant 2, or vowel 4, consonant 11, instead.

The last word in this chapter goes to Philolaos, one of the most influential disciples of Pythagoras. The name 'Philolaos' resonates with <u>vowel number 22, consonant number 22, name number 44</u>. And what did the Pythagoreans seek to demonstrate? The order of the entire cosmos, no less!

"I must create a system or be enslaved by another man's"
- William Blake, consonant 22

We now turn to the name number in detail.

Chapter 3

The Name Number

The Driving Force behind Your Ideals

Vowel and consonant combinations produce distinct patterns of sounds and letters. Children of multiple births exhibit different characteristics partly because they have different names. The name operates through the etheric body, which is the energy-body closely wrapped around the physical while the vowels operate through the astral and the consonants, the physical. Thus it is through the name that the ideal encoded in the date path connects with the astral, etheric and physical bodies. The three together - vowel, consonant and name – comprise the driving force behind the ideals encoded in your date path.

Calculating the Name Number

This is simply a matter of adding the vowel and consonant numbers together and reducing the outcome to a single digit, noting all the numbers involved in this process. A worksheet is provided at the end of the book. it is always important to calculate the original name because it exerts an influence throughout your life even if you never use it. Continuing with P!nk as our example:

Original Name

			16				5						17	Vowel Number = 38/11
1	5	9	1			5			6	6	5			
A	L	E	C	I	A	B	E	T	H	M	O	O	R	E	
3		3				2		2	8	4			9	
			6				12						13	Consonant Number = 31/4
														Name Number = 69/6

Looking to chapter 1 for assistance with interpreting number 69, we see that it is about realizing the inherent beauty of humanity. Add 6 and 9 and you get 15, which is focused on perceiving the perennial harmony with the apparent chaos of life. As a name number this is a motivating factor rather than an ideal. A good example of '69' is the song *We Are the World* in which Pink was the soloist for the 2010 remake.

Stage Name

				Vowel Number = 9
	9			
P	I	N	K	
7		5	2	
				Consonant Number = 14/5
				Name Number = 23/5

It is unlikely that Alecia was aware of it when she took the name Pink, but number 69, her original name number, is 3 times 23, which is her stage name number. Thus one supports the other. Number 5 is 'adventurous' and 'eclectic' and these are words that have been used to describe Pink. Specifically number 23 is about extending the boundaries of perception and you have to be adventurous to do that!

Married Name

				Vowel Number = 1 + 38 = 39/12
	1			
H	A	R	T	
8		9	2	
				Consonant Number = 19 + 31 = 50
				Name Number = 89/8

Chapter 1 stops at number 71 and so if your name number exceeds that, turn to chapter 5. There, it is noted that being a prime number, 89 is individualistic and has maverick tendencies. Mostly, a person with this number wants to serve as part of a team of people who are working towards something worthwhile. Name 8 matches with Alecia's birth day 8 and could either make her obsessive about this or simply more effective in its execution.

Interpreting Name Numbers

Name Number 1 - see Name Number 10

Name Number 2

Name Number 2 comes with a healthy drive to bond with other people. With 2 as your name number, you are motivated more or less consciously by the drive to experience love. By loving and by being loved you can develop faith in the process of life and eventually surrender the fear-based need to control it. As a part of this, you must cultivate receptivity to other people and develop your ability to work and play within a team setting. You may be more sensitive to people than you realize and you will need to learn how to recognize who it is that nurtures your energy and who depletes it. Listening to your intuition and respecting its guidance is vitally important to your health and wellbeing. Your personal ability to interact with other people is needed to fulfil the potential of your date path. If number 11 appears in the calculation, see also name number 11.

Name Number 3

The drive encoded in name 3 is to express the joy in one's heart. With 3 as your name number, you are motivated more or less consciously by the need to express yourself. For this reason you like to congregate with like-minded people, share your ideas, and listen to theirs. You like to chatter about most topics and learn from other people. Number 3 involves realizing that as you think so you speak and thus create. There's a cheeky and cheerful side to Name 3 that is yours to explore. You could develop the gift of using your voice to spread joy. You can also use it to bring out the best in other people. The advice offered to people with Name 3 is to choose your words thoughtfully, imaginatively *and* honestly because by the way you express yourself so does your date path unfold. If number 12 appears in the calculation, see also name number 12.

Name Number 4

Encoded in name number 4 is the drive to tap into one's strengths and use them in the material world. With 4 as your name number, you are motivated more or less consciously to create something that improves the quality of life. The advice offered to you is to take pride in your work, however insignificant it may seem to you. It is through your *attitude* to your work that you have the opportunity to contribute to the overall wellbeing of the planet. Keep in mind that small things matter as much as great things and quality is as important as quantity and more so in many cases. The more integrity that you put into your work, the more likely you are to actualize the ideals encoded in your date path.

Name Number 5

Name number 5 comes with a healthy drive to promote growth on all levels. With 5 as your name number, you are motivated more or less consciously by the need to evolve and to help others evolve. '5' will help you to appreciate the gift of life and what it has to offer you. Your name number will encourage you to use your talents to make progress in the material world and ultimately to overcome its denser and darker tendencies, which would inhibit such progress. The process of personal growth will help you to understand that life is your teacher and that every outer 'teacher' reflects the inner teacher. It is by making the most of the opportunities in each and every moment that the ideals encoded in your date path will unfold.

Name Number 6

The driving force behind name number 6 is to unite with others in order to accomplish something of mutual benefit. With 6 as your name number, you are motivated by a healthy drive to bring like-minded people together. You will have a common purpose in mind; probably something to do with health and wellbeing or a service of benefit to the community. Education and the arts often find their way into these broad topics. You may have a strong sense of the inter-relationship between education, the arts, health and community. So that you don't burn out, you need to develop the subtle art of observing people and learn to discriminate between their motives. It is the way that you manage your relationships with other people that will determine how your date path unfolds.

Name Number 7

Name number 7 comes with a healthy drive to discern fact from fiction. With 7 as your name number, you are motivated more or less consciously by the need to live truthfully. You will learn that it is not so much by speaking but rather by listening that truth emerges. Listening works two ways: listening to other people and listening to yourself. You need to be honest with yourself before you can be truly honest with others. It's a life-long process to strip away dishonesty and be 'real' with yourself. Seven is an enigmatic number and 'your truth' will be uniquely your own. You can change your truth and there is likely to have been a time in your life when you did exactly that; 'coming out' about something that you previously guarded as a secret. It is your personal spin on the truth that will determine how your date path unfolds.

Name Number 8

Name number 8 stands for nothing short of the drive towards complete self-mastery! With 8 as your name number, you are motivated more or less consciously by the drive to work hard and make a difference. Name Number 8 comes with a healthy drive to network with lots of different people. You care about people and about life, and you take people and life seriously. You are quite ambitious and you dislike wasting time. You thrive on a good challenge and will take risks to accomplish your goals. Until you learn how to balance working and resting, you will tend to oscillate between passive and aggressive behaviour. It is the way that you manage your personal resources that will determine how your date path unfolds.

Name Number 9

People with name number 9 typically feel propelled to help humanity attain the greatness that they perceive it is capable of. With 9 as your name number, you want to understand how the world ticks. You have your own ideas and possibly your own theory on what life is about. Although the circumstances that surround your life may be somewhat dramatic at times and feel very personal, of all the numbers, 9 is the least personal. What you need to understand is that spiritual forces aimed at benefiting humanity as a whole, are working through you. For this reason you may find that your quest for meaning becomes a journey shared with others. If your idealism is to enrich humanity on any scale, you must come to terms with the bigger picture and recognize where each point of view fits in. It is the meaning that you attach to life that will determine how your date path unfolds.

Name Number 10

Name number 10 comes with a healthy drive to pioneer something that will endure the test of time. With 10 as your name number you are motivated more or less consciously to work constructively with other people. You are ambitious and you want to do something worthwhile. Formulating a set of principles that work for you will help you to accomplish this. You have leadership potential and you need to develop the ability to stand in your own strength without relying on someone else's approval. You could become a pillar within your community; someone that other people can depend on. It is by becoming an authority in a field that interests you that the ideals in your date path will unfold to their highest potential.

Name Number 11 - see Master Numbers

Name Number 12

Name number 12 accompanies a healthy drive to renew something. With 12 as your name number you are motivated more or less consciously by the urge to dedicate your life to an ideal, and you will want to add a fresh approach to this ideal. Your perceptive powers are likely to be well developed; granting you the ability to see things from many different angles and points of view. Fact and fiction can merge here and produce some sparkling creativity. By uniting the abstract and the tangible, the ideal and the practical, over a period of time something of *lasting* value can emerge. You have the capacity to help people to see the world in a completely different way.

Master Numbers

Some people are given a name at birth that resonates with a master number, whilst others adjust their original name (often unintentionally) so that it becomes a master number. Either way, the master number comes to dominate the etheric field because it is twice as strong as a single number. If you have altered your name so that it is now a master number, consider how it modifies your original pattern, which will always be there, even if only in the background. If you have moved away from the master number of your original name, you may feel the tension slacken almost immediately. Its energy will always be there for you to access, but your new name number will modify it. Whatever your double number may be, read name number 11 first because it is a factor of all the others.

Name Number 11

Name number 11 comes with a healthy drive to express inspired ideas. With 11 as your name number you are motivated more or less consciously by futuristic forces. Whether you are aware of it or not, you are attuned to the distant drum-beat. It is as if the next generation seeks a voice through you. When you are working with number 11 rather than number 2, you are ahead of your time. Symbolically 11 is a double-1, and as such you need to keep an eye on the tendency to want to 'clone yourself', i.e. to wish that everyone was more like you. Who you adopt as a role model is critical to your state of mind, for 11 is primarily a 2 and thus highly impressionable. Your date path will develop in tandem with your ability to walk a path that benefits future generations.

Name Number 22

The drive behind the double- 2 is to build something of real benefit to other people. The name Buddha resonates with number 22; it is quite rare. If it happens to be yours, you need to make your visions and ideas tangible.

Name Number 33

Gathering and sorting information is the drive that comes with the double-3. Also unusual, name 33 resonates with 'Culhwch', the Celtic archetypal hero, who accomplished thirty-nine impossible tasks by applying the art of delegation, par excellence. Now 39 impossible tasks might be asking too much of you, but the art of delegation is something that you can learn.

Name Number 44

Behind the double-4 is the drive to contribute something of lasting value to future generations; something that builds on the best of our heritage. The name "Johann Strauss" resonates with the pattern vowel 11, consonant 33, name 44. Famous as a composer of dance music, Johann Strauss Senior set the foundations for his sons to carry on his musical dynasty.

Name Number 55

The double-5 brings a healthy drive to re-invent oneself over and over again. As your name number, 55 fuels the motivation to pioneer and create. The pen name 'Eliphas Levi' resonates with this number. He was a prolific writer on magic, some of which was original. His motto was "I don't teach; I awaken"; in other words he was an initiator. If you have name number 55 you might be able to relate to that.

Name Number 66

The double-6 accompanies the healthy drive to circulate compassion. This number elicits a strong urge to aid society as evidenced in Elisabeth Kubler-Ross (name 66). You want to serve (i.e., do your bit) for the love of it, but keep an eye on expectations: are they realistic or are you expecting too much of yourself or other people? Be clear about the boundaries of your responsibilities. In common with all 12's, number 66/12 necessitates believing in people and by so doing, bringing out the best in them. Further examples include Horatio Nelson - vowel 33, consonant 33 – famous for his service in the Royal Navy, and Avram Noam Chomsky –vowel 22, consonant 44 – famous for his service to linguistics.

Name Number 77

The double-7 comes with a healthy drive to break new ground and discover a deeper layer of truth. With name number 77 you will quest for the truth through participation in the life stories of other people. '77' will help you to see yourself reflected in others, and the creative force reflected in you. It will strip away falsehood and encourage you to evolve. An example is Jean Iris Murdoch (known as Iris Murdoch) - vowel 33, consonant 44, name 77 – novelist and philosopher, who probed 'truth' in her own unique way.

Name Number 88

The double-8 fuels a healthy drive to achieve something of enduring benefit to other people. With 88 as the driving force behind your date path, you will want to unify divergent points of view. You will find that the most effective way to do this is by networking. You are learning to listen to variations of the truth and integrate them. Agnes Gonxha Bojaxhiu, better known as Mother Teresa of Calcutta, exemplified the disciple that accompanies this number. She led a devoted and balanced lifestyle that enabled her to respond to the situation at hand with good-humoured efficiency. Magdalene Mary Szubanski – vowel 33, consonant 55, name

88 – comedy actor, writer and producer, with drive and determination in abundance, provides another example.

Name Number 99

The double-9 fuels the drive to live a meaningful life. The motivation encoded in name 99/18/9 is the same for all 9's: the quest for meaning, but here it is as if the heat has been turned up. The struggle against injustice gets you all fired up. With 99 as the drive behind your date path, you need to be aware that tremendous willpower, a creative imagination, and a generous heart, need harnessing to a just cause. An example is William Henry Cosby Jr. (vowel 44, consonant 55, name 99).

The Leading Letter of Your Name

Like the numbers, the letters have their own unique energy. The first letter of your first name initiates the whole name, and as such it indicates the way that you approach life in general. Because it is a part of your name, the first letter impacts on your inner growth, energy levels, health and well-being.

Head Letter A

Whether the A in your name is long as in Ailsa or short as in Adam your general approach to life is one of self-reliance. "A" as the first letter and vowel of the English alphabet, comes with a pioneering spirit. Consequently your natural approach to life is direct and spontaneous. You can be quite fearless at times; a tendency that benefits from being harnessed to long-range plans. That said it is by exercising initiative that you inwardly grow and develop.

Head Letter B

At the beginning of your name, the letter B indicates that your natural approach to life is self contained and somewhat restrained. You might feel as though you are bursting to express yourself, but then something seems to hold you back. Naturally this passes with age, yet you will always tend to remain sensitive to the reaction of others. This resonance will nurture your growth as you nurture the growth of others.

Head Letter C

Creativity is the keynote here. C at the beginning of your name indicates that your natural approach to life is optimistic, imaginative, playful, and mostly cheerful, although you will naturally have days when the word contrary seems more appropriate. Companionship is vital to you and some friendships will last a lifetime. Intellectual curiosity accompanies the letter C and will aid your inner growth and development.

Head Letter D

The letter D is dynamic and it will deepen your feeling life, drawing out your creative potential. If you accommodate the creative process within you, even though it's two steps forward and one back at times, you will steadily lay the foundation of your future. D will help you to create something of value, step by patient step. D at the beginning of your name indicates that your natural approach to life is self-contained (just like the shape of the letter). Attitude matters much here: look to the standard that you set for yourself.

Head Letter E

As the second vowel and equivalent to the eclectic number 5, E excites our emotions. Whether the sound is long as in Elizabeth or short as in Emma, E facilitates progress in the material world. E as the first letter or first vowel in your name stimulates the more versatile side of your nature. Your natural approach to life is enthusiastic and progressive. You may have more than one talent and you probably enjoy showcasing your talents in a way that benefits others. Exercising your entrepreneurial streak in a socially responsible way will aid your inner growth and development.

Head Letter F

This letter facilitates the flow of ideas within the mind. And it's what you choose to do with this wealth of ideas that will make all the difference in your life. F will test your mettle, your character, and your integrity. F at the beginning of your name indicates that your natural approach to life is serious and probably steadfast, particularly as you grow older. You may feel somewhat burdened by the conflicting urges to 'take root' somewhere and to be 'free'. Finding a creative way to combine the two will aid your inner growth and development.

Head Letter G

This letter will help you to speak your truth, even if others don't like it. There is an enigmatic quality about this letter and so do not be surprised if it is difficult for others to figure you out. You can be quite critical and controversial at times. G at the beginning of your name indicates that your natural approach to life is resilient and tenacious. Knowing when to forge ahead with guns blazing and when to wait until the tide turns, will aid your inner growth and development.

Head Letter H

At the beginning of the name this letter is always a consonant, yet H can never be entirely divorced from the soulful quality of the vowels. H at the beginning of your name indicates that your natural approach to life is serious, perceptive, and thoughtful. The letter H is obviously upright and well balanced but you may have to struggle to attain such qualities. You are probably ambitious, perhaps more than you realize, and quite capable of fulfilling your ambitions. Drawing on the innate resourcefulness and tenacity of your soul will aid your inner growth and development.

Head Letter I

The letter "I" generates energy within the emotional (or astral) body. It will thus amplify your emotions. The form of the letter obviously resembles Number 1 and as such your approach to life could be quite spontaneous. You want to act independently of other people but know that you must consider them. If you drive yourself too hard, you risk emotional burn-out. Keeping your eye on the bigger picture and thinking about the significance of your actions will aid your inner growth and development.

Head Letter J

As a derivative of the letter I, J corresponds to 10 in the old Chaldean system. 10th is also the ordinal position of J in the English alphabet. And number 10 suggests self-determination. J at the beginning of your name indicates that your natural approach to life is judicious and thoughtful. In modern numerology, 10 reduces to 1, which suggests that you can be wilful too, when you so choose. Moving towards your designated goals with quiet determination supports your inner growth and development.

Head Letter K

The letter K stimulates intuition and can inadvertently strain the nervous system. Charisma may provide some compensation for the tension that accompanies this multi-faceted resonance. K at the beginning of your name indicates that you approach life as an individual yet one who wants to establish meaningful rapport with other people. You tend to be idealistic and your ideals will either attract or repel other people. Learning the art of 'give and take' will aid your inner growth and development.

Head Letter L

The letter L will encourage you to look deeply at life from varying angles and points of view. "L" stimulates social conscience. Thus L at the beginning of your name indicates that your approach to life is social, idealistic, and imaginative. You have very strong emotions and you tend to approach other people in a thoughtful and compassionate way. Applying such qualities aids not only the society and community in which you live, but your personal growth and development as well.

Head Letter M

The letter M will encourage you to explore the word 'interdependence'. There are many way to be with other people and to blend stability and freedom within relationships. "M" encourages the type of creative thinking that finds ways of being with people within a mutually supportive structure. Your inner growth and development comes from making connections with other people and allowing them to transform you.

Head Letter N

The letter N is mental and transformative in nature. It inclines you towards adventures that may turn out to be bigger than you bargained for. N at the start of your name indicates that your approach to life is intellectual and discerning – yet discernment may be exactly your challenge. You tend to jump in where angels fear to tread because it seems like a good idea at the time. Behind this lies the urge to live in the 'Now!' N symbolizes a restless current that likes to investigate its options. It tends to instigate social action. Developing your ideas into practical outcomes will aid your inner growth and promote your personal development.

Head Letter O

The vowel sound "O" is sensitive vibration that is loaded with potential in all of the arts, including the domestic arts, music and poetry. Your inner growth and development is thus enhanced by exploring your rich emotional life through the arts. O as the first letter or vowel in your name can strengthen the emotional side of your nature if you are open to the huge variety of experiences that life offers you. With O as the first letter of your name, your approach to life leans towards social responsibility. Your powers of expression in this realm may be much greater than you realize.

Head Letter P

At the beginning of your name, P indicates that your approach to life is intellectual and self-sufficient. You may think you are being direct, yet people will sense an indefinable 'something' ticking away behind the scenes. There is likely to be more going on in your head than you let on. You like to keep quiet and observe until you have all of the facts, and have had time to think them over, before sharing your thoughts. It may feel quite foreign to you to share your thought processes, yet this is exactly how you can enhance your inner growth and development.

Head Letter Q

This powerful resonance enhances leadership ability. Q at the beginning of your name indicates that your natural approach to life is intuitive and cautiously ambitious. Your inner growth and development is enhanced by working sincerely with your intuition. As you strengthen your relationship with your mind, outer growth and development will follow. By listening to your intuition the more refined qualities of your mind can guide your life. If you persevere with the process, you will notice an increase of synchronicities in your life.

Head Letter R

At the beginning of your name "R" indicates that your natural approach to life is forthright and ambitious. You are a self-starter who can swing others into action, especially when your humanitarian instincts have been roused. If you choose a specific role through which you can express your feelings and ideas, then everyone else will know where they stand. Actively promoting the welfare of others without expecting anything in return, will aid your inner growth and development.

Head Letter S

At the beginning of your name "S" indicates that your natural approach to life is serious and possibly studious as well. You need to work by yourself and exercise your intuition in the development of whatever project you are engaged in. S stands for serpent, and it will encourage you to periodically shed whatever obstructs the flow of your creativity. The way that you exercise your imagination, will significantly affect your health. It will also impact on the development of your ability to interact with the rest of humanity.

Head Letter T

The letter T at the beginning of your name indicates that your natural approach to life is earnest (or at least determined), purposeful, and sincere. Nothing lightweight here, you are inclined to put others before yourself. Beware of any tendency you may have to control those you are close to especially if being 'in control' is an issue for you. 'T' relates to the tree-of-life and the cross-of-matter, and as such, can feel restrictive. Yet its propensity is to transform energy into tangible outcomes. Your health, inner growth and development, hinges on how creatively you manage this.

Head Letter U

As the first letter or vowel in your name "U" nurtures the more intuitive side of your nature. Your natural approach to life is thus congenial and receptive. You may be inspired yet unwilling to trust it; artistic, yet only partially express it; idealistic yet vacillating. Being near the end of the alphabet suggests that this resonance comes into its own later in life when the collective volume of your striving builds up momentum. In the meantime, focus on building a relationship with the powers of your mind so that your intuition can help you make a useful contribution to the collective thought of humanity.

Head Letter V

At the beginning of your name V indicates that your natural approach to life is achievement-orientated. This resonance targets the victory of spirit over mortal limitations. Our powerful 22nd letter catalyzes the realization that inspiration and sensitivity are practical tools from which many can benefit. It is receptive to revelation and can convert visions into dynamic plans that work. You have the ability to cut straight to the heart of the matter. Your health, inner growth, and personal development hinge on what you co-create with other sensitive and caring people.

Head Letter W

At the beginning of your name W indicates that your natural approach to life is versatile, adaptable, and adventurous. In your early years you might be inclined to overindulge your senses, but if your willpower is sufficiently strong, you will transform yourself into a person who knows where true happiness lies. You can use the highly magnetic energy of 'W' to promote your ideas, and the ideas of others. Helping other people to scale the heights and depths of everyday enlightenment in some form of co-operative adventure will enhance your inner growth and personal development.

Head Letter X

At the beginning of your name X indicates that your approach to life is either materialistic or idealistic. The choice is always yours and at some time in your life you may switch camps. Initially your ideals will be quite personal but as you mature they will become increasingly universal. 'X' can precipitate a crisis of consciousness, and this could be the very thing that changes your attitude to life. It could transform the self protective tendencies of your ego into the desire to protect others. Reconciling matter and spirit will enhance your development.

Head Letter Y

At the beginning of your name Y indicates that your natural approach to life is philosophical. You are sensitive to what is going on around you, which may at times cause you to vacillate. The letter Y will bring you continually to a point of choice until you learn to make decisions that support your higher-self. The letter Y will encourage you to weigh things up and consider a variety of viewpoints in your quest for the truth. Time to sit quietly by yourself and think about the choices you make is necessary to your health, inner growth, and personal development.

Head Letter Z

At the beginning of your name Z indicates that your natural approach to life is direct, confident, inspired, and dynamic. You will certainly get noticed. 'Z' stirs up a depth of feeling-life that can be used to understand what motivates other people. This resonance will help you to co-create networks between people and to keep such networks healthy and strong. Active diplomacy that creates peace between people will promote your inner growth and development.

The first letter of the name is not only important because it defines your approach to life but also because its vibration is felt throughout life in a cyclic pattern that will be explained in chapter 11.

Your Growth Number

As well as the individual letters, you need to be aware of your first name as a whole. Even if you never use this name, it is a part of the matrix of vibrations that holds your subtle bodies together and identifies who you are. Thus your first name subconsciously stimulates your inner growth throughout your life. Add up the letters of your first name, reduce to a single digit, 10, 11, 12, or 22, and then read the relevant interpretive statement.

Growth Number 2

Because your first name reduces to Number 2, your inner growth and development comes through patience, sensitivity, and co-operation with other people. But try to do it without selling yourself short! A sense of personal self-worth is mandatory here. Once you have secured that, the world is yours to enjoy. Examples: Athol, Brett, Bryon, Catherine, Charlie, Collin, Dillon, Elissa, Isis, Josephine, Kathy, Kelly, Leanna, Lynn, Maisie, Robyn, Rosie, Shawn, Sonya, Stephan, Thom, Ursula, Vijo, Watson, Wolf, Yusuf, Zita and ZsaZsa.

Growth Number 3

Because your first name reduces to Number 3, your inner growth and development comes through expressing whatever it is that gives you joy. Number 3 stimulates the imagination and you will need to learn how to apply this beneficially within a social context. Your friends will be your greatest allies in the development of this skill. Examples: Alice, Brien, Charles,

Cathy, Deanna, Debra, Deryck, Dillon, Frances, Geoff, Graham, Isabel, Karol, Kris, Nancy, Quinn, Rose, Sunday, Susanne, Tobias, Trudey, Vidal, Verona, Wendell, Yoko and Zublin

Growth Number 4

Because your first name reduces to Number 4, your inner growth and development unfolds through self-discipline. Taking one step at a time works best for you. Your personal growth needs to focus on building an *inner* sense of security. Outer security will naturally follow. Examples: Allan, Bradley, Christopher, Darrel, Engelina, Fairley, Gaven, Herbert, Istvan, Joan, Jesse, Kathleen, Lee, Merv, Nicolette, Orford, Quincey, Robin, Roslyn and Trixie

Growth Number 5

Because your first name reduces to Number 5, your inner growth and development comes through learning to go with the flow and expressing your talents within whatever situation you find yourself. Versatility works best for you. Continual change is something that you must learn to turn to your advantage. Examples: Alyssa, Caroline, Derrick, Elise, Emma, Fay, Gayle, Isla, Janet, Joanne, Joy, Leigh, Mai, Neal, Rashid, Robina, Rosanne, Sophia, Tommy, Trude, Vigil, Woodrow, Yasmine, Yvonne, Zack and Zina

Growth Number 6

Because your first name reduces to Number 6, your inner growth comes through service to others. But if you are to grow inwardly then service cannot be a drudge. Choose a way to serve that gives you personal satisfaction. Examples: Adair, Ailsa, Camilla, Cleveland, Dean, Daria, Enzo, Fabian, Hector, Isaac, Joel, Leanne, Maria, Moshe, Nalani, Robert, Rasheed, Sheehan, Sorrel, Tobe, Turner, Vanda, Victor, Winston, Wynford, Yutta, and Zohara

Growth Number 7

Because your first name reduces to Number 7, your inner growth and development comes through finding your own truth – and living that truth. Although '7' is somewhat of a solitary number, it is only by navigating 'truth' within the arena of your personal relationships that you will grow and develop beyond where you are now. Examples: Alyn, Anne, Bard, Catharine, Carl, Deana, Derrek, Francine, Huw, Jack, Kathryn, Kelley, Lynne, Noam, Quin, Rosalie, Sian, Susannah, Terri, Thor, Trudy, Vicky, Xavier, Yuan, and Yvette

Growth Number 8

Because your first name reduces to Number 8, your inner growth and development comes by managing your personal resources. Not just outwardly but also inwardly, you need to be able to sustain yourself within the milieu of life. Examples: Allen, Alicia, Anabel, Athene, Barrie, Bobbie, Brian, Colin, Darrell, Elysia, Gabrielle, Hugh, Jasmin, Jess, Karmen, Krishna, Loughlin, Susanna, Travis, Vikki, Vince, Wilder, Xenia, and Yves

Growth Number 9

Because your first name reduces to Number 9, your inner growth and development comes through giving with no strings attached. But it must be what you *want* to do, rather than what you feel you ought. '9' will continually broaden your outlook on life, and as you develop from within, your attitude to life will become increasingly generous. Examples: Allon, Anita, Bert, Carmen, Carole, Charley, Elisha, Francoise, Jeff, Johanna, Karina, Leith, Maisey, Otis, Roanna, Shaun, Sophie, Sue, Venus, Vicki, Woodley, Yarra, Yasmin and Zeva

Growth Number 10

Because your first name includes Number 10, your inner growth and development comes by taking the initiative and acting decisively. It is vital to your sense of wellbeing that you learn to stand on your own two feet, and stand firm with what you believe to be right and true. You must learn how to defend your point of view and take it forward. This is a Number that people mature into and things will become easier for you once you have established a definite role in life. Examples: Adam, Alan, Alyce, Barry, Bob, Carolina, Dan, Darrin, Elsa, Faye, Hercules, Israel, Jayne, Joanna, Joye, Kimberley, Lexie, Mae, Neale, Nancie, Ola, Peg, Phoenix, Rod, Roseanne, Saxon, Suzanne, Tatam, Urana, Waldo, Yasmeen Zane, Zara, and Zoe

Growth Number 11

Because your first name includes Number 11, your inner growth and development comes from acting on your most benevolent and inspired thoughts. Examples: Andrew, April, Bridget, Bligh, Cate, Charlie, Dennis, Doris, Felix, Gypsy, Heather, Ivy, Lucas, Max, Oma, Pierce, Rachel, Reuben, Susan, Sydney, Ted, Trish, Violet, Wylie, and Zenanda

Growth Number 12

Because your first name includes Number 12, your inner growth and development comes from cultivating a social ideal. Over the course of your life you are likely to encounter many different perspectives of the truth and you will grow inwardly in tandem with your efforts to reconcile these with your own ideal. Examples: Anna, Amos, Ben, Ella, Fae, Jane, May, Roberto, Sean, Sigrid, Silvester, Tom, and Zac

Growth Number 22

Because your first name includes Number 22, your inner growth and development comes through work that benefits and inspires others. '22' will challenge you to apply common sense to inspiration, and help you to orchestrate large-scale projects. Examples: Annabel, Athena, Blake, Carol, Danny, Darel, Ester, Gina, Huon, Joyce, Kara, Luke, Megan, Nathan, Owena, Ruth, Ryan, Sonia, Steven, Thomas, Tobey, Walton, Yani, and Zalman

The Name Table

At the top of each column write one component of your name (first name in first column, second name in second column etc). Then separate the letters of each name into their numerical equivalents and total each row.

Letter/ Number	Name:	Name:	Name:	Name:	Name:	TOTAL	Bench mark
1. (A,J,S)							4
2. (B,K,T)							2
3. (C,L,U)							3
4. (D,M,V)							2
5. (E,N,W)							5
6. (F,O,X)							2
7. (G,P,Y)							2
8. (H,Q,Z)							1
9. (I,R)							4

Three Key Questions:

Is a link provided for the date path? (When the primary date path number is in the name, the ideal that it encodes is easier to manifest)...

Are the numbers that are absent in the date of birth represented somewhere in the name? (This gives the energy a way in)...

Is there an Intensity Number?

To have an intensity number requires that one number *alone* be above the bench-mark. When there are two or more numbers that are above the bench-mark (per the final column in the name table above), they neutralize each other and there is no intensity number. (Although, realistically, all letters above average in number reveal an accentuated drive). When an intensity number does turn up it suggests a very strong focus in the area that the number represents particularly if the rest of a person's astronumerology supports this. The following career trends and public figures were carefully selected to represent the strongest trends.

Intensity Number 1: five or more 1's and no other number above the bench-mark

*Sports were strongly represented by number 1, e.g. Nigel James Smart, AFL

*Music was also strongly represented by number 1, e.g. Sergio Santos Mendes (with date path 1, vowel 1, growth 1) and LaDonna Adrian Gaines (Donna Summer - name 1)

*The sciences were also well represented by number 1, e.g. Clarissa Harlowe Barton, nurse, Jonas Edward Salk, immunologist, and Svante August Arrhenius, chemist

*Activists, eg Aaron Ronald Castan, legal activist, (with consonant 1), and Wangari Muta Maathai (supported by primary date path 1 and birthday 1)

Intensity Number 1 helps people to begin projects and initiate action.

Intensity Number 2: three or more 2's and no other number above the bench-mark

*The sciences were very strongly represented by number 2, e.g. James Tyler Kent, physician and forefather of modern homeopathy, (with primary date path 2 and consonant 11/2).

*Musicians also scored well here, e.g. Keith Lionel Urban and William Beckett, both with vowel 11

*Several politicians had intensity number 2, e.g. Bruce Edward Babbit, who sought to revitalize National Parks in the US; note the B as the head letter, reinforced by the B at the start of the surname, name number 11/2.

*Peter Bradford Blazey represents two trends: activism and writing (with consonant 11/2)

Intensity Number 2 can assist with teamwork.

Intensity Number 3: four or more 3's and no other number above the bench-mark

*There were more scientists with intensity number 3 than any other intensity number, e.g. Carolus Linnaeus, botanist (with consonant 30), Ella Sophia Bulley (Armitage), archeologist & historian, (consonant 30, birthday 3), and Linus Carl Pauling, immunologist (supported by growth 3)

*The arts also scored well, e.g. Anya Gallaccio and William Dobell

*Writers were strongly represented by number 3, e.g. Clive Staples Lewis, Colin Milton Thiele, Samuel Taylor Coleridge (all with primary date path 3), and Eugene Louis Vidal (with date path 3, growth 30, birthday 3), his penname "Gore Vidal" resonating with vowel 21/3, consonant 48/12/3.

Intensity Number 3 catalyzes a love of learning.

Intensity Number 4: three or more 4's and no other number above the bench-mark

*There were more sporting stars with intensity number 4 than any other intensity number, e.g. Arnold Daniel Palmer, golf, (with primary date path 4), Eamon Wade Sullivan, swimming, (vowel 4), and Lionel Edmund Rose, boxing, (date path 4, growth 4)

*The arts also scored well, e.g. Diane Nemerov Arbus, photographic artist (vowel 4, consonant 4), who worked under the name Diane Arbus (name 40); Herbert Edward Read, art historian (vowel 4, birthday 4), and Mirka Madelaine Zelik (Mora), painter and sculptor (supported by vowel 4)

*Writers were well represented, e.g. Andrew Marvell, Edith Maud Gonne and John Middleton Murry (all with name 4), as did Primo Michele Levi (with primary date path 4)

*There was also a strong cluster of activists and politicians with intensity number 4, e.g. Mary Jane McLeod (Bethune), educator and civil rights leader, Michael Donald Kirby, judge and law reformer (both with name 4)

Intensity Number 4 can assist with materializing anything the heart desires.

Intensity Number 5: six or more 5's and no other number above the bench-mark

*There were more actors with intensity number 5 than any other intensity number, e.g. Goldie Jean Hawn (with vowel 5), Irene Marie Dunne (consonant 5), Marie Susan Etherington (date path 5), Nigel John Dermot Neill (Sam), (consonant 5, name 5, birthday 5). *And fields that relate to acting, e.g. Carson Wayne Newton, entertainer (date path 5), John Clement Seale, cinematographer (birthday 5), Leslie Townes Hope (Bob), comedian, (vowel 5), and Steven Allan Spielberg, film director (date path 5)

*Writers were well represented by number 5, e.g. Jeannette Walls (with date path 5)

*Sports scored well, e.g. Kieran John Perkins, swimming (with birthday 5) and Raelene Ann Boyle athlete, (supported by consonant 5)

Intensity Number 5 can help a person to shine in any field.

Intensity Number 6: three or more 6's and no other number above the bench-mark

*There were more artists with intensity number 6 than any other intensity number, e.g. Leonard Lloyd Annois, painter (with date path 6, consonant 6, growth 6), and Yoko Ono, conceptual artist, musician, designer, composer, poet & performer (vowel 6)

*Musicians in general were strongly represented, e.g. John Robert Williamson and Olivia Newton-John (both with vowel 6), Lionel Leo Hampton and Paul Leroy Robeson (both with name 6)

*Writers were well represented, e.g. Chloe Ardelia Wofford (Toni Morrison), Esther Louise Forbes (both with consonant 6), Francis Thompson (consonant 6, date path 6), Francis Ford Coppola (date path 6), and Margaret Eleanor Atwood (date path 6, name 6)

Intensity Number 6 emphasizes the mental faculties such as imagination and criticism.

Intensity Number 7: three or more 7's and no other number above the bench-mark

*Intensity Number 7 scored well in the 'other' category verifying its inclination to be 'different'. Examples include **G**raham Cyril Kennedy, a unique television personality, (primary date path 7) and Poppy Cybele King, entrepreneur (growth 7)

*Sciences, e.g. György Pólya, mathematician noted for his work in heuristics and education (growth 7), Joseph Priestley, chemist, dissenting clergyman, and natural philosopher (maturity 7), Stephen Jay Gould, paleontologist (date path 7)

*Actors, e.g. Eldred Gregory Peck (name 7) and Phylis Lee Isley (Jennifer Jones, date path 7)

*Spiritual, e.g. Kuppuswamy Iyer (name 7) and William Gordon Gray (birthday 7)

Intensity Number 7 emphasizes the inclination to assert how things should *not* be, without necessarily offering an alternative.

Intensity Number 8: two or more 8's and no other number above the bench-mark

*There were more musicians with intensity number 8 than any other intensity number, e.g. John R Cash, singer/songwriter and Yehudi Mnachin (Menuhin), violinist, conductor, and humanitarian (both with consonant 8)

*Politics and activism were strongly represented by number 8, e.g. Elizabeth Gurney (Betsy Fry), prison reformer, and Meg Heather Francis (Lees), a leader within the Democrats (both with vowel 8, consonant 8)

*Writers were also well represented, e.g. Joseph John Campbell (consonant 8, birthday 8) and Kenneth Grahame (vowel 8, birthday 8) and also Baruch Spinoza (growth 8)

*Sports e.g. Sarah Michelle Ryan and Shane Elizabeth Gould, both swimmers, the former with consonant 8 and the latter with vowel 8

Intensity Number 8 highlights the process of integrating the various parts of oneself, with the data suggesting that this can be done through a variety of means such as music, writing and politics.

Intensity Number 9: five or more 9's and no other number above the bench-mark

*Writers, e.g. Andrea Rita Dworkin and Eric Arthur Blair (George Orwell), (both with consonant 9), Gloria Marie Steinem, editor and most noted feminist of her time (with date path 9), and Robin Francis Blaser, poet, essayist & translator (birthday 9)

*Musicians, e.g. Glenn Barrie Shorrock, Richard Lynn Carpenter, and Russell Norman Morris (all with consonant 9)

*Actors, e.g. Candice Patricia Bergen (vowel 9), and William Penn Adair Rogers (name 9)

*Sciences e.g. Rita Levi-Montalcini, neurobiologist (with date path 9, name 9)

Intensity Number 9 emphasizes lofty ideals.

One in three people have an intensity number and so they are not unusual. To further understand what your intensity number might mean for you, turn to chapter 7 and interpret as a name challenge.

Chapter 4

The Birth Day Number

Opening Acts on the Stage of Life

Your birth day is the most tangible aspect of your date path and indicates an attitude that you need to adopt in order to move forward in the material world. It acts through your personal willpower but is modified by the collective will. Through this number, your personal potency in the material world is pitted against the collective response, and may in turn influence it. The five numbers presented in the first four chapters of this book represent the core numbers of your numerology. It is important to distinguish between them but also to see them as members of a team. The date path defines an ideal within your mind. In the vowel number resides a longing and in the consonant number an inheritance. The name unites these to provide the driving force behind the date path. And whilst the name provides the password to your inner life, the birth day makes the date path ideal more accessible to your creative will. Your birth day number represents a quality that is recognizable to other people and generally agreeable to you.

Calculation: The number of the day on which you were born is your birth day number. If you were born on the 1st day of the month then 1 is your birth day number. If you were born on the 10th, 19th, or 28th of the month, then 1 is still your primary birth day number because each of these numbers reduces to 1 (e.g. 2+8 = 10 = 1+0 = 1). The same rule applies to all of the other numbers.

A Brief Overview of the Birth Day Numbers

The Ones

Birthday 1, 10, 19, 28

With your birthday event happening on the 1st, 10th, 19th or 28th of the month, you were born to lead. If there were adverse circumstances in your childhood you may attempt to subdue this impulse, but the fact is that doors will begin to fly open for you when you take the initiative and act with clear determination. If you were born on the 10th, 19th or 28th, see also the tens, below.

The Twos

Birthday 2, 11, 20, 29

Entering the world of duality on the 2nd, 11th, 20th or 29th of the month means that diplomacy works best for you. Establishing rapport between people is your specialty. Work out what is truly of value to you and then be prepared to stand by your conviction. In the things that you value, be sure to include working with other people in ways that are mutually rewarding. If you were born on the 11th or 29th (which is a complex type of '11') you will find a separate section for birthday 11 towards the end of this chapter.

The Threes

Birthday 3, 12, 21, 30

Celebrating your birthday on the 3rd, 12th, 21st, or 30th of the month means that developing a socially engaging style of expression get things happening for you. Your words need to be clear and concise with an easy, familiar style that people can readily relate to. Imagination is the key here. You have the ability to think in pictures and shape images within your mind. If you were born on the 12th it is your capacity to see things from another person's point of view that is critical to success.

The Fours

Birthday 4, 13, 22, 31

Success in the arena of number 4 means providing ideas with a tangible form. Because you entered the world on the 4th, 13th, 22nd or 31st of the month, you are most likely to get results by being well organized and committed to the task at hand. The ability to work effectively, regardless of circumstances, is the hallmark of number 4. For those born on the 22nd, a separate section has been created near the end of the chapter.

The Fives

Birthday 5, 14, 23

Your arrival on the 5th, 14th, or 23rd of the month means that you get things happening by exercising your enthusiasm, flexibility and versatility. Your ability to think outside the square is one of your greatest assets. You can make the most of the inner freedom and outer opportunities that come with '5' by focusing on one goal at a time and directing your creativity to that end.

The Sixes

Birthday 6, 15, 24

Celebrating your arrival on the 6th, 15th, or 24th of the month, means that bringing people together works for you. You are advised to focus on a particular social issue that you are passionate about and that other people might be interested in sharing with you. As with number 3, so with 2 x 3: imagination holds the key. Here you are specifically endowed with the ability to apply your imagination to ways and means of assisting your community.

The Sevens

Birthday 7, 16, 25

Entering the world on the 7th, 16th, or 25th of the month, means that you will find doors opening for you as you learn how to live your truth in a world that may be indifferent to it. The 7's are an enigmatic group of numbers and there will be times when you feel that no-one understands you. You may have a highly developed aesthetic sensibility such as we see in artists, poets or musicians. The natural world holds the key for you; be sure to visit it often.

The Eights

Birthday 8, 17, 26

Making your grand entry into the physical world on the 8th, 17th, or 26th of the month, means that you will open the doors of opportunity by the way you manage your personal power. Beware of feeling powerless to change something because it indicates that you have turned this energy in on itself. Number 8 is naturally passionate, social, and resourceful.

The Nines

Birthday 9, 18, 27

Success in the arena of number 9 means exercising your idealism. Because you entered the world on the 9th, 18th or 27th of the month, doors will open when you make your ideals relevant to the society that you are a part of. Aim to achieve peace and wholeness within yourself before attempting to change the world at large. As with number 3 and 2 x 3, so with 3 x 3 imagination holds the key but here it is applied more globally.

The Tens

Being born on the 10th, 19th or 28th indicates that a part of taking the lead and showing initiative is learning how to stand on your own two feet and hold an opinion. It's also about being willing to go the long haul with your idea rather than simply striking a match and running.

The Birth Day Number as a Career Indicator

Several numerologists claim that the birth day number provides a vocational guidance indicator. This makes sense because it describes the path of least resistance. Combine it with the date path and you have the means of bringing the date path ideals into your daily life, especially your career-life.

The Birthday Numbers in Greater Detail with Examples

Birth Day – Date Path Combinations:

Making the Most of the Opportunities That Come Your Way

People with birthday number 1 are most successful when they act with self-reliance. It does not necessitate belligerence but it does suggest that instead of looking to others for the answers, you realize that your sovereignty comes from within yourself. With birthday number 1, you need to instigate action based on your own innate wisdom. Once you've got the ball rolling, stay tuned to how things are progressing.

Birthday 1, Date Path 1

With this dynamic combination an active life is inescapable and success comes to those who take the reigns. With the double 1 as your pattern, the world is all yours, but never forget that 1 + 1 = 2, which in human terms means being considerate of others. Team-work is your ultimate goal. Examples include: *Cinematographer: Michael Longford, *Photographer: Auguste Lumiere, *Composers: Alberta Hunter and Richard Rodgers and *Singers: Janis Joplin and Mohammed Assaf, *Mathematicians: Ada Byron and Blaise Pascal (also a physicist & theologian).

Birthday 1, Date Path 2

It may not be easy but with a little imagination, self-reliance and the need for a significant-other *can* combine just as willpower can overcome hesitancy and common sense can subdue arrogance. With 1/2 as your combination, your goal is to develop clear and effective communication skills so that you can move easily between the lead and support roles. Examples include: *Actors: Ann-Margret, Jayne Mansfield, Kathy Bates, Kenneth Branagh, Meg Ryan, Omar Sharif, Poppy Montgomery, Richard Burton, Tasma Walton, *Welfare workers: Bon Hull, Clara McBride Hale and Rania Mc Phillamy, *Writers: Beatrix Potter, Bertolt Brecht, Edgar Allan Poe, James George Frazer, and Penelope Ruth Fletcher (Mortimer).

Birthday 1, Date Path 3

Self-reliance, thoughtfulness and integrity are the essential ingredients to career success for you. You may shy of it at first but the lead role is where you naturally gravitate, and so it pays to learn to express yourself effectively. Yet the factor that will make all the difference in your life is teamwork. Examples include: *Actors: Alan Alda, Helen Hayes, Judy Garland, Lisa McCune, *Dancer: Edward Villella, *Gymnast: Monique Allen, *Swimmer: Missy Franklin, *Presidents: Indira Gandhi and Kenneth Kaunda and *Politician: Peter Duncan.

Birthday 1, Date Path 4

With 1/4 as your combination, self-reliance, integrity and enthusiasm are the combination that you need to explore. The way that you express your ideas will be critical to your success. Add a touch of imagination to your presentation and people will show interest in what you have to offer. Examples include: *Musical composer & pedagogue: Carl Orff, and *Singers: Bono and

Nellie Melba, *Educator, Secretary of Labor & social worker: Frances Perkins, *Magistrates/ judges or senators: Hassen Mall, George McGovern, and Pat O'Shane.

Birthday 1, Date Path 5

Self-reliance, enthusiasm and compassion will set your creativity and ingenuity in motion but organization is also necessary if you want to succeed and remain successful. Inherent to this pattern is the drive to make it to the top in your field with your integrity intact. Examples include: *Actors: Bette Midler, Denzel Washington, Dudley Moore, John Meillon, Lily Tomlin, Ron Howard, *Artist: Paul Cezanne, *Chemist: Linus Pauling, *Medical missionary: Wilfred Grenfell, *Physicists: Auguste Piccard and Maria Mayer.

Birthday 1, Date Path 6

Self-reliance, compassion, and self-honesty will help you to realize the value of your creativity to others. If your life is one of continual change, try to turn this situation to your advantage. With date path 6 you will feel most at peace when you know that your efforts are benefiting your community in some way. Examples include: *Artists: Barbara Hepworth, Edgar Degas, Jackson Pollack, James Whistler, *Dancers: Fred Astaire and Mikhail Baryshnikov, *Musicians: Giuseppe Verdi and Vladimir Horowitz, *Presidents: Mustafa Kemal Ataturk (founder of modern Turkey) and Ho Chi Minh (founder of modern Vietnam).

Birthday 1, Date Path 7

Self-reliance, self- honesty, and resourcefulness will bring forth lasting achievements *if* you don't give up. Although you may like solitude, your most significant work will probably be accomplished in the social arena. Think of ways that self-employment could benefit your community. Examples include: *Activist & founder of Mother's Day: Anna M Jarvis, *Dramatist, historian, philosopher & poet: Friedrich Von Schiller plus several other writers: Emily Dickinson, Janet Frame, Joseph Pulitzer, *Spiritual leaders: Teresa of Avila, Sri Yukteswar, Robert Milburn, William Booth and Rabbi Zelman. And a <u>special case:</u> *Marcel Proust: birthday 10/date path 7 matched by vowel 10/consonant 7 in his full name.

Birthday 1, Date Path 8

Self-reliance, resourcefulness and a generous attitude will serve your career goals and unfold your ideals. If you want to succeed on a long-term basis then honesty is definitely the best policy. Numbers 1 and 8 form a potent partnership offering both leadership and organizational skills. Put them to work on a worthy project. Examples include: *Actors: David Gulpilil and Robert Reed, *Television presenter: Richard Wilkins, *Doctors: Alexis Carrel, David Livingstone, Jonas Salk, and William Harvey, *Engineers: Ferdinand de Lesseps (Suez Canal) and James Watt (steam engine), and *Motor Racing champion: Mario Andretti.

Birthday 1, Date Path 9

Self-reliance and a generous attitude are the keys that unlock the potential here. The way that you deal with your alternating surges of power and feelings of powerlessness is critical to your success. These strong emotional currents need a set of principles to contain them and an ideal to aim for. Resource-management is vital. Examples include: *'Hellraiser' on issues related to exploitation: Mary Harris Jones, *Politicians: Hattie Wyatt Caraway, Neville Bonner and Yitzhak Rabin, *Writers: Colleen McCullough, Elbert Hubbard and Rachel Ames.

Birthday 1, Date Path 11

Whenever you take the time to listen to the inspiration flowing through you and give it some form of expression, you are enacting the potential of this combination. It offers you the ability to see life from many points of view, not just your own, although with all of those 1's your own viewpoint may be strong. Principles matter. Examples include: *Artists: Albert Namatjira, and Camille Pissarro; *Patron of the Arts: Lorenzo de Medici, *Meteorologist: Luke Howard, *Nuclear engineer: Nunzio Joseph Palladino, and *Musician: Johnny O'Keefe.

Birthday 1, Date Path 22

Imagination is the key to success here because this combination generates inspired and creative works. You are probably far-sighted and extremely sensitive. Use these qualities to consider the effects of your words and deeds on the people around you, and structure your message accordingly. Examples include: *Anthropologist: Ashley Montagu, *Camping equipment manufacturer: Paddy Pallin, *Meteorologist: Inigo Jones, *Vulcanologist: Peter William Francis, *Poets: Joseph Addison and Robert Lowell, and *Singer & social activist: "Bono".

People with birthday number 2 are most likely to succeed when they learn to appreciate the value of their sensitivity. Empathy does not necessitate becoming a doormat but it does imply adopting an attitude of being willing to listen to the perspective of another person before rushing headlong into a decision, which may be regretted later. With birthday number 2, you are learning ways to cooperate with other people, and elicit their cooperation, because partnerships are important to you.

Birthday 2, Date Path 1

With 2/1 as your combination, sensitivity and self-reliance is the mix that you must master. Your teamwork skills must develop hand in hand with your leadership skills. Developing clear and effective communication is essential to your success. Examples include: *Adventurer, engineer, manufacturer, physician & surgeon: Lewis Lanyon, *Astronomer: Eleanor Burbridge, *Philosopher: Susanne Langer, *Presidents: Mikhail Gorbachev and Lech Walesa.

Birthday 2, Date Path 2

The double 2 implies working patiently towards your goals in a step-by-step sort of way. Integrity is paramount to your success. Examples include: *Diplomat: Abba Eban, *Doctors: Benjamin Spock and David Reuben, *Physiologist: Winifred Cullis, and *Educator & politician: Joan Kirner.

Birthday 2, Date Path 3

Sensitivity and imagination are in ample supply here and begging for expression. To succeed career-wise you also need to apply a measure of self-reliance and establish your 'centre' in a world that is constantly changing. Enterprise is called for here – enterprise based on initiative, effective communication skills and teamwork. Examples include: *Astronomer: Edwin Hubble, *Geographers: John Terence Coppock and William Rollinson, *Writers: Arthur Rimbaud, C. S. Lewis, and Thomas Hardy.

Birthday 2, Date Path 4

With this pattern you are so empathetic, sympathetic and compassionate that you may have to work hard to simply maintain your boundaries. Put that fertile imagination of yours to use and consider ways that your ability to attune to others can benefit your community without compromising yourself. Integrity is vital to your success. Examples include: *Actors: Irene Dunne, Johnny Weissmuller, Justine Saunders, Nicole Kidman, Nina Foch and Oprah Winfrey, *Artist: William Ricketts (sculptor), *Spiritual leaders: Mirza Ali Mohammed, Cardinal Vincentas Sladkevicius, and Swami Siva (Francesco Lopez).

Birthday 2, Date Path 5

Empathy and enthusiasm come naturally with this combination but they must blend with a solid core of self-honesty if your career path is to develop. Enterprise, teamwork and imagination are vital to you. The way that you express your thoughts and emotions will shape your success. Examples include: *Actors: Gwen Plumb, Michael Redgrave, Sidney Poitier, and Stacey Keach, *Mathematician, mental health care reformer & physicist: Marion Beefort, *Writers: Alex Haley, Anna L. Aiken, Hermann Hesse, Jack Davis, James Joyce, Joy Adamson and Nancy Cato, and *Screenwriter, film director: David Lynch.

Birthday 2, Date Path 6

Sensitivity, compassion, and resourcefulness are inherent to this pattern and they are obviously useful qualities in most careers, but there is a need here to give them form. If you shape them in a way that reflects your personal values, you are well on your way to success. Organization and integrity are vital. Examples include: *Doctors: Ian Stahle and Molly Newhouse, *Chemist: Leonard Weickhardt, *Social activists: Diane Graham, Eleanor Roosevelt, and Pearl Bailey, *Writers: D. H. Lawrence, Henrik Ibsen, Judith Guest, and Novalis.

Birthday 2, Date Path 7

Sensitivity, self-honesty and a generous attitude will assist the unfolding of your ideals but your life may have many strange twists and turn. This versatile pattern will encourage you to turn unexpected events to your advantage. Examples include: *Actors: Edward Furlong, Farrah Fawcett, Frank Thring, Jennifer Jones, Michael Moore, Myrna Loy, Peter O'Toole, and Richard Attenborough, *Artist: Max Ernst, *Astronaut: Edwin Eugene Aldrin, *Physician: Betsy Ancker-Johnston, *Philosopher and poet: John Moriarty.

Birthday 2, Date Path 8

What we have here is sensitivity and compassion on the one hand, and resourcefulness and ambition, on the other. Once each of these components is acknowledged within you, their synthesis follows. A set of principles upon which you can maintain your life is necessary here.

Base these on what you value. Examples include: *Judges: Paul Hatfield and Roma Mitchell, *Physicists: Aleksandr Mikhailovich Prokhorov and William Henry Bragg, *Writers: Eduoard Schure, Emanuel Swedenborg, Enid Blyton, Francesco Petrarch, Graham Greene, Isabel Allende, Sigrid Undset, Upton Sinclair, and Vera Brittain.

Birthday 2, Date Path 9

The willingness to listen to the inspiration flowing through you will steadily unfold once you set your mind on a workable ideal. Shadowing your natural tendency to be idealistic is self-honesty, which suggests that in order to succeed you may need to firstly accept yourself as you truly are. Examples include: *Cartoonist: Michael Leunig, *Comedians: George Burns and Harold Lloyd, *Judge: Thurgood Marshall, *Political activists: Angelina Grimke, Dean Acheson, Elizabeth Dole, Jeff Kennett, Niccolo Machiavelli, Robert Gordon Menzies, *Physicians: Hugh O'Hara and Richard Mead, and *Physiotherapist: Frederick Matthias Alexander.

Birthday 2, Date Path 11

Sensitivity and cooperation, self-reliance and inspiration, need to unite through self-discipline and a commitment to fulfilling one task at a time. Select one humanitarian ideal to focus your attention on and then work towards it, step by patient step. A personal transformation is imminent. Examples include: *Actors: Jennifer Aniston, Jessica Lange, and Lucy Lawless, *Environmentalist, humanitarian & mountain climber: Edmund Hillary, *Musicians: Edward Elgar, Karen Carpenter and Keith Potger, *Soccer Star: David Beckham (with vowel 11).

Birthday 2, Date Path 22

With this combination you are learning that inspiration, sensitivity, patience, integrity and compassion are practical tools that applied under the right circumstances can be of great benefit to yourself and other people. You probably have a keen eye for detail and if you don't then you need to cultivate it. Examples include: *Academic: Rene Pomeau, *Founder of institution caring for the terminally ill: Mother Alphonsa Lathrop, *Medical intuitive and author: Caroline Myss.

People with birthday number 3 court success by speaking thoughtfully. This does not negate spontaneity but it does imply caring that what you say impacts on the listener (and because what goes around comes around, this also ultimately means you). With birthday number 3, you are learning how to express yourself in a way that makes your meaning clear. You must to be willing to account for what you say, without loosing your natural joy and spontaneity.

Birthday 3, Date Path 1

Thoughtfulness and self-reliance are the key ingredients here. In other words success comes by initiating projects that other people wish they had thought of, and following them through to completion – with love, joy and integrity. The possibilities are limited only by your imagination, but team-work is vital. Examples include: *Artists: Pro Hart and Stanley Spencer,

*Fashion designer: Christian Dior, *Pioneer in automotive engineering & marketing: Henry Ford, *Pioneer Nurse: Florence Nightingale and *Pioneer Inventor: Alfred Nobel, *Politicians: Al Grassby, Benjamin Disraeli, Dick Cheney, and Don Chipp.

Birthday 3, Date Path 2

With 3/2 as your combination, thoughtfulness, sensitivity and enthusiasm probably come naturally to you. Such qualities can lead to any number of ingenious projects. Set them to work within a team-setting and you have the recipe for a successful career. It's up to you to exercise your imagination and get things happening. Examples include: *Educators: Charles Housden, Charles Dunford Rowley, and *Hanna Neumann: first female professor of mathematics in Australia, *Musicians: Brian Howard and Gordon (Tex) Beneke, *Pediatric Pathologist: John Emery, and *Psychoanalyst: Henri Rey.

Birthday 3, Date Path 3

Your birthday number and primary date path are developing in tandem with one another. The double 3 exerting a powerful influence on your mind especially your imagination. There is no limit to what can be accomplished here for people who can turn current trends to their advantage. Yet compassion is essential for lasting satisfaction. Think about ways to enrich your community with your gifts. Examples include: *Artists: Tracey Moffatt and Paul Avril and *Pottery maker: Elijah Wedgwood, *Educator & Entertainer: Bill Cosby, *Musician: Lionel Hampton & Singers: Celine Dion, Dionne Warwick, Nina Simone, and *Poet & Philosopher: S.T.Coleridge.

Birthday 3, Date Path 4

With 3/4 as your combination, thoughtfulness, integrity and self-honesty are the essential ingredients to career success for you. Shadowing these qualities is the need to lead or at least take the initiative and get the ball rolling sometimes. Several spiritual preceptors turned up here along with the following: *Artists: Amedeo Modigiliani, Charles Blackman, Jacques Louis David, *Sports careerists: Lionel Rose and Mike Tyson (boxing), Nadia Comaneci (gymnastics), Phillip Hughes (cricket) and Robert Kirkby (sports psychology), *Writers: Marion Zimmer Bradley, Mark Twain, William Inge, and Wystan Hugh Auden.

Birthday 3, Date Path 5

With this combination you could be racing to keep up with all of your ideas. The way that you organize your ideas is a critical factor to your success yet your style of communication is equally important. Enthusiasm is seldom lacking here and if you are able to apply sensitivity within a team setting, your input may have lasting impact. Examples include: *Anthropologist: Norman Tindale, and *Naturalist: Charles Darwin, *Artists: Joyce Wieland and Vincent Van Gogh, *Composer: Felix Mendelsson, *Writers: Ahmad Shamlu, Charlotte Bronte, Mudrooroo, and Paul Verlaine.

Birthday 3, Date Path 6

Highly inventive and creative people are found in abundance here – far too many to name – and as well as those careers named below there are several famous actors, artists, musicians and writers that could have been included. Thoughtfulness, compassion, and a generous attitude to life are critical to the unfolding of your ideals whatever they may be. Examples include: *Anthropologists: Adrian Adams and Jane Goodall, *Criminologist: Eleanor Glueck, and *Prison Reformer: Elizabeth Fry, *Inventor: Buckminster Fuller, and *Surgeon: Victor Chang.

Birthday 3, Date Path 7

A distinct style of presentation and a philosophical attitude to life characterize 3/7 people. The way that thoughts and words are given form is important to success here – even the way sound and silence are shaped - for there are several musicians with this pattern. Integrity and a set of principles are an essential part of this formula. Examples include: *Antiquarian, poet, & literary collector: Edward Williams ("Iolo Morganwg"), *Sports careerists: Chris Evert Lloyd (tennis), Doug Walters (cricket), Eamon Wade Sullivan (swimming), Ron Clarke (long distance running) and Yogi Berra (baseball), *Writers: Al Purdy, Andre Malraux, Fyodor Dostoyevsky, Gertrude Stein, Harold Robbins, Jonathan Swift, and Voltaire.

Birthday 3, Date Path 8

A diverse range of qualities constitutes the formula to success here, the way that you express your ideas being foremost. You will need to be resourceful, in a world that changes from day to day. Your impact on others may be greater than you realize especially if you are a far-sighted person. Examples include: *Doctors: Ainslie Meares (psychiatrist) and Elizabeth Blackwell, *Inventor & teacher: Alexander Graham Bell, *Mountain climber: Jordan Romero, *Musician: Johann Sebastian Bach (and several others).

Birthday 3, Date Path 9

The abilities to 'think in pictures', retain images within the mind, and mould them therein, are the inherent gifts of this combination. But this comes to very little unless you can share your ideas with others. Your willingness to explore perspectives other than your own will assist the unfolding of your ideals. Examples include: *Author & naturalist: Henry David Thoreau, and *Wildlife scientist: William Emison, *Geographer, cave explorer, professor, artist, writer: Friedrich Simony, *Novelists: Francoise Sagan, Joseph Conrad and Leon Uris, *Poet: Dante Gabriel Rossetti, *Lyric Poet: Rainer Maria Rilke, *Philosophical writer: Raymond Moody, *Singers: Amy Ray, Connie Francis, Glenn Shorrock, Judith Durham, and Lena Horne.

Birthday 3, Date Path 11

When the imagination and inspiration inherent to this pattern are channelled into a creative project that breaks new ground and helps us evolve, personal satisfaction is all but guaranteed. But you may have to learn how to roll with the punches in the process. Adaptability and resourcefulness are important to your long-term success. Examples include: *Astronomer

& mathematicians: Friedrich Wilhelm Bessel and Carl Friedrich Gauss, *Biologist: Oscar Hertwig, *Geologist/micro palaeontologist: Irene Crespin, *Entertainers: Benny Hill, Doug Henning, and Jaye P Morgan, *Presidents: John Adams (BD 3/DP 11), and son John Quincy Adams (BD 11/DP 3).

Birthday 3, Date Path 22

Most careers benefit from the empathy and inspiration, integrity and imagination, inherent to this pattern. The ability to formulate such qualities into something worthwhile will be a decisive factor in your life. Learn how to take the initiative and how to alternate between leading and supporting. Examples include: *Composer: Ralph Vaughan Williams, and *Record producer: George Martin, *Historian: Manning Clark, and *Politician: Alfred Deakin.

People with birthday number 4 succeed when they act with integrity even if it is not appreciated it at the time. This is neither stubborn self-righteousness nor intractability but what emanates naturally from a state of inner peace. For maximum efficiency in the working world, you need to formulate a set of emotional guidelines that enhance your state of well being so that you can make your contribution count. With birthday number 4, success comes by respecting what feels right for your body, mind and soul and, acting accordingly.

Birthday 4, Date Path 1

Integrity, self-reliance, and enthusiasm will support whatever goals you have in mind. Shadowing these qualities is the ability to give form to your mental meanderings. You may have to learn to live with uncertainty and be prepared to change course as need be. Nothing ventured nothing gained is the motto here. Examples include: *Doctor & educator: Maria Montessori, and *Eye surgeon: Albrecht Grafe, *Educator, family planner & midwife: Patricia Amicone, and *Inventor of a television system: John Logie Baird.

Birthday 4, Date Path 2

You have the numbers of rhythm and harmony working in your favour. Provided you schedule your life so that you allow some time just for you, and express your feelings rather than bottling them, you may be surprised by your creative capacity. Examples include: *Actors: Jamie Lee Curtis, Linda Blair, Matthew Newton, Michael Beck, Robert Downey Jr., Wesley Snipes, *Inventor: Erno Rubik, *Writers: Bettina Von Arnim, George Byron, Norman Mailer, and Robert Louis Stevenson.

Birthday 4, Date Path 3

You may have unique ideas to offer, but the way that you express these will be critical to your success. You need to strike a balance between being practical and being imaginative. Cultivating your own truth is fundamental to your success. Don't be afraid to take the lead sometimes. Examples include: *Activist & first Australian female political candidate: Catherine Helen Spence, *Anthropologist, biographer & historian: Marcia Langton, *Civic leader, doctor, and musician: Ella Stack.

Birthday 4, Date Path 4

The double 4 intensifies the need for order and organization, and its potency lies in being able to channel these into creative works. Examples include: *Landscape designer: Edna Margaret Walling, *Musicians: Elmer Bernstein, Hugo Wolf, Itzhak Perlman and Van Morrison, *Writers: Dorothy Leigh Sayers, Percy Bysshe Shelley, and Primo Levi.

Birthday 4, Date Path 5

If the number of sportspeople and explorers were anything to go by, this would have to be one of the most adventurous and energetic of combinations. 4/5's like to travel, in this world and in some cases, in other worlds as well. They are an expressive bunch too: actors, songwriters, educators, directors, magicians, writers and presidents are all represented. Here are just a few (and there are more in 22/5): *Doctors: Edward Keefer, Josephine Diaz Martin and Serge Preradovic, *Musicians: Adam Clayton, Beyonce, Kamal, Mike Stoller, Mitch Miller, and *Sailor: Richard Howard Bertram, with a matching vowel 5, consonant 4.

Birthday 4, Date Path 6

This pattern suggests that integrity and compassion find their unity through a set of principles that are anchored in love. These 'guidelines to decision-making' should be ones that ring true for you personally and allow you to express your creativity. Team-work is vital to your success. Examples include: *Historians: Jack Treasure and Muriel Wright, *Musicians: Arnold Schoenberg, Art Tatum, Dorothy Rudd Moore, George Benson, John Denver, Morrissey, Red Symons, Russell Morris, Stevie Wonder, Wilhelm Bach, and *Swimmer: Dawn Fraser.

Birthday 4, Date Path 7

Personal integrity and self-honesty are the key words here. Shaping their development is the desire to express an independent point of view. In everyday matters you are practical; but there is also an inspired mind here, one that can shape ideas and herald new concepts. Examples include: *Astronomers: Henrietta Swan Leavitt and Philip Keenan, *Baseball champion & civil rights activist: Jackie Robinson, *Campaigner for reconciliation, conservationist & poet: Judith Wright, *Educational reformer & poet: Gabriela Minstral, and *Film director: Scott Hicks.

Birthday 4, Date Path 8

Resourcefulness is put into action here, shaping projects that you feel strongly about. The willingness to see things from another person's perspective will facilitate the unfolding of your most cherished ideals. As well as those listed, the examples included several spiritual leaders, for this pattern grants the ability to probe deeply. Examples include: *Architects: Alfred Mosher Butts (inventor of Scrabble) and Justin Madden (also an AFL footballer & politician), *Astrologers: Dr John Dee (mathematician) and Michel Gauquelin (statistician), *Creator of a society & instigator of legislation for the blind: Cynthia Alden.

Birthday 4, Date Path 9

Continually changing circumstances are inherent to this pattern and must somehow be turned to your advantage. Ingenuity will therefore be required in whatever field you wish to succeed in. Examples include: *Aviation pioneer: Charles Lindbergh, *Inventor of shorthand: Isaac Pitman, *Entertainer, singer-songwriter: Robbie Williams, *Scientists: Rita Levi-Montalcini, and Robert Robinson.

Birthday 4, Date Path 11

Inspiration needs to be grounded in research if the career potential here is to be realized. You will do particularly well if you can discern the inherent rhythm and harmony in whatever your field of interest is. Self-honesty will enhance this development, because you will then be able to understand where you fit in and can make your contribution. Examples include: *Co-founder of the permaculture movement: Bill Mollison, *Musicians: Antonio Vivaldi, Eduard Lassen, Franz Schubert and Stephen Trier (instrument maker), *Politicians: Albert Gore, Constance Markiewicy, Hosni Mubarak, Jack Kemp, John Calvin Coolidge and Richard Gephardt.

Birthday 4, Date Path 22

A much more sensitive and complex pattern than it first appears, 4/22 compels people to formulate their own ideas on why the universe behaves as it does and why people behave as they do. It elicits the intuition that the world, individuals, and indeed all of life, operate by the same intrinsic law. Some of you will perceive this as a web of love. Examples include: *Physicists: J. R. Oppenheimer, Robert Boyle, and Robert Wilson, *Politician: Margaret Thatcher, *Psychotherapist and writer of books on druidry: Philip Carr-Gomm.

People with birthday number 5 invite success into their lives when they embrace opportunities with enthusiasm. This does not equate with recklessness but does imply exploring all the options before giving up on something, which may be more important than you initially realized. With birthday number 5, be aware that this vibration attracts a wide variety of experiences. You are learning how to manage all of your options in the most beneficial way.

Birthday 5, Date Path 1

Enthusiasm and self-reliance need to be anchored in a project that you can throw your heart into. The challenge is to develop your versatility without sacrificing your integrity. Tasks that benefit your community will give you the greatest satisfaction. Examples include: *Natural scientist: Alexander Humboldt, *Physicist: John Bardeen, *Psychiatrist: Milton Erickson, *Pioneers in the field of animation: George Lucas and Walt Disney, *Politicians: Poul Hartling, and Sallyanne Atkinson.

Birthday 5, Date Path 2

Research is favoured here, with success dependent on how well you present your ideas. Explore ways to balance your risk-taking instincts with your need for stability and security.

Examples include: *Actors: Clayton Moore, Emily Watson, Guy Pearce, and Robert Duvall, *Diarist: Samuel Pepys, and *Biographer: Walter Jackson Bate, *Painters: Klimt, Manet, Monet, and Turner.

Birthday 5, Date Path 3

This pattern will prompt you to find a way to express your empathy – with people and with the land - so that you are able to improve the way we relate to each other and our environment. Justice is high on the agenda here. Examples include: *Civil rights activists: Bernadette Devlin and Paula Masselos, *Civil rights lawyer: Elmer Gertz, *Politician: Cheryl Kernot, and *Zoology professor: Richard Eakin.

Birthday 5, Date Path 4

Technical skill and a novel approach to your ideals should bring you career satisfaction. Getting a balance between optimism and pessimism may prove challenging at times. Step-by-step research and the documentation of your findings will improve your chances of success. Examples include: *Actor: Diane Cliento, *Film director, producer, & screenwriter: Ingmar Bergman, *Doctor: Albert Claude (Nobel Prize Winner, 1974), *Economist and scholar: John Maynard Keynes.

Birthday 5, Date Path 5

Energetic and intuitive, you enjoy testing the boundaries in your field of endeavour. We are likely to find you attempting to a break a record, or in some other way going beyond what has been accomplished before. Getting ahead and making progress is important to you and the sky is the limit. A strong set of principles will keep you on track. Examples include: *Car racer: Joan Richmond, Cycle racer: Sid Patterson, and Horse racer (jockey): Roy Higgins, *Mathematician: David Hilbert, *Philosopher: Giambattista Vico, *News presenter: Eric Pearce, and *Politician: Gareth Evans.

Birthday 5, Date Path 6

Empathy, compassion and enthusiasm abound here and will unlock your creative ingenuity. Intuition and foresight are also a part of this pattern. Shadowing them is self-reliance. You must learn to trust your hunches and run with what feels right at the time. Examples include: *Barrister: Cherie Booth, *News presenter: Walter Cronkite, *Film makers/directors: Claude Autant-Lara and Pasquale Deleo, *Scientists: Albert Einstein (physicist) and Tycho Brahe (astronomer); together again as per vowel 7, consonant 11.

Birthday 5, Date Path 7

With 5/7 as your pattern, you will find that enthusiasm, honesty, and the willingness to see things from another person's perspective will liberate your ingenuity. It is the depth and sincerity that you put into your projects, in tandem with your ability to express your findings that wins the day here. Examples include: *Botanist & pioneer of taxonomy: Carl Von Linne, *Pioneering pathologist: Peter MacCallum, *Establisher of nurse-training colleges: Anna

Maxwell, *Playwrights/poets: Edwin Markham, Vaclav Havel, and William Shakespeare, *Singers: Bob Geldof, Clarence Carter, and Woody Guthrie.

Birthday 5, Date Path 8

Enthusiasm, resourcefulness and integrity will not only support your career goals but may eventually lead to a profound transformation of your values. The way that you structure and shape your ideas and present them to others will be critical to your success. As well as an extraordinary number of actors, the examples include: *Anthropologist: Ruth Fulton Benedict, *Historian: Arnold Toynbee, *Astronaut & first man to walk on the moon: Neil Armstrong, *Novelists: John Galsworthy and Nigel Godwin Tranter.

Birthday 5, Date Path 9

Fierce determination accompanies this pattern but it is your enthusiasm and a generous attitude that will release the creative ingenuity necessary to solve problems. Energetic and intuitive yet also practical and sensible, you could be a groundbreaker in you chosen field of endeavour. Examples include: *Mathematician: Amalie Emmy Noether (Noether's Theorem), *Medical missionary: Albert Schweitzer, and *Surgeon: Joseph Lister, *Tennis player: Steffi Graf, and *Aikido instructor: Leonie Mc Farlane.

Birthday 5, Date Path 11

This energetic combination can take you anywhere. Success hinges on your ability to be honest with yourself, and you need to find your own special niche in the market place of life. Do this, and you could become a 'market' leader. Examples include: *Explorer, geologist & scientist: Douglas Mawson, *Historians: Thomas Birch and Will Durant, *Musicians: Athol Guy, Charles Grover, Manuel de Falla, and Taylor Hanson.

Birthday 5, Date Path 22

Physical and mental dexterity combine here. An outgoing combination, 5/22 grants you the ability to understand what motivates people and the practical skills to do something tangible to help them with their problems. Inspiration and teamwork must combine. Examples include: *Authors: Harriet Beecher Stowe and Maureen Wheeler (travel guide), *Composer: Esther Rofe, *Philosopher: Thomas Hobbes, and *Psychiatrist: Helen Flanders Dunbar.

People with birthday number 6 set things in motion when they actively express their compassion. This does not mean neglecting your own needs and feelings but it does imply desiring to help when help is asked for. With birthday number 6, it probably comes naturally to you to contemplate the most effective way to be of practical assistance to those who are obviously in need of it. Consider how you can give to others without depleting yourself. It may take some lateral thinking, but it can be done.

Birthday 6, Date Path 1

Coherent action amidst changing circumstances is called for here. You will need to learn how to 'live in the moment' and make the most of whatever situation you find yourself in. Self-honesty is essential if your creative ideas are to be of real benefit to others. Examples include: *Civil rights campaigner: Martin Luther King Jr.,*Norman Cousins: world peace advocate; *Christmas Humphreys: judge, and author of *12 Principles of Buddhism*, *Environmental scientist: David Suzuki, *Healers: Hawayo Takata (Reiki), Helen Brooke Taussig (cardiology & paediatrics), Joao Teixeira Da Faria (spiritual healing), and Viktor Adler (general practice).

Birthday 6, Date Path 2

Compassion, sensitivity and resourcefulness will result in achievements that have lasting benefit *if* slotted into a durable framework *and* handled with integrity. Your actions must accord with your personal set of values. As well as a disproportionate number of Presidents and Prime Ministers, the following careers were represented: *Architect & designer: Charlotte Perriand, *Artist: Elizabeth Durack, *Cosmonaut: Valentina Tereshkova, *Metallurgist: Francis Arthur Fox, *Dancer and founder of a ballet school: Ninette de Valois.

Birthday 6, Date Path 3

Compassion, thoughtfulness, and a generous attitude will assist the unfolding of your ideals. You probably have good spatial awareness and a healthy imagination. Examples include: *Architect: Walter Burley Griffin, *Artist: Frida Kahlo, *Film producer: George Jackson, *Television producer: Penny Chapman, *Writers: E. L. Doctorow, Evelyn Underhill, F. Scott Fitzgerald, Robert Bolt, Robyn Davidson, and Walter Scott.

Birthday 6, Date Path 4

Compassion, integrity, and self-reliance will develop as you explore your potential through projects that you feel committed to and through which you can express yourself. Although this pattern indicates the need to co-operate with others, you will also need to explore your own ideas and generate own hypotheses. Examples include: *Actors: Helen Hunt, Jack Quaid, James Belushi, Steve McQueen and *Magician/entertainer: Paul Daniels, *Anthropologist: Thor Heyerdahl, *Architect: Charles-Edouard Jeanneret-Gris, *Medical pioneers: John Snow, Josef Breuer, and Sigmund Freud.

Birthday 6, Date Path 5

Compassion, enthusiasm, and a willingness to listen to your inspiration will help you to realize your dreams. To fulfil the potential inherent to this pattern you must dare to go beyond the contribution that others have made and exercise your own ideas. Examples include: *Astronomer: Williamina Fleming, *Astrophysicist: Charlotte Sitterly, *Medical researchers: Alexander Fleming, Florence Seibert, and Howard Florey, *Writers: Alan Watts, Alfred Tennyson, Aurobindo Ghose, Imgard Charlotte Keun, Jorge Luis Borges, Max Beerbohm, Myrtle Fillmore and Zelda Fitzgerald.

Birthday 6, Date Path 6

There's limitless potential here for original self-expression. You probably have a unique perspective on life: a conglomeration of ideas and images from a variety of disciplines, which you have synthesized in your own way. You need a career that encourages the application of your most promising thoughts. Examples include: *Musicians: Conrad Ansorge, Maria Theresia von Paradis, and Mary Carr Moore, *Physicist, mathematician & author: Freeman John Dyson (birthday and date path 15), *Writers: Alexandre Dumas (father), Christopher Marlowe, Elizabeth Barrett Browning, George Moore, Ram Dass, and Thomas Mann.

Birthday 6, Date Path 7

Sensitive yet also sensible, compassionate yet also practical, characterizes this pattern. You have a unique approach to problems and the mental dexterity to transform a difficult or discordant situation into a workable solution. The examples suggest that you may have an ear for music and/or an eye for composition as well. *Artists: Arthur Boyd (painter & sculptor) and William Morris (designer & poet), *Musicians: Alexander Scriabin, Alfred Schnittke, and Arman Khachaturian (composers), John Williams (classical guitarist) and Sarah Caldwell (conductor), and *Scientist: Pierre Curie.

Birthday 6, Date Path 8

This dynamic pattern blends compassion and resourcefulness in ingenious ways. Within your field of interest, you tend to shake things up and move things around. To make the most of the opportunities that 6/8 brings, firstly determine what is of value to you and then what needs to change in order to give these values a tangible form. Examples include: *Actors: Barbra Streisand and Lucille Ball, *Musician: Bob Dylan, *Artists: Michelangelo, Raphael and Rembrandt, *Geneticist: Spencer Wells, and *Inventor: George Westinghouse.

Birthday 6, Date Path 9

It is your deep compassion that will stimulate your creativity and unlock your ingenuity. Your presentation skills then become the linchpin of your success. A wide variety of occupations were evident in the examples, with an interest in global issues or universal themes as a common factor. Examples include: *Artists: Diego Rodriguez de Silvay Velazquez, Henri de Toulouse-Lautrec, Kahlil Gibran, Paul Lucien Dessau, and Phemie Bostock, *Religious leaders: Frank Woods, Maria Francesca Cabrini and Ranganathananda, *Singers: Kiri Te Kanawa, Mary Wilson, Richard Carpenter, Ricky Martin, Sly Stone, and Terence Trent D'Arby.

Birthday 6, Date Path 11

You need structure but it must be flexible. Hang on to whatever you consider valuable but not so tightly that unexpected developments are unable to enrich you. Compassion, resourceful, and inspiration must combine. Examples include: *Actors: Jill Ireland and Miranda July, *Arts patron & business tycoon: John Paul Getty, *Writers: Aleksandr Sergeyevich Pushkin, Annie Fellows Johnston, Baruch Spinoza, Elizabeth Goudge, and John Molony.

Birthday 6, Date Path 22

This is an extremely sensitive yet potentially practical pattern. It will help you combine compassion, integrity and inspiration in beneficial ways. Self-honesty is essential. 6/22 finds fulfilment in leadership and has a way of quickening the consciousness of the general population. Examples include: *Musician: Oscar Peterson, *Neurosurgeon: Charles Teo, *Spiritual leaders: HH, the 14th Dalai Lama of Tibet, and Sister Mary McKillop.

People with birthday number 7 get things happening once they adopt the attitude that 'honesty is the best policy'. This does not mean isolating oneself from those who are living a different 'truth' but it does imply researching and contemplating the matter of truth internally as well as externally. With birthday number 7, you will find that through self-honesty you will come to realize that truth is not a doctrine but an intuitive perception within the sanctuary of the soul and that it reflects itself, in some way, through every living entity.

Birthday 7, Date Path 1

With this combination you will find that self-honesty, self-reliance, and resourcefulness are necessary for lasting achievements. Focus your efforts on people's needs but don't get lost in their projections or expectations. Instead, cultivate your own ideas. As well as several famous actors, the examples include: *Anthropologist: Mary Shepardson, *Cardiothoracic surgeon: Victor Chang and *Pediatrician: Karl Konig, *Educator & poet: Rabindranath Tagore, and *Playwright: George Oppenheimer.

Birthday 7, Date Path 2

Self-honesty, sensitivity, and a generous attitude will assist the unfoldment of your ideas. When you can include change and unpredictability in your ideals and values, you are on the road to success. Examples include: *Artists: Florence Farr and Marc Chagall, *Diplomat: Ralph Johnson Bunche, *Politician: John Charles Bannon, and *Educational reformer: Susan Blow.

Birthday 7, Date Path 3

Research is favoured by 7/3, and so are editing skills. You will find that it is the principles that you live by, which hold the key to your success. Self-honesty is essential and will increase your ability to shape your ideas into a practical, yet flexible framework. Examples include: *Anthropologist: Margaret Mead, *Biologist: Nettie Stevens, *Economist & peace researcher: Frank Blackaby, *Linguist: Noam Chomsky, *Writers: Alice Bailey, Charles Dickens, and Colin Thiele.

Birthday 7, Date Path 4

This pattern supports the development of research projects enlivened by inspired thoughts, which can be put to use in any of the arts or sciences. With 7/4 social activism is common. You are a highly creative individual with a unique approach to your career. Examples include: *Artists: Ola Cohn (sculptor) and Russell Drysdale (painter), *Attorney, labour reformer & peace advocate: Crystal Eastman, *Musicians: Elton John (whose vowel and consonant pairing is also 7/4), Jean-Pierre Rampal, Maurice Ravel, *Scientists: Guglielmo Marconi, Marie Curie, and Stephen Salter (engineer).

Birthday 7, Date Path 5

Self-honesty, enthusiasm, and the willingness to see things from another person's perspective will set you on the road to success. The way that you present yourself and express your ideas will make all the difference. The examples suggest that your empathy should not be limited to people. Examples include: *Botanist: Luther Burbank, *Conservationist: Harry Butler, *Mathematician & scientist: Isaac Newton, *Scientific explorer: Roald Amundsen, *Nutritionist: Adelle Davis, and *Social anthropologist: Mary Douglas.

Birthday 7, Date Path 6

Mental dexterity comes with this pattern and a deep and abiding compassion as well. Shadowing these qualities is the need for scrupulous self-honesty, integrity, and self-reliance. 7/6 portends a personal transformation at some time during your life, and from it can emerge a more integrated and confident personality. Examples include: *Film makers: David Puttnam and Francis Ford Coppola, *Poets/writers: Francis Thompson, Ralph Waldo Emerson, and Robert Browning, *Politicians: Billy Hughes, Corazon Aquino, Keizo Obuchi, and James Madison.

Birthday 7, Date Path 7

Enthusiasm for the project at hand will release the floodgates of your creative ingenuity, which is boundless. Some truly groundbreaking work is possible with this combination. As your capacity for honest introspection increases, so will your insight. Double 7's are highly versatile people. Examples include: *Historical writers: Elizabeth Palmer Peabody and Marchette Gaylord Chute, *Musicians: Beethoven and Bernstein, *Dancer: Suzanne Farrell (with vowel & consonant 7, name 77), *Scientists: Alfred Alder, Ernst Haeckel, Galileo Galilei, and John Cornforth Jr.

Birthday 7, Date Path 8

Self-honesty and self-reliance, resourcefulness and compassion, are the keys to your success. The examples are loaded with unique individuals who blazed their own trail often amidst controversy. Reform is a consistent theme within the given field of interest. Examples include: *Cleric & founder of the Royal Flying Doctor Service: John Flynn, *Medical missionary: Dr Berke, and *Medical doctor & mystic: Anna Kingsford, *Popular historians: AJP Taylor and Thomas Babington Macaulay, *Writers: George S Kaufman, Mary Gilmore, Oscar Wilde, Thomas Keneally, and William Wordsworth.

Birthday 7, Date Path 9

Self-honesty and a generous attitude will assist the unfolding of your ideals and stimulate increasingly deeper levels of awareness. Your sensitivity may go unnoticed but to the extent that it helps other people, it will increase the value of your achievements. Yoke your activity to a solid core of research, internal as well as external. Examples include: *Actors: Anne Baxter and Henry Fonda, *Entertainer: Lauren Newton, *Social activists: Constance Cummings-John and Gloria Steinem, and *Surveyor & civic activist: Clem Jones.

Birthday 7, Date Path 11

Intuition, inspiration, constructive fantasy, and idealism, enhance the mental and physical dexterity this pattern offers. Research, observation, and self honesty shape its potential into worthwhile projects. Examples include: *Aeronautical engineer and inventor: Igor Ivanovich Sikorsky, *Conservationist: Marjorie Stoneman Douglas, and *Ecologist: Alton A Lindsey, *Sports careerists: Alberto Salazar, Cathy Freeman (running) and Gabriela Sabatini (tennis).

Birthday 7, Date Path 22

Social activism is common here, born of deep sensitivity. Sometimes this expresses itself through the creative arts too. With 7/22 comes political savvy. Examples include: *Historian: George Macaulay Trevelyan, *Religious leaders: Archbishop Desmond Tutu and Johann von Herder, *Sociological researcher, social reformer, and industrialist: Benjamin Rowntree.

People with birthday number 8 are efficiency-minded. They are also resourceful, intuitively knowing where to look for whatever is needed. The solution to a problem may not be immediately apparent but to those who listen, the answer usually comes. With birthday number 8, you are learning that the treasure trove 'within' is limitless and can supply you with everything you need. Until then, look after whatever you do have because resource management is the key to your efficiency in all spheres of endeavour.

Birthday 8, Date Path 1

Resourcefulness, self-reliance, and a generous attitude will serve your career goals and unfold your ideals. Self-honesty is critical here. You are probably a gifted problem-solver and strategist, and someone who can appreciate the bigger picture. Examples include: *Artist: Eugene Delacroix (painter), *Classical composer: Carl Vine, and *Singer/songwriter: Jim Morrison, *Writers: Andrea Dworkin and Sidney Sheldon.

Birthday 8, Date Path 2

Resourcefulness and self-reliance will unlock your potential but your powerful emotions need a set of principles to guide them and a clear goal to aim for. These guidelines must be your own and not merely a projection of community values. If you pursue your own ideas, you may invent something original. Examples include: *Analytic & linguistic philosopher: Ludwig Wittgenstein, *Nuclear physicist: Mark Oliphant, *Writers: Anne Bronte, Banjo Patterson, Eugene Ionesco, Jules Verne, and Morris West.

Birthday 8, Date Path 3

Being so profoundly sensitivity makes it difficult for you to cope with unforeseen circumstances. Yet turning challenging circumstances to your advantage may become precisely your forte. 8/3 is loaded with creative, charismatic, people-smart individuals. Examples include: *Actors: Anne Shirley, David Carradine, John Waters, John Wayne, and Kevin Spacey, *Musicians: Archie Roach, David Bowie, Enya, Micky Dolenz, and Olivia Newton-John, and *Television personality and comedienne: Joan Rivers.

Birthday 8, Date Path 4

The ability to design, i.e., to give shape to your ideas and images is strong here. To perceive pattern and order and formulate it into an original piece of work translates into a golden opportunity in the right hands. Integrity and willingness to see things from another person's perspective can led to achievements of lasting benefit to others. Examples include: *Architect, designer & photographer: Margaret Macdonald Troup, and *Photographer and poet: Walter Chappell, *Pianists: Billy Pierce and Nat King Cole, *Global electronics pioneer: Akio Morita, and *Seismologist: Charles Richter.

Birthday 8, Date Path 5

A personal transformation is imminent here, brought about by a combination of worldly activity and profound self-evaluation. Perhaps this is why so many healers turned up with this pattern. With 8/5 the way that you present and express your ideas, alongside your ability to adapt and evolve, will be the yardstick of your success. Examples include: *Medical Doctors: Albert Christian Billroth, Swami Sivananda and W.W.Westcott, *Politicians: Janine Haines, and Mao Tse Tung, *Scientists: Benjamin Franklin (electricity), George Batchelor (fluid mechanics) and Alfred Wallace (biologist and evolutionary theorist).

Birthday 8, Date Path 6

8/6 brings a longing to alleviate suffering, born of a deep sensitivity to the plight of other beings. This is a highly energetic pattern that promotes growth, both personally and within one's social arena. Resourcefulness, compassion, and adaptability are critical to your success. Examples include: *Composers: Arthur Fielder, James Galway, James Last and Robert Schumann, *Medical doctors: Anton Chekhov (physician & short-story writer), Christiaan Barnard (heart surgeon) and Elisabeth Kubler-Ross (psychiatrist), and *Toxinologist: Struan Sutherland, who developed a life-saving spider antivenin.

Birthday 8, Date Path 7

This pattern invites the widest possible range of career options. Writers, clerics and scientists are well represented and within these fields of activity, expression varies greatly. Resourcefulness and adaptability are the norm, and there is an interest in synthesis as well. The success and value of your synthesis hinges on self-honesty. Examples include: *Chemist: Humphry Davy, *Engineer: Jack Pittam, *Physicist: Stephen Hawking, *Doctors: Edward Jenner, and Susan LaFlesche Picotte, *Writers: A. E. van Vogt, Arthur Miller, Joseph Campbell, Kenneth Grahame, Martin Heidegger, and Pearl S Buck.

Birthday 8, Date Path 8

Resourcefulness and self-honesty are necessary to manage the power built into 8/8. If you refrain from deferring to others and blaming them when things do not go well and make time daily for quiet reflection, your potential for success is limited only by your imagination. Keep in mind that this pattern measures success in the long term and that increasingly profound levels of awareness are inevitable. Examples include: *Actors: Paul Newman and Sandra

Bullock, *Evolutionary biologist: Richard Dawkins, *Health promoter: John Harvey Kellogg, *Playwrights: George Bernard Shaw and Margaret Ayer Barnes.

Birthday 8, Date Path 9

With 8/9 as your pattern, it is resourcefulness, rational thinking, and a generous attitude that will unfold your career goals. Learn to temper any impatience you may feel and take one day at a time for the goals here should be long-term. As well as several famous actors, singers and spiritual leaders, the examples include: *Architect: Frank Lloyd Wright, *Artists: Clifton Pugh and Olive Crane, *Aviation engineer & novelist: Nevil Shute, *Industrialist: John D. Rockefeller, and *Photographer: Dorothea Lange.

Birthday 8, Date Path 11

Resourcefulness will unfold your potential *if* you are willing to listen to your inspired thoughts and act upon them. Conditional to your success will be the way that you express yourself. You must learn how to share your ideas and feelings without getting over emotional and choreograph your actions in co-operation with others. Examples include: *Inventor of calculating machines: Charles Babbage, *Musicians: Adrian Boult, Domenico Scarlatti, Lynn Anderson, Mandawuy Yunupingu, and *Scientist: William Thomson (later Lord Kelvin: pioneer in thermodynamics).

Birthday 8, Date Path 22

Resourcefulness, integrity and inspiration are your most effective tools. As the powers of your mind unfold and the power of your words and deeds to motivate others becomes increasingly apparent, satisfaction is yours. 8/22 people are typically large-hearted, their empathy finding expression in creative yet at the same time practical, projects. Examples include: *Author of *The Lotus and the Spinning Wheel*, environmental lobbyist, mountain climber, solicitor, and social justice campaigner: Marie Byles, *Composer: Jean Julius Christian Sibelius, and *Humanitarian: Betty Ford, founder of the Betty Ford Clinic.

People with birthday number 9 are learning to embrace an attitude of abundance. This is not to imply giving away what you need in order to survive and live joyfully, but it does mean giving away any fears that are impeding the free flow of your creative vitality. The creative force that sustains life is continually pouring forth its bounty in accordance with natural law but the fear of being left out causes us to block its flow. To dispel such a negative thought pattern requires faith in yourself and the meaning that you attribute to life.

Birthday 9, Date Path 1

Fearlessness is called for here: the ability to make up your own mind and proceed along the course dictated by your conscience. A natural leader, you have but to take the initiative in order to get things happening. Resourcefulness will be necessary as you learn how to balance going with the flow and directing the flow. Examples include: *Activists: Catherine Stuber Scheel, Doug Nicholls, and Mairead Corrigan, *Politician: Paul Keating, *Artists: Frans Pieter

ter Meulen, Paul Klee and Raphael Sanzio, *Writers: John Dryden, Leo Tolstoy, Simone de Beauvoir, and Susan Faludi.

Birthday 9, Date Path 2

Going beyond the boundaries set in the past is a common theme here but this sensitive pattern needs careful handling. Success hinges on honesty and remaining true to yourself. If you are willing to listen to the inspiration flowing through you and allow it to shape your activity, you may be surprised by the impact of your endeavours. Examples include: *Chess player: Bobby Fischer, *Composer: Nikolai Andreyevich Rimsky-Korsakov, *Diplomat: Henry Kissinger and *Financial adviser: Sylvia Porter.

Birthday 9, Date Path 3

Social conscience and imaginative solutions to problems come with this combination. You are highly sensitive to the environment and to the impact of actions rendered therein. Your powers of observation, both socially as well as within your chosen field of endeavour, are critical to your success. Examples include: *Bowen therapist: Tom Bowen, *Chemist: Dmitri Mendeleev, *Physicist: Wilhelm Von Roentgen, *Engineers: Frederick Henry Royce and Randolph Creswell, *Film directors & producers: Frank Capra, formerly a chemical engineer, and Kevin Costner, now also working on environmental advancements in the use of energy (Kevin is one of several actors with this pattern).

Birthday 9, Date Path 4

With 9/4 as your combination, you will find that a generous attitude to life and uncompromising integrity will not only lead to the unfolding of your ideals but a personal transformation as well. Examples include: *Ballet artist & choreographer: Roslyn Ann Watson, *Director: Antoinette Perry (her awards becoming known as the Tony's), *Writers: Alexandre Dumas II, Amy Lowell, Bertha Suttner, and Mickey Spillane.

Birthday 9, Date Path 5

With this energetic and intuitive combination you will find your thoughts wandering into the magical realm of possibility and your deeds preparing the way for the future. Yet 9/5 can also be practical, which enables you to concentrate on one thing at a time, and metaphorically at least, to turn the soil and break up the clods as need be. Examples include: *Actress: Marlene Dietrich, *Film director & producer: Steven Spielberg, *Engineer: George Stephenson, *Zoologist: Michael James Tyler, *Philosophers: Bertrand Russell, and Georg Hegel.

Birthday 9, Date Path 6

This combination elicits compassion and the impulse to express your ideas on how humanity could do things better. A strong humanitarian streak is generally evident with 9/6, and so you will try to walk your talk. Yours is a sincere striving towards a more ideal existence. As well some famous actors the examples included: *Mathematician, photographer & writer: Lewis Carroll, *Politicians: Glenda Jackson, Lynn Arnold, Pauline Hansen, Richard Nixon, and Robin Millhouse, *Priest/social worker: Gerard Tucker, and *Reporter: Paul Makin.

Birthday 9, Date Path 7

Sincerity is the key here. If you want to be successful in a way that also benefits others, you will need to keep an eye on your motives. You are creative and versatile and perhaps more sensitive and emotionally volatile than you realize. A feeling of kinship with nature will stimulate deeper levels of understanding and unfold your ideals. Examples include: *Doctor: Fred Hollows (eye surgeon), and *Medical scientist: Louis Pasteur, *Inventor, MD & Thesaurus writer: Peter Roget, *Inventor of the diesel engine: Rudolf Diesel, *News presenter: Jane Doyle, and *Singer & human rights activist: Joan Baez.

Birthday 9, Date Path 8

9/8 tends to engender rational thinking along with an intrinsic sense of the pattern and order within life. If you are clear about where you want to direct your energy and why, your career objectives will steadily unfold despite any obstacles you may encounter. Examples include: *Astronaut: Alan Shepard, *Astronomer: Johannes Kepler, *Medical researcher: Alice Hamilton, MD (occupational health & safety), *Writers: C. S. Forester, Brendan Behan, and Gail Godwin.

Birthday 9, Date Path 9

This is a most singular pattern, its thrust being to align your personal will with the 'greater will'. Seldom is this accomplished without drama and most 9/9's feel as if they have run the gauntlet of human experience before this point is reached. Once it is, everything becomes possible. As a first step, try to recognize the polarities within yourself and initiate dialogue between them. Examples include: *Aviator: Charles Kingsford-Smith, *Engineer & inventor: Nikola Tesla, *Psychiatrist: Roberto Assagioli (founder of psychosynthesis), *Writers: Barbara Cartland, Henry Longfellow, John Milton, and Rosa Praed.

Birthday 9, Date Path 11

A generous attitude and a willingness to listen to the inspiration flowing through you, will gradually unveil your light to the world. Team-leader is the vocation that beckons, for you are sensitive to the needs and feelings of others; yet you also need to stand out in some way. As well as a number of spiritual leaders and some equally profound writers, the examples include: *Ambassador: Helen Kirkpatrick, *Soldier: Doug Miller, *Musician: W. A. Mozart, *Politicians: Catherine May, and Ruth McCormick Simms.

Birthday 9, Date Path 22

Integrity is the key to your success. The expression 'one percent inspiration and ninety-nine percent perspiration' might have been written by a 9/22. Your goals may be honourable, but only consistent work will accomplish them. Your innate sensitivity and practicality are a winning team. Examples include: *Entrepreneur: Richard Branson, *Marine biologist & writer: Rachel Carson, and *Ski instructor: James Riddell.

People with birthday 11 need to steady their nerves and develop self-awareness so that the inspiration coursing through them can come to fruition. Once you understand the futuristic nature of this number, you will discover that you excel within a team situation.

Birthday 11, Date Path 1

Your natural leadership ability, empathy, and unique perspective on life must combine around a core set of principles that you can live comfortably with. From this base, you can launch your far-sighted ideas. Examples include: *Inventors: Jacques-Yves Cousteau and Sidney Jefferson, *Musicians: Sergio Mendes, Carrie Jacobs Bond and Clarence Clemons, *Writers: Barbara Cummings, O. Henry, Oliver Wendell Holmes, Osho, Susan Bogert Warner, and Torquato Tasso.

Birthday 11, Date Path 2

Supporting others comes naturally to you and it may take a personal transformation to develop your own ideas. Integrity and organization are vital to your success. The meaning that you attribute to life affects the long-term outcome of your activities. Examples include: *Entrepreneur: William Butlin, *Golfers: Ben Cranshaw, and Fuzzy Zoeller.

Birthday 11, Date Path 3

This is a versatile pattern replete with creative souls who want to participate in the progress towards a more enjoyable lifestyle for all people. Shadowing their efforts is the need to constantly adapt to and make the most of changing circumstances. Your mental depth and dexterity seek a project you can bring to fulfilment. Examples include: *Bacteriologists: Alice Evans and Robert Koch, *Engineer: George Washington Goethals, *Dancers: Vaslvav Nijinski and George Sampson (both with birthday 11/date path 12), *Social workers/reformers: Ann Lee, and Julia Clifford Lathrop.

Birthday 11, Date Path 4

This pattern offers mental and physical dexterity, and enhances your problem-solving skills and techniques. A steady commitment to something that inspires your creativity will generate work that gives you lasting satisfaction. Being honest with yourself and with others is vital to your long-term success. Examples include: *Biologist & environmental scientist: Paul Ehrlich, *Geologist: Vivian Ernest Fuchs, *Miner: George Manwaring, *Musicians: Abe Lincoln (trombonist), and Thomas Beecham (conductor).

Birthday 11, Date Path 5

Your quick, sharp mind and sense of adventure need to find a project that you are happy to research and commit your talents to. 11/5 is a volatile and versatile combination, and so periodically you must decide where you would like to direct your energy. Be aware of projections, both upon you and from you, and maintain a high level of personal honesty. Examples include: *Musicians: Gioacchino Antonio Rossini, Graham Cyril Russell, Irving Berlin, *Politicians: Julius Chan and Sebastian Coe (also an athlete), *Scientists: Annie Jump Canon, Allen DuMont, Christiaan Eijkman, and Mary Jane Rathbun.

Birthday 11, Date Path 6

Your compassion and inspiration can bring hope into the lives of others but you must make the most of the opportunities that come your way and manage your resources effectively. At some point you may find that something has to be sacrificed in order for further progress to be made. Examples include: *Actors: Don Cheadle and Kim Delaney, *Inventor: Thomas Edison, *Musicians: Duke Ellington, Michael Jackson, and Richie Sambora.

Birthday 11, Date Path 7

11/7 offers mental and physical dexterity plus the ability to perceive pattern in the natural world. It is vital to stay centred on the one project that truly fascinates you and bring it to fulfilment. Examples include: *Activists: Jeannette Rankin, Ron Castan and Rosika Schwimmer, *Co-founder of Apple Computer: Steve Wozniak, *Computer scientist: Stephen Wolfram, *Musicians: Arnold Ross (jazz pianist), and Zubin Mehta (conductor).

Birthday 11, Date Path 8

When profoundness and inspiration unite and are expressed in a way that people can relate to, the overall consciousness of the population is quickened, even if only on a small scale. That's the potential here. Your ability to make a difference needs to be tempered by your personal values: those things that you know are truly important. Examples include: *Conservationist: Minard Crommelin, *Inventors: Ambrose Fleming and Charles Macintosh, *Lawyer/politician: Gough Whitlam, and *Lawyer/reporter: Lisa Allen.

Birthday 11, Date Path 9

You will know that you are working with 11/9 rather than 2/9 when you begin to sense the ebb and flow of the universe; perhaps this is why so many musicians have this pattern. As this super-sensitive pairing attunes you to increasingly refined vibrations, you will need to cultivate a core set of values that embrace every situation that you are likely to encounter. Examples include: *Musicians: Chuck Mangione, Jimmy Dorsey, Lester Bowie, Pablo Casals, Peter Sculthorpe, Richard Strauss and William Beckett, *Writers: Antoine De St Exupery, E. B. White, Francis Stuart, G. K. Chesterton, Louisa May Alcott, and Maurice Maeterlinck.

*Special case: Loletha Elaine Falana ("Lola Falana"): dancer, pianist, violinist, recording artist, Broadway & Los Vegas star, film & TV actor, commercial spokesperson and author: birthday 11, date path 9 with vowel 9, consonant 11.

Like the 11's, birthday 22's need to steady their nerves and develop self-awareness so that the inspiration coursing through them can come to fruition. They too can excel within a team situation. You must make time on a regular basis, to listen to the inspiration that is guiding you towards the enactment of practical projects. The comments below add to what has already been written in the birth day 4 section.

Birthday 22, Date Path 1

Some of you will pioneer new frontiers but seldom alone, although you may sometimes feel alone. The ability to direct the team travelling with you requires energy, imagination, versatility and a far-sighted ideal to work towards, and that is precisely what 22/1 offers. Examples include: *Actors: Drew Barrymore and Jack Nicholson, *Novelist, poet & short story writer: Stephen Vincent Benet, and *Welfare worker: Colleen Shirley Smith ("Mum Shirl").

Birthday 22, Date Path 2

You have extraordinary patience with details. They may drive you mad at times, yet you continually check and restructure them. 22/4 combines inspiration and integrity within a practical framework. Your sensitivity needs to be embraced as an asset: a gift that helps you to attune to what is going on around you. Examples include: *Biophysicist: H. Keffer Hartline, *Conservationist: Ladybird Johnson (wife of President Linden Baines Johnson), and the *Mother of another US President: Rose Kennedy, and *Tennis player: Boris Becker.

Birthday 22, Date Path 3

With 22/3, inspiration and creative activity go hand in hand. Express yourself so that others can understand what you want to achieve. To the extent that you are able to promote goodwill, through whatever you do, you will find lasting satisfaction. Examples include: *Ichthyologist: Marie Fish, *Physicist: Robert Andrews Millikan, *Musicians: Kathleen Ferrier, Kris Kristofferson, Robert Rosen, Maurice & Robin Gibb, *Writers: Andre Gide and Helen Andelin.

Birthday 22, Date Path 4

22/4 has much to offer: sensitivity, resourcefulness, integrity, idealism, and the ability to create your own mythology or synthesis. Through this dynamic combination, inspiration and perception mature steadily as you develop projects that improve the lives of others or restore beauty, peace and harmony to your environment. Examples include: *Actors: Bill Bixby, Catherine Deneuve, Gary Sweet, Marcel Marceau, Tom Richards, *Artists: Anthony van Dyck, Norman Lindsay, and Robert Rauschenberg, *Chemist and physicist: Michael Faraday (inventor of the dynamo).

Birthday 22, Date Path 5

There's a tremendous amount of drive here to accomplish one ideal in particular, which may become the dominant theme of your life. This is common to both 4/5 and 22/5 but there's an element of sacrifice operating here as well. A meaningful relationship with nature and the natural rhythm of life is vital to your sense of well being. Examples include: *Physician & writer: Arthur Conan Doyle, *Tennis players: Billie Jean King, and Mats Wilander, *Travel agent pioneer: Thomas Cook.

Birthday 22, Date Path 6

22/6 lends itself to increasingly profound levels of awareness of one's place in the 'big picture'. You will find yourself continually drawn into the everyday concerns that we all share, and you will need to maintain a solid core of personal truth therein. Examples include: *Environmentalist: Steve Irwin, *Physiologist: Andrew Fielding Huxley, *Secretary General for the United Nations (1961-71): U Thant; *Writer, philosopher, critic and dramatist: Gotthold Ephraim Lessing.

Birthday 22, Date Path 7

With 22/7 as your pattern, you are running on your highly-strung nervous system. Related to this, you need physical work that directly benefits others. You are moving from 4/7 to 22/7 when you are able to orchestrate a large-scale project without losing your nerve. 22/7 requires courage and the ability to roll with the punches. Examples include: *Biologist: Julian Sorrell Huxley, *Musicians: Daniel Paul Johns, Franz Liszt, Frederick Chopin, Yehudi Menuhin, *Writers: Doris Lessing, George Eliot and James Russell Lowell.

Birthday 22, Date Path 8

You are moving from 4/8 to 22/8 when your sensitivity and practicality start to focus on one specific project that breaks ground in your field of endeavour. Your enthusiasm for this project will convert the work involved from merely a routine that enables you to pay the bills; to something you actually enjoy developing. Examples include: *Actors: Charlotte Rae and Laurence Olivier, *Aviator & writer: Anne Morrow Lindberg, *Businesswoman: Wendy McCarthy, *Poets: Edna St Vincent Millay, and Johann Fercher, and *Novelist: Vladimir Nabokov.

Birthday 22, Date Path 9

9/22 tends to target an ideal but it's an ideal that is likely to transform over time. Through a variety of life-experiences - trying your hand at this and that – the one project that you would like to devote yourself to, gradually takes shape. Examples include: *Golf champion and golf course designer: Amy Alcott, *Lawyer, philosopher & statesman: Francis Bacon, *Soldier and founder of the Boy Scout Movement: Robert Baden-Powell.

WHEN THE MASTER NUMBERS DOUBLE UP

Charisma is yours to make the most of, and another quality of the master numbers, is their high energy level. You are running on 'nervous excitement' and therefore must beware of burn out. Make relaxation a part of your daily routine. For better or worse, master numbers act like powerful magnets.

Birthday 11, Date Path 11

The hypersensitive 11/11 offers several choices. As 2/2 the emphasis is on order, integrity, and self-discipline, while 2/11 introduces a political overtone. Numbers 11/2 suggest transformation at some time in your life. This will bring with it a set of values that you can call your own.

11/11 elicits the practical application of far-sighted ideals. Examples include: Futurist: Robert Theobald (*Reworking Tomorrow*), *Painters: Albert Tucker and John Constable, *Political advisors & writers: Abigail Smith Adams and Julia Montgomery Walsh, and *Occult writer: Dolores Ashcroft-Nowicki.

Birthday 11, Date Path 22

When the lightning is flashing in your mind, revealing to you the way that one idea connects with another, then you know that 11/22 is operating. Ideally this inspiration finds expression through practical yet creative activities that synthesize many viewpoints and harmonize on a grand scale. Examples include: *Philosopher: John Locke, *Physicist: Enrico Fermi, *Photography pioneer: Henry Talbot, *Priest: Francois Beranger Sauniere, and *Writer: Ezra Jack Keats.

Birthday 11, Date Path 33

There are several choices here: 2/6 offers patience and perseverance and 11/6 ingenuity. 11/33 elicits practical yet creative goals that embrace the best from the past whilst laying a foundation for the future. When you are working as a part of a community and loving it, you are engaging in 11/33. Examples include: *Doctors: James Parkinson and William James Mayo, and *Naval Captain: Gerald Mellor Haynes.

Birthday 11, Date Path 44

44 equates with 'master commitment'. You are working with 11/44 when you are able to invent a project and dedicate your complete time and energy to it. That said, you are also capable of letting go of your project when it has run its course, and stepping into something new with just as much dedication. Examples include: *Aviator, engineer & inventor: Lawrence Hargrave, *Composer: William Turner Walton, and *Major General: Franklin Gardner.

Birthday 11, Date Path 55

A rare combination this one; at its best it implies being able to take hold of your most compassionate ideals and make them work – now and in the future. Consistency is the challenge here, and an awesome level of commitment is required of you. Examples include: *Australian's first female Prime Minister: Julia Gillard.

Birthday 22, Date Path 11

What has been written about birth day 11/date path 22 applies equally here. Number 22 relates directly to the body of the 'earth as mother', so we know that 22 is expressing itself when interest is shown in planet earth as a conscious, living being. 22/11 will help you to synthesize and enact your most noble ideas. Examples include: *Astrologer: Lois Rodden and *Astronomer: Adolphe Quetelet (both fastidious about data), *Composers: Andrew Lloyd Webber, Benjamin Britten, Claude Debussy, Giacomo Puccini and Stephen Sondheim, *Artist: Worthington Whittredge, and *Master Mason: John Sebastian Marlowe Ward (wrote several books on the history and spiritual meanings of Freemasonry e.g. *Freemasonry and the Ancient Gods*).

Birthday 22, Date Path 22

The magic of the physical world is brought to the fore here, the examples displaying some of the delightful ways that this can express itself. This number pattern suggests an interest in sacred geometry, best exemplified by Swami Satchitananda who designed a temple in the shape of a 12-petalled lotus to embrace all of the world's religions - past, present and future. Further examples include: *Composer: Richard Wagner, *Philosophers: Dugald Stewart, Immanuel Kant, and Pierre Gassendi (mathematician).

Birthday 22, Date Path 33

22/33 offers high energy levels and the ability to re-create yourself over and over again. Whatever the circumstances, you should be able to perceive a way to make the most of the opportunities that come your way. These could be considerable. Examples include: *Actors: Hoagie Carmichael (and musician), Lindsay Wagner, and Meryl Streep, *Scientist: Ian Clunies Ross (veterinary scientist), and *Writers: Dorothy Parker, and Emma Lazarus.

Birthday 22, Date Path 44

Real, hands-on commitment is required here. If you have been able to achieve a synthesis of the information available in your line of work, 22/44 will add a redemptive quality to it. 22/44 offers the ability, by your presence, to act as a harmonizing agent within your environment. Betty Williams' Community of Peace People exemplifies 22/44 hard at work in the community. Further examples include: *Actress & belly-dancer: Tahia Carioca (significantly, she was described as 'an artist who could sing with her body'), and *Artists: Mary Cassatt & Sidney Nolan (painters), and Randolph Caldecott (illustrator).

Core Numbers

In the *Pan's Script* system of numerology the core numbers are:

1. The date of birth and the *original name* constitute the warp and weft of the subtle fabric encasing us from birth. They are therefore always important although subsequent names can modify their effect.
2. The *original vowel* number and *original consonant* number, as aspects of the name
3. The *date path* to represent the ideal(s) behind the incarnation
4. The *birthday* number, as an aspect of the date of birth

A Handy Summary:

The date path and birth day are always on our mind, consciously or otherwise.
The name number works through our vital body or etheric double.
The vowel number emanates from our soul.
The consonant number is an instinct that we have inherited from our distant ancestors. If it is the same as the date path *or* vowel number *or* name number, it will help to ground those vibrations (but don't overdo a good thing!)

Relationships

There are a few numerology books that compare numbers within a relationship along that lines that 3 and 6 go well together and 3 and 8 don't. In this chapter and in chapter 2 it has been demonstrated that *all* numbers can work together if heed is paid to the formula: subtract the numbers lowest from highest to reveal where the stress lies and add the two numbers together to reveal where the 'glue' lies. You can apply this formula to any of the core numbers. For example: person A was born on the 3rd of the month and person B on the 8th. The stress between them is symbolized by number 5 (8 -3 = 5) and indicates that they need to be flexible with each other. The 'glue' that unites them is represented by number 11 (3 + 8 = 11) and indicates that if they share a vision that each is passionate about, then their relationship is likely to work out well (all other factors considered of course).

...

In chapter 2 we combined vowels and consonants and in this chapter, birth day and date path numbers; in the next chapter we will consider what happens when another pair of these core numbers combine.

Chapter 5

The Mature Personality

When the ideal of the date path and the vitality of the name combine your true personality comes into its own. Because it takes time and effort to develop these core aspects of your numerology, their combination has been called the maturity number. Like the ego, the personality has been given a bad name in some quarters but it is essential to discriminate between the authentic and counterfeit in both cases. The true ego and personality are transpersonal in nature. Unlike their fashionable counterparts, they accompany the soul when the body is left behind. As we mature a conglomeration of hereditary and environmental, personal and transpersonal influences mix and mingle like the colours on a paint palette, producing images or ways of projecting ourselves that suit the occasion and help us to survive. These are influenced by the real personality, which lies behind the experiments, but how are we to discern the authentic from its mask? The maturity number provides the definitive clue and you should be able to identify it as one of the roles that you play. The materialization of the ideal encoded in your date path is dependent upon the maturation of your personality and vice versa.

Calculating the Maturity Number

To calculate your maturity number, simply add the highest number in your date path to the highest form of your original name number. For example: if your highest date path number is 26 and your name number is 80, your maturity number is 106, which is primarily a 7. To the general awareness that as you mature you will become more discriminating in your search for the truth (7), is added the knowledge that this necessitates becoming more self-reliant (1), realizing your greater potential (0), and developing a sense of responsibility within your community (6). A second example will highlight an important point. Dion Fortune, a writer on the Qabalah, had the date path 36/27/18/9 and name number 60 but her maturity number was not 96 because Dion Fortune was not her original name. The original name is the only one that will disclose the maturity number. Dion Fortune was born on December 6, 1890 as Violet Mary Firth. Her original name number is 84 and thus her maturity number was 120.

Interpreting Maturity Numbers

To get you started, twelve archetypal personalities are listed below. Your Maturity Number will fall into one of these broad categories. Beyond that, the Numbers 72 to 180 are detailed as personality types. If your Maturity Number is less than 72, use what has been written in chapter 1 to gauge what it might mean in terms of your personality.

The Twelve Archetypal Patterns

Maturity Number 1: The Warrior

Maturity Number 2: The Companion

Maturity Number 3: The Communicator

Maturity Number 4: The Designer

Maturity Number 5: The Advocate

Maturity Number 6: The Orchestrator

Maturity Number 7: The Preceptor

Maturity Number 8: The Networker

Maturity Number 9: The Humanitarian

Maturity Number 10: The Champion

Maturity Number 11: The Visionary

Maturity Number 12: The Interpreter

...Continuing the Numbers from Chapter 1...

Maturity Number 72/9

The Philosophical Humanitarian

When '7' comes first, the quest for truth comes first. '2' as the second number suggests the desire for companionship in such quest. 9 as the total indicates that the quest for truth and companionship are necessary components of the meaning that you give to life. 2 subtracted from 7 equals 5, which warns that flexibility and versatility are critical factors in the development of your personality. The multiple factors of 72 suggest that there are multiple ways to structure and develop your ideals. For example, 72 as 2 x 36 would have you apply your imagination to the questions that interest you and 3 x 24 would have you apply your imagination to the practical welfare of others. Examples: Ida Lupino, John Bateman (later Batman), and Thomas Hardy

Maturity Number 73/10

The Champion of a Philosophy

Number 7 up-front represents an abiding quest for the truth. Number 3 lends its support in such quest through its own drive for information. 10 as the total indicates that truth, research, and the ability to ask questions, and share your findings, are essential components of your unique and individualized personality. 73 is a prime number, further emphasizing the individuality of your personality. It's the 21st prime, further indicating the need to develop your communication skills in a world that needs to hear what you have to say. The maturation of your personality requires honesty, refined communication skills, and the willingness to stand up for what you believe in.

Maturity Number 74/11

The Philosophical Visionary

7 represents the quest for truth and 4 the necessity of giving your truth form or format. '11' implies action based on a vision or ideal. The reduced form of 11 (2) will serve to remind you of the need to be considerate of others and not let your ego get out of hand. '74 as 2 x 37' implies that 'breathing new life into timeless truths' is a likely aspect of what you will do in your mature years. This necessitates considering points of view that are the polar opposite to yours and weighing up their merits. For your personality to mature, the creative powers of your imagination must be applied in a consistent and constructive fashion. An interesting example is Nikola Tesla who was born at midnight on either July 9 or July 10. If he were born on the 9th then this would be his maturity number and on the 10th then it would be 75. I think Number 74 works better for him and may indicate that he was born just before midnight. Further examples include Blaise Pascal, John Addey, Raoul Dufy, William James, William Lilly, Yoko Ono

Maturity Number 75/12

The Interpreter of a Philosophy

7 represents your quest for the truth and 5 your personal ingenuity in that quest. Their total signifies the ability to see truth from different points of view and to blend them in a way that is uniquely your own. The factors of 75 emphasize the need for flexibility. 'Going with the flow' and evolving alongside others will enhance the mature form of your personality. The factors would also have you develop coherence in your thinking and a sense of responsibility for what you say and do. In its mature state, this personality serves to clarify varying points of view and facilitate the exchange of information. 'I have learned to live by inward joy. It is the most beautiful thing life can offer': Example and quote: James Jesse Lynn; another example being Loretta Webb (Lynn)

Maturity Number 76/13/4

The Philosophical Designer

7 represents the quest for truth and 6 the quest for coherence or consistency. '13' suggests that your thinking will transform as you mature. Number 4 is always about form and also integrity; your ideas need a coherent and consistent format that feels absolutely right for you. Subtract 6 from 7 and you are left with 1, which means that you could be your own worst enemy or best friend; take some initiative and act boldly! 76 as 2 x 38 brings in the qualities of cooperation, teamwork, vision, imagination and organization. It would have you find a way to blend popular culture with timeless wisdom. As you find ways to amalgamate these influences, your personality will become increasingly resourceful. Examples: Emanuel Kant (aka Immanuel Kant), Joan Marshall (Grant), John Dalton

Maturity Number 77/14/5

The Advocate of a Philosophy

The 7's bring an intense quest for truth and understanding and 14 suggests that you may experience a real breakthrough. Number 5 is always about evolution on some level and as you mature, so will your personality evolve. 77 as 7 x 11 catalyzes inspiration and insight and hence the potential for a breakthrough in consciousness. Although you might want to spend your days studying all manner of ideas, you will make more progress if you harness your thoughts to a particular philosophy and explore it thoroughly from the inside out. The maturation of your personality requires self-honesty, integrity, courage and robust participation in all aspects of life. Examples: Annie Wood (Besant), Alvin Ailey Jr., Jane Austen, John Aubrey, Louis Braille, Kate Lee Langley (Bosher), Mary Wilson, Thomas Hobbes

Maturity Number 78/15/6

The Philosophical Orchestrator

7 up-front represents an ongoing quest for the truth and the 8 behind it probes for depth. This combination will support whatever research you chose to engage in. 15 will add originality and ingenuity to what you do, whilst the 6, as the final outcome, insists on cohesion and consistency. Subtract 7 from 8 and you and you are back at number 1, which means that the onus is on you to make things happen. The factors of 78 tell us that believing in yourself and humanity is important and so too is weaving a web of love in your social circle. The maturity of your personality can thus be enhanced in a variety of ways. You need to find your own unique way to orchestrate them. Examples: James Galway, John Meillon, Judith Sussman (Judy Blume),

Maturity Number 79/16/7

The Philosophical Preceptor

7 represents the quest for truth and 9 the quest for meaning. 16 indicates that as your personality matures, illusions must yield to a more honest appraisal of the world in which you live. 7

subtracted from 9 is 2, which warns that your quest for truth and meaning must not become too clinical but should be considerate of others. As a prime number, 79 is individualistic in nature and just so, you are 'one of a kind', yet 79 is the 22nd prime, making teamwork essential to the development of your personality. Number 22 is about demonstrating that qualities such as sensitivity, cooperation and insightfulness are practical tools from which others can benefit. Example: Tracey Emin

The 80's and realizing the Soul's Capacity to have and To Hold:

<u>Maturity Number 80</u>

The Networker Who Considers All Possibilities

'8 up-front' places resourcefulness up-front; the powerful resourcefulness of number 8 here raised by 10. '80' has multiple factors giving you multiple ways to manifest your resourcefulness. 80 as 5 x 16 will strip away illusions and encourage you to evolve. 80 as 2 x 40 will help you to develop moral fibre so that you can cope with opposition to your ideas while the complementary 4 x 20 encourages you to explore your potential within a team setting. As you integrate such layers and levels of who you are, so will your personality mature. Examples: Jacob Ezra Katz (Ezra Jack Keats), James Todd Spader, John Wesley, Joseph Addison, Robert Theobald

<u>Maturity Number 81/9</u>

The Forthright Humanitarian

8 and 1 are a potent partnership. They offer you resourcefulness and initiative. As you place such qualities at the service of humanity, so will your personality mature. 81 as 9 x 9 indicates that you have within you the courage and ability to organize and network on a large scale. The first steps include making a decision as to what you want your contribution to be and then researching your chosen field in depth and breadth. So armed, and with a commensurate awareness of yourself, you will be overcome the challenges that you will face. Subtract 1 from 8 and you arrive at '7', which warns that you must be honest with yourself and with other people for your personality to mature. Examples: Augusta Ada Byron, Étienne Pascal, Jelena Dokic, Mikao Usui, Paul Hogan, Yitzhak Rabin

<u>Maturity Number 82/10</u>

The Resourceful Champion

'8 up-front' represents resourcefulness and 2 behind it, the willingness to share such resources. 10 as the total of 8 and '2' indicates that your personality will mature in tandem with your willingness to stand up and be counted. Number 10 will insist that you live by a set of principles that make you a more effective person within your society. 6 as the difference between 8 and '2' warns that your thoughts and speech must be coherent if you are to develop your full potential and that need to cultivate compassion. 82 as 2 x 41 suggests that the theme of 'enhancing evolution by stabilizing one of your initiatives' might be a task that interests you in your mature years. Examples: Edgar Poe, Joan Chandos Baez, John Marwood Cleese, John Dryden, Samuel Johnson

Maturity Number 83/11

The Resourceful Visionary

8 represents resourcefulness and 3 communication. 11 as their total indicates action based on such qualities. 5 as the difference warns that you must be willing to go with the flow and evolve alongside your friends, co-workers and partners. 83 as a Prime Number heightens the individuality of your personality. The maturation of your personality hinges on being willing to listen to your intuition and working with it within a team setting. Ideally this process works outwardly and inwardly simultaneously. In other words, teamwork means being able to work productively with other people and with your 'inner team' as well. Examples: Jonathan Edwards, Patsy Lou Neal ("Patricia Neal"), Sushil Kumar, Ustad Inayat Khan

Maturity Number 84/12

The Motivator

8 and 4 are the numbers of order and organization. '12 as their total' applies such qualities to its agenda, which is about believing in your ability to create a change of consciousness, by exercising your imagination and expressing your ideas. The development of your personality depends on cultivating this ideal and may also include some of these themes from the multiple factors of 84: choosing a campaign, restoring something to harmony, stabilizing your most promising project through teamwork, and perceiving order where others can see only randomness. 84 is practical, serious, and ambitious. Examples: Darren Scott Lehmann, Edris Stannus, better known as Ninette de Valois, Johannes Brahms, Joseph Lister, Paul Klee, Robert Peel, Paul Thomas Mann

Maturity Number 85/13/4

The Resourceful Designer

8 and 5 are social in nature: 8 representing resourcefulness and 5 evolution, here within a social context. '3' as the difference between them signifies the importance of imagination to their development. By exercising imagination, your thoughts about your social group and society in general will evolve, and as they do so, you will become increasingly resourceful. Your network of friends will grow and become more varied. 13 as the sum of 8 and 5 indicates that as your thoughts about society transform, so too does your personality. '85 as 5 x 17' suggests that self-analysis and appropriate self-sacrifice alongside education and initiative will enhance the maturation of your personality. Examples: David Home (Hume), Giuseppe Balsamo ("Cagliostro"), Jeremy Bentham, John R Cash (Johnny), John Milton, Julian Paul Assange, Juno Belle Kapp (Jordan), and Zena Chlarson ("Zenna Henderson")

Maturity Number 86/14/5

The Resourceful Advocate

86 combines the complementary powers of organization and cohesion. Their sum of 14 applies such abilities to the task of reshaping entrenched thought patterns, inwardly as much as outwardly. The difference between 8 and 6 is 2, which means that team-work is essential to your success in this task. 86 as 2 x 43, makes this number distinctly different from 68 and involves the theme of using a cultural framework to express your truth and resolve polarities. As you mature and your personality develops, this theme may become important to you. It could help you to break new ground. Examples: Anne Inez McCaffrey, Carol Joan Klein (Carole King), John Constable, Kathe Schmidt (Kollwitz), Mukunda Lal Ghosh (Paramahansa Yogananda), Stuart O'Grady

Maturity Number 87/15/6

The Insightful Orchestrator

Within the number 87 resourcefulness and insight combine in the service of one's community. The sum of 8 and 7 is 15, which is about perceiving harmony where others see only chaos or perceiving pattern and order where others see only randomness; a skill that is useful in any community. 87 as 3 x 29 can serve to remind you of the importance of imagination and vision. You need to be able to 'see' a brighter future if there is to be one. Applying your imagination and resources to the task of 'thinking globally and acting locally' will enhance the development of your personality. Noble ideals can be fulfilled with the help of this Number but you may need to step up and take the lead. Examples: Ella Sophia Bulley (Armitage), Elizabeth Blackwell, Francis Bacon, Jesse Louis Burns ("Jesse Jackson"), Paul Foster Case, Paul Cezanne, Robert Schumann

Maturity Number 88/16/7

The Powerful Preceptor

The keywords for 8 include resourcefulness, organization and networking. Such qualities are here laid at the service of Number 16, which is about appreciating the subtleties going on around you and within you. 16 can catalyze sudden and significant shifts in perspective. As you mature you could experience a crisis of faith and need to withdraw for a while but if you are willing to engage in some serious self-honesty, there's boundless potential here. 88 as 8 x 11 can awaken inspiration and bring fresh and exciting insight. You will need to keep your ego in check though and be willing to cooperate with other people. Number 88 will help you to grow from within. Examples: Ernö Rubik, Jack French Kemp, James Dewey Watson, Jason Sean Donovan, John Locke, John (Newman) Morris, Marlon Brando Jr., Masaru Emoto, Rickie Fataar

<u>Maturity Number 89/17/8</u>

The Global Networker

89 is a prime number, which places an emphasis on individuality and could make you a 'maverick zealot' if you are not careful. Or you could place your organizational skill at the service of an ideal such as caring for your family, initiating a community project, or improving your work environment. What is important to 89 is that you are convinced of the importance of what you are doing and can place it within the bigger picture. Being the 24th prime highlights the significance of teamwork and service. As your inner world becomes increasingly integrated with your outer world, you will find it easier to apply your idealism in a way that truly benefits those you care about. Examples: Glenda May Jackson, Herman Hesse, Leon Marcus Uris, Mary Wein ("Lady Fairfax"), Thomas Cook

The 90's and realizing the Ego's Capacity to Enact a Global Ideal:

<u>Maturity Number 90</u>

The Exuberant Humanitarian

When 9 comes first, ideals come first. The zero then magnifies the possibilities. Your personality develops through your willingness to put your talent 'out there' for the benefit of others, regardless of whether they appreciate it or not. The multiple factors of 90 inform us that self-expression and a creative imagination are vital to this process but your personal principles should never be compromised. By helping the world become a better place you simultaneously develop your mature personality. Examples: Augustus Saint-Gaudens, Gustave Flaubert, James Earl Carter ("Jimmy"), James Parkinson, Kathleen Jean Mary Ruska, Lech Walesa, Lhamo Dhondup

<u>Maturity Number 91/10</u>

The Champion of an Ideal

'9 up-front' means that you must specify your ideals and put them up-front so that people can see them as a part of your personality. The second number – 1 – will encourage you to step forward and make your contribution count, as will number 10. The difference between 9 and 1 is 8, which warns that you must get organized if the full potential of your personality is to develop. '91 as 7 x 13' suggests that insight and transformation will accompany you throughout your life. Number 91 is nurturing your executive abilities. It will help you to manage large-scale projects that aid the environment. Examples: Emma Lazarus, Gertrude Stein, Isabel Allende Llona, Jacques Yves Cousteau, Margaret Mead, Martin Luder ("Luther"), Ruth Denis, Thomas Carlyle

Maturity Number 92/11

The Idealistic Visionary

'9' represents ideals and '2' teamwork; thus your personality will mature as you learn how to manifest your ideals within a team setting. The total of 9 and 2 is 11, which adds a futuristic quality to your ideals. Commitment to a far-sighted ideal that involves the cooperation of other people could revolve around the themes of 92's factors. 92 as 4 x 23 is about giving form to a new idea, and it will help you to maintain your integrity as you do so. 92 as 2 x 46 involves establishing principles upon which other people can depend regardless of whether they are with you or against you. The difference between 9 and 2 is 7, serving to warn you that honesty is the best policy at all times. Examples: Aung San Suu Kyi, Abraham Lincoln, Benjamin McLane Spock, Coretta Scott (King), Ilsa Konrads, James Ford Cairns, Steven Paul Jobs

Maturity Number 93/12

The One Who Perceives the Relationship between the Way and the Goal

9, 3, and 12 are a part of the number-family that stimulates the imagination and the impulse to express one's imaginings. The difference between 9 and 3 is 6, which serves to warn you to take responsibility for what you imagine and what you create. '93 as 3 x 31' places the focus on formulating an idea that is ready to enter the mainstream of human awareness. It would have you inject your imagination into something from your culture that you want to present from a fresh perspective. Number 93 operates through a compassionate social conscience. Examples: Elisabeth Kübler (Ross), Harry S Truman, Joanna Lamond Lumley, John Clement Seale, Louis Pasteur, Martha Graham, Michael King (Martin Luther King)

Maturity Number 94/13/4

The Designer Who Transforms

In '94' idealism seeks form. This sounds easy enough but the 13 suggests that as you transform something so it will transform you. '94 as 2 x 47' asks you to discern the value of your insight and inspiration and then put it to practical use. To make the realization that 'as we do to another, so we do to ourselves' a functional reality, is the goal here. It will help you engineer ideas into workable plans, goals, and outcomes. The difference between 9 and 4 is 5, which means that to bring out your potential and enhance your personality, you must be willing to be flexible and evolve alongside the people that you share this planet with. Examples: Edith Maud Gonne, Johanna Mansfield Sullivan, John Keats, Mary Jean Tomlin (Lily Tomlin), Richard Alpert ("Ram Dass"), Thomas Alva Edison

Maturity Number 95/14/5

The Global Freedom Fighter

Through number 95 idealistic and progressive thinking seeks practical and ground breaking application. '95 as 5 x 19' highlights the evolutionary potential available to you, personally and also in what you choose to focus on doing. The maturation of your personality hinges on keeping the balance between your inner (personal/spiritual) life and your outer (working/family/community) life. "To be free is not merely to caste off one's chains, but to live in a way that respects and enhances the freedom of others" Nelson Mandela wrote the above on the final page of his autobiography; his original name was Rolihlahla, maturity number 95, the quote incorporating its essential theme. Other examples include Edward Gough Whitlam, Elizabeth Tudor, George Eastman, Kathryn Dawn Lang (k.d.lang), Kamala Reddy ("Mother Meera"), and Marjory Stoneman (Douglas). A special case is Barack Hussein Obama II. His highest date path is 29 and his name number without the ii is 64/10; maturity number 93. However this would be his father's. I believe that 2 must be added to this for the President's maturity number.

Maturity Number 96/15/6

The Idealistic Orchestrator

The idealism of number 9 and the cohesion of number 6 can here combine in a 'cohesive ideal'; this number offering you the power to 'see' the harmony within the chaos of everyday life. The difference between 9 and 6 is 3, which means that your imagination holds the key. The multiple factors of 96 tell us that you must not limit your imagination but apply it to several ideals, faiths and perspectives. The 'cohesive ideal' of monastic life is insufficient here as this is more of an 'interfaith number'. 96 as 2 x 48 will urge you to apply your most innovative thought in a practical way and to embrace opposition. Similarly 96 as 4 x 24 enables connections between people for purposeful outcomes. Examples: Arthur Tatum Jr., David Russell Lange, Dugald Stewart, Elizabeth Moulton (Barrett-Browning), Elmer Gertz, Marc Edmund Jones, Mary Jane McLeod (Bethune), Miriam Simos ("Starhawk"), and Narendranath Datta (Swami Vivekananda)

Maturity Number 97/16/7

The Global Preceptor

Within your maturity number idealism (9) and insight (7) combine and the possibility exists for genuine insight to stimulate productive ideals. To ensure that your insight is genuine you must be ruthlessly honest with yourself, as indicated by the 16. This number has the propensity to strip away illusion and falsehood so that the truth can take their place. 97 is a prime number, making the quest for truth and understanding a personal and individualized one. Yet it is the 25th prime, which will help you to empathize with an increasing range and variety of people as you mature. The difference between 9 and 7 is 2, making team-work an essential part of the process. Examples: Edith Joy Scovell, George Wald, James Young Simpson, Paul David Hewson ("Bono"), Phoebe Ann Moses ("Annie Oakley"), Samuel Barclay Beckett, Roy Eugene Davis, Stuart Wilde, Thomas Paine

<u>Maturity Number 98/17/8</u>

The Humane Networker

In 98 the idealism of number 9 draws on the resourcefulness and efficiency of 8. The theme of number 17 shows the way; it would have you forge insight (and understanding) through contemplation, education, organization and networking. Put another way, the development of your personality hinges on honest self-appraisal as the basis for action. '98 as 7 x 14' extends this theme to personal honesty as the basis for ground-breaking work. 98 as 2 x 49 suggests that by adopting the axiom that "honesty is the best policy" and applying it to your ideals, you are likely to experience a transformation in your thinking, which will filter down to you mode of operation in the world. Examples Alexander Graham Bell, Edward Bach, George Everest, John Manuel Neri, Phylis Lee Isley ("Jennifer Jones"), Thomas Jefferson

<u>Maturity Number 99/18/9</u>

The Global Myth Maker

The natural power, drive, and efficiency of the numbers 1 and 8 here propel the benevolence that accompanies Number 99. Together these three numbers will support your engagement in big projects with far-reaching consequences. You lead by example and you teach through selfless acts. Practical and creative activities of a philanthropic nature are supported by number 99 and will support the development of your personality. Number 99 offers you the ability to see the bigger picture, draw your own conclusions, and act on them. As 9 x 11 it has plenty of inspiration to offer you. Examples: Anna Mary Sewell, John Flynn, Joseph Levitch ("Jerry Lewis"), Michael David Rann ("Mike"), Stephen Jay Gould, Sydney Omarr (Sidney Kimmelman), William Osler

The 100's and realizing the Soul's Capacity to fulfill its Potential:

<u>Maturity Number 100</u>

The Champion of Human Potential

'10' is here multiplied by itself, making the theme of stabilizing your ego's potential core and centre. Being decisive and acting on your own inner authority are thus critical to the development of your personality. The other factors of 100 highlight the significance of number 5 to this process and would encourage you to express your personal ingenuity. They would also advise flexibility. 100 as 4 x 25 suggests that as you gain strength and learn how to go with the flow without compromising your integrity, so will you be able to empathize with an increasing range of people. You will then be able to help them in real and practical ways. Examples include: Abraham Harold Maslow, Gareth John Evans, James Munroe, Jean Henri Dunant, Mark Gordon Ella, Mary Ann Evans (George Eliot), Mary Baker Morse (Eddy), Thomas Clayton Wolfe

Maturity Number 101/2

The Warrior-Like Companion

With the Number 10 up-front, there's plenty of room here to explore your potential. 101 as a prime number has an individualistic nature yet the fact that it is the 26th prime indicates that it's not all about you. 26 is about weaving a web of love, which implies that as you take up the challenge suggested by its theme, so will you grow in real strength as an individual. 101 is aesthetically a well balanced number; it can thus help you to see both sides of any situation and act appropriately. The maturation of your personality requires assertiveness (1), teamwork (2), and the ability to stand firm within your society and make a unique contribution (10). Examples: Bette Davis Midler, Gladys May Aylward, Henry Steele Olcott, Robert Burns

Maturity Number 102/3

The Forthright Communicator

The number 10 up-front places your potential up-front, here supported by number 2, which would suggest that your potential to make a contribution to society is governed by your ability to work within a team. Number 3 as the total indicates that the way that you express yourself and the image that you present, are critical factors in the development of your potential and your personality. 102 has several factors, each of which tell us something of its unique nature: 2 x 51 involves reconciling inner drive and outer expectation, 3 x 34 is about applying constructive imagination in your quest for the truth, while 6 x 17 adds a hefty dose of compassion and contemplation to the mix. Examples: Albert Namatjira, Andrew Marvell, James Cleveland Owens, Lucille Desiree Ball, Nathan Birnbaum ("George Burns"), Nicolas Poussin, Margaret (Peggy) van Praagh

Maturity Number 103/4

The Engineer of Reform

Number 10 up-front places your potential up-front, here supported by number 3, which would suggest that your potential to make a contribution to society is governed by your ability to communicate effectively. Number 4 as the total indicates that you must give your ideas form or format. As a prime number, 103 has an individualistic nature supporting 10's agenda to stand solidly on your own two feet and make a unique contribution to society. It's the 27th prime and number 27 is about learning to appreciate that human love is a reflection of something 'greater' (which is yours to interpret). This is the theme that will unfold the potential of your personality. Examples: Anna Mae Bullock ("Tina Turner"), Eugene Louis Vidal ("Gore Vidal"), Joscelyn Godwin, Marian Wright (Edelman), Sigrid Undset, William Quan Judge

Maturity Number 104/5

The Practical Advocate

Number 10 up-front places your potential up-front, here supported by number 4, which would suggest that your potential to make a contribution to society is governed by your ability to turn ideas into realities. Yet it is actually your imagination that will assist you with this task, and you won't get as far as you could, without it. 104 as 2 x 52 is about promoting love and truth, 4 x 26 will engage you in weaving a web of love, while 8 x 13 suggests that you will undergo at least one transformation in your life. Such factors will help you to integrate the various facets of who you are. Numbers 1+ 0 + 4 = 5, which can serve to remind you that your personality will evolve as you embrace change. "We cannot change anything until we accept it"- Example and quote: Carl Gustav Jung; further examples include Aurobindo Ghose, Josef Anton Bruckner, Kathleen Mary Kenyon, Myrna Adele Williams (Loy), Norman Cousins, Paula Lexine Masselos

Maturity Number 105/6

The Enterprising Orchestrator

In 105 initiative, enterprise and compassion combine. '10 up-front' puts your potential to make a contribution to humanity by applying such qualities, up-front. 105 as 5 x 21 will prompt you to choose a campaign and then advocate for it; (this could be personal, political, spiritual, or social). 7 x 15 necessitates forming a more cohesive view of reality. '15' shares the same digits as 105, making it especially important. It will teach you that even the most mundane tasks and chaotic events stand in connection with the universe as a whole, as does the mystical, fantastical and philosophical. Your maturing personality is wrapped around this theme. Examples: Albert Einstein, Cecil John Rhodes, Donald Allan Dunstan (Don Dunstan), George Benson, Helen Reddy, Lydia Emma Pinckert (aka Jeane Dixon)

Maturity Number 106/7

The Forthright Preceptor

In '106' initiative, compassion and truthfulness combine to serve your greater potential and the greater potential of your society. Number 106 has but a single factor: 2 x 53, and number 53 is about perceiving the interconnection of all forms of life. This will be a profound experience for some of you, and it will of its own accord, enrich your personality. The difference between 10 and 6 is 4, which means that giving form to your ideas is an important part of this process. More personally, number 4 is about maintaining your integrity regardless of what life throws your way. Examples: Eileen Mary Challans (Mary Renault), Joseph Priestley, Jules Gabriel Verne, June Marie Salter, Louisa May Alcott, Lucille Frances Ryan (Lucy Lawless), Muriel Sarah Camberg (Spark), Nicholas John Tate, William Blake

Maturity Number 107/8

The Forthright Networker

In '107' initiative (1), truthfulness (7) and resourcefulness (8) combine to serve your greater potential, as represented by Number 10 up-front. Subtract 7 from 10 and you get 3, which makes imagination important to the development of your personality and potential. As a prime number, 107 is individualistic; it's the 28th prime, and the theme of number 28 is stabilizing your most promising initiative through teamwork. This is where you need to apply honesty, organization, and constructive imagination. The maturation of your personality requires courage, and the willingness to sacrifice misconceptions. Examples: Cecilia May Gibbs, Doreen Edith Dominy (Valente), James Dixon Swan (Jimmy Barnes), John Isaac Hawking, John Maynard Keynes, Thomas Jones Woodward

Maturity Number 108/9

The Dynamic Humanitarian

The multiple factors of 108 explain much, most importantly 108 as 6 x 18. Bearing the same digits as 108, 18 will prompt you to commit to an ideal that makes sense to you. 9 x 12 will insist that you believe in your ability to co-create a change of consciousness within your society. 4 x 27 will encourage you to see ideal love within human love and have you do something practical with this realization. 3 x 36 can unite the creative forces within your mind and 2 x 54 will help you to identify your own wholeness within the dualities of life. Recognizing the impact that a single person can make will help you to unfold the power and potential of your personality. Examples: Alexander Toth, Ethel Mae Blythe (Barrymore), Gordon Lavers, Joan Alston Sutherland, Jonathan Coleman, Kenneth Douglas Lay, Martin a Beckett Boyd, Mary Emma Woolley

Maturity Number 109/10

The Champion of a Global Mythology

10 up-front puts potential up-front, here backed by the idealism, humanitarianism and myth-making capacity of Number 9. The difference between 10 and 9 is 1, which means that initiative is vital to the development of your personality. 109 is a prime number, compounding the importance of developing the qualities that are uniquely you. It's the 29th prime, and number 29 is about visioning a brighter future for humanity. It would have you cultivate the strength and motivation to stand for something along those lines. Examples: Clarissa Harlowe Barton (aka Clara Barton), Dolores Ashcroft (Nowicki), Dustin Lee Hoffman, Harrison Ford, James George Frazer, James Maitland Stewart (Jimmy), Nathaniel Adams Coles, Nigel James Smart, Philip Mountbatten

Maturity Number 110/11

The Sensitive Visionary

'11 up-front' puts the scintillating intuitive facilities of your mind up-front. '11' catalyzes inspiration, and being a double-1, you will want to act on it. If you are able to work with this heightened mental stimulation, you may produce something unique and inspiring. If not, work with 11 as a 2 and be content to support someone else's ideas. Team work is important to you either way, whether you are leading or supporting. There's a futuristic quality to 110 but as 11 x 10, the latter number would have you keep your feet firmly on the ground and in the present tense. Likewise 110 as 5 x 22 can serve to remind you that cooperation and sensitivity are tools that you need if your vision is to become a reality. Examples: Baruch Spinoza, Deepak Chopra, Douglas James Henning, Kathleen Mary Timpson (Ollerenshaw), Mary Jean

Cameron (Gilmore), Mary Stevenson Cassatt, Michael Hayden Walsh (Mike), Morgan Scott Peck, Ursula Kroeber (Le Guin)

Maturity Number 111/3

The Dynamo

'11 up-front' places your intuition up-front and three number 1's places a heavy emphasis on your ego. This suggests that your ego would be best placed at the service of your intuition. Subtract 1 from 11 and you get 10, which sounds the warning note: your ego and intuition both need to be harnessed to something solid and useful within your society. This is what will 'grow' your personality. '111 as 3 x 37' represents the theme of breathing new life into timeless truths. The 3's associated with 111 indicate the importance of communication skills, imagination and lucid thinking. "Become a dynamic personality. Through pure thought you can revolutionize the world": Example and quote: Kuppuswamy Iyer (Swami Sivananda); further examples including Elizabeth Garrett, Elsie May Wheeler, Harriet Martineau, Imgard Charlotte Keun, James Antony Brayshaw, Luciano Pavarotti, and Ronald David Laing.

Maturity Number 112/4

The Visionary Designer

The key to understanding number 112 lies with its multiple factors. 2 x 56 will help you to mobilize the collective consciousness and resolve polarities as you do so. 4 x 28 will grant you the ability to stabilize your projects through networking and teamwork. 7x16 encodes insight and honesty and will help you to appreciate the subtleties going on around you. 8 x 14 is about reshaping entrenched thought patterns (including your own), and breaking new ground. Such are themes you can explore as your personality matures. Although the 11 up-front catalyzes inspiration, 112 is essentially a 4; a number that insists on giving form to ideas. Examples: Edmond Halley, Esther Freda Rofe, Margaret Mary Tew (better known as Mary Douglas), Michael Andrew Fox (aka Michael J Fox), Alecia Beth Moore ("Pink"), Thomas Ambrose Bowen, William Ralph Blass

Maturity Number 113/5

The Inspired Advocate

'11 up-front' places inspiration up-front and makes listening to your intuition important to you. Behind it lays number 3, which is about imagination and communication; fact and fantasy intermingle here and you'll need to sort them out. 11 subtract 3 is 8, which means that integration is the aim. It warns of the need to organize your notes and network with colleagues. 113 is a prime number, giving you a somewhat singular personality. It's the 30th prime and the theme of that number is realizing the power and potential of your imagination. 1 + 1 + 3 = 5, a number that will help you to evolve and showcase your talents. Examples: Albert Schweitzer, David Daniel Kaminski (Danny Kaye), David Livingston, Martina Subertova (Navratilova), Mary Fairfax (Somerville), Pearl Mae Bailey, Percy Wells Cerutty, Raelene Ann Boyle, Vanessa Redgrave, William Butler Yeats

Maturity Number 114/6

The Inspiring Orchestrator

11 up-front and 4 behind would have you give your most inspired ideas a format. '6' promotes cohesion and common sense. The difference between 11 and 4 is 7, which insists on honesty, especially self-honesty. The factors of 114 provide further clues as to how you can develop your personality. 114 as 2 x 57 will help you to stimulate a change in people's perspective, especially when they are insisting that an issue cannot be reconciled. 3 x 38 will further encourage you to turn obstacles into challenges that can be met and overcome by communication. 6 x 19 will prompt you reconcile your personal ego with the rest of humanity and put yourself at the service of your community. Examples: Andre-Aime-Rene Masson, Anna Maria Grosholtz (Madam Tussauds), Helen Adams Keller, Maria Ellen Mackillop, Rabindranath Tagore, Walter Whitman, William Alan Shatner

Maturity Number 115/7

The Cutting Edge Preceptor

11 up-front and 5 behind blends inspiration, ingenuity, initiative and enterprise. The number's total of 7 makes honesty the focus; it would have you check your mental meanderings for truthfulness. Number 6 as the difference between 11 and 5 further warns of the need for cohesion, consistency and discrimination. This becomes more important when we take into account the fact that '115 is 5 times 23'. With so much 5 energy injecting its creativity into the mix, the development of your personality hinges on keeping the rein on forces that are quickening your consciousness and extending the boundaries of perception, without losing momentum or enthusiasm. Examples: George Orson Welles, Helen Flanders Dunbar, Isambard Kingdom Brunel, Jack Henry Quaid, Joan Alexandra Molinsky (Rivers), John Winston Lennon, Joseph-Maurice Ravel, Marie Beuzeville Byles, Reinhold Ebertin, William Morris

Maturity Number 116/8

The Networker with Far-Sighted Ideals

11 up-front and 6 behind blends inspiration and cohesion; the number's total of 8 helping to integrate these two distinct impulses. 5 as the difference between 11 and 6 would suggest flexibility. It would allow your creativity flow and then organize it later. '116 as 4 x 29' means visioning a brighter future for humanity and doing something practical about it. 116 as 2 x 58 would have you transform the positive and negative aspects of life into something of substance and significance. Blending these forces takes an ingenious and peaceful mind. It defines what you need to do to mature into your personality. "Do you want to be power in the world? Then be yourself!":Example and quote: Ralph Waldo Trine; further examples including Franklin Albert Jones (Adi Da), Johanna von Caemmerer (Hanna Neumann), Jewelle Lydia Gomes (Jewelle Gomez), Maria Salomea Sklodowska (Marie Curie), Nova Maree Peris, and Paul Leonard Newman.

Maturity Number 117/9

The Inspiring Humanitarian

Its single factor – 3 x 39 – provides a vital clue for understanding 117. 3 x 39 will stimulate your imagination so that you can see new possibilities for humanity. It will help you to believe in the essential goodness of humanity and to discern how things could be. 3 x 39 will encourage you to see that the same creative energy moves through all people, although it takes different forms of expression. Number 4 as the difference between 11 and 7 would have you give your inspiration (11), insight (7) and generalizations (9) a form. "We really here live and walk as little universes, carrying both heaven and the world": Example and quote: Emanuel Swedberg (later, Swedenborg); further examples including Barbara Ellen Wilson, Hans Christian Andersen, John Calvin Coolidge, Lidia Matticchio (Bastianich), Paul Leroy Robeson, and Ruth Fulton Benedict.

Maturity Number 118/10

The Champion of a Vision

'11 up-front' places intuition in the foreground and puts the onus on you to learn how to work with the intuitive powers of your mind. Number 8 will encourage you to organize your ideas, with number 10 insisting that they be put to good use. 118 as 2 x 59 will help to liberate and expand your thinking. It will encourage you to break free from conditioned thought patterns and explore a broader frame of reference. The difference between 11 and 8 is 3, which means that imagination holds the key for unlocking and developing your personality. 3 is also the number of communication and it would encourage you to express the outpourings of your mind. Examples: Emmeline Goulden (Pankhurst), Henrietta Swan Leavitt, Ernest Evan Thompson ("Ernest Thompson Seton"), Margaret Ayer Barnes, Percy Bysshe Shelley, Roberta Cleopatra Flack, Ronald William Howard, Victor Cousin, Walter Felt Evans

Maturity Number 119/11

The Humanitarian Visionary

Numbers 11 and 9 are both idealistic in nature. The difference between them offers both a warning and a way for working with them. 11 – 9 = 2 and 2 is about cooperation. It would remind you that the manifestation of ideals takes a team effort. '119 as 7 times 17' provides further clues for growing with and learning from this Number. Number 17 stimulates insight through introspection, study, research, and contemplation. The amplification of the 7 intensifies the need for truthfulness. 119/11 stimulates the intuitive faculties of your mind; it is an active and assertive combination. Harnessing its idealistic and futuristic tendencies to a just cause will enhance the development of your personality. Examples: Barbara Joan Streisand, Edith Louisa Sitwell, George Walton Lucas Jr., Gertrude Vanderbilt, Irene Crespin, Joseph John Campbell, Sidney Robert Nolan

<u>Maturity Number 120/12</u>

The Interpreter

With 12 up front, believing in your ability to create a change of consciousness within your social group is the key to developing your personality. 120 as 3 x 40 will help you imagine and articulate ideas that extend the limitations of people's thinking while 4 x 30 insists that you formulate your ideas. 5 x 24 will suggest ingenious ways to serve your community though practical and supportive projects. 8 x 15 will help you to see harmony where others can only see chaos. It will support your networking efforts and encourage you to promote an increasingly integrated view of life. 6 x 20 and 2 x 60 will encourage you to seek the wisdom of your soul and apply it within your home and work places. Examples: Alice Mildred Cable, Doris May Tayler (Doris Lessing), George Russell Drysdale, George Edward Negus, Jawaharial Nehru, Laura Elizabeth Ingalls, Violet Mary Firth (Dion Fortune)

<u>Maturity Number 121/4</u>

The Perceptive Designer

Number 12 leading the way will help you to 'see' things from multiple points of view, and believe in your ability to influence people's thinking (rather than assume that you are powerlessness). It would have you exercise your imagination in finding solutions to problems and expressing your ideas in a way that people can readily understand and relate to. Number 11 is also strong here: the difference between 12 and 1 is 11 and 121 is 11 x 11. With 11 comes inspiration and number 4 as the total of 1+2+1 will insist that you give your brightest ideas form. The maturation of your personality requires a blend of initiative (1), teamwork (2) inspiration (11) and above all, integrity (4). Examples: Albert Watson Newton (Bert), Edith Dircksey Brown (Cowan), Elizabeth Gurney (Betsy Fry), Henry Ross Perot, John Logie Baird, John Hoyer Updike, Magdalene Mary Szubanski, Natasha Jessica Stott Despoja, Robert James Lee Hawke

<u>Maturity Number 122/5</u>

The Perceptive Advocate

'12 up-front' puts believing in yourself up-front. The extra 2 behind it emphasizes team work: 122 is about believing that you can work as a part of a team and influence people. 122 as 2 x 61 indicates that as you carve out an authentic existence for yourself (within the company of other people), so does your personality mature. Number 5 as the total of 1+2+2 will encourage you to go with the flow and allow yourself to evolve. However number 10 as the difference between 12 and 2 would warn you to stand by your principles and remain true to yourself at all times. The ultimate expression of this personality is to demonstrate compassion, and to infect others with it. Examples: Edna St. Vincent Millay, Helen Marie Gurley, Ieoh Ming Pei, Eugenie Sinicky ("Jenny George"), Linda Denise Blair, Linus Carl Pauling, Maria Goeppert

Maturity Number 123/6

The Perceptive Orchestrator

This run of Numbers unites initiative (1), teamwork (2) and imagination (3). Their sum of 6 indicates that placing these qualities at the service of your family or community will enhance the development of your personality. The difference between 12 and 3 is 9, which would have you broaden your thinking and become increasingly inclusive. '123' has a single factor, 3 x 41, and in 41 initiative unites with integrity. This combination would encourage you to either establish or support the establishment of a structure (physical, social, intellectual or spiritual) upon which others can depend. By so doing you are enhancing the growth of other people and laying a foundation for the future. Examples: Edwin Eugene Aldrin, Eldred Gregory Peck, Francesco di Petracco, Harry Maurice Miller, Henry Fielding, Isobel Selina Miller (Kuhn), John David Newcombe, Leslie Townes Hope (Bob Hope), Morris Langlo West, Wilella Sibert Cather ("Willa")

Maturity Number 124/7

The Constructive Preceptor

With '12' up front you will need to believe in your ability to create change and hone your communication skills. The difference between 12 and 4 is 8, and '8' will insist that you get organized and network with other people. 124 as 2 x 62 complements the general trend: outwardly it injects compassion into teamwork whilst inwardly encouraging you to integrate the various aspects of yourself so that your work is more effective. This operates in tandem with 4 x 31 which is about formulating an idea of practical benefit to your social group and generation. The maturation of your personality requires blending spontaneity (1), teamwork (2), and practical application (4), with insight (7). Examples: Arthur Robert Ashe Jr., Eugene Curran Kelly (Gene Kelly), Francis Thompson, Herbert Edward Read, Ralph Waldo Emerson, Victor Marie Hugo

Maturity Number 125/8

The Perceptive Networker

'12 up-front' puts believing in yourself up-front. It will encourage you to express your ideas as effectively as possible – especially with Number 8 as the total of 1+2+5. '8' will insist that you get organized and get your ideas 'out there'. '125 as 5 x 25' informs you that as your personality matures, so will you be able to relate to an increasing range of people. '125 as 5 x 5 x5' highlights the progressive and proactive nature of your Maturity Number. 12 - 5 = 7, which would warn you to speak and promote the truth. The maturation of your personality requires blending initiative (1), teamwork (2), lots of ingenuity (5), and constructive ambition (8). Examples: Elizabeth Anne Bloomer (Betty Ford), Elwyn Brooks White (E. B. White), Frank MacFarlane Burnet, Marguerite Ann Johnson (Maya Angelou), Mary Elizabeth Donaldson, Phillip Calvin McGraw, Roma Flinders Mitchell, Samuel Leonard Lewis

Maturity Number 126/9

The Perceptive Humanitarian

'12 up-front' places believing in yourself up-front. 9 as the total of 1 +2+6 will use the qualities of initiative (1) and cooperation (2) to serve an ideal. The multiple factors of 126 provide further clues: 3 x 42 will help you to perceive the order within the universe while 2 x 63 encourages you to understand yourself as a co-creator. 6 x 21 would have you create or support initiative within your community. 7 x 18 will support your commitment to an ideal that you can throw your heart and soul into while 9 x 14 facilities your ground- breaking efforts to make the world a better place. Number 6, which is strongly represented here, warns that ideals must be tempered with compassion. Examples: Andrew Carnegie, Edna Margaret Walling, Goldie Jeanne Hawn, Nicole Mary Kidman, Ludwig Van Beethoven, Robin Francis Blaser, Stefanie Maria Graf

Maturity Number 127/10

The Champion of a Whole New Perspective

The maturation of your personality hinges on your skill in blending personal initiative (1), teamwork (2), and insight (7). Uniting these qualities is number 10, which will encourage you to stand strong in the belief that you can make an impact on the status quo. 127 is a prime number, which means that the way you blend the above will be uniquely your own. It's the 31st prime, and 31 is about formulating an idea due to enter the mainstream of consciousness; an ideal of practical benefit to your generation (and possibly future generations as well). The difference between 12 and 7 is 5, warning you to not become overly rigid but to maintain flexibility as your ideas take shape. Examples: Heinrich Cornelius Agrippa, Helen Elizabeth Hunt, John Ernst Steinbeck Jr., Joseph Chilton Pearce, Margaret Louise Higgins (Sanger), Stella May Henderson (Allan)

Maturity Number 128/11

The Perceptive Visionary

'12 up-front' puts believing in yourself up-front. Supporting this is number 8, which impels you to get organized. Their sum – 11 – needs such qualities if its altruistic tendencies are to amount to anything substantial. The difference between 12 and 8 is 4 and it will insist that you put your visions, ideas and revelations to practical use. 128 as 2 x 64 will help you to overcome the fear of being the guide to your own destiny, select a project to focus on, and take part in our collective evolution. 4 x 32 will encourage you to formulate your most promising ideas while 8 x 16 helps you to appreciate the subtleties of life. Your personality matures by devoting energy to a worthwhile cause. Examples: Amalie Emmy Noether, Angelina Jolie Voight, Charles Robert Darwin, Douglas Ralph Nicholls, Katherine Isabel Hayes ("Isabel Barrows"), Mairead Corrigan (Maguire), Mary Louise Streep (Meryl), Nancy Grace Augusta Wake, Nicholas Culpeper

Maturity Number 129/12

The Interpreter of a Global Ideal

Number 12 is all-important here and number 12 is about believing in yourself and your ability to influence people. It grants you the power to see multiple points of view. Number 9 backing this 12 will encourage you to broaden your thinking and embrace multiple perspectives. 129 as 3 x 43 is about using a cultural framework to express your ideas. Imagination holds the key here. The maturation your personality hinges on applying initiative (1), teamwork (2) and imagination (12 – 9 = 3) to your most promising ideal (9). 'The choices we make are our own responsibilities': Quote from Anna Eleanor Roosevelt; other examples include Charlotte Wolff, Carol Diahann Johnson ("Diahann Carroll"), Donald Leslie Chipp, John Ronald Reuel Tolkien, Stephen William Hawking

Maturity Number 130/4

The Designer Who Transforms Our Perception of Reality

'13 up-front' indicates transformation. As you mature, it is likely that your thinking will transform, i.e. change completely just as a caterpillar transforms into a butterfly. The number 4 does not change however and it will forever insist that you give your ideas form and act with integrity. '130 as 10 x 13' suggests that your creativity needs not only form but real and lasting substance as well. 130 as 2 x 65 will encourage you to share the delight of helping to fulfil the needs of your community while 5 x 26 bids you apply ingenuity as you weave a web of love around such community. Your personality matures as you embrace such themes. Examples: Barry Alan Crompton Gibb, Constance Elizabeth D'Arcy, Derryn Nigel Hinch, George Harrison, Grace Patricia Kelly, Henry James Elliott, John Robert Williamson, Oscar Emmanuel Peterson, Rachel Louise Carson, Thomas Lanier Williams

Maturity Number 131/5

The Advocate Who Gets the Ball Rolling Along a New Track

In 131/5 the forces of change, initiative and transformation combine. Subtract 1 from 13 and you get 12, which is about believing in yourself and your ability to communicate your ideas to other people. 131 is a prime number and so your way of working with such forces will be uniquely your own. As the 32nd prime, it will have you shifting and re-structuring your perception of life (possibly more than once). The numbers indicate that your personal evolution is intimately connected with the growth that you catalyze in other people. Your personality matures as you learn ways to grow in tandem with others. Examples: Catherine Greenaway (Kate), Denise Elizabeth Swan, Florence Nightingale, Helen Frankenthaler, Howard Andrew Williams ("Andy"), Jean Marc Gaspard Itard, Mary Wollstonecraft, Richard Howard Bertram, Thomas Stearns Eliot

Maturity Number 132/6

The Orchestrator Who Initiates and Transforms

At first glance 132 is about blending initiative (1), imagination (3), and teamwork (2) and putting such qualities to work within your community (6). However '132' also has extraordinary factors and if you subtract 2 from 13 you arrive at 11, which is common to them all: 2 x 66, 3 x 44, 4 x 33, 6 x 22 and 11 x 12. 6 x 22 is about demonstrating that cooperation, inspiration, and sensitivity are practical tools that can benefit your community while 2 x 66 circulates compassion to friends and foes alike. 33 x 4 and 4 x 33 are about gathering and sorting information from diverse sources in order to give them form. 11x12 is about believing in yourself and your ability to communicate your ideas. Examples: Cherilyn Sarkisian (Cher), Keith John Taylor, Maria Francesca Cabrini, Marie-Rosalie Bonheur (Rosa), Poppy Cybele King, Ronald Leslie Greenaway, Sigismund Schlomo Freud (Sigmund), Venkataraman Ayyar, William Wynn Westcott

Maturity Number 133/7

The Preceptor Who Transforms by Being Well-Informed

13 up-front means that your concept of 'truth' (7) is likely to transform as you mature. The difference between 13 and 3 is 10, which would warn you to keep your ideas on solid ground. Have a set of principles to live by but don't be unnecessarily rigid about them. 133 as 7 x 19 would have you keep a constant eye on your motives. You may have some excellent ideas, but don't forget to do your research. Gather and sort information from diverse sources and then allow insight to emerge from them. As your personality matures, let initiative (1), imagination (3), and truth (7) be your guide. Examples: Algernon Charles Swinburne, Chloe Ardelia Wofford ("Toni Morrison"), Clive Staples Lewis, Frank Lincoln (Lloyd) Wright, Judith Louise Jackson, Kylie Ann Minogue, Neville Thomas Bonner, Steven Allan Spielberg, Stephen Joshua Sondheim

Maturity Number 134/8

The Networker Who Transforms the Status Quo

'13 up-front' guarantees transformation. 134 as 2 x 67 compounds this theme (because 13 is embedded in 67), and so you can expect your personality to undergo transformation as you mature. Number 8 would have you become increasingly integrated within yourself and within your community as such transformation takes place. The theme of 67 is 'dancing between harmony and chaos', which sets the backdrop for transformation. The difference between 13 and 4 is 9, which would have you wrap transformation (13), initiative (1), imagination (3), practicality (4) and organization (8) around an ideal that rings true for you (7) and benefits your community (6 & 9). Examples: Elizabeth Ann Bayley (Seton), Ernest Henry Shackleton, George William Russell (AE), Joan Elizabeth Hood (Kirner), Marie Dionne Warwick, Michael Rubens Bloomberg, Rita Levi-Montalcini, Robin Hugh Gibb, William Lyon Mackenzie

Maturity Number 135/9

The Humanitarian Who Transforms the World as they Transform Themselves

'13 up-front' puts transformation up-front as a quality inherent in your personality. 135 as 3 x 45 will have you exploring ways to exercise your free will within the concept of universal law while 5 x 27 has you balancing generalization and truth, and 9 x 15, ideals and enterprise. All of the factors of 135 contain the number 5, and the number will stimulate the growth and evolution of your personality. Subtract the 5 from the 13 and you arrive at 8, which will insist that you get organized and network with other people. The maturation of your personality requires initiative (1), imagination (3), personal ingenuity (5), and humanitarian ideals (9). Examples: Caroline Chisholm, Nancy Fotheringham Cato, Norbert Wiener, Rachel Faye Wright, Shirley MacLaine Beaty, Stephen Edwin King, Williamina Paton Stevens

Maturity Number 136/10

The Champion of a New Frame of Reference

'13 up-front' implicates transformation in the development of your personality. It is backed by number 6, which suggests that compassion and service within your community will contribute to such transformation. 6 subtracted from 13 equals 7, which warns of the importance of honesty. 136 as 4 x 34 will help you to inject new life in ideas from the past; it will insist on integrity in all things. '136 as 8 x 17' emphasizes the importance of education, networking and organization to you. The maturation of your personality requires initiative (1), imagination (3), coherent thinking (6), and the ability to stand on your own two feet within the community you serve (10). Examples: Angela Bridget Lansbury, Filippina Lydia Arena (Tina Arena), Gerald Michael Riviera, Hunter Doherty Adams ("Patch Adams"), and Robert Ranke Graves

Maturity Number 137/11

The Visionary Who Transforms Ideas

'13 up-front and 7-behind' indicates that as your perception of truth matures and transforms, so will your personality. Number 11 suggests that intuition will play an important part in the process. 13 subtract 7 is 6, which would remind you that compassion is always important. 137 is a prime number which heightens your individualistic tendencies. It's the 33rd prime, and number 33 is about gathering and sorting information. You are going to feel the urge at some point to synthesize what you have learned. The more coherent your thinking is, the more likely that you will create something that breathes new life into timeless truths and changes the way we think. Examples: Aretha Louise Franklin, Cynthia May Westover (Alden), Edwin Powell Hubble, Evelyn Sybil Mary Eaton, Johann Gottlieb Fichte, Justine Florence Saunders, Leonie Elva Hazlehurst (Noni), Mary Tyler Moore, Olivia Newton-John

Maturity Number 138/12

The Interpreter of Transformation

'13 up-front' places your ability to transform yourself up-front. With 6 x 23 to help you, what you believed were irreconcilable differences, may reveal their commonalities as you mature. 3 x 46 would have you expressing, in your own unique way, the principles that guide your life and help you to maintain integrity and sanity. 2 x 69 will help you to see the inherent beauty of humanity, with all of its contradictions. Your personality thrives on sharing its discoveries, insights, and flashes of inspiration about the deeper meaning of life. It offers initiative (1), imagination (3), and the ability to network (8), and will help you to develop the capacity to see the world through the eyes of other people (12). Examples: Aldous Leonard Huxley, Elizabeth Palmer Peabody, Harold (Harry) George Belafonte Jr., John Barry Humphries, Lyndon Baines Johnson, Marcia Lynne Langton, Mohandas Karamchand Gandhi, Richard Francis Burton, Suzanne Arundhati Roy

Maturity Number 139/13/4

The Designer Who Transforms a Belief System

13 up-front and 9 behind signifies that as your idealism matures and transforms, so will your personality. 4 as the total means that creative ideas need to find practical applications. Subtract 9 from 13 and you arrive back at 4, further supporting the need to give your ideas and ideals form and format. It also warns that you must maintain your integrity throughout. 139 is a prime number, which will accentuate your individualistic tendencies. It's the 34th prime, and 34 is about applying imagination to the quest for truth. It reinforces the importance of integrity as your personality matures. Examples: Alfred Bernhard Nobel, Alfred Emanuel Smith, Gloria Marie Steinem, Esther Louise Forbes, Frederick Cossom Hollows, Kerri-Anne Wright (Kennerley), Mary Barbara Hamilton Cartland, Meg Heather Francis (Lees), Pearl Sydenstricker (Buck)

Maturity Number 140/5

The Groundbreaker

'14 up-front' means that your personality matures through practical initiatives that break some new ground. 140 as 2 x 70 will stretch your thinking beyond the obvious and into the philosophical. 4 x 35 will catalyze fresh and productive ideas within your mind, and bring the best of them into reality. 5 x 28 will sharpen your people skills. '7 x 20' favours research and stimulates profound soul-searching. 10 x 14 will encourage you to stand firm in your convictions that the improvements you want to make are beneficial for your community. All such factors are enhancing your teamworking skills. Examples: Carlos Filipe Ximenes Belo, David Herbert Lawrence, James Ephram Lovelock, John Geddes MacGregor, Michael Joseph Jackson, Raymond Douglas Bradbury, Travers Christmas Humphreys, Valerie Jane Morris-Goodall

Maturity Number 141/6

The Ground-Breaking Orchestrator

'14 up-front' means that your personality matures through practical initiatives that demonstrate compassion and break some new ground. The difference between 14 and 1 is 13, and that means celebrating transformation within you rather than resisting it. 141 as 3 x 47 will help you to discern the value of your inspiration and give your best ideas form. It will encourage you to see your inner self reflected in the outer world and articulate the insight this gives you. 141/6 requires you to blend initiative (1) and integrity (4) in a consistent and coherent way (6). Examples: Cathryn Antoinette Tennille ("Toni"), Crystal Catherine Eastman, Donald George Bradman, Edvard Hagerup Grieg, John Winston Howard, Kim Christian Beazley, Shane Elizabeth Gould, Stephen Phillip Bracks, Vera Mary Brittain

Maturity Number 142/7

The Ground-Breaking Preceptor

'14 up-front' indicates that your personality matures through practical initiatives that demonstrate the truth that you live by. The number 2 indicates that teamwork is an essential part of such initiatives. The difference between 14 and 2 is 12, which means that perception holds the key to unlocking the potential of your personality. Keep in mind that to some extent, your world is what you perceive it to be. 142 is 2 x 71, which suggests that daring to be a little different to everyone else would further enhance the development of your personality. Your task is to formulate a cohesive view of reality from all of the contradictions that you have encountered. Examples: Ernest Ashley Dingo, Georges Pierre Seurat, Henry Alexander Simon, José Manuel Ramos-Horta, Julian Sorrell Huxley, Madeline Gail Wolfson (Kahn), Margaret Elaine Dovey (Whitlam), Ross Gerald Gregory, William Henry Gates

Maturity Number 143/8

The Ground-Breaking Networker Who Remains Faithful to a Particular Cause

'14 up-front' indicates that your personality matures through practical initiatives that require you to network with other people. The number 3 behind this '14' is stimulating your imagination and indicates that communication skills are vital to your success. Subtract 3 from 14 and you arrive at 11, the double-1 warning of the need to rein in your ego and give it something substantial to do. 143 as 11 x 13 will stimulate your mind with plenty of fresh ideas and possibly some real inspiration. It will help you to transform those aspects of your personality that let you down. Number 8 will use all such qualities in its drive to organize, network and achieve. Examples: Charles Lutwidge Dodgson (aka Lewis Carroll), Elizabeth Jane Campion, Henri-Louis Bergson, Kathleen Mary Ferrier, Kenneth George Coles, Margaret Madeline Chase (Smith), Michael Francis Moore

Maturity Number 144/9

The Ground-Breaking Humanitarian

'14 up-front' indicates that your personality matures by undertaking practical initiatives that demonstrate your ideals (or the meaning that you give to life). Solid, practical, step-by-step work is implicated in this set of numbers. 144 as 12 x 12 wants you to see the world through the eyes of other people and cultivate multiple points of view. 3 x 48 will help you to apply your most innovative thoughts to practical situations and 8 x 18 will encourage you to harness your willpower to a just cause. 9 x 16 might bring a crisis of faith but ultimately strengthen your sense of meaning and purpose. Examples: Auberon Alexander Waugh, Haldan Keffer Hartline, Melville Louis Kossuth (Melvil) Dewey, Samuel Coleridge Taylor, William Edward Ricketts

Maturity Number 145/10

The Champion of a Progressive Line of Thought

'14 up-front' puts ground-breaking initiative up-front, the 5 increasing ingenuity, which the number 10 applies to something useful. Subtract 5 from 14 and you get 9, which means that the maturation of your personality requires initiative (1), integrity (4), personal ingenuity (5), steadfastness (10) and humane ideals (9). 145 = 5 x 29, adding sensitivity, and vision to the mix. It increases the ingenuity factor, making flexibility paramount. It also increases idealism. Number 29 is about visioning a brighter future for humanity. The presence of number 2 in 5 x 29 indicates that making the world a better place necessitates working alongside other people. Examples: Cynthia Morris Sherman, Helen Paull, Kirkpatrick, Margaret Evelyn Hookham ("Margot Fonteyn"), Robert Edward Turner, Stephen Robert Irwin, Theodore Roosevelt

Maturity Number 146/11

The Ground-Breaking Visionary

'14 up-front' indicates that your personality matures through undertaking initiatives that are both inspired and practical, and which benefit your community. If you subtract the 6 from the 14, you arrive at '8', which warns of the need to develop your organizational and networking skills. '146 as 2 x 73' highlights the need for honest communication. You may have an outstanding vision to work from (that's 11) but it won't make any difference to other people unless you work on your communication skills. The maturation of your personality hinges on initiative (1), integrity (4), cohesive thinking (6), honesty (7), teamwork (2), and respect for your intuition (11). Examples: Annette Marie Sarah Kellerman, Evonne Fay Goolagong (Cawley), Norman Vincent Peale, George Stanley McGovern, Oprah Gail Winfrey, Philip Childs Keenan

<u>Maturity Number 147/12</u>

The Interpreter of a Progressive Line of Thought

'14 up-front' indicates that your personality matures through undertaking initiatives that allow for multiple points of view (such as interfaith initiatives). The 7 in 147 is more significant than it initially appears. $14 - 7 = 7$, and $147 = 3 \times 49 = 3 \times 7 \times 7$. Seven is about honesty and the whole concept of truth. Here it relates to acknowledging that 'truth' is a matter of perspective. 147 would have you maintain your personal integrity and self-honesty alongside respect for other people's truth and integrity. The development of your personality depends on how well you blend initiative (1), integrity (4), insight (7), and imagination (3) with your ideals (9 & 12). Examples: Arthur Francis Grimble, Harriet Elisabeth Beecher (Harriet Beecher Stowe), Helen Beatrix Potter, Herbert George Wells, Jose Placido Domingo Embil, Margaret Eleanor Atwood, Norman Kingsley Mailer, Robert Andrews Millikan

<u>Maturity Number 148/13/4</u>

The Designer Who Transforms Tradition

'14 up-front' indicates that your personality matures through practical initiatives that transform the status-quo. Yet 4 – the number of form and integrity – is dominant here and so although transformation and breaking new ground are implicated in 148, stability is the goal. In this light, 148 as 4×37 can be interpreted as giving timeless truths a form that is relevant to the times in which you live. Your personality will develop as you apply your most innovative thoughts to practical situations. Combining initiative, imagination, common sense, honesty and a willingness to grow and change will bring out the best in your personality. Examples: Frances Theresa Densmore, Glenda Myrtle Saunders, John Francis (Jack) O'Hagan, Laurence Kerr Olivier, Oliver Wendell Holmes, Terence Hanbury White

<u>Maturity Number 149/14/5</u>

The Ground-Breaking Advocate

14 up-front and centre places ground-breaking initiative up-front and centre. '149' is essentially a '5' and so for your personality to mature you must learn to befriend change. The '9 behind 149' means that this is not frivolous change, but change in service to an ideal that is personally meaningful. 149 is a prime number which means that the changes that you initiate will have a distinctly personal quality. As the 35th prime, it will catalyze fresh and productive ideas. Your task is to sort through these and select those that you would enjoy 'growing and shaping' in a manner of speaking. 149 as your maturity number will help you to shape your ideals so that they have real and lasting value. Examples: Blanche Rachel Mirra Alfassa (The Mother of Pondicherry), Charles Richard Foster Seymour, Hilma Dymphna Lodewyckx, Max Karl Ernst Ludwig Planck

Maturity Number 150/6

The Life-Affirming Orchestrator

'15 up front' puts initiative and ingenuity up front. It necessitates thinking outside the square and coming up with viable solutions to existing problems. As you mature, you may become increasingly proficient at creating harmony between people. '150' has several factors to assist in this process. 5 x 30 is stimulating your imagination; it would have you field new ideas, mediate between warring parties, and motivate people to make change. 2 x 75 will help you to research and clarify opposing points of view while 6 x 25 facilitates your efforts to empathize with an increasing range of people. As you mature, 150 will help you to become a more versatile and engaging human being. Examples: Carol Creighton Burnett, Frances Eliza Hodgson (later Burnett), Helen Patricia Sharman, Martin Heidegger, Pierre-Auguste Renoir, Pieter Cornelis Mondriaan, Raymond George Grace ("Ray Martin"), Samuel Langhorne Clemens

Maturity Number 151/7

The Life-Affirming Preceptor

'15 up front' puts initiative and ingenuity up front; it implies that thinking outside the square and coming up with viable solutions to existing problems will stimulate the development of your personality. 15 – 1 = 14, the number of ground-breaking change; it would warn you to maintain your integrity throughout the process of change. '14' begets change of the practical kind. Number 7 as the total, applies all of the above in its quest for the truth. It would have you do your research thoroughly. As a prime number, your efforts will have a distinctly personal quality and as the 36th prime, imagination as well. '36' bestows the power to unify the creative forces at work within your personality. Examples: Catherine Helen Spence, Cynthia Kathleen Gregory, Jean-Paul Charles Aymard Sartre, Lena Mary Calhoun Horne, Michael Solomon Gudinski, Nigel Godwin Tranter, Peter John Hollingworth, Philip Richard Carr-Gomm, Alfred Rupert Sheldrake

Maturity Number 152/8

The Life-Affirming Networker

'15 up front' puts initiative and ingenuity up front; it necessitates thinking outside the square and coming up with viable solutions to existing problems. The 2 behind the 15 makes team-work equally important to the development of your personality. Subtract the 2 from the 15 and you get 13, the number of transformation. This warns that you must allow things to take their natural course. 152 as 2 x 76 will encourage you to dance between chaos and harmony as you steadily transform your thought patterns. 4 x 38 will help you to turn obstacles into practical outcomes, and encourage you to turn those flashes of insight and intuition that enter your mind, into achievements that inspire others. Examples: Jean William Fritz Piaget, Jeannette Pickering Rankin, Judith Arundell Wright

Maturity Number 153/9

The Humanitarian Who Appreciates the Intricacies of Life

'15 up front' puts initiative and ingenuity up front and implies that thinking outside the square and coming up with viable solutions to existing problems will stimulate the development of your personality. The 3 behind the 15 injects imagination into your ideas and would have you articulate them in a way that is relevant to your generation. Subtract 3 from 15 and you arrive at12, which warns that you must try to see things from more than one perspective. 153 as 3 x 51 will encourage you to reconcile inner drives with outer expectations while 9 x 17 insists that you do your research and think big. As with all 9's, this one will insist that you put your ideas to work in the everyday world. Examples: Diana Ernestine Earle Ross, Edmund Percival Hillary, Howard Walter Florey, Kerry Kathleen Fitzpatrick (Kate), Merwan Sheriar Irani, Michael Robert Willesee, Penelope Ruth Fletcher (Mortimer), William Gordon Gray

Maturity Number 154/10

The Champion of Life's Integrity

'15 up front' puts initiative and ingenuity up front; it necessitates thinking outside the square and coming up with viable solutions to existing problems. The 4 behind the 15 makes integrity equally important to the development of your personality. Subtract the 4 from the 15 and you get 11, the number of inspiration and high-minded idealism. It lies behind the factors 2 x 77 and 7 x 22 and indicates that maturity for you is about demonstrating that cooperation, inspiration, and sensitivity are practical tools that can benefit many people regardless of whether other people approve of your way of doing things or not. This sounds awesome but could be as simple as helping a friend in need. Examples: Carl Heinrich Maria Orff, Michael Scudamore Redgrave, Peter William Francis, Paulus Henriqus Benedictus Cox (Paul Cox), Roger Tory Peterson

Maturity Number 155/11

The Visionary Who Sparks the Collective Imagination

'15 up front' puts initiative and ingenuity up front; it necessitates thinking outside the square and coming up with viable solutions to existing problems. The number 11 always injects inspiration into the other numbers. It is implicated in the '55' part of 155. So much 5 and 11 energy will make you restless but also innovative. '11' is futuristic in nature and blends well with 155 as 5 x 31 because number 31 is about formulating an idea that is due to enter the mainstream of human consciousness. '31' can put the inspiration that comes with Number 11 to good use. Subtract 5 from 15 and you get '10', which warns of the need for principles if your endeavours are to have a lasting impact. Examples: Alan Richard Griffiths, Elizabeth Jane Coatsworth, Elizabeth Rosemond Taylor, Francois-Auguste-Rene Rodin ("Auguste Rodin"), Henri Francois Rey

Maturity Number 156/12

The Interpreter of Life in All its Colours

'15 up front' puts initiative and ingenuity up front; it necessitates thinking outside the square and coming up with inspired but viable solutions to existing problems. '156 as 2 x 78' necessitates self-honesty and tangible achievement within a teamwork situation. 3 x 52 will remind you to apply ingenuity and imagination to whatever projects you turn your mind to. 4 x 39 is about believing in the essential goodness of humanity and committing yourself to projects that aid humanity. 6 x 26 is about weaving a web of love within your community. 156/12 symbolizes the ideal of unity within diversity. It would have you regard the world through multiple points of view. Examples: Christine ("Chris") Marie Evert, Elizabeth de Beauchamp Goudge, Johann Wolfgang Goethe, Julia Clifford Lathrop, Michael Philip Jagger (Mick), Sigrid Madeline Thornton

Maturity Number 157/13/4

The Designer of a Service that Promotes Life

15 up front puts initiative and ingenuity up front and implies that thinking outside the square and coming up with practical solutions to existing problems will stimulate the development of your personality. The 7 behind the 15 will insist on honesty so that it can offer you genuine insight. The 13 in the middle symbolizes the need to allow things to take their course and transform over time. Subtract the 7 from the 15 and you arrive at '8', which warns of the need to get organized. 157 is a prime number, emphasizing the individualistic side of your personality. As the 37th prime, it would have you breathe new life into timeless truths. This is a theme for your personality to explore. Examples: Alexander Murray Palmer Haley, Heinz Alfred Kissinger (Henry Kissinger), Patrick Michael Rafter, Roger Robert Woodward, William Penn Adair Rogers

Maturity Number 158/14/5

The Advocate Who is Not Afraid to take Centre Stage

15 up front puts initiative and ingenuity up front and implies that thinking outside the square and coming up with practical solutions to existing problems will stimulate the development of your personality. Subtract the 8 from the 15 and you arrive at '7', which warns of the need for honesty. 158 as 2 x 79 unites truth and idealism within a team setting. It would have you work in cooperation with other people to fulfil an ideal that you share. There's a hint of transformation in this number, and so don't expect to be the same person all of your life. With 158 to guide you, take the initiative, apply some personal ingenuity, and ground-breaking achievements are possible. Examples: Berthe Marie Pauline Morisot, Francis Harry Compton Crick, Frederick Ronald Williams, Glenn Barrie Shorrock, Henry Wadsworth Longfellow, Muriel Hazel Wright, Orlando Jonathan Blanchard Bloom, Paul Guillaume André Gide

Maturity Number 159/15/6

The Orchestrator Who Dares to Do things Differently

'15 up front and centre' puts initiative and ingenuity up front and centre. It means that thinking outside the square and coming up with practical solutions to existing problems will stimulate the maturation of your personality. '159 as 3 x 53' bestows imagination and will help you to perceive the interconnection of all life forms. '159' stimulates spontaneity, and activates the restless search for something to believe in. It facilitates coherent thinking as a counterpoint to the diversity that comes with the 5's. Applying initiative and ingenuity to ideas that serve your community will enhance the development of your personality. 159 will help you blaze a trail that liberates yourself and others. Examples: André Leon Marie Nicolas Rieu, Francis Scott Key Fitzgerald, Jean Louis Rodolphe Agassiz, Jean-Francois Champollion, John Fitzgerald Kennedy, Jorge Mario Bergoglio (Pope Francis 1), Richard Buckminster Fuller

Maturity Number 160/7

The Truthful Preceptor

'16 up-front' places initiative and service up-front. It will help you to appreciate the subtleties of life. Paired with number 7, the emphasis here is on 'truth'. The multiple factors of 160 suggest that you will explore many facets of that word as you mature. 2 x 80 necessitates sensitivity and resourcefulness. 5 x 32 will extend the boundaries of your perception as it injects enthusiasm, imagination, flexibility and ingenuity into your personality. 8 x 20 wraps achievement around teamwork. 4 x 40 adds a hefty dose of integrity to the mix. 10 x 16 would have you create a set of principles through which you can investigate all of the possibilities available to you. Examples: Charles Sherlock Fillmore, Christina Georgina Rossetti, Franklin Delano Roosevelt, Ivan Sergeyevich Turgenev, Katharine Houghton Hepburn

Maturity Number 161/8

The Compassionate Networker

16 up-front places initiative and service up-front; and it will help you to appreciate the subtleties of life. Subtract 1 from 16 and you get 15, which will insist that you think outside the square and create practical solutions to existing problems. 161 as 7 x 23 will help you to find where the truth lies and to reconcile opposing points of view. What you believed were irreconcilable differences may reveal their commonalities when you investigate further. Transforming the perception of polarity into the perception of unity will come to you through honest introspection. All of the above is used by achievement-orientated number 8 and therein lays the key for the maturation of your personality. Examples: Charles Robert Redford Jr., Robindro Shaunkor Chowdbury ("Ravi Shankar"), and Wesley Eugene Roddenberry ("Gene")

Maturity Number 162/9

The Compassionate Humanitarian

16 up-front places initiative and service up-front; and it will help you to appreciate the subtleties of life. 16 subtract 2 equals14, which warns you of the need to be daring yet practical. 162 as 2 x 81 will encourage you to work hard and do something beneficial for humanity. 3 x 54 will help you to become more aware of the impact that you are having on evolution. It grants you the imagination to see your personal story within the greater story of humanity, and would encourage you to share your understanding. 6 x 27 will help you to reconcile polarities in the name of truth. The maturation of your personality requires initiative (1), coherent thinking (6), teamwork (2) and idealism (9). Examples: Catherine Elizabeth Middleton, Isobel Marion Dorothea Mackellar, Gilbert Keith Chesterton, Henry Spencer Moore, Walter Burley Griffin

Maturity Number 163/10

The Champion of Compassion

16 up-front places initiative and service up-front and it will help you to appreciate the subtleties and complexities of those qualities. The 3 behind the 16 injects imagination into the mix. 16 subtract 3 equals 13, the Number of transformation, and so you must expect your personality to transform as you mature. 163 is a prime number, which tends to highlight the more individualistic side of your nature. It's the 38th prime, and that will help you to bridge contemporary and ancient wisdom. The maturation of your personality requires initiative (1), coherent thinking (6), imagination (3) and the willingness to stand for something within your community (10). Examples: Frederic Alan Schepisi, Ezra Weston Loomis Pound, Isabella Henrietta Younger (Ross), Johann Heinrich Pestalozzi, and Mikhail Sergeyevich Gorbachev

Maturity Number 164/11

The Compassionate Visionary

'16 up-front' places initiative and service up-front. It will help you to appreciate the subtleties and complexities of blending those two qualities, and also their potential. The 4 behind the 16 will insist on integrity. 16 subtract 4 equals '12' which warns that you must try to see things from more than one perspective. '164 as 2 x 82' compounds the sensitivity of this Number but also adds a hefty dose of resourcefulness. '164 as 4 x 41' emphasizes practicality. Your personality matures as you undertake service-oriented projects within your community. However the total of 1 + 6 + 4 is 11, which means that you must also find a way to express your own unique ideas. Examples: Frederick Matthias Alexander, George Hubert Wilkins, Marion Robert Morrison (John Wayne), Minard Fannie Crommelin, Richard Evelyn Byrd

Maturity Number 165/12

The Interpreter of a Popular Ideal

'16 up-front' places initiative and service up-front. It will help you to appreciate the subtleties and complexities of blending those two qualities, and also their potential. The 5 behind the 16 assists with its flexibility and versatility. 16 subtract 5 equals 11 which would warn you to keep the reins on your ego and listen to your intuition. 165 as 5 x 33 will encourage you to gather and sort information from diverse sources. It likes nothing better than to explore every lead but the ultimate aim is synthesis. '165' enhances initiative (1), coherent thinking (6), and personal ingenuity (5). It encourages you to see multiple points of view, and stimulates curiosity and imagination. Examples: Catherine Fabienne Dorléac (better known as Catherine Deneuve), John Christopher Williams

Maturity Number 166/13/4

The Compassionate Designer

'16 up-front' places initiative and service up-front, with the emphasis on service. 16 subtract 6 equals 10 which would warn you to keep your feet firmly on the ground and stand for something in this life. '166 as 2 x 83' stimulates the imagination and adds resourcefulness to your personality. It would have you find ways to reconcile opposing viewpoints. The '66' aspect of 166 enhances compassion and inspiration. It makes you socially responsive. 1 + 6 + 6 = 13, which is the number of transformation, and so you must expect your perspective on life to change completely in your mature years. The total is 4, the number of form. It will insist that you give your most compassionate ideas form. Examples: Catherine Rosamund FitzGibbon (Sister Irene), Catherine Astrid Salome Freeman, Ernest Miller Hemingway, Katheryn Elizabeth Hudson (Katy Perry)

Maturity Number 167/14/5

The Compassionate Advocate

'16 up-front' places initiative and service up-front. The 7 behind the 16 will insist on honesty. 16 subtract 7 equals 9 which would warn you to avoid rash generalizations. 1 + 6 + 7 = 14 = 5, increasingly the likelihood that you will break some new ground in the development of your personality and extend yourself further than you would have thought yourself capable. 167 is a prime number, which highlights the individualistic side of your nature. As the 39th prime, it is stimulating your imagination and encouraging broad-mindedness. '167' enhances initiative, critical and coherent thinking, integrity, and personal ingenuity. It will help you to break new ground within your community. Examples: Brigitte Anne-Marie Bardot, Céline Marie Claudette Dion, Henry Maximilian Beerbohm, Mervyn Gregory Hughes, Nirmala Sundari Bhattacharya (Anandamoyee Ma), Richard Tiffany Gere

Maturity Number 168/15/6

The Compassionate Orchestrator

'16 up-front' places initiative and service up-front; the 8 behind the 16 insisting that you get organized. As 2 x 84, 168 will help you to motivate people and network. As 3 x 56 it is stimulating your imagination, ingenuity and compassion. As 4 x 42 it adds a strong dose of integrity to your personality. As 6 x 28 it will stabilize your projects and as 8 x 21 it is resourceful. Several of these factors suggest that teamwork is vital to your success. This multi-faceted number will encourage you to take the initiative, think coherently, and apply your personal ingenuity to community needs and interests. Your initiatives have the potential to motivate and mobilize a wide range of people. Examples: Andrew Sydney Withiel Thomas, Conrad Nicholson Hilton, Gottfried Wilhelm Von Leibniz and Helen Charlotte Isabella Fraser ("Helen Gwynne-Vaughan")

Maturity Number 169/16/7

The Insightful Preceptor

'16 up-front' places initiative and service up-front. It will help you to appreciate the subtleties and complexities of blending those two qualities, and also their potential. The 9 behind the 16 adds an idealistic note to your personality. You may want to put all of your initiatives and compassion-orientated service under the banner of an ideal. Subtract 9 from 16 and you get 7, which is also the total, and 7 warns of the need for honesty. It will have you do your research before proclaiming that something is a 'fact'. 169 is uniquely 13 x 13 and 13 is the number of transformation. You must expect transformation within your life and subsequently your personality. Examples: Philip Peter Ross Nichols, Richard Charles Nicholas Branson, Joseph Rudyard Kipling

Maturity Number 170/8

The Studious Networker

'17 up-front' puts initiative and honesty up-front. This number will demand that you release the dishonest and unproductive aspects of your personality. 17 favours education and research, particularly of the kind that leads to productive action. 2 x 85 will encourage you to shape your environment so that you can more effectively express your personal ingenuity. It will insist on team work and would have you transform yourself as your team transforms. 170 as 5 x 34 will stimulate your imagination, demand integrity, and encourage you to apply such qualities in your quest for the truth. 170 is the effective networker who is prepared to make personal sacrifices for a goal. Examples: Fryderyk Franciszek Chopin ("Frederic Francois Chopin"), Henriette Rosine Bernard ("Sarah Bernhardt"), Hilaire-Germain-Edgar De Gas ("Edgar Degas")

Maturity Number 171/9

The Studious Humanitarian

'17 up-front' puts initiative and honesty up-front. This number will demand that you release the dishonest and unproductive aspects of your personality. 17 favours education, particularly of the kind that leads to productive action. 171 will support research projects with an ideal behind them. Subtract the 1 from the 17 and you get '16', which warns that your actions should not just serve yourself but others too. As 3 x 57, 171 will stimulate a shift in your perspective so that in your later years your thinking could be radically different to what it was when you were younger. It will inject imagination and ingenuity into the work you choose to do for humanity and the environment. Examples: Maria Corazon Sumulong Cojuangco (later Corazon Aquino),

Ernestine Jane Geraldine Russell, George Gordon Noel Byron, Henry Franklin Winkler, Norman Alfred William Lindsay, Paul Ambrose Toussaint Jules Valery

Maturity Number 172/10

The Champion of Truth and Justice for All

'17 up-front' puts initiative and honesty up-front. Number 172 stimulates initiative and insight, sensitivity and sincerity. '172 as 2 x 86' combines the complementary powers of organization and coherence. It will encourage you to work as a part of a team and resolve differences as they occur. You can break new ground with this number if you want to. 4 x 43 adds integrity and imagination to your personality. It will encourage you to use an established cultural framework to express your ideas. Subtract the 2 from the 17 and you arrive at 15. This number warns of the need for flexibility. It would have you act with courage and determination in an eclectic sort of way. Examples: Christine Campbell Thomson (Hartley), Joseph Mallord William Turner

Maturity Number 173/11

The Studious Visionary

'17 up-front' puts initiative and honesty up-front. In particular 173 supports research projects with imagination and vision. 17 subtract 3 is14, which would warn you to remain flexible as your personality develops. Both 173 and 137 are prime numbers and as such, will draw out the more individualistic side of your nature. Both stimulate initiative, insight, imagination, and intuition and would encourage you to become a better team player. Whereas 137 is the 33rd prime, number 173 is the 40th. As such, 173 wants practical outcomes based on solid research. Examples: Dorothea Margaretta Nutzhorn (Lange), Francis Scott Key Fitzgerald, Howard Hoagland Carmichael ("Hoagy Carmichael"), Maria de Lourdes Farrow (Mia)

Maturity Number 174/12

The Student of the Mysteries

'17 up-front' puts initiative and honesty up-front. 174 will support practical research projects that deal with unusual topics. 17 subtract 4 is 13, warns that you must expect your personality to completely transform as you mature. '174 as 2 x 87' emphasizes the importance of teamwork, organization, and truthfulness to your personality. 3 x 58 would add imagination and ingenuity to the mix. It will help you to transform the positive and negative realities of life into works of substance and significance. 6 x 29 symbolizes sharing a vision with your community and helping them to make it real. 174 is a multi-faceted Number that will help you to see life from many points of view. Example: Robert Stephenson Smyth Powell (better known as Robert Baden-Powell).

Maturity Number 175/13/4

The Studious Designer

'17 up-front' puts initiative and honesty up-front. This number will demand that you transform the dishonest and unproductive aspects of your personality. 17 favours education, particularly of the kind that engenders action. 17 subtract 5 equals '12', which warns of the need to consider multiple points of view; try to see life through other people's eyes. 7 x 25 will help you to empathize with an increasing range of people and thereby grow increasingly honest with yourself. 3 x 35 reinforces the imagination and ingenuity of 175. The total of 4 demands integrity and practicality while the 13 will help you to transform those aspects of your personality that you are not happy with. Examples: Ethel Florence Lindesay Richardson (aka Henry Handel Richardson), Margaret Mary Emily Anne Hyra (aka Meg Ryan), Miranda Jennifer Grossinger (July)

Maturity Number 176/14/5

The Studious Advocate

'17 up-front' puts initiative and honesty up-front, 176 helping you to change the dishonest and unproductive aspects of your personality. 17 subtract 6 equals 11, which stimulates the intuitive faculties of the mind. The factors of 176: 2 x 88 add empathy and organizational skill and 4 x 44 a hefty dose of integrity while 8 x 22 would have you demonstrate that such qualities are practical skills that really help people. '176' offers inspiration, insight, coherent thinking, and the opportunity to conduct some ground breaking work. In return it requires that initiative, self-honesty, and ingenuity be placed at the service of your community. Examples: Henry Wadsworth Longfellow, Johannes (Hans) Franciscus Catharinus Klok, José Montserrate Feliciano Garcia ("Jose Feliciano"), Kenneth George Cunningham, Mary Wollstonecraft Godwin (Shelley), Robert Frederick Zenon Geldof ("Bob")

Maturity Number 177/15/6

The Studious Orchestrator

'17 up-front' puts initiative and honesty up-front. '17' favours education, particularly of the kind that engenders action and productivity. 17 subtract 7 equals 10, which would warn you to keep your feet on the ground and suggest that standing up for something within your community will stimulate the development of your personality. As three times the eclectic 59, 177 will blaze a trail that will liberate your consciousness on multiple levels. It will enhance your ingenuity, and expect you to fully engage in life in return. As 1-77 this number stimulates insight and catalyzes inspiration. It helps to break new ground. 177 does all this in the name of enhancing the community life that you are a part of. Example: Marie Charlotte Carmichael Stopes Stephanie Marie Elisabeth Grimaldi (Princess Stephanie of Monoco)

Maturity Number 178/16/7

The Studious and Dedicated Preceptor

'17 up-front' puts initiative and honesty up-front. '17' favours research and education of the kind that engenders action and productivity. 17 subtract 8 equals '9', which would warn you of the need for broad-mindedness. Your personality matures in tandem with your willingness to interact with a diverse range of people in an honest and productive way. The factors 2 x 89 emphasize the '8' aspect of 178, which means that organization is important to the maturation of your personality. The '9' would put all of your hard work into the service of an ideal, with the '2' reminding you of the importance of team work. In '16' – the middle number – initiative and service seek to blend. Example: Maria Tecla Artemesia Montessori

Maturity Number 179/17/8

The Scholarly Networker

'17 up-front and centre' places initiative and honesty up-front and centre. '17' favours education and research, particularly of the kind that leads to productive action. This number will insist that you release the dishonest and unproductive aspects of your personality in the name of authenticity. 17 minus 9 equals 8, which warns of the need for organization. 179 is a prime number, highlighting the individualistic side of your nature. It's the 41st prime, and within that number, initiative and integrity join forces. Number 8, as the total, will help you to integrate the various facets of your personality. In your mature years, this number expects you to achieve something of real benefit to others. Examples: Henriette Theodora Marković (aka Dora Maar), Mary Therese Winifred Bourke (Robinson), Michelle Marie Pfeiffer

Maturity Number 180/9

The Humanitarian Who Makes Us Re-think the Way that We are Heading

'18 up-front' places the potent partnership of initiative and organization up-front. The zero indicates all of the potential available to you in this arena. The total is 9, indicating that all such effort must be done in the name of an ideal that is personally meaningful; an ideal that you are passionate about; an ideal that is humane. '180' has multiple factors, giving you plenty of ideals to choose from: 2 x 90, 3 x 30, 4 x 45, 5 x 18, 6 x 15, and 9 x 10. At least one of these numbers will relate to the ideals encoded in your date path making it the one most relevant to you. Revise the meaning of your chosen number in chapter 1 and use it to create a goal for yourself. Number 180 will help you to set goals worthy of your mature years, and lend you the power to achieve them. Examples: Flora Sydney Patricia Eldershaw and Francisco José de Goya y Lucientes.

Chapter 6

The Date Chart

In this chapter we will consider the usefulness of a little 3 by 3 grid as a means of arranging the date of birth so that intrinsic patterns of intelligence become evident. Upon the assumption that the numbers symbolize mental impulses, the hypothesis is that a sequential arrangement of the grid provides an indication of the *type* of intelligence a person is likely to have been born with. It cannot be stated too emphatically that the chart does not measure the amount of intelligence a person may have. I believe that people are universally intelligent but in different ways. The pioneer in formalising the idea of multiple intelligences is Howard Gardner. Throughout this chapter the concept of multiple forms of intelligence will be compared with energetic patterns in the date chart.

The Pythagorean Cross

In *The Theology of Arithmetic* Robin Waterfield has drawn a diagram that is very similar to the date chart. His book is a translation from the notes of a Greek scholar, schooled in the ways of Pythagoras. This fourth century student refers to a diagram wherein the sum of the diagonal corners is ten. And because the 'decad' was sacred to the Pythagoreans, the grid was called the Pythagorean Cross. The diagram below is a variation of this cross. It provides the underlying structure of the date chart.

3	6	9
2	5	8
1	4	7

Date Chart Examples

To demonstrate how to create your own date chart here are some examples. Author and playwright, Alexandre Dumas – pere – was born on July 24, 1802. His date chart therefore looks like this:

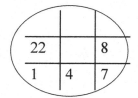

To find a father and son with almost identical charts is quite rare yet, playwright and novelist, Alexandre Dumas, son to the above, born on July 27, 1824, has a date chart which has only a slight variation of the same basic pattern to his father's:

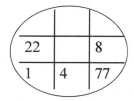

The grandfather, General Thomas-Alexandre Dumas, born on March 25, 1762, was a soldier rather than a writer. There are some similarities, but his date chart is actually quite different from those of his descendants, indicating that he had a very different type of intelligence:

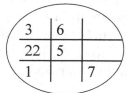

Date Chart – Yours

You now have all of the clues that you need to create your own date chart:

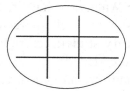

Introversion and Extraversion

Initially my definition of these terms aligned solely with the idea that introversion and extraversion relate to the way that one source's one's energy supply. By that definition, extraverts are energized by interacting with other people whilst introverts recharge their batteries from within and therefore need a place completely free of others in order to do so. Gradually it was realized that to be consistent, the classification of introversion and extraversion must *also* relate to patterns of intelligence. Interestingly Gardner's intelligences are all extraverted in nature. His definition of an 'intelligence' as "a biopsychological potential to process information that can be activated in a cultural setting to solve problems or to create products that are of value in a culture" (1999), is an extraverted one. For Gardner to classify it as an "intelligence" it must useful in an outward sort of way. In some texts, introversion has been mistaken for an emotional state. Introversion has even been described as an illness, curse and affliction. Even within the jargon of intelligence studies, the introverted states are sometimes referred to as 'weak'. Introversion and extraversion are neither emotional, nor strong or weak states, but energetic dispositions underscored by a common intelligence. In terms of intelligence, introversion and extraversion represent a polarity and operate on a continuum, which makes them potentially complementary.

Keirsey and Bates noted that we all draw from both sources – internal and external - but one way is preferred. The date chart supports this finding and demonstrates that most people have a fairly even mix of extraversion and introversion, which makes extremities noteworthy. The date chart method for discerning a person's natural inclination towards introversion or extraversion could not be simpler: Count up the number of squares that have numbers in them and those that don't. For example, with five numbered squares and four unnumbered squares, both Alexandre Dumas' had a bias towards extraversion. Within the Date Chart, nobody can have a number in every square. Seven is the maximum number of occupied squares, e.g. June 23, 1958, whilst eight is the maximum number of vacant squares possible, e.g. February 2, 2000. Because of the odd number of squares, the grid reveals that we do not draw evenly from both sources but are predisposed to draw more from one than the other.

If you discover that you have seven extraverted squares, you are probably so busy that you barely take time to sleep. If on the other hand, you have seven introverted squares, you need lots of time to recharge your batteries or you may suffer from nervous exhaustion. People with four or five numbered squares have the fortunate balance of introverted and extraverted energy.

Clusterings

In some date charts the numbers cluster into lines or distinct energy patterns. We will be relating these to various types of intelligence.

Types of Intelligence Chart

LINE	TYPE OF INTELLIGENCE
1-2-3	Linguistic Intelligence
Missing 1-2-3	Linguistic Intelligence (Introverted)
4-5-6	Kinesthetic Intelligence
Missing 4-5-6	Kinesthetic Intelligence (Introverted)
7-8-9	Logical- Mathematical Intelligence
Missing 7-8-9	Logical- Mathematical Intelligence (Introverted)
1-4-7	Survival Intelligence
Missing 1-4-7	Survival Intelligence (Introverted)
2-5-8	Interpersonal Intelligence
Missing 2-5-8	Interpersonal Intelligence (Introverted)
3-6-9	Spatial Intelligence
Missing 3-6-9	Spatial Intelligence (Introverted)
1-5-9	Self Intelligence (Worldly)

Missing 1-5-9	Self Intelligence (Introverted)
3-5-7	Self Intelligence (Cultural)
Missing 3-5-7	Self Intelligence (Introverted/Existential)

If you have any one of these forms of intelligence, you can probably relate to its inverse quality. You probably value it and strive towards it. This is because the pairs gravitate towards each other. Exploring the polar aspect of your intelligence type unfolds more of its potential.

We are now going to explore each line and type of intelligence systematically. To make it easier for you to locate a particular chart, we will proceed in the following order: Vertical lines first: 1, 2, 3 then 4, 5, 6, and then 7, 8, 9. Horizontal lines next: 1-4-7, then 2-5-8, and then 3-6-9. And then finally the diagonals: 1, 5, 9 and 3, 5, 7. The extraverted bands are examined first and then their introverted counterparts.

The Three Vertical Bands

Line 1, 2, 3

Linguistic Intelligence

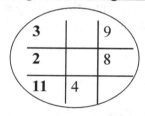

The numbers 1, 2, 3, render the following definition of linguistic intelligence:

- The ability to apply speech in order to accomplish desired effects (relates to number 1)
- Sensitivity to the spoken word (relates to number 2)
- An intuitive awareness of the form of language (relates to numbers 2 and 3)
- The perception of the interrelationships between words (relates to Number 3)
- The capacity to explore the meaning of words and the impact of language on others (a more sophisticated expression of Number 3).

From the *Pan's Script* data bank of one thousand names there were thirty-one examples of people with linguistic intelligence, as represented by the line 1, 2, 3 and with no other lines. The chart shown is that of Herbert Read, born on December 4, 1893. He was an art historian and advocate of contemporary British art. Howard Gardner also selected Herbert Read as an example of a person with linguistic intelligence. The other thirty examples included writers, musicians, actors, social activists, sporting legends, scientists, artists, spiritual leaders, an entrepreneur and a philosopher. Obviously people put their Linguistic Intelligence to different use. You don't need the whole of the line 1, 2, 3 to be an accomplished writer. Gardner claimed that linguistics is an intelligence that is democratically shared across the human species. He describes it as the pre-eminent instance of human intelligence, a statement that is also relevant to this numerological model. Language is sufficiently important that in very young children it will develop in the right hemisphere of the brain if the left is unavailable. Perhaps having the line '1, 2, 3' makes certain aspects of the linguistic process easier.

Variations of Linguistic Intelligence

<u>1, 2, 3, with 1 – 4 - 7</u>

Linguistic and survival intelligence combines. Number 1 is pivotal. Chart below: Francesco Petrarch, poet, born on July 20, 1304.

3		
2		
1	4	7

<u>1, 2, 3, with 2-5-8</u>

Linguistic and interpersonal intelligence combines. Number 2 is pivotal. Chart shown: Lady Gregory, dramatist, folklorist, and theatre manager, date of birth: March 15, 1852.

3		
2	55	8
11		

<u>1, 2, 3, with 3-6-9</u>

Linguistic and spatial intelligence combines. Number 3 is pivotal. Chart shown: Blaise Pascal, mathematician, physicist, inventor, writer, philosopher, born June 19, 1623.

3	66	9
2		
11		

<u>1, 2, 3, with 1, 5, 9</u>

Linguistic and self-intelligence (worldly) combines. Chart shown: Benjamin Spock, paediatrician, born on May 2, 1903.

3		9
2	5	
1		

1, 2, 3 with 3, 5, 7

Linguistic and self-intelligence (cultural) combines. Chart shown: John Dee, mathematician and medical astrologer, born on July 13, 1527.

3		
2	5	
11		77

1, 2, 3 with missing 4, 5, 6

Linguistic and kinesthetic intelligence (introverted) combines. Chart shown: Gene Kelly: Although he was a fabulous dancer, he always thought of himself, first and foremost as a choreographer, which is a useful way to think of kinesthetic intelligence. DOB: August 23 1912. A more recent example is Prince George of Cambridge born on July 22, 2013.

3		9
22		8
11		

1, 2, 3 with missing 7, 8, 9

Linguistic and logical-mathematical (introverted) intelligence combines. Chart shown: Christopher Wren, architect, born on October 20, 1632.

3	6	
22		
11		

Variations of 1, 2, 3 with 4, 5, 6

1, 2, 3 with 4, 5, 6 and 1-4-7 and 3, 5, 7

Linguistic, kinesthetic, survival, and self-intelligence (cultural) combines. No examples were found but one possible date from history is April 23, 1765 and from the future: June 17, 2345. The primary date path will always be 1.

3	6	
2	5	
1	4	7

1, 2, 3 with 4, 5, 6 and 3-6-9 and 1, 5, 9

Linguistic, kinesthetic, spatial, and self-intelligence (worldly) combines. This highly extraverted chart is equally that of golfer, David Graham, born on May 23, 1946, and skier, Donna Weinbrecht, born on April 23, 1965.

3	6	9
2	5	
1	4	

1 2, 3, with 4, 5, 6, and missing 7, 8, 9

Linguistic, kinesthetic, and logical-mathematical (introverted) intelligence combines. Chart shown: William Shakespeare, playwright, born on April 23, 1564. Christopher Marlowe and Francis Bacon had similar charts to Shakespeare but he is the only one who had this triple formation. It is an unusual chart, which is due to return on May 16, 2034.

3	6	
2	5	
1	44	

Variations of 1, 2, 3 with 7, 8, 9

1, 2, 3 with 7, 8, 9 and 1-4-7

This trough formation combines linguistic, logical-mathematical, and survival intelligence. The chart shown is equally that of two musicians: Jean Redpath, born on April 28, 1937, and Brian May, born on July 28, 1934, and two engineers: George Julius, born on April 29, 1873, and John Madsen, born on March 24, 1879.

3		9
2		8
1	4	7

1, 2, 3 with 7, 8, 9 and 3-6-9

Linguistic, logical-mathematical, and spatial intelligence combines. Chart shown: Bruce Babbit, politician and author of *Cities in the Wilderness: A New Vision of Land Use in America,* born June 27, 1938.

3	6	9
2		8
1		7

Variations of 1, 2, 3 with 1-4-7

The Number 1 is pivotal in all of these charts and some also feature a secondary number as well.

1, 2, 3 with 1-4-7 and 2-5-8 and 3, 5, 7

Linguistic, survival, interpersonal, and self intelligence (cultural) combines.

3		
2	5	8
1	4	7

The chart shown is equally that of Walter de la Mare, poet and novelist, born on April 25, 1873, and Wilhelm Von Roentgen, who discovered X-rays; date of birth: March 27, 1845.

1, 2, 3 with 1-4-7 and 3-6-9

Linguistic, survival, and spatial intelligences combine in this boomerang-shaped chart. Chart shown: Bryan Brown, actor, born on June 23, 1947, his linguistic intelligence being particularly evident. He was the only example in a data pool of 1000 people.

3	6	9
2		
1	4	7

1, 2, 3 with 1-4-7 and 3, 5, 7

This one-sided configuration combines linguistic, survival, and self-intelligence (cultural). Chart shown: Joseph Turner, artist, born on April 23, 1775. There were two further examples: Franz Anton Mesmer who formulated the theory that magnetic fields affect human health and mind, and Catherine of Sienna, mystic and hospital executive.

3		
2	5	
1	4	77

1, 2, 3 with 1-4-7 and 1, 5, 9 and 3, 5, 7

Linguistic, survival, and self-intelligence (worldly & cultural) combines. The chart shown is equally that of Elton John, musician, born on March 25, 1947, and Roslyn Ann Watson, ballet artist, choreographer and teacher, born on March 27, 1954.

3		9
2	5	
1	4	7

Variations of 1, 2, 3 with 2-5-8

The social consciousness of 1, 2, 3 is here facilitated by the interpersonal intelligence of 2-5-8.

1, 2, 3 with 2-5-8 and 3-6-9 and 1, 5, 9

Linguistic, spatial, interpersonal, and self-intelligence (worldly) combines. Chart shown: George Stephenson Beeby, born on May 23, 1869 - an active chart for an active life - he was at different times a teacher, accountant, manager of local newspapers, solicitor, barrister, politician, reformer, judge and writer.

3	6	9
2	5	8
1		

1, 2, 3 with 2-5-8 and 1, 5, 9

Linguistic, interpersonal and self-intelligence (worldly) combines. The chart shown is equally that of Sean Connery, actor, born on August 25, 1930, and Pro Hart, artist, born on May 30, 1928. There were only four further examples in a data pool of one thousand.

3		9
2	5	8
1		

1, 2, 3 with 2-5-8 and 3, 5, 7

Linguistic, interpersonal and self-intelligence (cultural) combines. Chart shown: Anne Tracy Morgan, social activist, born on July 25, 1873, who was awarded the Croix de Guerre for relief work during World War 1. She demonstrated 'people intelligence' by setting up shelters for the homeless.

3		
2	5	8
1		77

Combining the two previous charts, we arrive at the highly extraverted:

<u>1, 2, 3 with 2-5-8 and 7, 8, 9 with 1, 5, 9 and 3, 5, 7</u>

Linguistic, interpersonal, logical-mathematical, and self-intelligence (worldly and cultural) intelligence combines. Chart shown: Grace Munro who was co-founder of the Country Women's Association from which base she lobbied for better health care facilities for countrywomen and children. She used the energy and intelligences available in her chart to the 'max' establishing no less than one hundred branches! Her date of birth was March 25. 1879.

3		9
2	5	8
1		7

Variations of the complementary pair: 1, 2, 3 and 3-6-9

<u>1, 2, 3, with 3–6–9 and 1, 5, 9</u>

Linguistic, spatial, and self-intelligence (worldly) combines. Chart shown: George Orwell: By being called 'the social conscience of his time' he exemplifies one of the most consistent themes in this set of charts. His date of birth was June 25 1903. Three further examples included an historian, a medical missionary, and a cardiothoracic surgeon.

3	6	9
2	5	
1		

<u>1, 2, 3, with 3 – 6 – 9 and 1, 5, 9 and 3, 5, 7</u>

Linguistic, spatial, and self-intelligence (worldly & cultural) combines. The chart shown is equally that of Glenn Murcutt, architect, a profession that requires spatial intelligence; date of birth: July 25, 1936, and Keizo Obuchi, politician, a profession that requires linguistic and self intelligence; date of birth: June 25, 1937.

3	6	9
2	5	
1		7

<u>**1, 2, 3 with 1, 5, 9 with 3, 5, 7**</u>

Linguistic and self-intelligence (worldly & cultural) combine. Chart shown: Gotham Chopra, spiritual leader & counsellor, born on February 23, 1975.

3		9
22	5	
1		7

1, 2, 3, with missing 4, 5, 6, and an extraverted 7, 8, 9

Linguistic, kinesthetic (introverted), and logical-mathematical intelligence combines. Three prominent doctors share this configuration: Norman Gregg, the ophthalmologist who discovered the link between rubella in pregnancy and congenital blindness and deafness; DOB: March 7, 1892, John Newman-Morris, another surgeon renowned for his philanthropy; DOB: March 2, 1879, and Victor Coppleson, surgeon and pioneer of post-graduate medical studies; DOB: February 27, 1893. These doctors provide us with an interesting perspective of 'internal kinesthetics' working in tandem with linguistic and logical-mathematical intelligence.

3		9
2		8
1		7

1, 2, 3, with missing 4, 5, 6, and missing 7, 8, 9

Linguistic, kinesthetic (introverted), and logical-mathematical (introverted) intelligence combines. Chart shown: Jonas Berg, actor, comedian, and musician, born October 13 2001.

3		
2		
111		

Moving across to the central vertical band

Line 4, 5, 6

Kinesthetic intelligence

	6	
	5	8
11	4	

In the definition of what he called bodily kinesthetic intelligence, Howard Gardner unites two capacities. The first is the ability to control one's bodily motions, and the second to handle objects skilfully. His definition embraces the using of one's body as a whole and the parts of one's body (such as the hand or the mouth) to solve problems or to fashion products. We are going to have to split these two intelligences because the theoretical model that we are working with, dictates it so. The vertical Line 4, 5, 6 will be called kinesthetic intelligence and its horizontal counterpart - line 1-4-7 - called survival intelligence and dealt with later. Kinesthetic and survival intelligence are complementary and united by the number 4. In relation to linguistic intelligence this number helps us to give language form. Kinesthetically, it is used to formulate a sequence of motions.

With the above in mind, the numbers 4, 5, 6, render the following definition of kinesthetic intelligence:

- The ability to coordinate body motion as a whole (relates to number 4)
- The ability to judge the timing, force, and extent of your movements and to make necessary adjustments en route (a combination of numbers 5 and 6)
- The ability to sense direction: an awareness of the way that a sequence of motions is proceeding (combines 4, 5, and 6)

From the *Pan's Script* data bank of one thousand names there were only seven examples of people with kinesthetic intelligence, as represented by the line 4, 5, 6 with no other lines. The chart shown above is that of Anna Jarvis born on May 1, 1864, who successfully launched a campaign to have the second Sunday of May set aside to honour mothers. She has been selected because social activism seems to go in tandem with this line. There was a single musician and four writers, noticeably on serious subjects and with somewhat of an educational bias: Elizabeth Palmer Peabody, born on May 16, 1804, who founded the first kindergarten in the United States, Myrtle Fillmore, born on August 6, 1845, who started an alternative school and later co-founded the Unity Movement with her husband, Charles, Mary Eliza Fullerton born on May 14, 1868, who has been called 'Australia's Mary Wollstonecraft' because she took up the banner of the women's suffrage movement, and Grant Watson born on June 14, 1885, who was a natural science graduate and biologist; also a traveller and writer, and much concerned with social issues as were all of the other examples.

We may not have turned up any body builders or sporting stars here, but perhaps this is a limited definition of kinesthetic intelligence. People with this line up are typically *socially dynamic*: 'movers and shapers'. Team players, they can be found right at the heart of social change. As this chapter unfolds we will see that kinesthetic intelligence often blends with other intelligences as in the case of Suzanne Farrel, who was one of Gardener's examples of bodily kinesthetic intelligence.

Variations of Kinesthetic Intelligence

<u>4, 5, 6, with 1-4-7</u>

The complementary kinesthetic and survival intelligence combines. Chart shown: Johann Friedrich Herbart, philosopher and writer on psychology and education; DOB: May 4, 1776. We will see this chart again in 2045.

	6	
	5	
1	4	77

4, 5, 6 with 2-5-8

Kinesthetic and interpersonal intelligence combines. Chart shown: Maybanke Anderson, editor, feminist, reformer, and teacher, instrumental in establishing kindergartens and playgrounds in Sydney, Australia; date of birth: February 16, 1845.

	6	
2	5	8
1	4	

Further examples include Saint Rose of Lima, who was also active in the area of social welfare, and Viktor Adler, a physician; instrumental in uniting the socialist parties in Austria, who devoted his life to universal suffrage and world peace.

4, 5, 6 with 1, 5, 9

Kinesthetic and self-intelligence (worldly) combine. Chart shown: Candice Bergen (aka Murphy Brown), actor, born on May 9, 1946.

	6	99
	5	
1	4	

More complex variations of 4, 5, 6 uniting it with the complementary line 1-4-7:

4, 5, 6 with 1-4-7 and 2-5-8

Kinesthetic, survival, and interpersonal intelligences combine. This tightly woven chart is always accompanied by the date path 51/33/15/6, emphasizing the qualities of number 6. It is equally represented by Rose Cecil O'Neill, artist, born on June 25, 1874, John James Audubon, ornithologist and bird artist, born on April 26, 1785, and Henri Farman, a pioneering aviator and aircraft designer, born on May 26, 1874.

	6	
2	5	8
1	4	7

4, 5, 6 with 1-4-7 and 1, 5, 9

Kinesthetic, survival and self-intelligence (worldly) combines. Chart shown: Bob Connolly, filmmaker, born on June 7, 1945. Andrew Gaze, basketballer, born on July 24, 1965, provides a second example.

	6	9
	5	
1	4	7

<u>4, 5, 6 with 1-4-7 and 3, 5, 7</u>

Kinesthetic, survival, and self-intelligence (cultural) combine. Chart shown: Michelangelo, artist, born March 6, 1475. Although renowned as a painter, it was the physical experience of sculpting that he loved best. It has been said that he sensed the resonance of the marble he fashioned, its sound and rhythm patterning his every move. Michelangelo sought the natural forms within the stone, capturing universal themes and dynamics. Rather than oral speech (1, 2, 3), his was 'tactile speech' (4, 5, 6).

3	6	
	5	
1	4	7

<u>4, 5, 6 with 2-5-8</u> and 1, 5, 9

Kinesthetic, interpersonal and self-intelligence (worldly) combine. Chart shown: Jimmy Barnes, "wild man of Australian rock", born April 28, 1956.

	6	9
2	5	8
1	4	

<u>4, 5, 6 with 3-6-9 and 1, 5, 9</u>

Kinesthetic, spatial, and self-intelligence (worldly) combine. Chart shown: Christopher Keith Wallace-Crabb, critic and poet, who once said that he wanted "to see how far the lyrical, Dionysian impulses can be released and expressed without loss of intelligence" - a comment relevant to this pattern; date of birth: May 6, 1934.

3	6	9
	5	
1	4	

<u>4, 5, 6 with missing 7, 8, 9</u>

Kinesthetic and logical-mathematical (introverted) intelligence combines. Chart shown: Isaac Newton born December 25 1642. The 4, 5, 6 is evident in his *Principia*, which set the cornerstone for the understanding of *dynamics* and *mechanics*. The missing 7, 8, 9 is evident by the way he investigated deeply buried wisdom and esoteric insight to push forward the theoretical boundaries of science. Together, these intelligences promoted the demonstration of his ideas through practical research and complex mathematics. The fact that he made use of the images and tools of his research into ancient models of the universe to construct a workable celestial mechanics is relevant to this pattern. Further examples include the famous writer, Christopher Marlowe, and astronomers Galileo Galilei and Tycho Brahe.

	6	
222	5	
11	4	

Moving across to the third vertical band

Line 7, 8, 9

Logical-Mathematical Intelligence

	6	9
2		8
11		7

The Numbers 7, 8, 9, render the following definition of logical-mathematical intelligence:

- The capacity to analyze problems logically (relates to number 7)
- The ability to carry out mathematical operations (relates to number 8)
- The ability to investigate issues scientifically and draw conclusions (relates to number 9's inclination to generalize but is really a combination of these three numbers)

Some people with this line might not think that they have logical-mathematical intelligence but were they to explore the root meanings of the words 'logic', 'mathematics' and 'science' they may realize that it may be only the emphasis on technical competence that appears to exclude them. Throughout this book we are exploring the broader implications of the original definitions because only by so doing can we discern how these intelligences are working through a whole range of people.

Broadly speaking logic is any system of reasoning and inference, and the word can be applied to any sensible, rational thought and argument (rather than ideas influenced by emotion or whim). Logic has a predictive component when it reveals an inescapable relationship and a pattern of events. Mathematics is the study of relationships using numbers and science is the systematic study of the physical world and its manifestations. Thus, if one contemplates the broader implications of these three words, it will be seen that no one need be excluded from logical, mathematical and scientific intelligence.

From the *Pan's Script* data bank of one thousand names there were eight examples of people with logical-mathematical intelligence, as represented by the line 7, 8, 9 with no other lines. The chart shown is that of Georg Riemann born on September 17, 1826. He is also one of the people that Howard Gardner chose as an example of logical-mathematical intelligence. By posing deep questions about the relationship of geometry to the everyday world, Georg Riemann was half a century ahead of his time, the mathematical structure he set up eventually finding its niche in the theory of relativity. The other seven examples of this solitary line comprised three medical practitioners, two musicians, an artist and an engineer.

As with linguistic and kinesthetic intelligences, it is obvious that human beings can adapt these intelligences to whatever interests them. And as Howard Gardner points out, there is a logic to language and a logic to music, which operate according to their own rules. Undoubtedly there is an 'artist logic' too, which like the others is neither superior nor inferior to mathematical and scientific logic.

Regardless of how it is used there is one style of thinking that seems to prevail here and that is the process called deduction. To deduce is to reach a logical conclusion based on evidence and after much consideration. It includes the ability to categorize, define, probe, research, and notice pattern and order. Deduction necessitates hindsight and grants the power of prediction based on careful observation, analysis, and the systematic recording of findings.

Variations of logical-mathematical intelligence

<u>7, 8, 9 with 1-4-7</u>

Logical-Mathematical and survival intelligence combines. Chart shown: Marjorie Stoneman Douglas, conservationist, providing an obvious application of these two intelligences; date of birth: April 7, 1890.

<u>7, 8, 9 with 2-5-8</u>

Logical-Mathematical intelligence teams up with its counterpart, 2-5-8: 'people intelligence'. It pivots around the number 8. Chart shown: August 9, 2057, when this energy pattern begins.

<u>7, 8, 9 with 3-6-9</u>

Logical-Mathematical and spatial intelligence combines. The chart shown is equally that of Flora Eldershaw, born on March 16, 1897, and Gail Godwin, born on June 18, 1937. Both were writers.

3	6	9
		8
11		7

7, 8, 9 with 1, 5, 9

Logical-Mathematical and self-intelligence (worldly) combine. Number 9 is pivotal, implying that people with such charts are likely to be concerned with global issues. Chart shown: Richard Branson, entrepreneur, born on July, 18 1950.

		9
	5	8
11		7

More complex variations of 7, 8, 9:

7, 8, 9 with 1-4-7 and 2, 5, 8 and 1, 5, 9

Logical-Mathematical, survival, interpersonal and self-intelligence (worldly) combines. This highly extraverted chart is that of William Wilberforce, who actively campaigned against slavery. He was born on August 24, 1759.

		9
2	5	8
1	4	7

7, 8, 9 with 1-4-7 and 1, 5, 9

Logical-Mathematical, survival and self-intelligence (worldly) combines. Chart shown: Brooks D Simpson, historian; date of birth: August 4, 1957.

		9
	5	8
1	4	7

7, 8, 9 with 2-5-8 and 1, 5, 9

Logical-Mathematical, interpersonal and self-intelligence (worldly) combines. Chart shown: Buckminster Fuller: as the inventor of the geodesic dome, he exemplifies the logical-mathematical type of intelligence in particular. His date of birth was July 12, 1895.

		9
2	5	8
11		7

7, 8, 9 with 1, 5, 9 and 3, 5, 7

Logical-Mathematical and self-intelligence (worldly and cultural) combines. The chart shown is equally that of Noni Hazlehurst, actor, singer, and television presenter, active in children's welfare organizations, born August 17, 1953, and Lloyd Rees, artist, conservationist, teacher, and visionary, born March 17, 1895.

3		9
	5	8
11		7

7, 8, 9 with missing 4, 5 6

Logical-Mathematical and kinesthetic intelligence (introverted) combines. Chart shown: Nelson Mandela, revolutionary politician, born on July 18, 1918.

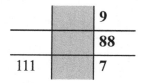

The Three Horizontal Bands

Line 1-4-7

Survival Intelligence

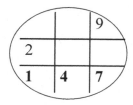

The numbers 1-4-7 render the following definition of survival intelligence:

- The ability to use your hands, feet, mouth or some other specific body part, to fashion products and solve problems in order to enhance the likelihood of survival (that's number 1 in action)
- The capacity to perform a sequence of fine motor activities that become steadily internalized and integrated, leading consequently to a feeling of competence within your environment (relates to number 4)

- Where appropriate, the capacity to substitute a tool that can do the task more quickly and effectively (another facet of number 4)
- The ability to construct a method to affect all of the above, firstly by trial and error, then gradually refining the process through sustained effort, feedback, and reflection (a combination of 1, 4, and 7).

From the *Pan's Script* data bank of one thousand names there were thirty-two examples of people with Survival Intelligence, as represented by the line 1-4-7 with no other lines. The chart shown is that of Ravi Shankar born on April 7, 1920. He was a master sitarist, a versatile composer, a teacher, and a writer. Renowned for bringing Indian music to the 'West', he is one of four musicians within the data bank. The other thirty examples comprised two more musicians, eight artists, five writers, five social activists, three scientists, three sports stars, an actor, an architect, a chef, and a spiritual leader.

What is similar to the 4, 5, 6 line is the social consciousness powering creative works. The lines 4, 5, 6 and 1-4-7 are loaded with people who care passionately about social issues. Whether they demonstrate this through music, art, invention, or direct action, these people are engaged body, mind and soul, in effecting change wherever they perceive it is needed. These are people whom literally 'walk their talk'. People with the line 1-4-7 are problem-solvers of the hands-on kind. Self-motivated and inventive, they like to craft, fashion, fix and restore things; in their own way and within their own timeframe.

Survival intelligence is three times more prevalent than its kinesthetic counterpart. Being also four times more prevalent than logical-mathematical intelligence, and as common as linguistic intelligence, makes 'survival' a significant intelligence.

Variations of survival intelligence

1-4-7 with 1, 5, 9

Survival and self-intelligence (worldly) combine. Number 1 is pivotal. Chart shown: Ernst Walter Mayr, leading evolutionary biologist of the twentieth century; date of birth: July 5, 1904.

```
        │   9
 ───────┼───────
     5  │
 ───────┼───────
  1  │ 4 │ 7
```

1-4-7 with 3, 5, 7

Survival and self-intelligence (cultural) combine. Number 7 is pivotal. Chart shown: Alice Green, Irish historian and senator, born on May 30, 1847.

3		
	5	8
1	4	7

<u>Combining the previous two chart: 1-4-7 with 1, 5, 9 and 3, 5, 7</u>

Survival and self-intelligence (worldly & cultural) combine. Chart shown: Doug Henning, magical performer, born on May 3, 1947.

3		9
	5	
1	4	7

<u>1-4-7 with missing 2-5-8</u>

Survival and interpersonal (introverted) intelligence combine. Chart shown: Alexander Humboldt, who was acknowledged by Charles Darwin as the greatest naturalist in the world. Humboldt demonstrates the integration of survival intelligence with its introverted counterpart. He was an ecologist before the word existed, and it was his sensitivity to the beauty, nobility, and harmony of nature that opened his eyes to the link between place and species, which was a radical, new concept in his time. His copious volumes of scientific observations display a respect for the grand design behind nature, which he perceived as essentially spiritual. Alexander Humboldt was born on September 14, 1769.

	6	99
11	4	7

<u>1-4-7 with missing 3-6-9</u>

Survival and spatial (introverted) intelligences combine. Chart shown: Albrecht Dürer, who stated that geometry and measurement were the keys to understanding the art of the Italian Renaissance. His date of birth was May 21, 1471. There were a further sixteen examples from many different walks of life.

2	5	
111	4	7

More complex variations of 1-4-7:

<u>1-4-7 with 2-5-8 and missing 3-6-9</u>

Survival, interpersonal, and spatial (introverted) intelligences combine. Chart shown: All three types of intelligence were evident Ernest Henry Shackleton, the explorer, born on February 15, 1874. To follow the story of the way he kept his men alive during the eighteen months they were stuck in Antarctica during winter is to understand what 'survival' and 'people intelligence' really means. Shackleton had the knack of bringing out the best in people and encouraging them to go beyond what they thought they were able to endure. He kept the group united, continually coming up with new ways to offset despair. On a previous expedition he had turned back just a hundred miles from the Pole, rather than lose a man. He was rightly hailed a hero. On the strength of his leadership, practicality, and powers to motivate depended the sanity of the marooned crew - and he got every one of them through. The 'missing 3-6-9' may encode his navigational intelligence.

2	5	8
11	4	7

<u>1-4-7 with missing 2-5-8 and 3-6-9</u>

Survival, interpersonal (introverted), and spatial intelligence combines. Chart shown: Andreas Corvus (a.k.a. Barthélmy Cocles), palmist, born on March 9, 1467.

3	6	9
1	4	7

<u>1-4-7 with missing 2-5-8 and missing 3-6-9</u>

Survival, interpersonal (introverted), and spatial (introverted) intelligence combines. Chart shown: William Wordsworth, poet, born on April 7, 1770. Through his empathy with nature as expressed in his poetry, we witness the introverted aspect of survival intelligence. Wordsworth deduced that poetry such as his, which he believed expressed the soul of nature, exerted a moral influence on human thought and feeling.

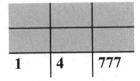

1	4	777

Moving up to the central horizontal band

Line 2-5-8

Interpersonal Intelligence

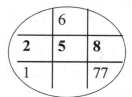

The numbers 2-5-8 render the following definition of interpersonal intelligence:

- The ability to affect diplomacy, taking polarities into account (that's number 2)
- The capacity to demonstrate your social ingenuity within a particular cultural setting (that's number 5)
- The ability to network between divergent populations (that's number 8)
- The capacity to understand the motivations of other people and consequently, the capacity to work effectively with them (that's 2, 5, and 8 in combination)

From the *Pan's Script* data bank of one thousand names, there were seventeen examples of people with interpersonal intelligence, as represented by the line 2-5-8 with no other lines. These comprised five musicians and five people who broadly represent the 'sciences'. There were also three social activists, a writer, an actor, a dancer, and a spiritual leader. The chart shown is that of Carl Jung, born on July 26, 1875. Jung realized that only a doctor who knows how to cope with his/her own problems would be able to teach others to do the same.

The line 2-5-8 will be a common one in the third millennium for the obvious reason that everyone will at least have the first number. We should therefore expect to witness more 'people intelligence'. We will hopefully see more negotiation and networking between diverse as well as likeminded people.

Variations of interpersonal intelligence

2-5-8 with 1, 5, 9

Interpersonal and self-intelligence (worldly) combine in this extraverted chart.

		9
22	5	8
111		

Chart shown: John Paul Getty, business tycoon, born on December 15, 1892.

2-5-8 with 3, 5, 7

Interpersonal and self-intelligence (cultural) combine. This extraverted chart begins on August 7, 2035.

3		
2	5	8
		7

2-5-8 with missing 1-4-7

Interpersonal and survival (introverted) intelligence combines. Ancient dates of birth are notoriously unreliable but if Alexander the Great, King of Macedonia, *was* born on June 28, 356 then he exemplifies this pattern. A much more recent date with this pattern is May 8, 2003.

3	66	
2	5	8

2-5-8 with missing 3-6-9

Interpersonal and spatial (introverted) intelligence combines. Chart shown: Florence Nightingale, nurse, her interpersonal intelligence required with patients and patrons alike. Her date of birth was May 12, 1820. There were thirty-three further examples including Francois Sauniere who apparently used his spatial intelligence (introverted) to locate a buried treasure!

22	5	8
11		

2-5-8 with missing 1-4-7 and missing 3-6-9

Interpersonal, survival (introverted) and spatial (introverted) intelligences combine in this highly introverted chart. Chart shown: Maya Bond, singer-songwriter, born on August 5, 2000.

2	5	8

Moving to the top of the chart and the third horizontal band

Line 3-6-9

Spatial Intelligence

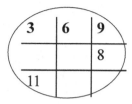

The numbers 3, 6, 9 render the following definition of spatial intelligence:

- The capacity to conjure up a mental image within one's mind (refers to number 3)
- The ability to recognize the constancy of something from different angles (that's 6)
- The ability to think in terms of geometric relationships including ones in which the problem solver is a part of the problem to be solved (3, 6, and 9 in combination)

The line 3-6-9 would seem to correlate with Howard Gardner's spatial intelligence and the recognition and manipulation of patterns in space. Gardner was careful to distinguish between spatial and visual-spatial because although it relates to some form of vision, this intelligence can develop in people who are physically blind. This line is counterpart to 1, 2, 3 (linguistic intelligence), the two lines pivoting around the number 3, and thus the ability to project one's imagination.

From the *Pan's Script* data bank of one thousand names there were twelve examples of people with spatial intelligence, as represented by the line 3-6-9 with no other lines. These comprised three writers, two singers, an actor, a comedian, a financial adviser, a politician, a chemist, a spiritual leader, and an artist, whose chart is shown: Stanley Spencer, born on June 30, 1891. Artists such as him get a special mention in Gardner's book. Their type of spatial intelligence demonstrates "sensitivity to the various lines of force that enter into a visual or spatial display... the feelings of tension, balance, and composition that characterize a painting" (*Frames of Mind*).

Gardner noted that spatial intelligence is "an amalgam of abilities", yet people with spatial intelligence demonstrate that their preferred mode of solving imagery problems is typically through the positing of an internal mental image that can be manipulated as one would if an actual object were actually present. Also important to our model is this statement: "Just as musical and linguistic processing are carried out by different processing centers and need not interfere with one another, so, too spatial and linguistic faculties seem able to proceed in relatively independent or *complementary* fashion" (*Frames of Mind*; the emphasis not part of original text but relevant to the complementary nature of the lines 1, 2, 3 and 3-6-9). Some people display spatial intelligence through sketching, painting, cartography, photography or some other form of composition, but just as often, such composing is about the manipulation of imagery through the medium of words.

Variations of spatial intelligence

<u>3-6-9 with 1, 5, 9</u>

Spatial and self-intelligence (worldly) combine in this is an extraverted chart. Chart shown: Rene Descartes, philosopher, who worked from the premise that god is rational and therefore the design of the universe is completely rational. His date of birth was March 31, 1596.

33	6	9
	5	
11		

<u>3-6-9 with 1, 5, 9, and 3, 5, 7</u>

Spatial and self-intelligence (worldly and cultural) combine in this extraverted chart.

3	6	9
	5	
1		7

Chart shown: His Holiness the 14th Dalai Lama of Tibet: July 6, 1935.

<u>3-6-9 with missing 1-4-7</u>

Spatial and ecological intelligence combines. If it is correct that Caesar Augustus was born on September 23, 63 BCE, then this was his date chart. A much more recent birthday is that of Xia Vigor, actor and television host, born on June 23, 2009.

33	6	9
2		

<u>3-6-9 with missing 2-5-8</u>

Spatial and interpersonal (introverted) intelligence combines. Chart shown: Gary Kasparov, spatial intelligence being obviously useful to a chess champion; date of birth: April 13 1963.

33	6	9
11	4	

The Two Diagonal Bands: the polarising and reconciling currents

Line 1, 5, 9

<u>Self-Intelligence (Worldly)</u>

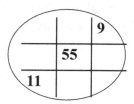

The numbers 1, 5, 9 render the following definition of self-intelligence (worldly):

- The ability to know yourself as unique among other individuals (that's number 1)
- The capacity to demonstrate your personal ingenuity within your social setting (5)
- The ability to draw conclusions about yourself as a part of the human race (1, 5, and 9 in combination)

What will here be called self-intelligence is similar to what Howard Gardner called intrapersonal intelligence. Gardner presented the Personal Intelligences, as he called them, together, on the understanding that intrapersonal intelligence must develop within a social context and that mixing with other people develops self-intelligence. In our model interpersonal or 'people intelligence' is symbolized by the horizontal line 2-5-8 while intrapersonal or self-intelligence is symbolized by the diagonal lines 1, 5, 9 and 3, 5, 7. At the intersection of these three lines is the number 5.

We have in other parts of this book equated number 5 with ingenuity, and here we can apply this to social and personal ingenuity. The Ancient Greeks called 5 the "marriage number" because it weds the even 2 and the odd 3. Here it stands for the union of interpersonal and intrapersonal intelligences. Number 5 unites or 'weds' the two types of intelligence. In *Pan's Script* we not only distinguish between interpersonal and intrapersonal intelligences but also between four types of self-Intelligence, two extraverted and two introverted.

In astronumerology number 5 also represents our ability 'to shine' and like a sun or star, to generate our own energy and maintain it. And it is on this level that we should discuss the numbers because the numbers represents energetic principles, rather than emotions, which are a secondary factor. In this way we part company with any definition of interpersonal or intrapersonal intelligence that involves emotions. The problem is that whilst it is possible to train people to identify their emotions, such labelling is subject to cultural conditioning. For example, what might generate pleasure in a person of one culture may be distressful to a person in another culture. The numbers suggest an alternative way to distinguish what is happening to oneself in any socially dynamic situation. Because they are impersonal, unemotional and impartial, the numbers would have us firstly take note of what is happening to our energy level. Is the particular person we are with or the particular situation we are in raising or lowering our energy level? There is also a third state wherein we simply feel at peace because our energy is in balance. Thus the numbers would have us define intrapersonal intelligence as the management of our personal energy system within a social situation.

It is the pair of numbers either side of the number 5 that distinguish inter and intra-personal intelligences. Numbers 2 and 8, the pair related to interpersonal intelligence, are even numbers and thus tend to 'hold things together'. Congruent with 'people intelligence' numerologists have been known to call 2 and 8 'relationships numbers'. On the other hand, numbers 3 and 7 and 1 and 9, the pairs associated with intrapersonal intelligence, are odd: a law unto themselves, in a manner of speaking. They are not relationship numbers and we are therefore justified in equating them with self-intelligence.

A frequent line in the twentieth century, over eighty examples of the line 1, 5, 9 turned up within a data pool of one thousand. Uniquely, this line could stand-alone during the twentieth century. The chart shown is that of Richard Marshall Eakin, Professor of Zoology, born on May 5, 1910. The line 1, 5, 9 meets the line representing logical-mathematical intelligence (7, 8, 9) in number 9: consciousness of generality, the former as it applies to oneself and the latter as it applies to science, mathematics and logic.

Noticeably people with the line 1, 5, 9 in their date chart tend to define themselves and others in terms of roles. For example a person might say: "I am a wife and this is how a husband and wife should behave towards one another" or "I am a grandson and this is how a grandfather and grandson should behave". The line 1, 5, 9 offers the capacity to understand yourself within the context of the world as a whole, and it is through the process of experimentation with the various polar extremities of worldly life that you learn to understand your own strengths and weaknesses. The 1, 5, 9 line stands closest to Howard Gardner's concept of intrapersonal intelligence. As such, he emphasized the importance of having a viable model of yourself and being able to draw effectively on that model in making decisions about your life.

Line 3, 5, 7

Self-Intelligence (Cultural)

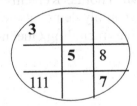

The Numbers 3, 5, 7 render the following definition of self-intelligence (cultural):

- The ability to imagine and articulate your role within your culture (that's number 3)
- The capacity to demonstrate your personal ingenuity within a particular cultural setting (that's number 5)
- The ability to refine your role within your social group, via the process of reflection (and that's number 7)

In his chapter on the personal intelligences, Howard Gardner draws the reader's attention to the fact that many of the world's cultures are vastly different from what is generally called the 'Western' variety, where the locus of the self inheres to the specific individual. In more traditional societies this may not be the case at all. In such settings, the expression of one's self-awareness is largely shaped by the culture into which one is born, and individuals are thought of in terms of the role they play within such a society.

Distinguishing this type of personal intelligence from the others, we firstly note that this line does not begin with number 1 as 1, 5, 9 does, nor number 2 as 2-5-8 does, but that it begins with number 3: consciousness of image. Its home base is not the self (1) or another (2) but an *image* of self (3).

From the *Pan's Script* data bank of one thousand names there were seven examples of people with self intelligence (cultural), as represented by the line 3-5-7 with no other lines. These comprised three socially or politically active people, two musicians, a philosopher, and a theologian. The chart shown is that of Alva Erskine Smith, who founded the Political Equality Association. She was born on January 17, 1853.

The shortage of examples suggests that this is not a common form of intelligence; however the fact that this line (without other lines) was not available in the twentieth century is partly responsible for this. The heyday of cultural intelligence will be the fourth millennium, which provides us with a clue as to where humanity is heading.

One way to think of 3, 5, 7 is to consider the culture within yourself. Self-Intelligence (Cultural) is that type of personal intelligence that facilitates understanding 'the culture' within your own mind. Role-play assists the development of this type of intelligence.

Self Intelligence - both Cultural and Worldly

1, 5, 9 with 3, 5, 7

This extraverted pattern combines self-intelligence, cultural and worldly. The chart pivots around the number 5: consciousness of growth and evolution. Chart shown: Thomas Keneally, whose books, such as *The Chant of Jimmy Blacksmith* and *Schindler's List* amply demonstrate these intelligences; DOB: October 7 1935. There were five further examples including Queen Elizabeth I.

3		9
	5	
11		7

The Eight Introverted Bands

Missing Clusters

There are many charts with lines of 'missing numbers' and we will be studying them with the intention of revealing their hidden potential. We are going to be exploring the idea that numbers missing from the date chart are operating outside of the 1-9 range. And so if number 1 is missing, the person may actually be attuned to number 10. Similarly, if number 2 is missing in the date chart, the person may be attuned to number 11, and so on. In chapter 1 it was noted that as the numbers go higher, the level of consciousness deepens. Thus these missing numbers, particularly a whole set like 2-5-8, may be difficult to access in one's early years of life and could leave a young person feeling somewhat inadequate, misunderstood, and vulnerable. In chapter 1 it was also noted that missing numbers usually turn out to be very important in people's lives. Rather than simply saying that people with missing lines are inept with words, awkward or weak-willed, irrational, impractical, defensive, uncreative or forgetful, disengaged from life or unmusical, as others have done, we need to look for the *gift* that people with these subtle forms of intelligence can tap into and cultivate. If the numbers represent specific forces of consciousness, then their absence suggests a more pliable energy field.

The Three Vertical Bands Introverted

Missing 1, 2, 3

Linguistic Intelligence (Introverted)

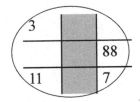

The Missing Numbers 1, 2, 3 render the following definition of linguistic intelligence (introverted):

- The capacity to 'hold one's own' in a situation that involves some form of communication with another entity (that's number 1 operating as number 10)
- The ability to establish rapport with another person through an agreed form of language (that's number 2 operating as number 11)
- The ability to perceive something from multiple points of view and express such perception (and that's number 3 operating as number 12)

As the inverse of linguist intelligence, missing 1, 2, 3 could indicate the ability to communicate without words, i.e., telepathically, but we won't know for a very long time because this line is not possible until the year 4000. However, everyone with linguistic intelligence could tap into the inverse qualities of this intelligence.

Moving across to the Central Vertical Band

Missing 4, 5, 6

Kinesthetic Intelligence (Introverted)

Missing Numbers 4, 5, 6 render the following definition of kinesthetic intelligence (introverted)

- The ability to transform motion in one's mind and imagine a whole new direction that something could take (that's number 4 operating as number 13)
- The ability to re-shape a sequence of motions or thought-patterns (that's number 5 operating as number 14)
- The ability to engage in 'mental gymnastics' in any field of human endeavour that you can imagine (that's numbers 13/4, 14/5, and 15/6 working together)

The versatility of this intelligence was born out in the thirty examples of this intelligence in our data bank of one thousand people. These comprised six writers, four artists, three actors, three sports stars and three spiritual leaders, two musicians, a politician, an entrepreneur, and a historian.

The chart shown is that of Dr. Maria Montessori, the famous educator who observed the tendency of children to repeat the same task over and over again, with concentrated effort that did not fatigue them but which actually brought them to a state of restfulness. She discovered that repetition is a spontaneous phenomenon that not only led to a feeling of peace but to an openheartedness that deepened the person's ability to participate in socially beneficial work. Montessori noticed that through self-willed repetition, disorder fell away and self-discipline emerged, accompanied by a heightened interest in life and sense of dignity. She came to realize that this process was a part of the universal discipline that keeps everything in the universe on course. This tells us much about kinesthetic intelligence. Maria Montessori's date of birth was August 31, 1870.

Variations of Kinesthetic Intelligence (Introverted)

Missing 4, 5, 6 with missing 1-4-7

Kinesthetic (introverted) and survival intelligence (introverted) combine. Chart shown: Kalani Hilliker, dancer, model, and television personality, born September 23, 2000.

3		9
22		

Missing 4, 5, 6 with missing 2-5-8

Kinesthetic (introverted) and interpersonal (introverted) intelligence combine. Chart shown: Reverend Desmond Tutu, Archbishop of Capetown, born on October 7, 1931. There were a further eleven examples, including four musicians.

3		9
111		7

Missing 4, 5, 6 with missing 3-6-9

Kinesthetic (introverted) and spatial (introverted) intelligence combine. Chart shown: James Cook, navigator, explorer, and cartographer, born November 7, 1728.

2222		8
1		7

Missing 4, 5, 6 with missing 1, 5, 9

Kinesthetic (introverted) and self-intelligence (other worldly) combine. Chart shown: Maggie Batson, actor, business owner, and philanthropist, born August 7, 2003.

3		
2		8
		7

Missing 4, 5, 6 with missing 3, 5, 7

Kinesthetic (introverted) and self-intelligence (existential) combine. Chart shown: Martinus Thomsen, a simple farm-hand barely schooled, his consciousness suddenly began to expand until over the course of a lifetime he developed a comprehensive cosmology. DOB: August 11, 1890.

		9
		88
111		

More complex variations of missing 4, 5, 6:

Missing 4, 5, 6, with missing 7, 8, 9, missing 1-4-7, and missing 1, 5, 9

Kinesthetic (introverted), survival (introverted), logical-mathematical (introverted), and self-intelligence (other worldly) combine in this highly introverted pattern. Three young sports people currently represent this pattern: Colton Herta, race car driver, Naina Jaiswal, table tennis player, and Nahida Akter, cricketer, born March 2, 2000, per chart shown.

3		
22		

Missing 4, 5, 6, with missing 1-4-7 and missing 1, 5, 9

Kinesthetic (introverted), survival (introverted), and self-intelligence (introverted) combine. Chart shown: Catherine Lyons, artistic gymnast, born on August 30, 2000.

3		
2		**8**

Missing 4, 5, 6, with missing 1-4-7 and missing 3, 5, 7

Kinesthetic (introverted), survival (introverted), and self-intelligence (existential) combine.

		9
22		**8**

Chart shown: Frankie Jonas, actor, born September 28, 2000.

Missing 4, 5, 6, with missing 1-4-7, missing 3-6-9, missing 1, 5, 9 and missing 3, 5, 7

Kinesthetic (introverted), survival (introverted), spatial (introverted), and self-intelligence (existential and otherworldly) combine. Chart shown: Jaylen Arnold, activist, philanthropist, and actor, born on August 28, 2000.

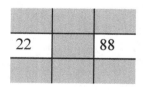

Missing 4, 5, 6, with missing 7, 8, 9, missing 1-4-7, missing 3-6-9, missing 1, 5, 9, & missing 3, 5, 7

Kinesthetic (introverted), logical-mathematical (introverted), survival (introverted), spatial (introverted), and self-intelligence (existential and other worldly) combine. Chart shown: Maria Lyle, parasport athlete, born on February 20, 2000.

Missing 4, 5, 6, with missing 2-5-8 and missing 3, 5, 7

Kinesthetic (introverted), interpersonal (introverted), and self-intelligence (existential) combine in this introverted chart. Chart shown: Peggy van Praagh, dancer, born on September 1, 1910, obviously exemplifying kinesthetic intelligence.

Missing 4, 5, 6, with missing 3-6-9 and missing 1, 5, 9

Kinesthetic (introverted), spatial (introverted) and self-intelligence (other worldly) combine. Chart shown: Troy Glass, actor and cook, born on July 27, 2000.

Missing 4, 5, 6, with missing 3-6-9 and missing 3, 5, 7

Kinesthetic (introverted), spatial (introverted), and self-intelligence (existential) combine. Chart shown: Leo Tolstoy, writer, born on August 28, 1828.

Missing 4, 5, 6 with missing 7, 8, 9, missing 3–6-9 and missing 3, 5, 7

Kinesthetic (introverted), logical-mathematical (introverted), spatial (introverted), and self-Intelligence (existential) combine. Chart shown: Ren Qian, diver, born on February 20, 2001.

Moving across to the third vertical band

Missing 7, 8, 9

Logical-Mathematical Intelligence (Introverted)

```
    |  6 |
 22 |  5 |
 111|    |
```

The missing numbers 7, 8, 9, render the following definition of logical-mathematical intelligence (introverted):

- When introverted, logical-mathematical intelligence can slough off the extraneous until only the essential remains (that's number 7 operating as number 16). In terms of logical-mathematical intelligence 'missing 7' implies 'no barrier' to the forces that distil information. It helps people to think abstractly and aesthetically.
- The ability to formulate insight into a symbolic system (that's number 8 operating as number 17). When introverted, logical-mathematical intelligence tends to take the essence of something and formulate it into symbolism, and there are many forms that symbolism can take. Language is a form of symbolism, so is religion, law, philosophy, the Kabala and astrology. Mathematics is the most abstract form of symbolism, and the ability to formulate an equation belongs here.
- The ability to generalize a symbolic system into a unified theory that embraces the greatest number of extreme examples (that's number 9 operating as number 18).

When introverted logical-mathematical intelligence tends to expand symbolism so that it embraces the greatest number of possibilities. The ability to generalize an equation and realize its broader applications is a mathematical expression of this type of intelligence.

Such lofty ideals require concrete examples to make them real. Our sample of one thousand persons revealed just six examples of logical-mathematical (introverted) but this is mainly because we have to look far back in history to find them. No 7, 8, 9 means effectively no examples in the 1700's, 1800's or 1900's.

The chart shown is that of writer, philosopher, lawyer and statesman, Francis Bacon, born on January 22, 1561. He has been selected to represent this intelligence because history would judge him as the father of inductive reasoning, and inductive reasoning seems to be what this configuration is about. Inductive reasoning means being able to create a generalization from observed instances. It places an emphasis on collecting instances rather than testing theories.

Variations of logical-mathematical intelligence (introverted)

Missing 7, 8, 9 and missing1-4-7

Logical-Mathematical (introverted) and survival (introverted) intelligence combines. Chart shown: Jared Scott Gilmore, actor, born on May 30, 2000.

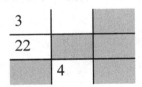

Missing 7, 8, 9, with missing 2–5–8

Logical-Mathematical (introverted) and interpersonal (introverted) intelligences combine. Chart shown: Regiomontanus, astrologer, born on June 16, 1436

3	666	
11	4	

Missing 7, 8, 9, with missing 3-6-9

Logical-Mathematical (introverted) and spatial (introverted) intelligence combines. Chart shown: Leonardo Da Vinci whose far-sighted inventions and designs amply demonstrate this combination of Intelligences; DOB: April 15 1452.

2	55	
11	44	

Missing 7, 8, 9, with missing 1, 5, 9

Logical-Mathematical (introverted) and self-intelligence (other worldly) combine. Chart shown: Chloe Kim, snowboarder, born April 23, 2000.

3		
22		
	4	

Missing 7, 8, 9 with missing 3, 5, 7

Logical-Mathematical (introverted) and self-intelligence (existential) combine. Chart shown: Marcus Aurelius, the 14th Roman Emperor, best known for his *Meditations, Writings to Himself*. He financed all four philosophical schools: The Lyceum, The Garden, The Academy and The Stoa, which was his favourite. Thus he exemplifies self-intelligence (existential) in particular; DOB: April 26, 121. This pattern has now returned and a much more recent example is Mo'ne Ikea Davis, baseballer, born on June 24, 2001.

	6	
22		
11	4	

More complex variations of missing 7, 8, 9

Missing 7, 8, 9 with missing 1-4-7 and missing 3-6-9

Logical-Mathematical (introverted), survival (introverted), and spatial (introverted) intelligence combines. This chart appeared on February 5 2000 when the Year of the Dragon began. Chart Shown: Claire Liu, tennis player, born May 25, 2000.

22	55	

Missing 7, 8, 9 with missing 1-4-7 and missing 1, 5, 9

Logical-Mathematical (introverted), survival (introverted), and self-intelligence (introverted/other worldly) combine. Chart shown: Sena Miyake, figure skater, born on March 26, 2002.

3	6	
222		

Missing 7, 8, 9, with missing 1-4-7, missing 1, 5, 9 and missing 3, 5, 7

Logical-Mathematical (introverted), ecological, and self-intelligence (existential and other worldly) combine. Chart shown: February 6, 2000.

	6	
22		

Missing 7, 8, 9, with missing 2-5-8 and missing 3, 5, 7

Logical-Mathematical (introverted), interpersonal (introverted) and self-intelligence (existential) combine. Chart shown: William Penn, an English real estate entrepreneur, philosopher, Quaker, and founder of the Province of Pennsylvania. An early champion of democracy and religious freedom, his good relations with the Native Americans exemplifies interpersonal intelligence. Penn's date of birth was October 14, 1644.

Missing 7, 8, 9, with missing 3-6-9 and missing 3, 5, 7

Logical-Mathematical (introverted), spatial (introverted), and self-intelligence (other worldly) combine. Chart shown: Alexa Gerasimovich, actor, born on April 11, 2002.

Missing 7, 8, 9, with missing 3-6-9, missing 1, 5, 9 and missing 3, 5, 7

Logical-Mathematical (introverted), spatial (introverted), and self-intelligence (existential and other worldly) combine. Chart shown: Abigail Duhon, musician and actor, born April 20, 2000.

Missing 7, 8, 9, with missing 1, 5, 9 and missing 3, 5, 7

Logical-Mathematical (introverted) and self-intelligence (existential and otherworldly) combine. Chart shown: Julio Alfredo Chiappero, chess prodigy, born on April 2, 2006.

The Three Horizontal Bands Introverted

Missing 1-4-7

Survival Intelligence (introverted/ecological)

Chart shown: Ceren Akkaya, footballer, born on September 5, 2000

If the *Pan's Script* model is correct, then 'No 1-4-7' is the flipside of 1-4-7 (survival intelligence) and related to its counterpart 4, 5, 6 (kinesthetic intelligence, both internal and external).

Missing Numbers 1-4-7 render the following definition of survival intelligence (introverted), which could also be called ecological intelligence.

- The capacity to 'hold your own' within your environment (that's number 1 operating as number 10). Unhampered by a demanding number 1, your mind is open to subtle vibrations, which means that you may be able to detect subtle 'shifts' in the environment. It doesn't take much imagination to relate this to survival.
- The ability to transform your environment as it transforms you (that's number 4 operating as number 13). People with neither 1 nor 4 in the date chart may be able to sense the primal harmony that exists between living things and the land.
- The ability to perceive the natural order behind life, its subtle truth, and timeless reality (that's number 7 operating as number 16).
- The capacity to discriminate among similar species is the core ability most people would associate with ecological intelligence. Howard Gardner noted that this obviously relates to survival because one must be able to discriminate between predators and food-sources, competitors and supporters, in order to maintain the health and status of one's energetic system. Relating this to 'missing 7' it is noted that this intelligence is operating at a subtle level and developed via the process of reflection rather than external manipulation. Understanding the essential differences between living things comes about by a 'not this; not that' type of thinking within the mind. It predisposes you to a certain type of aesthetic appreciation of nature.

It was in 1999 that Gardner presented 'naturalist' as the eighth distinct type of intelligence in his theory of multiple intelligences defining it as the ability to recognize and classify the numerous species of flora and fauna that exist in one's environment. My preference is for the term ecological intelligence, taking my cue from Thomas Berry's book, *The Dream of the Earth*. We agree that ecological intelligence is not simply about physical survival, but a matter of surviving as unique, affectionate, creative and imaginative individuals, capable of enjoying life, inwardly rich and concerned with the integrity of the whole organism called Earth. We also agree that this is not a utopian vision, but one fundamental to survival. We both use the term ecological in its primary meaning as the relationship of an organism to its environment and as an indicator of the interdependence of all living and nonliving systems of the Earth.

Variations of survival intelligence (introverted)

Missing 1-4-7 with missing 1, 5, 9

Ecological and self-intelligence (introverted/other worldly) combine. Chart shown: Emma Rayne Lyle, actor, born on August 26, 2003.

3	6	
22		8

Missing 1-4-7 with missing 3, 5, 7

Ecological and self-intelligence (introverted/existential) combine. Chart shown: Akim Camara, musician, born on September 26, 2000.

	6	9
22		

Missing 1-4-7 with missing 3, 5, 7 and missing 1, 5, 9

Ecological and Self-Intelligence (Existential and Other Worldly) combine.

	6	
2		8

Chart shown: Hayes Grier, internet personality, born June 8 2000.

Moving up to the next horizontal line

Missing 2-5-8

Interpersonal Intelligence (introverted)

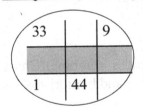

Missing numbers 2-5-8 render the following definition of interpersonal intelligence (introverted).

- The ability to establish rapport with another person by empathizing with them (that's number 2 operating as number 11). In regards to interpersonal intelligence, number 2's consciousness of duality expressed inwardly could empower a person to go within their mind and intuit what is similar between themselves and another person and what is different, and use this information to figure out how to relate to the other person. However it may be difficult to harness this tendency in an intelligent way because until sufficient mental fortitude is developed, 'no 2' means literally 'no barrier' between self and another.
- The ability to re-shape conditioned thought patterns within oneself and then by sympathetic resonance, within a larger social setting (that's number 5 operating as number 14). Number 5's consciousness of evolution manifesting in an inward sort of way would impress upon the mind the possibility of progress, in this case in the domain of relationships between people. In other words, missing 5 might predispose you to

remaining at the negotiation table when others have given up. You would explore every possible avenue, learn from your mistakes, and adapt yourself accordingly.

- The ability to appraise oneself honestly and make necessary sacrifices for the greater good. Action is based on personal insight rather than external reward (that's number 8 operating as number 17).
- The ability to help another person to attain their goals as you attain yours is missing 2-5-8 working in unison and interpersonal intelligence in top gear.

All of the above interactions are a two-way process; as one of two parties achieves a breakthrough so does the other. When introverted, interpersonal intelligence helps us to see ourselves in others and thus, to know how they feel. It offers the gift of social sensitivity. Missing 2-5-8 has the same 'other person' focus as 2-5-8, which is what distinguishes this pair from the intrapersonal intelligences. The difference between 2-5-8 and missing 2-5-8 is that the latter sources ideas about people differently. People with missing 2-5-8 source their ideas about other people from within themselves, by reflecting upon how they would feel in similar circumstances. If this is your pattern, be aware that you are wide open to the influence of others and choose your acquaintances carefully.

From the *Pan's Script* data bank of one thousand names came seventeen examples of people with interpersonal intelligence (introverted) as represented by the missing line 2-5-8 with no other lines. They represented an approximately equal measure of musicians, writers, artists, politician, activists, inventors, psychologists, anthropologists, mathematicians, physicists, chess champions and spiritual leaders. The chart shown is that of Jane Goodall, who was born on April 3, 1934. Her empathy extended to primates other than human.

A variation of interpersonal intelligence (introverted)

Missing 2-5-8 with missing 3, 5, 7

Interpersonal (introverted) and self-intelligence (existential) intelligences combine. Chart shown: Steve Bhaerman (aka Swami Beyondananda), an author, educator and humorist, who helps us to laugh at ourselves; DOB: October 9, 1946.

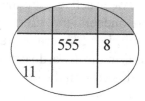

Missing 3-6-9

Spatial Intelligence (introverted)

	555	8
11		

Missing numbers 3-6-9 render the following definition of spatial intelligence (introverted):

- The ability to perceive something from multiple points of view and articulate such perception (that's number 3 operating as number 12). In terms of spatial intelligence, 'no 3' implies 'no barrier' to the host of imagery in the prototypical or ideal worlds. This would predispose you to thinking in terms of ideal images. Until you are able to apply such images to the material world, you may be accused of having 'airy-fairy' ideas.
- The ability to perceive the intrinsic order of something and apply it to an image (that's number 6 operating as number 15). In terms of spatial intelligence 'no 6' implies 'no barrier' to the forces that reconcile the critical and the creative tendencies of the mind. In its immature expression Missing 6 might cause mental confusion but as mental fortitude increases, it becomes possible to 'take hold' of an ideal image and equip it with functional expression.
- The ability to synthesize the real and the ideal into a unified model that embraces the greatest number of possibilities (that's number 9 operating as number 18). In terms of spatial intelligence 'no 9' implies 'no barrier' to the forces that generalize your ideal and its functional expression.
- Spatial Intelligence (introverted) suggests an inner type of navigational intelligence such as being able to find your way around the in the world of ideas. In a similar way to designing a building, people with this type of intelligence can synthesize their ideas. Both the extraverted and introverted forms of this intelligence come with the ability to architect new ideas. The difference between them is that the person with the more introverted kind may need greater encouragement to share such ideas.

From the *Pan's Script* data bank of one thousand names there were fifteen examples of people with spatial intelligence (introverted) as represented by the missing line 3-6-9 with no other lines.

The chart shown is that of Sri Yukteswar who was born on May 10, 1855, and who, in keeping with 'internal spatial intelligence', rectified the cycle of the yugas. I cannot support the claim of an earlier numerologist that this line indicates a failing memory in old age. Sri Yukteswar and the other examples in this chapter demonstrate that there is absolutely no basis for this frightening assertion. Like Sri Yukteswar, William Blake who also had this line, lost none of his mental sharpness in old age. In fact, these examples and others such as Charles Fillmore, demonstrate the opposite: their mental capabilities *improved* with age.

Variations of spatial intelligence (introverted)

Missing 3-6-9 with missing 1, 5, 9

Spatial (introverted) and self-intelligence (introverted/other worldly) combine. Chart shown: Paula Leitón, water polo player, born on April 27 2000.

22		
	4	7

Missing 3-6-9 with missing 3, 5, 7

Spatial (introverted) and self-intelligence (introverted/existential) combine. Chart shown: Eduoard Schure, philosopher, author of an insightful book on Pythagoras, born on January 2, 1841; Georg Brandes, biographer, and William James, author of *Variety of Religious Experiences*, also exemplifying existential intelligence in particular.

2		8
111	4	

Missing 3-6-9 with missing 3, 5, 7 and 1, 5, 9

Spatial (Introverted) and Self Intelligence (Existential and Otherworldly) combine. Chart Shown: Keiron Williamson, artist, born August 4, 2002.

22		
	4	8

The Two Diagonal Bands Introverted

Missing 1, 5, 9

Self Intelligence (introverted and other worldly)

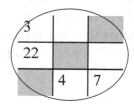

Chart shown: Amira Willighagen, musician, born March 27, 2004.

Missing Numbers 1, 5, 9 render the following definition of self-intelligence (introverted/ other worldly).

- The capacity to hold one's own in this world and others (that's number 1 operating as number 10). In terms of self-intelligence, 'no 1' implies 'no barrier' to your Self. A person unconcerned about impressing themselves on this world is better able to locate themselves within a greater world scenario.

- The ability to reshape conditioned thought patterns (that's number 5 operating as number 14). In terms of self-intelligence 'no 5' implies 'no barrier' to the forces that engender (personal) evolution. As such missing 5 represents the capacity to consciously evolve from within.
- The ability to generalize across the domains of the self and create a personal mythology to live by (that's number 9 operating as number 18). In terms of self-intelligence 'no 9' implies 'no barrier' to the forces that expand the mind so that it can locate the self within the greatest number of possibilities.
- To be able to locate yourself within worlds other than the immediate, obvious and tangible, is the core competence of self intelligence (other worldly). You do not need to imagine this to be extraordinarily difficult, occult or strange. Whenever a person describes themselves as 'A Leo' or a 'Sensory Feeling Type' or 'A Member of the Bear Clan', they are exercising an otherworldly schemata. As with all genuine forms of intelligence, such knowledge progresses from curiosity to competence. What the yogis have called knowledge of the astral and causal planes of existence, and Sufi and Buddhist masters have given similar labels to, are also 'other worlds'.

Some people have highly sophisticated abilities in this domain. By persistent mental discipline and extraordinary courage in the face of public scepticism, Robert Munro documented his out of body experiences. He discovered that many people have had such experiences, and so he continued to refine his methods until he was able to map several worlds. In one of these he located his deceased wife and communicated with her. Importantly, he knew precisely how to return at will. In *Black Elk Speaks* we learn that this traditional medicine man was communicate with beings living in other worlds and thus locate missing objects and people. Trained from childhood in the ways of his people, Black Elk illustrates what is possible for those with sufficient self-discipline.

Therefore we should not imagine that persons with this intelligence are 'away with the pixies', although in its immature state, this may the case and may even be a necessary stage in its development. But this is not the goal. In its mature form people with this intelligence would be engaged in making a difference within their social group; that would be to turn this intelligence inside out.

Like missing 1-4-7, this is a difficult pattern to comment on because it is only since the year 2000 that it became possible. Time alone will tell if it has been interpreted correctly. If this is your type of intelligence, you have the ability to reconcile polarities from within rather than having to act them out in the physical world.

Missing 3, 5, 7

Self Intelligence (introverted and existential)

Missing numbers 3, 5, 7 render the following definition of with self intelligence (introverted/existential):

- The ability to perceive the world from multiple points of view and express such perception (that's number 3 operating as number 12). In terms of self-intelligence (existential) 'no 3' implies 'no barrier' to the imagery that bombards the mind. This is likely to cause confusion and mental anxiety until you decide what you want to focus on.
- The ability to reshape conditioned thought-patterns (that's number 5 operating as number 14). In terms of self-intelligence (existential), 'no 5' implies 'no barrier' to the forces that generate (personal) evolution.
- The capacity to discern the subtle truth that lies just behind the visible world and the ability to reflect on life and decide what is real and what is not (that's number 7 operating as number 16). In terms of self-intelligence (existential), 'no 7' implies 'no barrier' to the forces that distil, whereby extraneous notions of the self are sloughed off until only the essence remains.

Within the *Pan's Script* data pool of one thousand names, self-intelligence (introverted/existential) was the most common. There were over a hundred examples of it with no particular vocation highlighted more than any other.

The chart shown is that of Emanuel Swedenborg whose life and ideas clearly demonstrate this intelligence. He was born on January 29, 1688. Swedenborg was an intellectual giant who was humble enough to admit that when it came down to it, he knew absolutely nothing. But he did know that he had to let go of preconceived ideas if he was to understand the nature and origin of things, and he realized that sensory data could only unite with intuition by rational thinking. He noticed inconsistencies in other people's ideas and sought to remedy them. He had an open mind that was imaginative and speculative yet also scientific and progressive. In these ways he exemplified self-intelligence (introverted/existential).

If you have this line of intelligence, it is likely that you are a 'mental purist'. You would rather believe in nothing that something you are not sure about. In other words, you are a true sceptic, who will persist with your inquires until a resolution is reached, suspending judgments and conclusions until such time. Initially you might be inclined to polarize existential issues but with practice your capacity to tolerate and integrate points of view other than your own, will naturally increase.

Missing 1, 5, 9 with missing 3, 5, 7

Self-intelligence (existential and other worldly) combine. Chart shown: Goo Seung-hyun, actor, born on June 28 2004.

	6	
22		8
	4	

Unlined Charts

Approximately five percent of charts do not have any of the lines we have considered, making it necessary to consider individual numbers. Charts without lines are always balanced in their extraversion/introversion ratio.

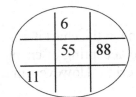

<u>Interpreting number by number</u>

The theory we have been working with grants three simple guides to interpretation:

1. A balance of a particular number grants ease of expression for any type of intelligence.
2. An abundance of any particular number creates a certain type of mental tension. If this is worked with constructively, it can bring forth a special gift or talent (our examples are loaded with them).
3. A missing number may be operating at a higher octave, for example, missing 1 might be manifesting as number 10, missing 2 as number 11 etc. You can refer to the date path numbers 10-18, in chapter 1 for further clues. In the next chapter we will consider missing and abundant numbers in more detail.

When is a Number balanced and when is it in excess?

<u>Number 1</u> relates to consciousness of self and when there is no number 1 in the chart, the person may lack self-projection in childhood, which could affect their self-confidence. Such a person is likely to develop strong principles on which to base their self-confidence (this would be number 10 exerting its influence). With just one number 1, a similar effort to assert oneself may be necessary but the person may not feel any great urge to do so. Two or three number 1's seems to grant a balanced proportion of self-projection. More than three 1's can make a person self-conscious to a degree that can be crippling in their early years but could then be turned to their advantage once a strong set of personal principles has been developed.

<u>Number 2</u> relates to consciousness of duality and when there is one or two in the chart, they can offer an intuitive knowing of where one person ends and another begins. Beyond two there may be a tendency to be overly reactive to other people and to take things too personally.

<u>Number 3</u> relates to consciousness of image and a singular 3 can be an asset in a person's social life. Double 3, just like date path 33, can overstimulate the mind with images and triple 3 even more so. If one's belief in oneself is sufficiently strong, missing 3 can operate as number 12

and the person could become a social force to be reckoned with, but it will probably take a radical shift of perspective in order to do so.

Number 4 relates to consciousness of form, and so a four in the chart is very handy. The more 4's there are, the more preoccupied the person will be with practicalities. There is some evidence that 4's engender dexterity with the hands or feet.

Number 5 relates to consciousness of evolution and when there is just one in the chart it gives the person adaptability and versatility. The more 5's there are the more accepting of change the person will be, which may facilitate their ability to respond to in a crisis. However three or more 5's could also make them restless to the point of recklessness.

Number 6 relates to consciousness of cohesion and so a singular 6 grants ease in unifying ideas. The more 6's there are the more the person is likely to feel burdened with the responsibility of trying to 'bring everything or everybody together'. The 6's were strongly represented in most of our sample charts, which indicates that awareness of cohesion is useful in every domain of human endeavour.

Number 7 relates to consciousness of differentiation and when there is one in the chart it helps a person to hone in on details and slough off the extraneous or irrelevant. The more 7's there are the more the person is likely to focus on what is not right rather than what is. The 7's also facilitate an affinity to the natural world, which in some people engenders a deep sense of appreciation.

Number 8 relates to consciousness of organization and in our sample charts every writer, every scientist, and most musicians had at least one. Two eights further sharpen perceptiveness and the powers of assessment. Most people can handle two 8's but beyond that, multiple eights tend to exacerbate any tendency the person may have to see themselves as a victim. It can also make people hyperactive. Use your 8's to organize, network, and achieve your goals.

Number 9 relates to consciousness of generality and when there is only one in the chart it is easy for the person to perceive how a particular event fits in to the bigger picture without getting carried away. The more 9's there are the more a person is likely to over-generalize and become impatient with the time it takes to prove that their conclusions are 'right'.

In our sample of one thousand people, there were fifty unlined charts from all walks of life. The chart shown is that of Mikao Usui, Reiki Master, born on August 15, 1865.

Concluding comments

Initially it seemed preposterous to suggest that it is possible to discern the types of intelligence that a person is predisposed to, from the date of birth. Could it really be that simple? Time will tell if it is true or not; it hinges on how accidental you think your birthdate is. *Pan's Script* presents a coherent hypothesis of which this chapter is a part. It is not a doctrine but an idea that may just turn out to be important. Intelligence is a complex matter, and hereditary, environmental, and physiological considerations must be taken into account, but if we know what a person's innate tendencies are, we may be able to help them to make the most of such potential. This work represents merely a drop in the ocean of research being done in the field of intelligence yet a potentially valuable piece of information because if it turns out to be correct, it is based on one of the most objective and ethical pieces of data we have available to us: the date of birth.

Chapter 7

The Challenges

So called because their nature is confrontational to the ego, the challenges stand before you as something that you need to acknowledge before you can fulfil the potential encoded in your date path. As in a work of art in which shadow provides light with form, so the challenges imbue human activity with depth and personal meaning. There are four challenges inherent in your date path and three within your name. To facilitate the process of perceiving where your challenges lie and how intense they are, you can complete the worksheet near the back of the book as you proceed through this chapter. Do not be concerned about getting the number of challenges in each row exactly right; the idea is to bring your challenges to light so that you know what you are dealing with.

Calculating the Challenges

Subtraction Reveals the Challenge-Pattern

In numerology the operations are significant in their own right, each having its own symbolic meaning. We will be applying the operation of subtraction to reveal where the tension lies between two Numbers.

The Four Challenges within the Date Path

1. The birth month and birth day are subtracted from each other, lowest from highest, to reveal the 1st challenge.
2. The birth day and the birth year are now subtracted from each other, lowest from highest, to reveal the 2nd challenge.
3. Now subtract the above sub-totals, lowest from highest, to reveal the whole-life challenge.
4. Finally, subtract the birth month and the birth year from each other, lowest from highest. We will be calling this 'the polarity challenge'.

Our example throughout this chapter is Jeannette Walls not only because her childhood was incredibly challenging but also because of the way that she has dealt with those challenges. Complex challenges are fleshed out in books such as *The Glass Castle*, Jeannette's best-selling autobiography. To begin with we will study the calculations and then move through ways to interpret the challenges before returning to Jeannette at the end of the chapter.

Challenges Great and Small

Jeannette Walls was born on April 21, 1960 and these are her date path challenges:

1. $21 - 4 = 17$ (birth day 21 - birth month 4)
2. $21 - 16 = 5$ (birth day 21 - birth year 16)
3. $17 - 5 = 12$ (subtracting the sub-totals)
4. $16 - 4 = 12$ (birth year 16 - birth month 4)

Jeannette's date of birth highlights a significant issue in regard to the challenges. It has been the common practice of numerologists to reduce all of the numbers before doing the subtractions. Here we have not done that because it would be inconsistent with our objective, which is to reveal all of the potentials within the date of birth by acknowledging the numbers in their full expression. As we did in chapter 1, so we do here: we keep the numbers whole in order to unveil their greatest potential before reducing them. The series $17 - 5 - 12 - 12$ represents a distinct set of challenges, shaping a distinct destiny.

If the numbers had been reduced before the subtraction was carried out, this set of numbers would have remained concealed. Here is the reduced set of calculations:

1. $4 - 3 = 1$ (birth month 4 – birth day 3)
2. $7 - 3 = 4$ (birth year 7 – birth day 3)
3. $4 - 1 = 3$ (subtracting the sub-totals)
4. $7 - 4 = 3$ (birth year 7 – birth month 4)

The reduced series is $1 - 4 - 3 - 3$. To keep things simple, the reduced series will henceforth be referred to as the small challenges and the unreduced series, the big challenges. Occasionally they are the same, and sometimes they reveal a higher octave of the same number, e.g. 13 instead of 4. In such cases the small challenges provide the launching pad to the big challenges.

Timing Date Path Challenges

The 1st challenge is a part of a person's energy pattern from birth. Because it is calculated from the left-hand side of the date of birth, it relates to the past. It is an issue that has arisen from a previous incarnation and it informs your first Saturn Return Cycle. This astrological conjunction takes place somewhere between 29 and 30 years of age as the planet Saturn returns to the position it was in when you were born. The 2nd challenge, being calculated from the right-hand side of the date of birth, is critical to your future development. Challenges 1 and 2 co-exist, together shaping the date path throughout life; resolving the 1st challenge facilitating the resolution of the 2nd. Both challenges can then be transmuted into assets. Not dealt with, they compound and have a detrimental effect on the whole-life challenge. The whole-life challenge is just that: it is with you throughout your life. It represents an on-going issue and can mediate between the other two. The trick is to see these three challenges as part of one story.

The polarity challenge also operates throughout life but becomes more significant after the second Saturn return at around 60 years of age. Sometimes it is the same as the whole-life challenge, as in Jeannette's case, but sometimes it is totally different.

The Three Challenges within the Name

1. By subtracting the number equivalents of the first and last vowels in the name, lowest from highest, we arrive at the vowel challenge.
2. By subtracting the number equivalents of the first and last consonants in the name, lowest from highest, we arrive at the consonant challenge.
3. Subtracting the above two numbers, lowest from highest, we arrive at the name challenge.

For example, Jeannette Walls, has a vowel challenge represented by the number **4** (i.e. 5 for the e minus 1 for the a), consonant challenge *zero* (i.e. 1 for the J minus 1 for the s). Her name challenge was therefore represented by number 4 (i.e. 4 minus 0).

Locating Missing Numbers by Comparing the Date Chart with the Name Chart

The Name Chart

In the previous chapter you were shown how to place the date of birth with the date chart. Now we will do the same with the name. We will place each letter into a 3 by 3 grid by applying the letter correspondences explained in chapter 2. This allows ease of comparison between the name and the date of birth numbers.

For example, Jeannette Walls had the following name chart:

ll		
tt	eee nnw	
aajs		

Not every number is represented (and there is an intensity number: 5).

Born on April 21, 1960 her date chart looks like this:

	6	9
2		
11	4	

Comparing the name chart with the date chart we note that there are two numbers missing in both her name chart and date chart: 7 and 8. (Jeannette's date chart indicates that was born with self-intelligence, introverted and existential, which would have helped her to navigate such challenges).

Karmic Challenges as Collective Issues

From somewhere is numerology's distant past, the Numbers 13, 14, 16 and 19 have become labelled 'karmic numbers'. And while some numerologists have rejected this notion outright, others have elaborated on the interpretation that they represent mistakes, which an individual person has made, in a past life. Within the overall paradigm upon which *Pan's Script* is based, a karmic number represents a *collective* issue, which is sorting itself out through certain individuals. Psychology encourages us to take responsibility for what is happening to us but we must also take into account that there are forces beyond an individual life. The fact that a challenge is collective in nature, but played out through individual lives, might not seem to make any difference: the individual still suffers. Yet to realize that the problem is collective in nature necessitates a different slant to the interpretation of these numbers.

Jeannette has two karmic numbers within her date of birth and date path, which might help to explain the nature of her challenges.

April 21 1960
= 4. 21. 16 = 41
= 4. 3. 16 = 23
= 4. 3. 7 = 14

$$\begin{array}{l} 4 \\ 21 \\ \underline{1960} \\ \underline{1985} = 23 = 5 \end{array}$$

Numbers 14, per her secondary date path and 16, per her year of birth are karmic numbers. With vowel number 17/8, consonant number 27/9, and name number 44/8, there are no further karmic numbers in Jeannette's core numbers.

Energy Crisis

Repeated numbers portend an energy crisis. There is tremendous potential, but applying it wisely is the challenge. People naturally avoid the full implications of this number until they feel ready to handle it. There is a pattern to the timing of the unfolding of these concentrations of energy.

If 2 numbers are the same in the date of birth, e.g. February 2, this slightly excessive energy balances itself at around **24** years of age. Prior to that people are likely to experience difficulty in applying the Number to their advantage. The same can be said when any two of these are the same:

The birth day and vowel
The birth day and name
Birth month and vowel
Birth month and name
Birth year and vowel
Birth year and name

The vowel and name (as in Jeannette's case)

The consonant is a special case. If the consonant number is the same as any other core number, the birth month, or birth year, it actually helps to make the energy readily accessible. However if the consonant number is the same as two or more core numbers, the birth month or birth year, it intensifies the crisis and must therefore be counted as a contributing factor (see 3 or 4 numbers the same).

If one of the date of birth numbers is the same as the date path, the energy crisis eases at around **36** years of age.

For example Alexandre Dumas was born on July 24, 1802 = primary date path 6, with primary birth day 6. Prior to his 36th Birth Day, he would struggle with the energy-pattern we call number 6, but after that time it would open up to him in a way not generally experienced by those who have not had this struggle. (He was 38 when he wrote the novel for which he is most famous, *The Three Musketeers*). The same principle applies equally with the birth month and birth year. For example, Andrew Carnegie was born on November 25, 1835, primary date path 8. The year 1835 also reduces to an 8 and so it would be 36 years before the potential of the number 8 would become fully accessible to him. (It was during his late 30's that Andrew Carnegie began organizing his philanthropic endeavours into trust funds and educational organizations).

When the following are the same, an energy crisis is likely for around 36 years:

The date path and the birth day
The date path and the birth month
The date path and the birth year
The date path and the vowel

When 2 numbers in the date of birth are primarily the same at the date path, the energy tends to balance itself and become easier to apply at around **48** years of age.

An example is Immanuel Kant, born on April 22, 1724 = **4**. 22/4.14/5 = 40/**4**.

Kant was actually 46 when he got the job he had been waiting for; the timing is not always exact. He then went on to become Dean of the Philosophy faculty at age 52.

When the following are the same, an energy crisis is likely for up to 48 years:

Date path, birth day, birth month
Date path, birth day, birth year
Date path, birth month, birth year
Date path, birth month or birth day or birth year, and the vowel number
Date path, vowel and consonant

Similarly, when the following are the same, an energy crisis is likely for around **48** years:

Birth day, birth month, birth year
Birth day, birth month, vowel

Birth day, birth month, name
Birth day, birth year, vowel
Birth day, birth year, name
Birth day, vowel, name
Birth month, birth year, vowel
Birth month, birth year, name
Birth month, vowel and name

For example William Blake: name and month 11/2, with year 20/2. At around 48 he realized that he had been selling his soul in the market place and determined to return to his own vision. Blake is an important example for those readers who assume that the end of the energy crisis will bring material wealth. It may, but the essential nature of the numbers is mental rather than material. Blake accepted the price of his decision and although poor, thrived on the freedom that came with it. Simultaneously, his work 'lightened up'.

When the date path and the name are the same, the strong energy of this pair finds its point of balance at around **48** years of age.

For example, Shirley MacLaine Beaty has a date path and name that are both represented by Number 9. In *Dancing in the Light* she writes something that throws light on the difficulty people experience with extremes of a single energy. "Resistance creates conflict. It causes the energy flow to turn back on itself". When a particular energy is felt intensely, we typically react by resisting it". On the same page Shirley has written: "The energy required to repress feelings causes strain in the body and in the spirit… If you allow any resistance to the flow of energy, you create polarity". Shirley was in her early 50's when she wrote this.

When the date path, name and another number are the same, this intense focus on one particular number creates an energy crisis that can last for up to **60** years.

For example, Jean Henri Dunant, born on May 8, 1828 with name, date path and month 5 must have very restless at times but what he achieved in founding the Red Cross to aid people in extreme crisis has left us an enduring legacy.

When the following are the same, the energy crisis can last for up to 60 years:

Date path, name, and birth day
Date path, name, and birth month
Date path, name, and birth year
Date path, name, and vowel
Date path, name, and consonant

When any 4 numbers are the same, the strain is felt right up until **60** years of age.

Samuel Taylor Coleridge provides an interesting example. His date path was 48/21/12/3, vowel 48, consonant 48 and being born on October 21, 1772 meant that his birth day also reduced to number 3. He was a brilliant poet but he also suffered from mental instability for much of his life. Between

March and August 1834, when he was 61, the 3rd edition of his *Poetical Works* was published in 3 volumes. He died on July 15, 1834 = 48/21/12/3.

<u>When the following are the same, an energy crisis is likely to last for 60 years</u>:

Date path, birth month, birth day, and birth year
Date path, birth month, birth day, and vowel
Date path, birth month, birth day, and consonant
Date path, birth month, birth day, and name
Date path, birth day, birth year, and vowel
Date path, birth day, birth year, and consonant
Date path, birth month, birth day, and name
Date path, birth year, vowel, and consonant
Date path, birth year, vowel, and name
Date path, birth year, consonant and name
Birth month, birth day, birth year, and vowel
Birth month, birth day, birth year, and consonant
Birth month, birth day, birth year, and name
Birth day, birth year, vowel, and consonant
Birth day, birth year, vowel, and name
Birth day, birth year, consonant and name

<u>When the challenges double up</u> i.e. when any two different repeating number patterns occur, the two challenges will run side by side.

For example the famous writer Stephen Edwin King, born on September 21, 1947, has number 3 as his primary birth day, birth year and name, while his primary date path, vowel and consonant are all 6. Each represents a crisis of 48 years. Not at all an easy situation, it seems to have come to a head between the years 44 and 52, i.e., four years either side of 48.

Whereas a 24-year crisis seems to hit its apex almost right on the 24th birthday, these more complex challenges can take a longer period of time to stabilize.

Occasionally, one number crisis runs longer than another does.

For example, William Butlin, born September 29, 1899 = **9**. 29/<u>11</u>. 27/**9** = 56/<u>11</u>/2

Hence, the 9 was only in crisis for 24 years, but the 11 remained in crisis for another 12 years. (It was just after his 36th birthday that Billy opened his first holiday camp).

You should never assume that an energy crisis means that nothing worthwhile can be achieved until a certain age is reached. The given examples and countless other people, in all walks of life, have achieved stunning heights before the age the effected energy balanced itself. An energy crisis actually stimulates creativity, its intensity providing the fuel for great works throughout life. What is noticeable is that it becomes easier to apply after the given age. Certain goals that have been stashed away in your 'wildest dreams portfolio' may suddenly become accessible. To those who have dared to live a full life, the way finally opens up to something wonderful within the realm of the number that has been intensified. If you have a repeating number, read everything you can about it in the interpretive section of this chapter because you will surely experience the full gamut of its expression.

Prioritizing Challenges

Karmic Challenges usually give people the most difficulty.

Challenging Core Numbers: the imbalance caused by repeated core numbers comes next in order of difficulty.

Challenged Core Numbers

This is when one of the core numbers is also a challenge number; it comes third in the order of difficulty.

- When a challenge and a vowel number are the same, the issue is one of allowing your soul to have a say in your life
- When a challenge and a consonant number are the same, an overly active survival instinct might be obstructing the flow of your energy
- When a challenge and the date path are the same, issues may arise related to enacting the ideals that inspired your life, and a change of attitude may be necessary
- When a challenge and the birthday are the same, you might wrestle with the attitude necessary to make your life a success
- When a challenge and the name are the same, the issues that the number represents will affect your energy levels. You might experience a lack of motivation.

The Whole-Life Challenge incorporates challenges 1 and 2 and is therefore somewhat of a triple whammy. It therefore comes next in order of difficulty.

Missing Numbers come next: those numbers that are neither in the name and date charts are energies that you may have trouble 'owning'.

The Most Frequent Challenge: If not already accounted for, the number most frequently appearing in the challenge chart must be considered. Sometimes this frequently appearing number is more of a bother than the 'missing' energies, because most people deny the latter.

The Vowel, Consonant and Name Challenge set come next.

Miscellaneous Numbers can usually be grouped with similar energies such as 3-6-9.

The date path challenges tend to present themselves 'out there' whereas the name challenges represent inner qualities that you need to address. All numbers connected to the date of birth are mental in nature, and so an abundance of one particular number can cause mental agitation. All numbers connected to the name affect your vitality.

Assigning a Total to the Number of Challenges

The exact number of challenges assigned to any particular number is less important than the overall prioritizing of the challenges, and the ability to see how certain challenges relate to each other. The rule of thumb is this: if in doubt, count it as a challenge, because it probably is!

Interpreting the Challenges

Interpreting Karmic Challenges

The date chart provides a clue as the meaning of these karmic challenges (and incidentally, an easy way to remember them).

```
       |   |
       | 5 |
       |(14)|
   ____|___|____
    1  | 4 | 7
   (19)|(13)|(16)
```

With the exception of 14, the karmic numbers sit on the bottom line of the chart like the line of survival intelligence. Number 14 creates a triangular relationship with them and progresses the line of kinesthetic intelligence. Interpreting them as collective issues in need of resolution through individual human beings, reveals that these four numbers comprise a set of issues that touch every life but impact on some more than others.

Karmic 13: The dance of life in which we all share, seems to move one step forward and then a part-step back when number 13 is involved. '13' brings with it a feeling of restriction. Try not to get depressed and give up. That's a part of the lesson here. Remember that in the science of numerology, $13 = 1 + 3 = 4$. This means that you (number 1) must use the powers of your imagination (number 3), to put your ideas into form (number 4). In other words, exercise your imagination and see yourself in the role that you would like, and then work to achieve it. Rather than fantasizing that it should be easy, be prepared for tests and obstacles. You have the courage to overcome whatever life throws at you, but you must allow life to transform you in its own good time: that's number 13 as the pivotal point between survival and kinesthetic intelligence (introverted). The only thing you can control here is your attitude. If you feel like you are working hard and getting nowhere, set yourself a clear and uplifting goal to aim for, and then move steadily towards it. As frustrating as it may be, simply keep plodding along in the desired direction. The collective issue is patience. See date path 13 in chapter 1 for further insight.

Karmic 14: In the science of numerology $14 = 1 + 4 = 5$, which means that you (number 1) can use your ability to impact upon your environment (4), to grow and evolve as other people grow and evolve around you (5), or you can wander around repeating the same mistakes over and over again. At any point in time you can break out of your conditioned thought patterns and create your own opportunities. The cycle of life waxes and then wanes before waxing again, giving you the chance to reflect upon your actions and integrate the lessons you have learned from them. A part of this reflection includes being prepared to let go of unhealthy mental habits. Refusing to reflect on the impact of your actions will cause you ill-health. Number 14 enhances ingenuity within the natural flow of life. It encourages presence of mind regardless of one's circumstances. You can make it work for you by perceiving change as an opportunity to break free of whatever is restricting your natural ability to shine. The collective issue is adaptability, and it relates to the way that we express our thoughts and feelings. Return to date path 14 in chapter 1 for further insight.

Karmic 16: This number portends a crisis: a point within your life, probably during adolescence, when you become totally disillusioned with the dance of life and feel that it is arbitrary, nonsensical and unfair. At that point, you may be able to see the falsehood but not yet the truth. Exacerbating the situation is the paradox that mistrustfulness tends to find itself mirrored in others, and so what can happen is that you find yourself unjustly accused of something. $16 = 1 + 6 = 7$, which means that you (number 1) must seek cohesion in your thinking (6) so that you can become increasingly truthful (7). If your thinking is confused, this will reflect itself in your relationships. Wanton pride is your enemy; introspection your friend. To turn karmic 16 to your advantage, take an impartial look at yourself. Self-honesty will reflect back to you as mutual trust, but you will have to work at it, for love's sake. Contemplate the significance of a single life, however humble that life may seem to be. The collective issue is honesty. Distilling the lies from the truth, changes the whole world. See date path 16 in chapter 1 for further insight.

Karmic 19: This collective issue touches every life, especially the lives of those born when the world numbers began with 19 (i.e. the previous century). It is also relevant to those of you who have it in your personal numbers. What is indicated here is that the noble number one is at risk of being weighed down by a rampant ego, which is inclined to forget that it is the companion of the soul. Just as 1 and 9 are the extremities of the primary digits, so 19 can behave in extreme ways. At one extreme are the people who are so immersed in their own life that they overlook the needs of others. At the other extreme are those who find it difficult to act independently. Either way, you need to clarify the difference between independence and domination. Number 19 will draw your attention to the distinction between healthy versus unhealthy ambition. If you don't make that distinction you could feel like you are flapping around everywhere and getting nowhere. Because 19 has turned up as a priority in your list of challenges, you need to focus on one healthy ambition that is truly your own, and stick with it. Endurance comes with this package, particularly enduring the egotism of other people. You might need to learn how to listen to other people without assuming that your story is more important than theirs is, and without assuming that their story is more important than yours is. The collective issue is the use of personal power to enact the ideal of a united humanity. Once you get a handle on this, you can do awesome things to help the world's people. See date path 19 in chapter 1 for further insight.

Interpreting the Challenge of Repeated Core Numbers

This set of interpretations relate to the challenge of repeated core numbers such as when the birth day and date path are the same, or the vowel and name number, name and birthday, name and date path, vowel and date path, or birthday and vowel.

In your early years you probably ran hot and cold like a heater with a broken thermostat. Feeling yourself becoming 'overheated' and fearful of the consequences, you might have tried to switch the energy off altogether. Naturally there would be times when the 'temperature' was just right. As you grow accustomed to your patterns of behaviour, you learn how to regulate your *inner* thermostat and stay 'just right' for longer periods of time. Extremities of behaviour are then less likely to occur. Read *everything* related to this number because you are likely to experience every nuance of it at some time in your life! The science of energy, of which numerology is a part, offers two complementary ways to direct strong energy. One is to add the numbers together and work with the total (i.e. double it). This could be called the homeopathic remedy. The other technique is to move it up to the next number. This could be called the odds and evens approach because it necessitates shifting from an odd to an even number, or vice-versa. Evens stabilize whilst odds catalyze change. Keep this simple formula in mind when dealing with strong energy patterns. The following advice is based on these techniques within the overall paradigm offered in *Pan's Script*.

Challenging Core Number 1

This is a dynamic energy that symbolizes a busy life. If you were born with challenging core number 1, outbursts of selfishness and even tyranny are likely until you learn how to control your emotions. Conversely, if aggression is feared and repressed, its opposite will appear as the tendency to lean on others instead of standing on your own two feet; but tumbling back into the invisibility of 'nothingness' fools no one, least of all you. Applying the principles of moving to the next number up or doubling the number and working with the total, indicates that there is just one way for you to go and that is to number 2. This means listening to others and relating to their needs in tandem with your own. Life will provide you with ample opportunity to create win-win situations, which you may come to excel at.

Challenging Core Number 2

The problem with 2's in abundance is nervous exhaustion brought on by an abundance of social interaction and insufficient quiet time. This will cause you to do whatever is necessary to protect yourself. One of the most useful questions to ask yourself in a crisis is: "Am I coming from love or fear on this issue?" If you suspect that it might be fear, explore your options further. Resilience in social situations is the challenge here. Avoiding others and falling back on number 1 is a reasonable strategy in some situations but not when it negates intimacy altogether. Whenever possible it is better to move forwards to number 3 and create friendships with a few like-minded people. Doubling the number means acting with integrity and placing the goal of your heart above all else.

Challenging Core Number 3

Challenging core number 3 usually indicates some difficulty in the expression of feelings and ideas in the early years of life, maturing into a great gift through the struggle to master the issue. On the one hand, you need to think before you speak whilst on the other, you need to let people know how you are feeling. The advice offered is to take responsibility for what you say and the effect that it has on other people, but also be aware that a refusal to speak up impacts on others too. You also need to find an outlet for your imagination: some form of creative expression that gives you joy. You will gain even greater satisfaction if your work brings hope and joy to those who need some. If your mind is over-active, i.e. inclined to fly from one thing to another, make a sincere effort to develop one of your interests to a greater level of depth and personal satisfaction. All of the above is one way of interpreting $3 + 3 = 6$, as numerology's homeopathic method of directing strong energy. The other way is to move up to number 4. These two methods are complementary for they both indicate the need to formulate the energy. Use it to give whatever is in your heart, tangible expression. The creation of lyrics to express your ideas and feelings is an ideal way to use the gift that comes with having challenging core number 3.

Challenging Core Number 4

With this challenge tunnel vision or an overwhelming feeling of victimization can spoil the opportunities that number 4 usually brings. If you feel that this applies to you, the advice based on numerology, is this: rather than getting lost in an underground emotional labyrinth, focus your thoughts and inspiration on something of real and practical value to yourself and others. From your rich feeling-life draw forth one clear goal that you can work steadily towards. It is an idea that must feel absolutely right in your heart. Once you have found an activity that gives you enjoyment, talk to other people about it and allow it to take on a life of its own. In other words, rather than trying to control life, give it room to grow organically. By so doing, you would be redirecting any excessive energy into number 5's domain. Moving up to 5 is one way; the other is doubling the 4 to arrive at 8. That would involve getting organized. It could also involve noticing the pattern, order and symbolism in the world around you. Several musicians have a challenging core number 4 including Andrew Lloyd Webber, Antonio Vivaldi, Elmer Bernstein, Hugo Wolf, Itzhak Perlman and Jean Sibelius. The pattern, order, and symbolism through which they direct their strong number 4 energy is rhythm and sound. Whether you are a musician or not, you have the opportunity to bring, pattern, order, organization, and common sense to any field of interest that takes hold of your heart.

Challenging Core Number 5

Challenging core number 5 nearly always accompanies an abundance of people, moving in and out through your front door. If you are working with this energy in a positive way then such people will be strengthened by the friendship they receive from you, and if not, you could be hurting them. The way forward is to find a means to express the tremendous amount of creative energy coursing through you. You move up to number 6 when focus your mind on the practicalities of your interest. Likewise, doubling the 5 suggests that one way to stem the scattering of your energy is to become an authority-figure in one particular field of endeavour.

Challenging Core Number 6

Challenging core number 6 can bring a fanatical sense of responsibility. If this is happening to you, you need to learn that caring for others should either be enjoyed or delegated to someone else. A related aspect of this challenge is criticism. If you find it difficult to function in chaos, you will tend to be critical of it. What you are actually seeking is consistency, for that alone would bestow peace of mind. However you may be looking outside of you for such consistency. It's not 'out-there' that you will find lasting peace but within you. Deal with your inner critic and the rest will fall into place. If you keep a diary you may discover why you take on so much or so little responsibility. This is to evoke number 7 and your innate powers of reflection. Doubling the 6 leads to 12, and that means believing in your ability to reverse your thinking. Your challenge is to maintain peace within you as you negotiate peace within your environment. Define the boundaries of your responsibilities and work vigilantly within those parameters. You have the opportunity to do some fabulously creative work within whatever domain of human endeavour comes most naturally to you.

Challenging Core Number 7

Aloofness and deliberate distancing are difficult to avoid with challenging core number 7. Contrariness is also quite common because 7's are prone to feeling misunderstood. And they very often are! Perhaps you became discrete about your 'differentness', or perhaps you became rebellious; probably both. If you can relate to any of this, aim to reach a point where you can perceive all of nature (including human beings) as a part of one dynamic matrix. By so doing, you effectively move into number 8's domain. You may then find it easier to accept the apparent imperfections in yourself and others. Doubling the number implicates the risk of learning as you go, and daring to move into number 14's realm. This involves reshaping conditioned thought patterns, including your own. At some point you will need to learn how to appreciate the moment at hand. Some people with challenging core number 7 excelled in one particular sport, perhaps because this allows their 'rebel energy' to play itself it. Artist, athlete, or something entirely different, the fact remains that once you are able to survey your environment and see yourself surrounded in beauty, you have discovered the hidden potential inherent in multiple 7's.

Challenging Core Number 8

Relentless once you have set your heart on something, you have what it takes to accomplish those long-term goals that other people allow to fall away. However this comes at the risk of obsession, which can lead to impatience with other people and the general flow of life. When zealousness becomes a substitute for mutually supportive relationships, you need to take a step back to number 7 and do some honest introspection. Significantly, doubling the 8 also results in 7, but a particular 7 - number 16 – and that brings an awakening to the subtle truth behind the natural world. By taking an interest in the bigger picture you move into number 9's realm. Placing your insight on higher ground and sharing it with other people indicates that you've got your abundance of 8's working in the most productive manner. You are a passionate individual and your greatest challenge is honouring the rhythmic cycle of activity and rest. You tend to want to keep going and never stop!

Challenging Core Number 9

Faith in your power to improve the state of the world will take some interesting twists and turns in your life, as you learn how to listen to points of view that conflict with your own. Cultivating *inner* tolerance is essential, along with the ability to perceive that everything has its place in the bigger scheme of things. Watch out for this cycle: fits of superiority and misplaced criticism alternating with bouts of inferiority and self-doubt (when people kick back). In some cases, challenging core number 9 results in hermit- like behaviour. But the spiritual potential here involves becoming a light bearer for others. Moving up to number 10 means letting the example of your life to be the way to effect change. It necessitates finding the courage to stand in your own light. Moving up to 10 involves creating a set of principles upon which you can build your life and upon which you can sustain your contribution to the greater good. Doubling the 9 results in '18' will result in a confrontation with your ego, and you will find it necessary to harness your willpower to a just cause. 9's in abundance is less common than the other numbers in abundance, and there is a higher proportion of spiritual people here than elsewhere. Realizing that as you change yourself, so you change the world is the challenge and opportunity here.

Challenging Master Numbers

The double numbers are very hard on the nervous system and can lead you to fantasy land as a means of escape. Yet fantasy can also enrich your imagination, and when applied to problems, can engender fantastic solutions. Your challenge is to encourage others to listen to such ideas, and if they don't understand, then to find another way to present them. Writing is an important tool to this end but not the only one. Sometimes music is more effective, and music lends itself to the master numbers. You may also need to broaden your circle of friends to include some that are aware that there is more to life that making money. This challenge involves honouring yourself as you learn how to honour the creative spirit in people who may not be able to understand a word you say. The challenge and the opportunity that the master numbers lay before you is to tap into a futuristic impulse and bring it into the present-day world.

Interpreting the Whole-Life Challenge

The term 'whole-life' is a deliberate play on words because in order to feel whole, this is a number that you must master, even if it takes you an entire lifetime to do so. Challenges 1 and 2 inform the whole-life challenge. As you work on this triad of challenges, the ideal encoded in your date path takes shape.

Whole-Life Challenge 1

With 1 as your whole-life challenge, you will find that circumstances force you to take charge of your life. The case histories reveal that if the willpower to become your own person is sufficiently strong, you could become very successful. However, if you are having trouble getting off the starting block, keep in mind that 'confidence comes not from always being right, but from not fearing being wrong'. The challenge is to create an intelligent set of guidelines that are authentically yours, and which allow others their rights without suppressing your own. You must determine the principles that you live by. Number 1 is the most common challenge and so here are some signs that you are working with the gifts that it promises to unfold:

- Daring to be true to your own, unique nature
- Refusing to see yourself as a victim to life circumstances
- Doing something that no-one has done before
- Pioneering new ideas
- Becoming a leader in your chosen field of expertise

<u>Whole-Life Challenge 2</u>

With 2 as your whole-life challenge, it is through partnerships that your date path matures. Such partnerships may in themselves be challenging yet to the extent that you are willing to keep working on your partnerships, so the potential of challenge number 2 can unfold. Challenge 2 usually involves a husband, wife or lover as the significant partner. Sometimes a love partner is supporting or challenging you on the one hand, while a business partner is supporting or challenging you on the other. The way to meet this challenge is to become a very good listener and work out how you can *both* win. Conversely, challenge 2 may put you in a situation where you must learn how to *receive* help from others. Either way, with 2 as a challenge, the patience and consideration that you give to others will be a critical factor in your life. The way that you react to your personal relationships will be a vital shaping force within your date path.

Challenge number 2 is almost as common as challenge number 1 and they often run side-by-side. Here are some signs that you are working with its gifts:

- Daring to be intimate with another human being
- Refusing to be someone else's doormat or punching bag
- Co-operating effectively with another person in a joint project
- Reaching out for support or advice when you need it
- Standing by your own set of values despite any opposition you may encounter

<u>Whole-Life Challenge 3</u>

With 3 as your whole-life challenge the ease with which your date path unfolds is dependent on the way that you express your personal ideals. If you are shy and fearful of criticism, you can recover your natural spontaneity by being genuinely enthusiastic about something. Many gifted speakers have this challenge and there is not a single case where it was easy.

Dale Carnegie provides one such example. Born on November 24, 1888, his small challenge set was 4 – 1 – 3 - 5 while his big challenge set was 13 – 1 – 12 - 14, the larger numbers providing specific information as to the nature of the shaping forces within his life. Not only was Dale's whole life challenge 3, but so were his name challenge and consonant challenge and so the pressure was really on. He seems to have taken this challenge to heart, becoming an exceptional trainer in the art of communication.

If you find it difficult to speak in public, here are some tips: observe accomplished speakers, attend personal development classes, rehearse, ask questions, and be willing to learn. Set your sights on a goal that you can focus your enthusiasm upon, and learn everything you can about your topic of interest. With number 3 as one of your challenges, it is the way that you express your thoughts, ideas and feelings that will make all the difference to the way that your date path unfolds.

Whole-Life Challenge 4

Whole-life challenge 4 typically presents a situation that rocks a person's sense of security. This catalyzes the need to determine your own means of survival in the material world. This challenge also turns up for people who live in the realm of ideas, prodding them to work towards materializing those ideas. Challenge 4 demands practicality. You need to set yourself tangible goals if you want to see your dreams become a reality.

Natural scientist, Alexander Humboldt, born on September 14, 1769, provides an example. His small challenges were encoded in the set of numbers 4 – 0 – 4 - 4, whilst his big challenges were represented by the pattern 5 – 9 – 4 - 14. Not content with merely reading about them, he led expeditions to the places he wanted to study. He was deeply moved by nature, sensing the immanence of the creator within it. Humboldt perceived a beauty and an order unnoticed by his contemporaries. He organized his ideas and observations into books with beautiful, accurate illustrations. Through his talks, Humboldt helped people to see nature through their feelings and their senses, and he understood the influence of such sensations on the moral development of his listeners.

Humboldt's life suggests ways of working productively with challenge number 4, wherever it appears. Dedication is the keyword. Study the ideals in your date path and create a 'dedication' based on them.

Whole-Life Challenge 5

Whole-life challenge 5 attracts circumstances that force you to deal with continual change. Life will invite you to put your talents to work within whatever circumstances you happen to find yourself in.

Sister Mackillop provides an example. Born on January 15, 1842, her small challenges were 5-0-5-5 while her big challenges were 14-0-14-14. Number 14 as a specific type of 5, tells us that reshaping entrenched thought patterns was a big challenge for her. And indeed it was, because her efforts to improve things were constantly hampered by the chauvinism of the priests. Time and again Mary was tempted to escape to an easier life, yet she persisted and defied the odds.

With 5 as a challenge, you are learning to make the most of opportunities as they arise in your life. It is mental dexterity that you need to cultivate. The ability to maintain faith in the task that you have set yourself, and faith in your ability to cope with whatever it brings you, will shape the way that the ideals in your date path materialize.

Whole-Life Challenge 6

With number 6 as your whole-life challenge, life will present you with the struggle to meet the expectations of other people and force you to discern the boundaries of your personal responsibility. The existential issue here is coherence versus chaos. You may find chaos difficult to live with, yet you will test its boundaries. And you are likely to probe other people's theories and ideas for inconsistencies, before sharing your own. Self-expression is therefore a critical factor to your success. You must learn how to shape your ideas and images so that they can be readily understood by other people. The feedback that you receive can then be used to modify your thoughts and springboard future developments.

Barry Humphries provides an example. Born on February 17, 1934, his small challenges are 6 – 0 – 6 - 6 and big challenges 15 – 0 – 15 - 15, the zero amplifying the 6 in general and 15 in particular. Number 6 materializes through our collective projections and the challenge of number 6 is to work creatively with these as Barry has done.

Through number 6 you are learning how to create solutions that engender harmony. Maintaining peace within yourself while attempting to create peace within your environment is therefore crucial to your success. Understanding that what you regard as reality is conditional upon the theory you subscribe to, will shape the way that the ideals in your date path unfold.

Whole-Life Challenge 7

With number 7 as your whole-life challenge, it is the way that you relate to other people that shapes your date path. By participating in relationships, of all kinds, your mind develops the power to reflect; to weigh things up, and to make decisions. This in turn leads to insight and understanding, and ultimately a peaceful state of mind.

An example is Sarah Frances Durack, born October 27, 1889; small challenges 8 – 1 – 7 - 7, big challenges 17 – 1 – 16 - 16. Sarah (better known as Fanny) wanted to swim in the Olympic Games but she had to confront powerful administrators who were hell bent on stopping her (challenge 8). She had to have tremendous faith in herself and her goal in order to get *to* the starting block let alone off it! (challenge 1). But she persisted, and the people who believed in her raised the funds. She did not let them down. She won the very first Gold Medal for female swimmers. By so doing she not only did something that had not been done before but something that had been severely frowned on in her day (competitive swimming was considered a men's-only domain). Her courage in the face of such adversity paved the way for others. Whole-life challenge 7 accompanies another theme as well. In every one of the case studies there was a secret sorrow in the life; something that had to be 'laid to rest' in a manner of speaking. (In Fanny's case this was the inability to have children).

The twin themes – being different and bearing a secret sorrow – will encourage you to promote a cause rather than yourself, and by so doing, you may become a specialist in your chosen field of endeavour. With number 7 as a challenge, your success hinges on being able to apply differentness to your advantage. Courage and self-honesty are vital to the process.

Whole Life-Challenge 8

With 8 as your whole-life challenge, you may have to confront oppression, jealousy or persecution, in the name of becoming a wiser and more resourceful person, whether you like it or not. In other words, life is presenting you with the opportunity to realize the depths of your potential and the omnipresence of your soul. The existential issue here is feeling powerful versus feeling powerless, and the way that you resolve this will shape the ideals in your date path.

Whole-life challenge 8 means that you have only zero and 8 in the small challenge set, the zero amplifying the impact of the 8 both positively and negatively. For example, Edgar Allan Poe, born on January 19, 1809, small challenges 0-8-8-8 and big challenges 18-1-17-17, was described by all of his biographers as his own worst enemy.

With 8 as a challenge, you have a real need for privacy because it is only within the tranquillity of your own company that you can tap into the depths of your soul. You also benefit from routine and ritual as these help to unify your outer and inner worlds. '8' involves recognizing that the law of cause and effect works on all planes of existence.

Whole-Life Challenge 9

As a challenge, number 9 can only appear when the numbers are left intact (i.e., not reduced before subtracting). Number 9 broadens or generalizes the implications of any other number in the series so that it becomes increasingly universal in its expression.

In the case of Sri Amritanandamayi, born on September 27, 1953, all of the small challenges are represented by zero and the big challenges by 9, including 18. This means that *everything* she does has far-reaching implications.

With 9 as a challenge it is your ability to think big and think generously that will unfold the ideals in your date path. Challenge 9 anywhere in the set, is inviting you to explore *every* facet of the other numbers in your challenge set within a worldly context. With number 9 on board you must always keep your eye on the bigger picture.

Whole-Life Challenge 0

Zero: A line prolonged infinitely in one direction, eventually to return to its starting point via its opposite direction. Like such line, you are being challenged to extend yourself as far as you can in one direction, while being prepared to, at some point, turn around and explore a completely opposing point of view.

Thomas Edison provides an example. Born on February 11, 1847, his small challenges were all zeros while his big challenges were 9 – 9 – 0 - 18. During his lifetime he was granted more than one thousand patents for his work (or work done by his team), and so he certainly explored his potential! Having initially wasted his time creating something that no one wanted to buy, he decided he would not invent anything unless there was a market for it. Yet he refused to patent one of his medical breakthroughs, the fluoroscope, so that people would not have to wait to benefit from it. That's where we see the influence of the number 9 shining through.

Challenge 0 is inviting you to explore *every* facet of the other numbers in your challenge set. With zero issuing a challenge, you will not feel completely at peace until you decide upon your central goal in life and then explore it from every possible angle. Study the implications of your date path thoroughly.

Interpreting Polarity Challenges

The polarity challenge resonates throughout life but its relevance increases with age. Being calculated from the date of birth, we know that the issue it represents is essentially mental or attitudinal in nature. It encodes both a warning and an opportunity, which, as you advance in age, will become increasingly relevant. Like the whole-life challenge, the following interpretations can be applied to other challenges calculated from the date of birth and thus related to the ideals encoded in your date path. Occasionally the polarity challenge is distinct from the other three in the set, which suggests that it has a unique contribution to make in relation to the date path. When the numbers are left intact (i.e. not reduced before subtracting); numbers greater than 9 sometimes appear. In such cases, you can read the primary number below and then consult chapter 1 for further details.

Polarity Challenge 1

Polarity challenge number 1 warns you to listen to your inner guidance and determine your own course of action. This challenge represents the need to progress in one specific direction, and become an 'expert' in your chosen field of endeavour. If you set your mind to it, you could pioneer a whole new idea.

Polarity Challenge 2

Polarity challenge number 2 warns you to never assume that you know how another person is feeling. This challenge represents the need for a mutually supportive relationship but you will have to work at it. You are learning to listen to other people and you are learning ways to have them listen to you. Valuing the significant people in your life and loving them, despite your personal reaction to them, is the challenge here.

Polarity Challenge 3

Number 3 warns that a few thoughtless words can escalate into huge misunderstandings. This challenge represents the need to link up with people who share similar ideals to you, but you will only find them if you speak up! If you give your imagination an airing and exercise your powers of self-expression you could make a real difference to other people.

Polarity Challenge 4

Number 4 warns you to maintain integrity at all times despite the temptation to do otherwise. Be sure to read all contracts carefully. Challenge 4 represents the need to be prepared for contingencies; to be practical and take the necessary precautions. If you pay attention to the details, the work that you commit yourself to could have a lasting impact.

Polarity Challenge 5

Number 5 warns that dealing with constant change is something that you will have to get used to. This challenge represents the need to adapt. If you maintain your centeredness, you will find that things usually fall into place of their own accord. Challenge 5 will encourage you to spot your opportunities and make the most of them.

Polarity Challenge 6

Number 6 warns that living up to the expectations of other people could become an issue for you. If you feel burdened at times by the weight of your responsibilities, check that you are not subconsciously attracting this experience from a need to feel appreciated, as this often the case with number 6. You cannot be everything to everybody. Challenge 6 represents the need to define the boundaries of your responsibilities so that you can work effectively within those boundaries.

Polarity Challenge 7

Number 7 warns that you are likely to find yourself out on a limb and in a situation that you can honestly say is not entirely your own making. Yet it may cause you to doubt yourself, which will lead to inertia and perhaps even depression for a while. The only way to avoid this situation or mitigate its impact is to be ruthlessly honest with yourself. You are probably well aware that you are different to other people in some way, and so what you need to do is to align that 'differentness' with a solid sense of purpose. Think about the unique advantages that your 'differentness' offers you.

Polarity Challenge 8

Number 8 warns about the use and abuse of power. The key question is: how do you want people to remember you: as a bully, victim, survivor, or<fill in the gap here>; the choice is yours. Think very carefully about your legacy. Once you are clear about this, you need to get organized. Prioritize your goals around your core values. Network with other people and let them know what you have decided to do. Wherever number 8 appears the effective management of one's personal resources (internal and external) is mandatory to success.

Polarity Challenge 9

Only possible when working with the higher numbers, polarity challenge 9 indicates that the themes contained within the other numbers in your challenge set will be generalized so that they are given the broadest possible application. Occasionally the entire set is represented by number 9, signifying the need for honesty regarding 'the myth' upon which you are basing your life. The meaning you attribute to our collective co-existence is critical to your success.

Polarity Challenge 0

With zero as your polarity challenge, you have the opportunity to do more than you ever thought possible. But be prepared for the 'unexpected'; you must embrace this as a part of your life's journey. Zeros amplify the other numbers in the challenge set. It is the other number (usually there is only one other number involved) that specifies the nature of your challenge. Explore every nuance of it.

Interpreting the Challenge of Missing Numbers

When a number is neither in the date chart or name chart it means that its energy is not operating in the 1-9 range. The ideal that the number represents probably appeals to you, but you may experience difficulty actualizing it. A missing number is not a blind spot. You are aware of it, but you tend to rationalize your lack of motivation to work on the issue involved. Because missing numbers implicate both the date of birth and the name, not only will your attitude be affected, but your vitality as well. The case studies revealed that missing numbers indicate a decisive factor in the life, for they are latent powers, which if unlocked, grant an extraordinary quality to you, provided that the attached warning label has been understood. The gift inherent in a missing number is not likely to fully manifest until your second Saturn return (around 60 years of age) and only then if you have been truly wrestling with it. But don't make the mistake of thinking that this means you will perform poorly in this domain before such time. Actually you will probably perform well because you work so damn hard at the issue involved; but you are likely to run hot and cold, going full pelt and then collapsing with exhaustion, or getting in a temper, or feeling terrible despair. Such reactions stabilize at around 60.

Missing numbers are not uncommon. You are twice as likely to have at least one missing number as you are to have no missing numbers.

One technique for accessing the energy of a missing number is to turn to the next number down and come at it from that angle. It is easier to go back to the familiar rather than forward to the unknown. For example, if number 2 were missing you could go back to number 1, strengthen that, and then approach '2' from that perspective. In keeping with the hypothesis advanced in chapter 6, missing 2 is actually trying to operate at its higher octave: 11. There is a pattern that states this in a simple formula:

'Missing 1' means going back to zero in order to materialize number 10.
'Missing 2' means going back to number 1 in order to materialize number 11.
'Missing 3' means going back to number 2 in order to materialize number 12.
'Missing 4' means going back to number 3 in order to materialize number 13.
'Missing 5' means going back to number 4 in order to materialize number 14.
'Missing 6' means going back to number 5 in order to materialize number 15.
'Missing 7' means going back to number 6 in order to materialize number 16.
'Missing 8' means going back to number 7 in order to materialize number 17.
'Missing 9' means going back to number 8 in order to materialize number 18.

We will now apply this formula to interpreting each missing number.

<u>Missing Number 1</u>

Returning to zero in order to materialize number 10

From the year 2000 it became possible to have no 1's in either name or date chart. When number 1 is missing there is less demand from the ego to prove itself in the material world. You are motivated from within rather than without. Rather than competing with others, you are more likely to compete with yourself and to try to improve your own performance in every way possible. This is how you move forward. Exploring your potential is equivalent to 'going back to zero'. Starting from scratch you can construct a set of principles that you want to live by. That's number 1 stepping up to number 10. People with missing number 1 are only in their early teens or younger, and so no examples can be offered here. However it is likely that some of these young people will mature into courageous individuals: people who will be remembered for their bravery. Some will even be described as heroes or heroines and they will inspire courage in others.

Missing Number 2

Returning to number 1 in order to materialize number 11

Impossible after the year 1999 and uncommon before that, missing number 2 indicates that the idea of working cooperatively with other people probably appeals to you but you may have difficulty accommodating all of the emotions that go along with it. You tend to fall back on number 1, which is okay provided that you don't give up on relationships altogether. Ironically, learning how to stand on your own two feet can enrich your appreciation of other people. Case studies reveal that when a person with missing number 2 unites with a group of like-minded souls and contributes to the group's development, happiness tends to follow them. Quality biographies and historical fiction will also help you to empathize with other people and understand what motivates them.

The extraordinary potential here can be seen through the life of Rolihlahla (the original name of Nelson Mandela), who forged a workable partnership between black and white South Africans. Number 2 was missing in both his name and date of birth yet his interpersonal skills were the keynote of his life.

The latent gift of missing 2 is to listen to both sides of a story and then unite the opposing factions by establishing common ground. Such common ground needs to include a vision shared by both sides; that's where number 11 enters the equation. The high incidence of scientists with missing 2 suggests that listening to both sides must be applied to listening to scientists who oppose your ideas, again with the view to establishing common ground. Number 2 is also about listening to the land.

Missing Number 3

Returning to number 2 in order to materialize number 12

Shyness is common when number 3 is missing. You may admire the ideal of effective communication but have difficulty practicing it in daily life. You can meet this challenge by keeping company with, and observing, people who have 3's in abundance. If you find yourself frustratingly tongue tied when you want to express your ideas, keep in mind that there is no quicker way to overcome the fear of speaking your truth than to be clear on what your truth is. Arm yourself with information and become an expert in your chosen field of interest or endeavour. Savour it from every angle, ask questions, exercise your imagination, seek advice, and meet contradictory evidence and opinions as opportunities for further growth and development.

An example is Ingrid Bergman. She was a shy child, who realized during her early adolescence that she could perform convincingly. Enthusiasm for acting, concentration and goodwill gradually melted her shyness. An initial step was the adoption of a role model. The right role model provides a bridge for this energy to move from the mental realm to the physical one. If your role model is a person who helps you to see yourself in a whole new way, then you have moved into number 12's domain. You are then not far from doing the same for someone else.

Acting and related fields score well here but the strongest representation of missing 3 comes from the sciences. Number 3 also scored well as an intensity number (per chapter 3), warning us not to interpret missing numbers as inverse to intensity numbers. Missing or intense, number 3 encourages people to ask questions and probe for answers, which is what the sciences are all about. It could be that people with missing 3 feel driven to work harder at communicating than people who have lots of them. Writers and spiritual people are also well represented in both categories. Not so in the arts where there is a clear contrast between an intensity number and a missing number: 3 scored higher in the fine arts than other intensity numbers but lowest as missing number 3. This is the type of contrast one might expect between missing and intensity numbers yet it only showed up in this one profession. In all cases please remember that this is only one factor in your astronumerology and that mitigating factors are entirely possible. However you choose to apply it what you have here is a latent gift.

Missing Number 4

Returning to number 3 in order to materialize number 13

The danger here is that people with missing 4's can adopt a utilitarian view of life, in which people (and other life forms) become objects in whatever system, goal or strategy they have thought up. Missing 4 is characterized by a fear of chaos and let's face it: life is can be extremely chaotic at times! Try as you might to put things in order, there is always going to be something or someone who messes things up. Proceeding towards number 13 involves allowing life to transform you (instead of trying to control it).

One in eight people have a missing 4 in their numbers and so they are not uncommon. All occupations are represented but there is an interesting relationship between sport and science here. As an intensity number, 4 scored highest in sport whereas as a missing number, 4 scored lowest. In keeping with the formative forces associated with number 4, having lots of 4's would aid body building and maintenance. If you are a keen sportsperson (and there are some top sporting stars with missing 4), your prowess is not coming from your missing 4 but another factors in your astronumerology. Sheer grit brings out the best of number 4's qualities and could take you to greater heights than those people who find mastering the necessary skills comes easily to them. Conversely as an intensity number, 4 scored below average in science whereas as a missing number, 4 scored highest.

An example of a scientist with '4' as his only missing number is George Keith Batchelor. Renowned for his contribution to fluid mechanics, he has been selected here because of the relationship between number 4 and the dynamics of earth and water. Fluid dynamics, which was George's speciality, is the natural science of fluids in motion. It studies the effect of forces on fluid motion. People with missing number 4 may find that it has much to teach them if they are willing to broaden the principles involved. The Archimedes principle would be a good place to start.

Several very famous classical musicians had number 4 missing in both their date of birth and their name including Franz List, Franz Schubert and Johann Sebastian Bach. Writers are well represented by all of the missing numbers but the interesting finding here was that several of the missing 4 writers wrote for children such as Annie Julia Johnston, Elizabeth Jane Coatsworth and Helen Beatrix Potter.

If number 4 is missing in your name and date of birth, spend time outside observing the natural world, and feeling a part of it. Do it with friends and you are working in number 3's domain. Rituals related to the cycle of the seasons will further help you. Notice how things change and evolve yet within a continual cycle. Then think about how this applies to your own life. You might even come to appreciate the laws that exist behind sudden and apparently senseless change. Applying what you have learned to initiating systems, strategies, literary forms, and scientific paradigms that transform people's lives for the better, is to work with missing number 4 as a gift.

<u>Missing Number 5</u>

Returning to number 4 in order to materialize number 14

The issue here is adaptability. You may want to 'go with the flow' but you find it really difficult. Perhaps that's because deep down you feel uncentered or insecure. In chapter 6 we noted that 'no 5' means 'no barrier' against all of the environmental influences that bombard the senses. This could lead to feeling overwhelmed much of the time. Applying the 'back to 4' principle, you must firmly establish the ground on which you stand. Ask yourself "What *really* matters? Where can I bend? Where must I stand strong?" Number 4 on the astral plane infused with the agenda of number 5 suggests shaping your ideas into some form of art but please interpret the word 'art' broadly.

Proceeding towards number 14 involves reshaping ideas that have become outmoded, without discarding those that still have value to you. Converting frustrated creativity into creative genius would require a change of attitude though. It might also require a change of heart. Increasing levels of adaptability will follow as you learn to accept the ebb and flow that is life and ride *with* its currents (rather than against them).

This missing number is quite rare: only .5% of people have missing 5 with no other missing number. In the *Pan's Script* data pool of one thousand people, these included Ada Norris who was a teacher and community welfare worker. She founded the UNAA National Status of Women Network and was awarded the UN Nobel Peace Prize, Dorothy Parker, a writer, critic and satirist, best known for her wit, wisecracks, and eye for 20th Century urban foibles, Gustav Klimt, symbolist painter, whose works are marked by a frank eroticism, Judith Durham, lead vocalist for *The Seekers*, and Lidia Bastianich, celebrity chef, author, television host and restaurateur. Such examples along with those people who had more than one missing number cover most professions except acting. Actors typically have lots of 5's. Number 5 encourages a person to take centre stage and showcase their talents. However, the above examples demonstrate that you can do this even when number 5 is missing. This is because your astronumerology is more than one factor. You may have a missing 5 but plenty of fire in your horoscope or number 5 may turn up at a certain time in your life, as a base or attainment – the subject of the next chapter.

Missing Number 6

Returning to number 5 in order to materialize number 15

The idea of a harmonious and loving home, family and work environment appeals to you but you have to work hard on yourself to materialize it. Because there is no direct passage through the astral realm, the energy that number 6 represents will slip into the number 5 stream and attempt to get through there. This will make you a bit of a rebel. Along life's journey you will probably come to realize that although people should be free to make up their own mind about things, opportunities can be lost without a tangible ideal to hold people together. You therefore need to create reasonable expectations for yourself and make sensible projections into the future. You will find that having a missing 6 then becomes an advantage, because once you commit to the task, you will create 'scaffolding' rather than rigid edifices for your ideas. These convenient frameworks suffice to grant you and your loved ones, a sense of security while remaining flexible enough to be negotiated and adjusted at any time.

Once the art of working in number 5's realm is effectively applied to number 6's agenda, you will then be able to proceed towards number 15 and begin to perceive something you once never thought possible: that there *is* harmony within the chaos of life on Earth! When such insight is communicated, or simply demonstrated by your example, it soothes other people's anxieties as well.

Numbers 6, 7 and 8 are the most common missing numbers. Approximately 16% of people have number 6 missing in both their date of birth and name. The statistics reveal that missing numbers – all and any – aid the work of writers and scientists. In Jules Verne we witness a combination of both. One of the founders of science fiction, '6' was his only missing number. He called his literary invention a *Roman de la Science* (novel of science). It allowed him to combine factual information, meticulously researched, from history, geography, science and technology with an engaging fictional story. His goal was to depict the earth and at the same time achieve the ideal of beauty and style in literature. By so doing he provided 'scaffolding' for modern science fiction.

Missing Number 7

Returning to number 6 in order to materialize number 16

The issue here is honesty, and this is not something achieved by isolating yourself from people. You need to learn the nature of dishonesty by witnessing it in other people. That means going back to number 6 and reflecting on your own behaviour in comparison to others. When you allow the dishonesty within yourself to fall away, you have stepped up to number 16.

'7' is the most common missing number: one in five people have a missing 7. The data pool turned up a 'group' of unusual people, from all walks of life, who can only be categorized as unique in some way. Their names ring out through the pages of history as 'one of a kind': Abraham Lincoln, Charles Darwin, King James I & IV, JRR Tolkien, John Lennon, Karl Marx, Neville Bonner, Louis Braille, George Burns, Tennessee Williams and Swami Vivekananda: all people whose only missing number is 7. At some time during their lives, each of these people would have felt 'different' – strange even – and at odds with their social surroundings and themselves. This would have resulted in lapsing back into 6 at times and trying to fit in with the collective consciousness. But each had a 'secret self' or at least some offbeat ideas, which they feared, would be rejected by the mainstream of society.

Similarly, you are an abstract or critical thinker that can spot dishonesty anywhere, and so fitting cozily into the collective seldom works for you. This paradoxical state of mind will torment you for as long as it takes for you to feel comfortable with having 'strange ideas' about things. Eventually you must come out of the closet and launch yourself into an uncharted realm with only your daemon to guide you, or lapse into hypocrisy. The successful people with missing 7 – and there are many – remain quietly faithful to a greater sense of purpose regardless of the changes going on around them. Establishing a joyful relationship with the natural world assists such development.

<u>Missing Number 8</u>

Returning to number 7 in order to materialize number 17

The idea of power intrigues you yet you tend to reject your personal power and make philosophical statements to justify yourself. (That's 8 hiding behind number 7). But this issue cannot leave you alone because the power emanating from the creative life force within you begs integration within the psyche, and so power - personal and collective - cannot simply be edited out of existence. Because the number 8 has to pass through number 7 to reach ground level, you need to be honest about what 'power' means to you. Number 7 acts like a taskmaster here, prodding you to reject dishonesty wherever it turns up. The most difficult part of this challenge is confronting the dishonesty within yourself, and this will be most evident whenever you claim that you are impotent to change an existing situation (and it is clear to everyone else that you *do* have a choice, at least in the attitude you adopt). Personal sacrifice is always a part of '17', and here it means sacrificing whatever is false or self-deceiving so that the truth can shine forth. Only love can measure up to this task.

Missing 8 is quite common, which implies that lots of people are struggling with the issue of power. It turned up equally in all fields of endeavour, spurring people on to greatness. Scientists and writers were again well-represented as per other missing numbers but here they were joined by actors, musicians, sporting stars, activists and politicians, the spiritually minded and a miscellaneous cluster of others, including Prince George who will surely have to deal with the issue of power as he matures.

'Missing 8' often accompanies a fascination with symbolism, which has a necessary place in helping you to understand the truth about power. The data relating to intensity number 8 (chapter 3) suggests that music is a form of symbolic language and so if you are struggling with issue of power there may be a way that music can help you. An effective symbolic system, whether it be music or whether it takes some other form, could help you express yourself in powerful and productive ways. The strong representation of successful actors, activists, sporting icons (including dancers), and spiritual leaders suggest further ways of dealing with the issue of power.

Missing Number 9

Returning to number 8 in order to materialize number 18

The idea of making the world a better place is definitely on your mind but you must get passed thinking that it is going to happen in some distant future and realize that the deeds of the future are incubating within you right now. The states of consciousness encoded in all missing numbers take time to develop and none more so than the number 9. The idealism that number 9 symbolizes must find its way through the depth sounding of the number 8 before it surfaces, but when it eventually does what is expressed may be wisdom of the most profound kind. However you must acknowledge any wild generalizations and prejudices that you are harbouring and reconcile them in a complete and meaningful philosophy that gives you faith in adversity and works in the world for the good of all people.

'9' is the rarest of the missing numbers. There were only twelve examples in the *Pan's Script* data pool but that could be because much of that pool comes from the 20th Century. Maybe this Century will bring more. One example from times long ago was Emanuel (later Immanuel) Kant. He was to become a great philosopher but his philosophy did not emerge easily; his *First Critique* taking eleven years to formulate. One biographer noted that when Kant first began to write he was a 'wild thinker', impetuous and fired up with all sorts of prejudices. This represents the number 18, towards which 'missing 9' is moving, but in an immature stage of development. Bear in mind that '18' is about initiating and organizing powerful works that benefit humanity and the environment of which we are all a part. With time you will be able to formulate an ideal that applies as much to you as to those around you, and express it in a way that appeals to others.

Runs of Missing Numbers

Occasionally several missing numbers appear when the date chart and name chart are compared and sometimes these are consecutive, such as 7 and 8. The guideline for interpretation remains the same: missing numbers represent a latent mental power that will seek 'ground floor' via the first number available to them.

An interesting example is newspresenter Barbara Jill Walters, born on September 25, 1931. The numbers 4, 6, 7 and 8 are all missing from her name and date charts. Currently in her 70's Barbara shows no sign of slowing down, the pleasure of her work overriding fatigue. This is missing 4 coming through number 3 (self-expression), enabling her to act as a transforming agent within society (13). Missing 6, 7 and 8 must all be 'earthed' through number 5. In Barbara's case this has given her versatility on the job and adaptability in relationships. Another gift emanating from this set of numbers is that she can navigate her way around an interviewee's perspective on personal responsibility (6), truth (7) and power (8). All three numbers, operating as they are on the mental plane, are contributing towards the materialization of numbers 15, 16 and 17 and have undoubtedly helped Barbara to appreciate the complexities of life.

During their period of incubation, which can be a considerable length of time, missing numbers tend to cause troublesome 'oversights' in your day to day dealings with other people. You must be firm yet patient with yourself as these latent powers mature. A missing number is usually present somewhere in your astronumerology. It could be your date path number, name, vowel, consonant, maturity, growth or birth day number. If it is not there, look for it in your birth month or birth year. In the next chapter it will become apparent that these two numbers can indicate *when* aid is likely to turn up to support the development of your missing number. Occasionally a missing number turns up nowhere in a person's numerology. In such cases, you must look to your horoscope for clues.

Locating the 'missing' energy within your astronumerology and understanding its significance, means that with a little prompting from life and the people you share it with, you will be able to mobilize your inner resources and convert this quality from a weakness to a strength. The struggle to come to terms with a weakness in your behaviour brings the issue into focus, and when you make a commitment to work with it, the way clears and the potential becomes actualized, sometimes in an extraordinary way. Children born in the early part of the third millennium may have several missing numbers. We can therefore predict that they will be 'late bloomers' and whilst they may do fabulous things during the first part of their lives, the second half of their lives will be even greater. But there is a proviso, and that is self-honesty. These gifts only unfold through honest introspection. You must first of all admit the 'weakness' of the ungrounded number and be willing to do something about it. The energy will then follow the way of your intentions.

Challenged Core Numbers

Each core number must be checked to see if it is the same as any of your challenge numbers.

If any challenge is the same as your date path, at least 40% of your mental energy will be engaged in agenda related to the number involved.

If any challenge is the same as your name, about 30% of your vital energy will be affected.

If any challenge is the same as your vowel, at least 10% of your emotional energy will be engaged in agenda represented by that particular number.

If any challenge is the same as your consonant, at least 10% of your energy will be in 'survival mode' per your consonant number.

If any challenge is the same as your birth day, at least 10% of your mental energy will be wrestling with the agenda of your birth day number.

If two percentages are identical, give priority to any karmic numbers or master numbers that might be involved and then the date path, name, vowel, and birth day.

In each case the state of consciousness represented by the particular number involved will exert a considerable shaping force upon your life.

Interpreting the Vowel, Consonant and Name Challenges

Whilst the challenges emanating from the date inform the mental attitude necessary to work with these forces in a constructive way, the challenges emanating from the name inform matters that impact on your sense of well-being. The vowel, consonant, and name challenges highlight issues that are likely to impact on your health and vitality. Listed below are some of the ways that a challenge might present itself. People who are severely stressed by the repetition of a number may exhibit some of the extreme qualities at times. Occasionally the energy will turn in on itself, particularly if repeated. This is similar to the hot and cold effect noted in the repeated core numbers section of this chapter. In most cases a mid-range interpretation is adequate. The best-case scenario is that the qualities represented by these challenges will bring out the best in you as you rise to meet them. The name challenges are more immediate and personal than the date path challenges. While the latter shapes your ideals, the former shapes your character. The following name challenge interpretations can be applied equally to your vowel and consonant challenges.

<u>Name Challenge 1</u>

Extreme – megalomania and egoism

Stressed – aggression, punitiveness and self-righteousness

Mid-range – bossiness, impatience, and single-mindedness (positive & negative)

Turned inward – cowardice, lack of initiative and slavishly looking to others for answers

The fear to be overcome is of being nothing and nobody (i.e. slipping back to 0).

Advice: find your inner authority, which is your authentic self, align with it, and stick fast to it. Examine your motives and ask yourself why you choose certain actions over others. Is what you do motivated by the highest and best within you?

The potential – initiative, decisiveness, and the courage to act upon your convictions

Sample Interpretation – extreme - Adolf Hitler

Number 4 challenged vowel 3

Number 5 challenged consonant 8

<u>Number 1</u> challenged name 11

His longing to feel a part of a group of like-minded people (vowel 3) was challenged by hatred and tunnel vision (challenge 4). His innate efficiency and tenacity (consonant 8) were challenged by recklessness (challenge 5). The drive to act as inspiration to others (name 11) was challenged by megalomania and egoism (challenge 1). In this extreme case the name challenge exaggerated the vowel and consonant challenges and polarized them instead of uniting them. It didn't need to be that way. His longing to feel a part of a group of like minded people, his innate efficiency, and his drive to act as an inspiration to others, could have been enriched by the initiative, decisiveness and courage associated with name challenge 1.

Name Challenge 2

Extreme – paranoia, vindictiveness, and slyness

Stressed – fearfulness, jealousy, and possessiveness

Mid-range – indecisiveness caused by repressed emotions and the need for approval. There may also be an inclination to pry, inappropriately, into the affairs of others.

Turned inward – delusions about yourself and insensitivity to others

The fear is of being alone, completely abandoned like a babe in the woods.

Advice: case studies turn up a strong connection to the mother in some way. Sometimes this accompanies a feeling of betrayal and sometimes obligation. Whatever happened, it colours relationships and may cause fantasies to arise as a substitute for unresolved issues. if this is your situation you need to name this for what it is, because only then will you be free to move on; (the verbalization of one's feelings being equivalent to stepping up to number 3).

The potential – the ability to give and receive love in a mutually supportive way.

Sample Interpretation – stressed – Charles John Huffham Dickens

Number 4 challenged vowel 3

Number **2** challenged consonant 4

Number **2** challenged name 7.

his longing to feel a part of a group of like-minded people (vowel 3) was challenged by his fear of losing the material security he had worked so hard for and returning to the awful poverty he knew in adolescence when his father was sent to debtor's prison (challenge 4). Repressed emotions and fears (challenge 2) challenged his innate dependability (consonant 4). His drive to know the truth (name 7) was challenged by issues that had arisen due to feeling betrayed by his mother. She had expected him to continue as a manual labourer because they needed the money. He felt misunderstood by her and it cut deep into his soul. Perhaps this explains his unreasonable vindictiveness toward his wife of 22 years who had borne him ten children and who, like his mother, had a pragmatic approach to life. He tended to fantasize his relationships with women and due to a lack of self-honesty (a number 7 issue), blamed his wife for 'the sins of the mother' in a manner of speaking. Yet this emotional turmoil is exactly what oiled the wheels of his creative genius!

Name Challenge 3

Extreme – spitefulness, bitterness, and blatant lying

Stressed – criticism, sarcasm, and indifferent silence

Mid-range – mindless chatter, flippancy with words, and general difficulties with expressing yourself including feeling tongue-tied and confused

Turned inward – shyness, timidity, and naiveté

The fear is criticism; it paralyses the joy of self-expression

Advice: there is nothing like genuine enthusiasm for overcoming shyness. Focus your attention on something that you would like to accomplish and work steadily towards it. if you are uncertain in group situations, keep in mind that companionship thrives when each member maintains his/her integrity, and hold tight to your own (that's stepping up to number 4).

The potential – verbal brilliance and realistic optimism; a peaceful mind, completely capable of working in harmony with others

Sample Interpretation – an unusual case - Margaretha Geertruida Zelle (mata hari)

Number 4 challenged vowel 5

Number 1 challenged consonant 3

Number 3 challenged name 8.

Her yearning to be free (vowel 5) was challenged by her lack of personal integrity (challenge 4). She didn't seem to care about the consequences of her actions. Her natural wit and charm, cleverness and joy-de-vie (consonant 3) were challenged by arrogance: she thought that she could get away with anything (challenge 1). Her drive for self-mastery (name 8) was challenged by verbal flippancy (challenge 3). She traded confidence for money and although there is no historical basis for saying that her pillow talk cost the lives of 10 000 men, her lack of verbal integrity certainly cost her own life. Difficulty in establishing credibility and being falsely accused is a dual theme that hovers around challenge 3. Use your powers of speech wisely.

Name Challenge 4

Extreme – hatred, despair, and chronic insecurity or guilt

Stressed – defiance, intractability, and the tendency to be pedantic

Mid-range –stubbornness, tunnel-vision, and incoherent emotionality

Turned inward – feeling victimized and deeply insecure, sometimes leading to chronic depression; and in turn, this would affect your health and vitality

The fear is a loss of material security or personal integrity, depending on the circumstances. Either way, fear of the future is implicated.

Advice: this corner of my research file is loaded with people who work until they drop. Challenge 4 suggests deep and powerful feelings of insecurity hidden beneath an avalanche of commitments. This is where the serious business of life justifies ignoring our secret fears. Organization is the key to turning this challenge into an asset, i.e. organizing time for work, time for enjoyment, and time for introspection.

The potential –dependability, integrity, and the feeling of 'coming home' can come with meeting this demand of this challenge number

Sample Interpretation – turned inward – Jacqueline Lee Bouvier (Kennedy/Onasis)

Number 4 challenged Vowel 11

Number 8 challenged Consonant 11

Number 4 challenged Name 4.

The yearning of the soul to act as an inspiration to others (vowel 11) was challenged by deep-seated insecurity (challenge 4), which began when her parents divorced. Her natural charm and charisma (consonant 11) was challenged by unrelenting media exposure of her private heaven and hell (challenge 8). In this case, power, fame and fortune extracted a terrible price. The drive to tap into subconscious strengths and use them in the material world (name 4) has turned in on itself. Jackie kept her secret feelings buried, even from her closest friends, which must have taken its toll on her body. It only happens occasionally that the name and the date path challenges are the same and it certainly compounds the issue, yet also strengthens the likelihood of engaging in meaningful work. A comment made about Jackie at the time of JFK's death demonstrates the potential here: 'she held us together' (challenge 4).

Name Challenge 5

Extreme – recklessness and the tendency to court danger

Stressed – addictions of all sorts and/or hyperactivity

Mid-range – restlessness, sensationalism and exaggeration

Turned inward – the inability to cope with change

The fear is a loss of options and subsequently, personal freedom.

Advice: you must dare to let your light shine regardless of circumstances, so that others can benefit from it. Ultimately this is a matter only your heart can resolve, but there are steps you can take that will bolster your courage. Firstly get enthusiastic about something and learn everything there is to know about it. Try to see your chosen interest from every angle you can think of. What questions are other people likely to ask about it? And how will you respond? Once you understand its history and current state of development, predict how your topic of interest might evolve in the future. All of this will grant you an understanding of the nature of change and how you can use it to your advantage.

The potential – to live at the cutting edge of progress and act as an evolutionary force in the world

Sample Interpretation – the potential - Kuppuswamy Iyer (Swami Sivananda)

Number 2 challenged vowel 10

Number 7 challenged consonant 6

Number 5 challenged name 7.

The desire to be authentic and fearless (vowel 10) was enriched by the opportunity to give and receive love in a mutually supportive way (challenge 2). 'I love the students' he would say, and he did everything that he could to accommodate their needs. His innate dutifulness (consonant 6) was enriched by the maintenance of inner peace (challenge 7). He worked in the world and for the world but never lost his emotional equipoise. The drive to know the truth (name 7) was enriched by living at the cutting edge of progress and acting as an evolutionary force in the world (challenge 5).

Name Challenge 6

Extreme – hypochondria: the power of the imagination to manifest symptoms

Stressed – feeling burdened by the weight of responsibilities

Mid-range – constant worry, particularly concerning the ability to meet the expectations of other people

Turned inward – the inability to accept responsibility

The fear that you will never be good enough paralyses your creativity. If you worry excessively about making a mistake or upsetting someone, the creative spirit finds itself blocked and this causes certain types of illness. You need to realize that mistakes are an important part of the creative process.

Advice: dialogue is the key to success here. 'Di' is a prefix for two, and so you can begin by listening carefully to others, not with an answer in readiness, but with the aim of improved understanding. Dialogue is a creative process that seeks synergy and produces undreamed of possibilities. Your responsibility lies with sharing your ideas as coherently as possible, while the way that people react is their responsibility.

The potential – creative brilliance and the exceptional management of 'people projects'

Sample Interpretation – mid-range - Charles Robert Darwin

Number 8 challenged vowel 16/7

Number 2 challenged consonant 11/2

Number 6 challenged name 9

The desire to awaken to a higher level of truth (vowel 16/7) was challenged by the fear of reprisal (challenge 8). His natural charisma and concern for others (consonant 11/2) was challenged by the need to love and be loved (challenge 2). The consciousness encoded in number 2 has turned in on itself causing immense emotional strain. In Charles Darwin's life story the issue of evolution versus religion polarized itself and this showed up first and foremost in his relationship with his wife, whom he adored. The drive to make a contribution to the body of knowledge available to humanity (name 9) was challenged by concern for his family (challenge 6). He literally worried himself sick about the ridicule he and his family would have to endure if his findings were published. Which was more important, protecting his family or expanding the parameters of global awareness? This very real and practical dilemma is typical of that confronted by people with challenge number 6: that the projections and expectations of other people become what one expects from oneself. Eventually life itself forced Darwin's hand and he published his work, bracing himself for the onslaught of public criticism. Resolving the issue of personal responsibility (eventually) resolved the other issues as well. His work paved the way to a higher level of truth and inspiration from which all of humanity would benefit.

Name Challenge 7

Extreme – cynicism, hypocrisy, and morbidity

Stressed –secretiveness, and strategic distancing

Mid-range – moodiness, contrariness, and defensiveness

Turned inward – self-deception and a guilty conscience; but also resentfulness at the very idea that someone should 'make' you feel that way

The fear is that someone will find out something about you, which you would prefer to remain private. Some people with name challenge 7 seem to live a double life. A walking paradox; they may even be a 'scoundrel-saint' like Oskar Schindler.

Advice: mythology, drama, poetry, history, biography, natural science, comparative religions and adventure stories all support the development of self-understanding. The big step for 7's is to join a group of like-minded people who share a common interest. Specialization is the key to turning this challenge to your advantage and that means becoming 'an expert' in the field of your research efforts.

The potential – coolness under fire, emanating from a profound sense of peace

Sample Interpretation – a wide range - Joseph Mallord William Turner

Number 1 challenged vowel 9

Number 8 challenged consonant 8

Number 7 challenged name 8.

The desire to contribute to the betterment of humanity (vowel 9) was challenged by irritability with people, yet turner was unafraid to express the injustice of human against human in his paintings (challenge 1). His natural efficiency, tenacity and resourcefulness (consonant 8) would have been challenged by feelings of powerlessness (challenge 8); perhaps this is why he often focused on the awesome powers of nature. The repetition of the number 8 would have contributed to his phenomenal output. He seems to have lived for his work. Challenge 7 is evident in his obsessive secretiveness, both personally and professionally. Only once did he allow someone to watch him work. As he aged he was increasingly called 'difficult', a word that often comes up with number 7. He was frugal to the point of being miserly, tight with both his money and affections. A bit of a loner, turner wanted both fame and anonymity; a paradox that often accompanies number 7. On the positive side, turner bequeathed humanity with an extraordinary legacy of powerful and unique paintings.

Name Challenge 8

Extreme – tyranny and the tendency to intimidate others; the might is right mentality

Stressed – oppressiveness, over-achievement, and vengefulness

Mid-range – the inclination to confront with combat in mind rather than negotiation

Turned inward – feeling powerless and impotent

The fear is reprisal, which may be real or imagined. The person may actually be justified in being concerned about what his or her personal convictions may cost, and will have to decide if it is worth it.

Advice: let your love for others provide the motivation for managing whatever resources you have in a manner that reaps benefits all around.

The potential – resourcefulness and self-mastery; the ability to turn pressure and setbacks into golden opportunities that have a healthy impact on your environment

Sample Interpretation – exemplary - Anna Lætitia Aikin (married name Barbauld)

Number 8 challenged vowel 10

Zero challenged consonant 6

Number 8 challenged name 7.

Her longing to have an independent voice (vowel 1) was challenged by the fear of reprisal by those in power (challenge 8). These were dangerous times for dissenters and reformers, and the Barbaulds feared that the royal proclamation against seditious writings and publications might be used against them. Her innate dutifulness (consonant 6) was challenged by the impulse to explore her complete, uncensored potential (challenge 0). Anna was a poet, but she also wrote essays on topics of social and political concern, such as abolition, freedom of religion, education and international policy. She published collective works and wrote biographies and critical reviews as well. Her ease of expression and the elegance of its structure can be partly attributed to consonant 6 (and the line 1, 2, 3 in her date chart), but the fact that she avoided clichés and spoke from personal conviction represents the force of number 8. Her drive to know the truth (name 7) was challenged by an awareness of what her personal convictions might cost her (challenge 8). Her final piece of published work was a criticism of England's war on France and contained a prophecy. She noted that because powerful countries in the past have eventually dwindled and been surpassed so would England's fortunes change. Such insightfulness relates to the combination of 7 and 8. Anna was severely criticized by those who thought England's resources were inexhaustible, but her courage did not fail her.

Name Challenge Zero

Extreme – perfectionism (i.e. disallowing mis-takes)

Stressed – splintering (i.e. completely axing people from one's life)

Mid-range – the tendency to be melodramatic ('over the top')

Turned inward – total confusion: not knowing which way to turn

The fear is madness (i.e. going 'over the edge')

Advice: zero amplifies the other number(s) in the set, which makes it absolutely necessary to know that number. In its immature expression, zero can amplify the more negative expressions of the number, such as aggressiveness when number 1 is involved. Action goes where thought leads, and so you need to stay focused on the positive potential of the number involved.

The potential –the opportunity to accomplish more than you thought possible

Sample Interpretation – exemplary - Billie Jean Moffitt (married name King)

Zero challenged vowel 8

Zero challenged consonant 7

Zero challenged name 6

The zeros amplify the innate tendencies of vowel 8, consonant 7, and name 6 as described in chapters 2 and 3. Extremities of behaviour are more likely, especially during one's early years. The potential to do something extraordinary is also there, once the extremities have been tempered by the lessons of experience.

Only rarely do we see a complete run of zeros such as this. Much more often the zero is accompanied by another number and amplifies it. For example in the Name 'Emma Bunton', the zero amplifies the number 1, in 'Diana Ross', the zero amplifies the number 3, in and 'John Lennon', the zero amplifies the number 4. The names Elvis Presley and Lisa Marie Presley share the same set of challenges: vowel challenge 2, consonant challenge zero, and name challenge 2, making this a family pattern.

Challenges Chart Example

The Challenge Chart for Jeannette Walls

Challenge	Where it appears	Totals
0	consonant challenge	1
1 & 10	1st small challenge	1
2		
3 & 12	whole life and polarity challenges 3 whole life and polarity challenges 12	4
4	2nd small challenge, vowel and name challenges	3
5	2nd big challenge	1
6		
7	missing number	1
8	repeated core number + missing number	2
9		
karmic numbers	secondary date path 14 birth year 16	2
master numbers		

Prioritizing:

1. karmic numbers 14 and 16
2. repeated core number 8: vowel and name number; missing number 8 must also be factored in here.
   Numbers 1 and 17 can be grouped with challenge number 8
3. Challenged core numbers: 3 and 5: date path 5 and birth day 3 are also challenge numbers. We will look at number 5 first because it relates to karmic 14.
4. whole life and polarity challenges 3 and 12
5. missing number 7
6. vowel challenge 4, consonant challenge 0, name challenge 4

Karmic numbers 14 and 16 are evident throughout Jeannette's memoirs. You could say they are the main theme: no sooner had Jeannette settled into one place than she suddenly had to leave and that meant leaving behind the things that she had grown fond of.

Repeated core number 8 in tandem with the fact that 8 is missing from both the name and date of birth brings the issue of power versus powerlessness into focus. Challenges 1 and 8 share a potent relationship; they symbolize the dynamic of action and re-action.

Challenged core number 5 is an aspect of karmic 14. In Jeannette's story it manifest through the constant and ongoing need to adapt in order to survive.

Whole-life challenge 3 is evident in the problem of image. Jeannette's whole life challenge 3 is specifically a 12 and there's a quote from Wayne Dyer that sums that challenge up perfectly: "If you change the way you look at things, the things you look at change."

Missing number 7 is an aspect of karmic 16. Jeannette definitely felt different to other folks as a child and consequently, she had a secret-self as an adult. That was until she decided to publish her story. There was no doubt in her mind when she wrote the book that she would lose everything by going public. As it turned out, people admired rather than scorned her.

Name challenge 4: look at the list of possibilities. How easy would it have been to hate your parents under such circumstances? Becoming chronically insecure or wracked with guilt is another possibility that Jeannette declined. Defiance however kept her going; she remained mentally defiant throughout. She could have sunk into depression and stayed there – many people would have. The potential of challenge number 4 shone through her integrity.

Chapter 8

The Attainments

Within your matrix of energy is encoded the blueprint of all of your personal development: past, present and future. This is neither static nor fated but in a constant state of flux, within a set of pre-dispositions. In this chapter we explore the pre-determined pathway that lies before you, as encoded by your date of birth. You will notice that the calculations take the form of a pyramid. And although these numbers are 'set in stone', just like a pyramid, there is an infinite number of ways of responding to the patterns that they reveal.

Calculating the Attainments

Throughout this chapter we will use the actor, Daniel Jacob Radcliffe as an example. He was born in London, England on July 23, 1989, date path 57/39/21/12/**3,** vowel 37/10, consonant 49/4, name 143/8, growth number 27/9, maturity number 143/8

Addition Reveals the Attainment-Pattern

We begin constructing the pyramid by placing the birth month, birth day and birth year as follows:

Daniel Radcliff, born July 23, 1989:

July	23	1989
month	day	year

All of the numbers related to the month, day and year are placed above this:

7	**23/5**	**27/9**
July	23	1989
month	day	year

We now add the month number to the day number, to begin building the pyramid.

In Daniel's case: 7 + 23 = 30

Next the day number is added to the year number.

Continuing our example: 23 + 27 = 50

These two totals are now added together, the third attainment building thus on the previous two.

30 + 50 =80

You may have noticed that the process is similar to calculating the challenges, except that now you are adding the totals instead of subtracting them. The challenges are thus the shadow or shaping forces of the attainments. Like the challenges the attainments are kept whole during the calculation process but with the attainments there is no need for two sets of calculation.

The final attainment sits at the apex of the pyramid and will be called the quest of the life. To discover what it is, add the birth month to the birth year.

In Daniel's case the quest is 7 + 27 = 34

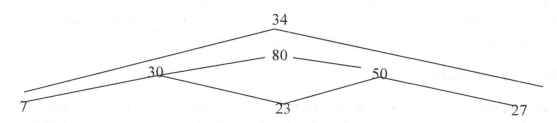

Numerologists have called each of the four totals 'attainments'; 'pinnacles' 'peaks' or 'pyramids'. Occasionally the first one is called 'the achievement number' because it represents just that: an achievement that is a necessary foundation for the others. It is used in this context in *Pan's Script*.

Life Cycles

There are actually two sets of numbers to interpret here and they are inter-related. The birth month, birth day and birth year form the base of the pyramid. They are typically named 'the life cycles' and you can see that they represent the foundation upon which the pyramid is built. The achievement, central attainments, and quest rise from them.

The birth month equates with what will here be called the first base. Being on the left side of the calculation, it pertains to the past (i.e. a previous existence). As such it is deeply subconscious and you might have to wrestle with it. Denial and projection are common. The first base is active throughout your childhood and will linger until you come to terms with the positive qualities that it represents.

The birth day equates with what will here be called the birthday base. It typically represents a more conscious quality than the first base. You know that you possess this quality. As explained in chapter 4, the birthday number encodes your winning attitude to life. The birthday base mediates between your past and your future. Especially whilst this quality is active in your life (during your middle years), re-read the overview of your birthday number and your birth day-date path combination in chapter 4.

The birth year equates with what will here be called the home base. Throughout your life you will work on getting the combination of first base and achievement number to a comfortable place. The birthday base and central attainments add specific details to this. If you are at odds with your first base or achievement number, you will probably struggle to reconcile all of these different influences. And if repeated core numbers are involved, then they will intensify the situation. The home base will attempt to reconcile everything so that you can live in peace with yourself.

Timing the Bases

Some numerology texts fail to align all of the cycles and this puts the timing out, but in this book several cycles have been synchronized, including key astrological cycles. The second base cycle begins on the personal year 1 closest to the 28th birthday and is related to the first Saturn return in astrology. (The personal years will be explained in the next chapter). Likewise, the third cycle begins on the personal year 1 closest to the 56th birthday, and relates to the second Saturn return.

Timing the Attainments

By subtracting the primary date path from 36, you can establish the year that the achievement number passes into the 2nd attainment. You then add 9 years (i.e. the sum of 3 and 6) to ascertain the start of the 3rd attainment and another 9 to establish the age at which the quest begins. The bases and attainments cycle in tandem with the personal years and thus the ages given are inclusive of each other. To get you started, the timing related to each primary date path has been calculated in the table below.

Base & Attainment Table

Date Path	First Base	Birthday Base	Home Base		Achievement	2nd Att.	3rd Att.	Quest
1	birth-26	27-53	54 -		birth-35	36-44	45-53	54-
2	birth-25	26-52	53 -		birth-34	35-43	44-52	53-
3	birth-24	25-51	52 -		birth-33	34-42	43-51	52-
4	birth-23	24-59	60 -		birth-32	33-41	42-50	51-
5	birth-31	32-58	59 -		birth-31	32-40	41-49	50-
6	birth-30	31-57	58 -		birth-30	31-39	40-48	49-
7	birth-29	30-56	57 -		birth-29	30-38	39-47	48-
8	birth-28	29-55	56 -		birth-28	29-37	38-46	47-
9	birth-27	28-54	55 -		birth-27	28-36	37-45	46-

For example: Daniel Radcliffe has primary date path 3. Subtracting 3 from 36, we see that his achievement number runs from birth to December 31st of the year in which he turns 33.

Adding 9:

$33 + 9 = 42$, and so between January 1st of the year he turns 34 and December 31st of the year in which he turns 42, he will be influenced by his second attainment.

Adding 9 again:

$42 + 9 = 51$, and so between January 1st of the year he turns 43 and December 31st of the year in which he turns 51, he will be influenced by his third attainment.

His quest number begins on January 1st the following year.

Attainments 2 and 3 only span nine years each, but the quest permeates the rest of the life. Quite often people only begin doing what they *really* want to do, once the quest number begins. They may then realize that the achievement and central attainments were opening and central acts in their personal drama on the stage of life. The achievement and central attainments are conscious milestones as the way unfolds to the climax of your personal story. This is the quest of your life. It may be a 'missing number' or one that you have been struggling with. Whilst the apex encodes the quest, the polarity challenge acts as its polar dynamic. Together, the challenges and attainments shape the way that your date path is fulfilled.

When you examine your life cycles, try to see your life wholistically, and the various phases as chapters in your story, rather than disconnected experiences. And don't forget your key players – your core numbers - because the potential of the attainments can only be realized if you have sufficient energy to capitalize on them. Hold that thought as you peruse the research findings related to the bases and attainments.

Interpreting the Bases and Attainments

The following interpretations are based on real case studies.

Base 1

Self-determination arises as a common theme in base 1. Ready or not, and with or without assistance, you will have to determine the course of your life.

First Base 1

January Birthdays

The files reveal that when the first base number is 1 the significance of the father is highlighted. Occasionally this was by his absence, rejection, or dominance. But not always; there were just as many fathers who provided a positive and sustaining role model for their children, including a few that had to take over because the mother was missing. 'Making father proud' is the underlying, often subconscious theme in First Base 1 and this tends to stimulate ambition. In many cases the father's state of mind and unfulfilled ambitions were absorbed into the young person's consciousness. Your accomplishments could be considerable, although this may not become fully apparent until later in your life.

Birthday Base 1

In Birthday Base 1 each and every person studied acted with great determination, often against considerable odds. In a few cases it was the death of a loved one that brought out a strength, which the person may not have known they had. In some cases we witness people so determined to carry out their mission or get their message across that not even jail or the threat of death could stop them! Usually however this is a productive time in which original ideas can be explored and showcased.

Home Base 1

Big breaks and new concepts - all successful in the long term- continued into Home Base 1. The hard work evident in earlier cycles continued in the later years but in this later cycle people were more likely to accomplish their goals *and also* find time to enjoy life. Sometimes they even refashioned their image. You can expect to feel that you have come home to yourself at some point during this cycle and wonder what took you so long.

With number 1 as one of your base cycles, you may find yourself in circumstances where you have to fall back on your own resources. Especially in first base 1, you might feel unsupported and alone. At all ages, base 1 brings unexpected change, which will make you think for yourself, strengthen your willpower, and develop your personal autonomy. You are learning how to lead, accept responsibility, and manage your own accomplishments. Rather than expecting other people to have the answers, you may need to become a guiding light for them!

Achievement 1

If your achievement number is 1, make sure that you initiate *something* this life time! Number 1 will stimulate your ability to make up your own mind about things and set your own course. It will encourage you to initiate and take the lead where necessary. Although there may be lots of other people involved, number 1 focuses on your personal story and development. You will learn that when you are being true to yourself, others are more likely to be true to themselves too. When you are not being authentic then others won't be either. When you not only initiate something but also build a solid foundation underneath it, you are working with Achievement number 10.

Attainment 1

As per Achievement 1, Attainment 1 focuses on your inner strength. You need to do something new and progressive during the time that this number is active. Start at the bottom and work your way up, if necessary.

Quest 1

Quest 1 typically indicates a 'new start'. In some way, probably due to circumstances beyond your control, you will have to 'start again' in some way. There's still plenty of time to initiate something and build it from the ground up, if necessary.

Base and Attainment 1 target the strengthening of your personal sovereignty, which is synonymous with authenticity. Being yourself naturally brings out the best in others too. When your activities involve the ideals in your date path, and the manner in which you accomplish them is in accord with your date chart, you will feel that you are really getting somewhere.

If any of your core numbers are 1, it will lend its strength to achievement, attainment or quest 1. Conversely, achievement, attainment or quest 1 activate a latent core number 1 and draw out its potential.

If one of your base or attainment numbers includes the number 10, read date path 10 to gain clearer insight into this number. If number 19 is involved, read not only date path 19 but also karmic 19 in chapter 7. Numbers 28, 37, 46 and 64 can be read about in chapter 1; number 55 is mentioned in chapters 1 and 3, and numbers 73, 82, 91 and 100 in chapter 5. Whichever member of the number 1 family your base or attainment belongs to, the following quote from Thomas Jefferson remains relevant: *"Do you want to know who you are? Don't ask. Act! Action will delineate and define you"*.

Base 2

Whether to comply or rebel would seem to be the issue that arises in base 2 and most people oscillate between the two.

First Base 2

February birthdays

Securing the means by which to enact one's dreams or fantasies seems to lie behind the various manoeuvrings witnessed in first base 2. You tend to react strongly to other people, liking or disliking them intensely. Mostly, such reactions accord with your perception of whether they like or dislike you. You tend to put up barriers to protect yourself against real or perceived opposition. These are some of the reasons why some people with first base 2 tend to move in and out of love-relationships. They settle down when they realize that the love comes from within, and that feeling secure relates to self-esteem. Once you learn to value yourself, such as you are, then other people are more likely to value you too, and your dreams are more likely to come true.

Birthday Base 2

Birthday Base 2 reveals a consistent pattern: initial struggle requiring persistent effort, but eventually leading to the fulfillment of a personal goal. Something akin to righteous indignation pushes these people forward, emerging as small-scale action. Then ever so gradually the person moves into increasingly bigger concerns until what they are doing may even have global implications. Success depends on how well the groundwork has been done.

Home Base 2

This above trend continues in Home Base 2. Life has been teaching you about intimate and personal relationships for a long time and it hasn't always been easy. You have been learning how to be your own best friend and less dependent on others for your sense of wellbeing. By connecting with your own soul you can also tap into a love that is not swayed, damaged, or in any way affected by the shenanigans of partners or other people in general.

With number 2 as one of your base cycles, your life-lessons include working as part of a team. This necessitates sensitivity to the feelings of other people, tact, and co-operation. Those who fare best in base 2 are people who nurture their dreams without expecting others to approve of them or even support them. Big dreams *are* often realized in base 2, and usually in cooperation with others, but you must be prepared to attend to the details, do the leg-work, exercise patience, tolerate setbacks, and cultivate the ground upon which they will materialize.

Achievement 2

You are learning how to apply receptivity and cooperation within a team setting. Your task is to *sense* a situation from both sides of the proverbial coin. You will need patience with other people, but more than that, you need to exercise patience with yourself. Becoming your own 'best friend forever' is the goal here.

Attainment 2

Anywhere in the cycle, number 2 reveals polarities and intensifies the awareness of any lack of wholeness in the individual psyche. To the extent that you feel whole within yourself, this cycle will attract complementary partnerships.

Quest 2

Demonstrating kindness to others and bringing more love into the world is your quest. No more need to be said except that it's only going to happen to the extent that you are loving and kind to yourself.

Through either base or attainment 2, you are learning to find balance by experiencing the polarity of extremes. Your interactions with other people are deepening your feeling-life and enabling you to find security within your relationships. You are learning to ride your emotions rather than be a victim of them. As you master this, you will feel increasingly at peace within yourself and with your partner. Life is teaching you ways to co-exist with other people.

If any of your core numbers are 2, it will lend its strength to achievement, attainment or quest 2. Conversely, achievement, attainment or quest 2 could help to materialize the latent potential in core number 2.

If one of your base or attainment numbers includes the number 11, read date path 11 to gain clearer insight into this master number. Similarly, numbers 29, 38, 47, 56, 65, 74, 83, and 92 can be read as extensions of master number 11. Number 20 has an energy of its own, which you can read about as date path 20 in chapter 1. Whichever member of the number 2 family your base or attainment belongs to, the following quote sums up the ideal behind base and attainment 2: *"Teamwork is the fuel that allows common people to produce uncommon results" – source unknown*

Base 3

Ready or not life gives people in base 3 a mighty push forward in the material world and quite often spiritually as well.

First Base 3

March birthdays

At first, shyness is common. Usually however this is not only overcome, but also overtured, with the person becoming skilled in communicating by adulthood. It is the struggle that has made them so. A related problem is that you may not be a good listener. You tend to speak and then listen rather than the other way around. One of your life-lessons is to learn to ask questions that open up new possibilities. Some of you will master this and excel at communication.

The case studies revealed that well into this cycle a critical decision had to be made. And this would mark the course of the life. Typically this involved a career decision although there was often a spiritual thread running parallel with it.

Birthday Base 3

Birthday Base 3 was usually less complex than the first cycle, the major decision at this stage being how to present one's ideas. Once the presentation that best suits one's nature is found, success generally follows. The case studies revealed that without exception, whatever a person set their mind to, whether constructive or destructive, came to fruition in this cycle, which makes it critical to work on one's attitude to life. This is an upwardly mobile cycle and intensely social in nature.

Home Base 3

The case studies revealed that Home Base 3 is often a controversial one. They turned up people who were judged harshly by some whilst being praised by others. You will feel that you have reached home base when you have developed, from within yourself, the ability to brighten people's lives; knowing that the joy of giving is sufficient unto itself. And you will find that the gift most appreciated is simply yourself, tried and true.

With number 3 as one of your base cycles, you will be given plenty of opportunity to learn from other people. Number 3 moves energy swiftly so that mean-spirited acts bring immediate retribution. It is therefore necessary to approach this cycle with humility and a clean heart - and to keep it clean - by listening to others and learning whatever you can from them. People who acted with the view of promoting a healthy culture within their sphere of influence did very well indeed.

Achievement 3

You are learning to appreciate the value of your creativity to brighten other people's lives. Tied in with this achievement, you are also learning to be accountable for your words and actions.

Be prepared to make a choice and then see it through. It might surprise you to learn that there is freedom in commitment. Once you have decided on a course of action, energy can flow in that direction, with number 3 to help it along.

Attainment 3

Anywhere in the cycle, number 3 presents opportunities to express yourself but if you scatter your talents all over the place, you will have little to show at the end of the cycle. Focus on one talent in particular. Learn everything you can about it, and then keep yourself up to date with the latest developments. If you let your life become too hectic with all of your interests, real opportunities may slip through your fingers. You could become prosperous in a 3-cycle but wind up spending as much as you gain. Similarly, you might find yourself spoiled for choice in a 3-cycle and that you need to keep your mind focused on the one thing that means most to you. Another scenario is that you fear getting what you want because that will give you even more to do. It is a matter of prioritizing your interests and concerns. Focusing on the one thing that you want most enables the energy to move in that direction.

Quest 3

The Quest is to finish the wonderful, imaginative things that you start. It is your willingness to take responsibility for your choices and actions that will make all the difference here.

Whether it be base or attainment 3 under consideration, the quote: *"You grow up the day you have the first really good laugh at yourself"* is relevant and second only to Joseph Campbell's advice to *"follow your bliss"*. '3' brings lots of opportunities for personal expression. It may also bring opportunities to travel and learn. This cycle will bring you lots of acquaintances and hopefully some like-minded friends among them. Through number 3 you are learning how to relate to people in social situations by understanding their behaviour. By so doing, you can better uplift and inspire them.

If any of your core numbers are 3, it will lend its support to achievement, attainment or quest 3. Conversely, achievement, attainment or quest 3 will draw out the latent potential in core number 3.

If one of your base or attainment numbers includes the number 12, read date path 12 to gain clearer insight into this unique number. Similarly, numbers 39, 48, 57, 66, 75, 84 & 93 can be read as extensions of number 12. You will also find number 12 mentioned in chapters 2 and 3. Numbers 21 and 30 each have a distinct energy, which you can read about as their equivalent date paths in chapter 1; and 102 as a maturity number in chapter 5.

Base 4

The motivation to make one's mark in the material world simmers, smoulders and periodically erupts throughout base 4 settling into consistent achievement with maturity.

First Base 4

April birthdays

The case studies revealed that suppressed rage was common in first base 4, although the person involved would probably only recognize it as such, with hindsight. Indeed many of the home environments evidenced in the case studies would be described as decent, conservative, orderly, well-disciplined, middle-class or traditional, yet the young person seems to pick up on the unlived life, the melancholy, or the sacrifices made. This makes them determined to do better than that for themselves, and their loved ones.

Birthday Base 4

During Birthday Base 4 a decision is typically made to improve the lives of others. Instead of taking cushy jobs, these people often take the more challenging option. In some cases victimisation was thrust upon them by circumstances beyond their control, leaving them with no choice but to either tough it out or give up in despair. The workings of number 13 are usually evident even when this is not the birthday, catalysing major transformations in one's relationships, image and concept of self. Those who took hold of their emotions, and shaped them in a beneficial way, found that they *were* able to make a difference *and* where it was needed most. Birthday base 4 indicates that you are learning to take one step at a time and to feel grateful for every gain along the way.

Home Base 4

Home Base 4 was remarkable for the additional status it cast upon the people. In every case there was a dramatic rise in the prestige of one's role in life and with it an awareness of the responsibility it carried. Yet it was not always a burden; the satisfaction it gave depending on the level of personal integrity brought to it. Whether it was 13, 22 or 31 the case studies revealed that it made no difference; it was the willingness to stand up and be counted that mattered. You know when you have reached home base when you feel content with being an ordinary human being.

With Number 4 as one of your base cycles, you will find yourself in circumstances where you will be required to act efficiently in the material world. It is the ability to set goals, time frames, and step by step plans that will move you (ever so gradually) through this period. You are learning to appreciate routine, budgeting, and procedures. If you have no 4's in your chart, this cycle will help you to become more practical. Those people who fare best use this cycle to build a solid foundation upon which long-term dreams can materialize.

Achievement 4

In your early years you may find that conflicting responsibilities catalyze extreme emotions because you don't know how to handle them. Being physical in a constructive way such as going for a walk would help you to regain your equilibrium if you find yourself loosing it. When the going gets tough and you don't let it get the better of you; that is a major achievement.

When the pressure is turned up and your drive increases, that's when you know that you have mastered your Achievement Number.

Attainment 4

Anywhere in the cycle, number 4 accompanies the lesson of being ready for anything, to think ahead of time, and be prepared. If you are willing to work in a consistent and methodical way, you can achieve much during this cycle. Status and prestige may not happen during the cycle but could come later, especially if you refuse to give up and if your personal integrity doesn't falter.

Quest 4

The Quest is to realize that although life is 'ordinary' it is loaded with potential. If you look at the world through the eyes of your soul, you will see yourself as a co-creator along with everybody else that you share this amazing planet with. When the implications of this sink in, you then become truly alive; you are fully present here and now. Noticing the patterns of the seasons and responding to them in small ritualistic ways will help you get there.

Base and Attainment 4 target working for the love of it. To take pride in your work, no matter how apparently insignificant, indicates self-mastery of the highest order and transforms the world we live in. The most apt quote for base or attainment 4 comes from Kahlil Gibran: *"Work is love made visible"*.

If any of your core numbers are 4, it will help you to master achievement, attainment or quest 4. Conversely, achievement, attainment or quest 4 will help you to materialize the latent potential in core number 4.

Number 40 is an extension of number 4 and you can read about it in chapter 1. If one of your base or attainment numbers includes the number 13, read date path 13 in chapter 1 and karmic 13 in chapter 7 to gain clearer insight into this unique number. Numbers 49, 58, 67, 76, 85 and 94 can then be read as extensions of 13. Number 22 is a master number with a distinct energy of its own; to learn more about it consult chapters 1-3.

Base 5

Progress comes with base 5; evolution and adaptation being the nature of this number.

First Base 5

May birthdays

First Base 5 is sometimes experienced as unsettling circumstances in childhood, such as multiple changes of home and schooling, often related to a parent's work. Even when this was not the case, there was usually a lack of certainty in the child's life, yet the case studies revealed that equally often, the young person received a high level of education, one way or another. Good fortune seems to come in this cycle but usually nearer to the end of it, once a necessary adjustment has been made.

Birthday Base 5

The above trend is often repeated in Birthday Base 5. It has a habit of bringing unexpected changes to people's lives. Not all of them difficult of course, but challenging in various ways, even accepting success, fame and fortune being a challenge for some people. Movements were often literal and occasionally involved separations. Liberation was a highly pronounced theme: liberation from the past (welcome or not), liberation for one's soul, and very often liberation for the souls of others too. Much creative work was accomplished - often one's greatest works takes place in Birthday Base 5. Indeed the only problem that emerged with this cycle came from failure to adapt to circumstances. With '5' as your birthday base you probably like a work environment that provides you with plenty of people to interact with. You need the stimulation that comes with variety.

Home Base 5

Home Base 5 usually brings increased personal power and radiance. This necessitates looking after the physical body, because things can move very fast in this cycle. More than ever there is a need for mental strength and clarity, and above all to remain centred in one's soul. You will know when you have reached home-base when every day becomes an adventure even if you don't leave home. You no longer need to run around all over the place to experience something new, yet you probably will continue experience a lot of new things, because of other people's need for you to share what you have learned.

With number 5 as one of your base cycles, the ground beneath your feet may feel like shifting sand. Just when you get used to one environment, and set of rules, everything changes. Try to accept life's fluctuations as opportunities and make the most of them. Make the most of the variety, and keep in mind that progress necessitates a calculated risk. Like Perceval, champion of the quest for the Holy Grail, you must be willing to ask the fundamental questions and extend the boundaries of your 'comfort zone' in order to prise the answers.

Achievement 5

Number 5 has a way of speeding things up and so if it is your achievement number you could find yourself in the fast lane. It will give you the thrill of feeling alive and encourage you to take risks. Packing so much into every day can be exhausting and you might find that you need long periods of rest at times. Fun is definitely on your agenda and there is nothing better than friends to share it with, and the more the better! You tend to hop from one experience to another, learning as you go. You are usually happy to try anything once. Achievement number 5 indicates that learning to go with the flow is an important life-lesson for you. Number 5 demands presence of mind under whatever circumstances you happen to find yourself and it will encourage you to apply your creative ingenuity to problems.

Attainment 5

Anywhere in the cycle, '5' will catalyze changes that stimulate the creative faculties of your mind. Your mental powers may strengthen during this time. The higher purpose of your fluctuating environment is to make you more adaptable and thereby elicit your unique gift to humanity. Whilst acknowledging that this can be painfully difficult at times, the advice offered is to continually exam your entrenched thought-patterns, assumptions and beliefs. And remember that people can benefit from what you have learned. There will be times when you feel uncentered and therefore quite unwell. At such times phone a friend and ask them to be your sounding board. If you pick the right person they can help you to focus on facts rather than emotions.

Quest 5

The Quest is to pass your knowledge onto others so that they can grow and evolve as you have done. You might also find yourself championing people who cannot do so for themselves. Advocating for people, plants, animals or places that need someone to speak for them, is likely to be a feature of your quest cycle.

Base and Attainment 5 will test your faith in the process of life, but as you become increasingly centred, those who have lost their centeredness will seek you out. They will also test the strength of your convictions so that they, too, may grow. Out of the struggle to adapt to a continually changing environment, you will evolve into a more resourceful and ingenious person. Lao Tzu wisely said: *"Life is a series of natural and spontaneous changes. Don't resist them – that only creates sorrow. Let reality be reality. Let things flow naturally forward in whatever way they like."*

If any of your core numbers are 5, it will enrich achievement, attainment or quest 5. Conversely, achievement, attainment or quest 5 will draw out the latent potential in core number 5 and help you to shine.

If one of your base or attainment numbers includes the number 14, read date path 14 in chapter 1 and karmic 14 in chapter 7 to gain clearer insight into this number. Numbers 59, 68, 77, 86, and 95 can then be read as extensions of 14. You'll find more about number 77 in chapters 3 and 5. Numbers 23, 32, 41 and 50 each have a distinct energy, which you can read about in chapter 1 as their equivalent date paths.

Base 6

Compassion and its offspring – service to others – is the key to success in base 6.

First Base 6

June birthdays

First Base 6 focuses on family ties and obligations. Typically it raises the feeling that one is responsible for the wellbeing of other family members. Caring for others may be admirable when it is a conscious choice but having to live up to the expectations of one's family can feel restrictive to a child. Feeling 'hemmed in' was a common finding but so too the adoption of a clever means to move beyond that feeling. With 6 as your first base, you are learning ways to use your skills alongside other people who may or may not be pulling their weight.

Birthday Base 6

Birthday Base 6 seems to begin in a similar way but the more mature person was better able to turn restrictions 'on their head' and make them work in a socially productive way than people with first base 6. Once this has been accomplished, success generally follows. The case studies suggested that where this process includes self-healing, the outcome could continue to benefit others beyond the person's life span. Your birthday base 6 is teaching you about commitment. You are learning that you can serve others through the commitments that you make and benefit yourself at the same time.

Home Base 6

The case studies revealed that Home Base 6 typically revolved around a social issue. Confronting the mentality of defeatism was common, and naturally this had to begin with oneself. People who were able to surf the tides of human emotions moved into the arena of alleviating suffering on a broader scale. Substantial and enduring legacies were the norm rather than the exception. You will know that you have reached 'home-base' when you can take full responsibility for the choices you make, and find the necessary sacrifices enjoyable.

With number 6 as one of your base cycles, you may need to *create* the means by which you can enjoy caring for others. Enjoying being a part of a 'family', despite the responsibilities it brings, is what base cycle 6 offers you, but you have to make it work. Rather than waiting for things to fall into place, you will need to piece the various aspects of your life together so that they work for you. If you can relax into your life's circumstances you may find that you can create an environment that is functional for you, and helpful to others as well. There is enormous creative potential here for people whose hearts are open to it. Once your heart and mind are reconciled, your intuitive faculties will unfold, and then wonders truly never cease.

Achievement 6

The Achievement is to maintain the balance between caring for yourself and caring for others. You may be sensitive to your social environment, picking up on the needs of others, and naturally want to respond to them. You are inclined to work hard to please others but sometimes that gets taken advantage of. You are learning to value everyone's contribution, your own included.

Attainment 6

Anywhere in the cycle, number 6 will bring issues relating to the family into the foreground, the research indicating the need to give the word 'family' a broad context. The community of which your family unit is a part comes into play and so too your 'homeland', even the 'family' of humanity' and ultimately the 'family' within your own mind, for those who delve deeply. Think about how you can blend your creative development and service to your community. Attainment 6 invites you to take a wholistic view of life in both its obvious, and its more subtle aspects.

Quest 6

The Quest is to live in harmony with the beauty of your own soul. This can only happen when you realize that despite the chaos of everyday lives, there is an intrinsic beauty within the world. Once you've come to terms with this, and nobody is saying that it's easy, the peace within your soul will radiate into the world and automatically make it a better place.

Base and Attainment 6 encourage the perception that the whole world is your family and the understanding that *"Home is where the heart is"* - it's old but still true! Opportunities abound here to help your human family by teaching, healing, counseling, and generally serving the community with an open heart. Let life transmute your powerful emotions and creative ideas into acts that synchronize with the efforts that others are making towards improving lives.

If any of your core numbers are 6, it will strengthen achievement, attainment or quest 6. Conversely, achievement, attainment or quest 6 will help you to materialize the latent potential in core number 6.

If one of your base or attainment numbers includes the number 15, read date path 15 to gain clearer insight into this number. Numbers 69, 78, 87, and 96 can be read as extensions of number 15. Numbers 24, 33, 42, 51 and 60 each have a distinct energy, which you can read about in chapter 1 as their equivalent date paths, and you will find more about number 33 in chapter 3.

Base 7

Upon reflection, most people would describe their base '7' cycle as difficult. Much of it successful, happy even, but 'something' seems to gnaw away from the inside out.

First Base 7

July birthdays

The case studies indicated that in first base '7' life somehow makes a person feel different to his or her peers. It might be a health condition or an embarrassing home-life for example. Whatever it is, it causes confusion until a resolve is made. The most helpful response from parents was to appreciate that whatever is making their child feel 'different' may actually be a gift incubating deep within. You are learning that another person's truth cannot work for you because that person is not you. Deep down only you know what is real and true for you.

Birthday Base 7

Birthday Base 7 can bring controversy, a host of contradictory behaviours, creative brilliance, and changes all round. Often the person feels that no one understands them and this may actually be true, especially if they are developing spiritually. The research findings clearly demonstrated the need for personal integrity throughout this cycle. Masked by a cool exterior, other people may not realize the torrid life going on within, but the person themselves certainly knows and must find a way to work with it. Only from the position of self-honesty can a life that works emerge. You might then find that you don't need to do anything to have enjoyable relationships with other people except be honest them.

Home Base 7

Home Base 7 enables a consolidation of one's life. Prestige may be offered but declined due to the felt need to work within a quieter space. This should not be interpreted as unsuccessful for this is anything but the case. Rather, it involves a reevaluation of one's situation within a current context, and a decision to be made that involves applying one's skills in a different way to earlier years. This is what the case studies revealed; for you, personally, you will know that you have reached home-base when you feel peaceful deep inside. Your relationships with other people may be as complex as they always were, because that's the nature of life, yet you will find it easier now to remain centered within your own soul.

With number 7 as one of your base cycles you may need to acclimatize to feeling different. While others expand, circumstances may cause you to contract and contemplate. You can make the most of this unique cycle by committing yourself to study, specializing in an area that holds your interest in a profound way. To offset any moodiness or feelings of alienation and loneliness that may arise, spend time in the natural world, as it will help you to unravel the truth you seek. Your mental accomplishments could be considerable, especially if you have done your research, analyzed different points of view, and sorted out the proverbial wheat from the chaff.

Achievement 7

The Achievement is to live passionately from your own truth. If you have a tendency to rely upon other people's truth in order to be happy, this cycle will help you to understand what is wrong with that. Number 7 will encourage you to connect with your own truth and find happiness from within yourself. You will find that being more honest with yourself opens the way for others to be more honest with themselves. Relationships will thus improve all around.

Attainment 7

The case studies revealed that anywhere in a cycle, number 7 will call upon your inner strength in the face of impersonal circumstances. The emphasis during this time is on study and investigation, research, and skill development. Some of you will be drawn to the physical sciences, others the metaphysical sciences, and a few of you will combine the two. You are also learning from relationships. Ways to restore your equilibrium within relationships is what each unsettling incident can teach you. You can then use the knowledge you have gained next time you confront a similar issue. Life is encouraging you to strike a healthy balance between work and relationships. During a 7-cycle (wherever it appears) you need to make time for personal reflection and insight.

Quest 7

The Quest is, quite simply, to live your own truth, fully and completely. Your soul is teaching you to trust yourself. Armed with your hard-won and deeply personal truth, you can make it through the complexities of life, including relationships. Not by detaching or withdrawing, although there is necessary place for these in the overall balance of each day, but by allowing life and its people to be your teachers, will you attain the inner peace that is possible here. You might constantly find yourself shedding: letting go of former modes of operation and learning more authentic (truthful) ways of being with others. Let nature help you with this. Go for walks in the bush and become a part of the beauty all around you.

Whether in Base or Attainment 7 contemplate this: *In the story of your life, include tales of overcoming hardships, and the insight gained from it. Fill your story with adventure, poetry, the unexplained, and some crazy contradictions. Make each chapter a reflection of time well spent. And keep these words from Harvey Fierstein in mind: "Accept no one's definition of life; define yourself"*.

If any of your core numbers are 7, it will enrich achievement, attainment or quest 7. Conversely, achievement, attainment or quest 7 will draw out the latent potential in core number 7.

If one of your base or attainment numbers includes the number 16, read date path 16 in chapter 1 and karmic 16 in chapter 7 to gain clearer insight into this number. Numbers 79, 88, and 97 can then be read as extensions of 16. Numbers 25, 34, 43, 52, 61 and 70 each have a distinct energy, which you can read about in chapter 1 as their equivalent date paths. You'll find more on number 77 in chapters 3 and 5.

Base 8

Determination to achieve one's goals, despite any opposition encountered, lies at the heart of base 8.

First Base 8

August birthdays

In first base 8 we typically witness young people setting their own course, making their own mistakes, and celebrating their own achievements. Education is a critical factor because it has long-term implications. A young person in base 8 would benefit from the most comprehensive education that is available to them.

Birthday Base 8

Birthday Base 8 requires not only mental fortitude but also the whole-hearted commitment to something substantial and worthwhile. Organization will help you to manage the contingencies that accompany this commitment provided you remain flexible. Surrendering to the will of others is likely to be difficult for you, but if you consider the possibility that their ideas might have some merit, and could improve on your own, you will find it easier to make the necessary adjustments. Negotiating win-win outcomes has as much of a place in number 8's domain as number 2's. You are a serious person, and you take your work and your relationships very seriously. Sometimes you push too hard and risk either burning yourself out, or making enemies, or both. Delegation is one of your life-lessons. '8' is teaching you ways to empower others as you empower yourself.

Home Base 8

Home Base 8 represents a busy cycle with disappointments to be reconciled, debts to be paid, and agreements negotiated. An appraisal of one's life and profession may be called for so that priorities can be set in place. Steadfastness is still required because other people's emotions can be challenging even if one has done one's personal 'homework'. It is common to see people making comebacks and finally being acknowledged for efforts they have made in the past. You will know that you have reached home-base when you lay down your battle gear because you have learned that life is less about winning and more about being the best person you can be.

With number 8 as one of your base cycles you will need to maintain a steady flow between incoming and outgoing energy in your life. Knowing when to listen and when to speak, when to trust others, when to trust your own perceptions, and when to seek advice, requires discernment, wisdom, and the ability to think around corners. Number 8 will tend to resurrect all those parts of yourself that you have denied and projected onto other people. You must courageously rise above any crisis this precipitates and allow it to transform you into a more compassionate human being. If you can tap into the strength of your heart-felt convictions and act on them in negotiation with others, this could be an enormously productive time in *all* facets of your life.

Achievement 8

The Achievement is to recognize that although you need to be able to manage your life, you cannot control life. Life is bigger than you are. Your task is to manage your resources – those within you as well as those around you – to the best of your ability.

Attainment 8

Anywhere in the cycle, number 8 concentrates on building an independent, well rounded human being. It will help you to manage your own success. A part of this involves networking, within your community, and within your mind. Number 8 expects you to organize your life so that you can achieve material independence and inner peace within a busy world. You are learning to exercise sound judgment and demonstrate the courage of your convictions.

Quest 8

The Quest is to relax and enjoy life instead of constantly worrying about what you 'should' be doing next. Number 8 will help you to plan wonderful accomplishments and achieve them, and if you allow room in all of that to simply go with the flow, you will enjoy your accomplishments much more. Number 8 is teaching you to value life for what it is rather than what you think it should be.

If any of your core numbers are 8, it will intensify your experience of achievement, attainment or quest 8. Conversely, achievement, attainment or quest 8 will draw out the latent potential in core number 8.

Numbers 17, 26, 35, 44, 53, 62 and 71 each have a distinct energy, which you can read about in chapter 1 as their equivalent date paths. You'll find more on numbers 80, 89 and 98 in chapter

5. Whichever number your 8 is, the saying: *"Some people dream of worthy accomplishments, while others stay awake and achieve them"* applies.

Base 9

The mind tends to wander into the future in base 9, creating images of how things *could* be (if only things were different).

First Base 9

September birthdays

In first base 9 people typically find their idealism confronted by circumstances that are anything but ideal. The case studies indicated that the child's environment may be emotionally charged, sometimes quite dramatically. In other households philanthropy was practiced but the child ignored. In most cases challenging circumstances served to stir creative passions, but the outcome of such passion may not be evident until much later in life.

Birthday Base 9

In Birthday Base 9, creativity and emotional release remain vital to emotional health. Creativity sometimes takes on political or spiritual overtones in Birthday Base 9. The case studies showed that there is often a huge leap forward professionally. A confrontation with corruption was evidenced in some cases and a confrontation with prejudice or vilification in others. Those who responded positively by moving elsewhere, taking the offenders to court, or creating a circle of peace within the external battlefield, did well in the long term provided their motives were squeaky clean.

You function well in roles where you can see a bigger picture or higher purpose. You can then hold to this for the benefit of everyone around you. When you accept a role within humanity, however humble or grand you think it is, you make the world a warmer and friendlier place for everyone. You are learning to be more broad-minded about how people operate and that being human is sufficient unto itself. Number 9 will encourage you to enjoy helping but *trying* to be helpful won't work; you will simply become resentful. You are at your happiest when you forget about yourself and become absorbed in the joy of doing something for someone else but when it stops being a joy, pause for a while and take a break. You probably find it easy to strike up a conversation with all sorts of people and this can be helpful in itself. You probably have strong opinions and you may have to work at listening to the other person before you speak to them. Interfaith activities may interest you because they allow you to explore the common factors in the world's belief systems.

Home Base 9

The famous examples with Home Base 9 blew the whole issue of number 9 wide open. Clearly witnessed were people who spoke much about world peace whilst waging war on those who loved them. Compromise was not necessarily the answer and sometimes a person had to leave in order to live peacefully and creatively elsewhere. Refusing to compromise their most sacred ideals, such people were sometimes able to forgive their persecutors while waiting for the tide to turn. Expansion was evident in *all* cases, embracing diversity an option taken up by some. You have reached home-base when you can effectively use your energy to support the needs of your environment and all of the life-forms that you share it with. Number 9 will help you to put your views across passionately and by so doing, you can liberate others of real or perceived injustices.

With Number 9 as a base cycle you will find that your ideals need to be generous but also feasible. Travel will help you to gain a broader perspective of the issues involved. Partnerships can be difficult: on the one hand you may want a partner who shares your ideals, whilst on the other hand you may be drawn to a person who challenges your ideals. If you can see opposition as an opportunity to embrace a broader perspective, then everyone stands to benefit.

Achievement 9

Achievement Number 9 is about trusting your inner wisdom. You are learning that by thinking and acting with positive intent, you can create abundance in your life, and not just for you but for others as well. Similarly, you are learning to be more broad-minded about how people operate. Interfaith activities may interest you because they allow you to explore various belief systems.

Attainment 9

Anywhere in the cycle, number 9 harnesses creative vitality to fascinating ideas. It can change the way that others see you and the way that you perceive yourself. It also seems to bring sudden change, just when you least expect it. Allow this to stir your creative juices, and express your feelings in broad terms. Number 9 expands the mind in all directions. It offers you a more universal understanding of life.

Quest 9

The Quest is to learn that receiving is a form of giving. The influence of number 9 catalyzes the urge to give to others but you will find that although other people appreciate your generosity, they also appreciate the opportunity to give to you sometimes. It uplifts them and makes them feel worthwhile, just as giving to others uplifts you, and makes you feel worthwhile. By allowing the cycle of giving and receiving to flow freely in both directions, you are creating more joy in the world.

Base and Attainment 9 invite you to engage in creative self-expression for the satisfaction, pleasure, and sheer joy of it! As you do so, contemplate these words by George Washington Carver: *"How far you go in life depends on your being tender with the young, compassionate with the aged, sympathetic with the striving, and tolerant of the weak and strong. Because someday in your life you will have been all of these"*.

If any of your core numbers are 9, it will intensify your experience of achievement, attainment or quest 9. Conversely, achievement, attainment or quest 9 will broaden the latent potential in core number 9.

Numbers 18, 27, 36, 45, 54, and 63 each have a distinct energy, which you can read about in chapter 1 as their equivalent date paths. You'll find more on numbers 72, 81, 90 and 99 in chapter 5, and the last-mentioned is also in chapter 3.

Base 10

<u>First Base 10</u>

October birthdays

Because your first base cycle resonates with number 10, what has been written about first base 1 will also apply to you but the zero may amplify your innate potential. For such potential to find fulfilment, you will need to formulate a personal set of principles to guide your way. Number 10 will help you to develop backbone, i.e., it will help you to stand up for what you know is right. Life may turn out to be more complex than you expected, but if your principles are in place, you will get through the hard times. Parents of children with first base 10 can help by modelling their own principles. The following quote is attributed to Buddha and relevant to both first base 1 and 10: *Be ye lamps unto yourselves, be your own reliance. Hold to the truth within yourselves, as to the only lamp.*

Base 11

<u>First Base 11</u>

November birthdays

Because your first base cycle resonates with number 11, what has been written about first base 2 will also apply to you but the double-one sharpens the focus on your personal response to life and makes teamwork more complex. Don't be surprised if you feel the need to find a special same gender friend. This is someone with whom you can share your deepest feelings and most off-beat ideas. Number 11 fills the mind with ideals that are slightly ahead of their time. Parents of children with first base 11 need to be aware that number 11 strains the nervous system and that it takes courage to reveal your dreams to someone. Refrain therefore from scoffing what you may not understand. The source of the following quote is unknown but relevant to number 11 wherever it is placed in your numbers: *"We all get lost in the darkness but dreamers learn to steer by the stars"*.

<u>Master Numbers</u>

If one of your cycles is a master number (11, 22, 33, 44 etc), keep this quote in mind: *"It isn't a calamity to die with dreams unfulfilled, but it is a shame not to dream. It is not a disgrace not to reach the stars, but life would be dismal if there were no stars to reach for"* (source unknown).

Base 12

<u>First Base 12</u>

December birthdays

What has been written about first base 3 will also apply to you but you are more likely to experience a 'moment of reckoning' in your life, when a critical decision must be made. And because number 12 is involved, your decision will not only impact on your life but on the lives of others as well. Befriending your intuition will definitely help you when the time comes. You probably have a naturally active imagination and this can be put to good use as well. Imagine how your world could be. As if you were looking through a multi-faceted crystal, gaze at your world through the eyes of several different people and contemplate what you see. You are learning to be adaptable in your opinions and ultimately generous with them. If you tend to think that you are always right, it could be that you fear that changing your point of view will bring up emotions that you would rather ignore. Remember that being inflexible to what the river of life brings to you, creates energy blocks in your body, and in turn, these block your creativity. Parents of children with first base 12 help them when they demonstrate that they have faith in them. Here is a quote from William James that is relevant to number 12 wherever it is in your numbers: *"Believe that life is worth living and your belief will help to create the fact"*.

The Pyramid Provides a Structure for the Unfolding Life Story

Returning to our example:

First Base 7 ran from Daniel's birth to the end of 2013. It is evident in the 'differentness' of his life in general: how many people rocket to international stardom during their twelfth year of life? It's also evident in the fact that he had a hard time at school because he suffered from a mild form of developmental coordination disorder, which in his own words "made him crap at everything." Once he became famous, attending school became even more difficult with some of his fellow students becoming quite abusive. He continued his education with on-set tutors and did well but mostly found school work useless. He already knew what he wanted to do with his life and college was not a part of it. He realized that a normal college life was never going to happen for him.

In January 2014 Daniel's base cycle shifted to 23/5 and he would have felt that shift at some level. Base 5 is typically easier to live with than base 7 but it does herald continual change. Since he is already thriving on the stimulation of changing movie roles and settings, Daniel is likely to find this energy to his liking.

Achievement number 30 will run until Daniel is 33 years of age before it passes the baton to second attainment 50 where it will join forces with birthday base 5 between 2023 and 2031. It will be a busy time indeed! Number 30 is about realizing the power and potential of the imagination and it would be hard to find someone who is doing that better than Daniel.

…

When a person stands at a crossroads in life or is experiencing difficulties, it is useful to consult their pyramid as outlined in this chapter, because it could shed light on what is happening. Unexpected changes can also be due to the personal year cycle, which operates within the base and attainment cycles, and which will be discussed next.

Chapter 9

The Personal Years

The nine-year cycle of personal years is a part of the base, attainment and challenge cycles of numerology and informs the progressed cycles of astrology. Your personal years are aligned with the calendar commonly used throughout the world for business transactions. The number cycles that we work with today are by no means arbitrary and are aligned with the evolution of humanity. Although the personal years inform our outer lives, these naturally affect us inwardly. That is why they are so useful: they tell us the most productive attitude to adopt to each year. What follows builds on what has been written by other numerologists. The metaphor of 'the tree' will be applied to a theoretical framework and accompanied by my personal research findings. The recommendations made are thus based on a model, a metaphor, and actual experience.

Calculating the Personal Years

The personal years are a personalized form of the world years. As a first step to determining your personal year you thus need to calculate the world year. Adding the numbers of the year together accomplishes this.

For example the year 1999 = 1 + 9 + 9 + 9 = 28 = 2 + 8 = 10 = 1 + 0 = 1 (i.e., world year 1)

The year 2000 = 2 + 0 + 0 + 0 = 2 (i.e., world year 2) etc.

To personalize the world cycle, the birth month and birth day must be added to it. 2014 was a world year 7 (2+0+1+4). If you were born on February 12, for example, you would therefore add 7 to your achievement number (2 for February plus 12 for your birth day = 14). The fact that this is the achievement number (discussed in chapter 8) implies that it is your achievement number that is being affected by the world cycle. Thus we could define the personal years as the way that the achievement number develops within the cycle of world years. When you add your achievement number to the world year, you have your personal year. So in the year 2014 a person with a birth day on February 12 experienced a personal year 3 (14 + 7 = 21 = 3) and in the year 2015, a personal year 4 (14 + 8 = 22 = 4) etc.

If the agreed 'global time' were to change, then this system would change with it. But for now, even those people who were born on December 31 have their personal years tick over on January 1st along with everyone else. No one stands apart from our global evolution.

The Personal Year = The World Year + Your Achievement Number

Interpreting the Personal Years

The personal years are one of the most widely researched and appreciated aspects of numerology. It is impossible and undesirable to avoid some repetition in this area, and I would encourage you to look at the personal years in context with your overall life story, as others have done. The personal years are the individual bricks in the pyramid and thus a part of a larger story. The core numbers, growth, maturity, and intensity numbers are your work crew, and so effectiveness in any year depends on how well you are able to apply available energies and compensate for 'missing' vibrations. When the personal year is the same as a core number it generally means that the person will be able to maximize the opportunities available, but only if the core number is not over-taxed. If it is, the person is likely to feel stressed much of the time. Likewise, if the personal year and the world year are the same, you may experience life racing along in one particular direction – each and every year!

Consider carefully the theme of the world year that your personal year 1 falls in. For example if your year 1 was in 2014, you may find that the power of truth (world year 7) is a major theme throughout this 9-year cycle, and it may seek to express itself through polarity (2), force (1) and form (4). Exploring the potential of your soul through teamwork (20) will be a part of this and could involve reshaping some entrenched thought patterns (14).

The pyramid described in the previous chapter demonstrates that subsequent attainments build on the initial achievement and so when interpreting a cycle of personal years you must consider not only the cycle at hand but also how your achievement number is continually developing. The cycles of 9 that are a part of the first base cycle are usually only understood with hindsight. Until the first Saturn return (in your late 20's), you may feel that life is beyond your conscious control and that things just happen. It is not until you contemplate a pattern such as that offered by numerology, that you gain an appreciation of the fact that you can maximize the opportunities that each year brings. Within the birthday base cycle there are either three or four cycles of 9 personal years, sitting (approximately) between the first and second Saturn returns. Many people can actually feel the beginning of a new cycle in their lives at the start of each 9-year cycle, however, rather than abrupt endings and beginnings, it is better to see the 9-year cycles as links in a chain moving through the 3 base cycles. The attainments, in turn, weave into these and are influenced by them. Like any new task that has several components, this may seem difficult at first to grasp, but these cycles are worth mastering. They hold the key for taking the reins of your life.

Within the *Pan's Script* model of Astronumerology, the personal years are a part of an overall paradigm, and so the imagery that follows is slightly but significantly different to that offered by other authors.

One Year at a Time...

<u>Personal Year One</u>

It is actually during year 9 that new seeds begin to germinate and so you need to reflect back on what new ideas sprang into your head last year. As soon as the old cycle has been released, these new ideas can move in. This germinating time, which begins in the mind, begins to attract a new round of external experiences, in accordance with the universal law of vibration. It is comforting to know that at the beginning of every 9-cycle you can start all over again, particularly if the previous cycle did not go well. Yet you need to contemplate whatever has happened, and then release it, keeping only its lessons, if you do not wish to repeat any mistakes that you might have made. Personal Year 1 will test your ability to project yourself and get things happening. The time is right to be daring: to go forth where you have not gone before and pioneer a new track. This is an active year, which will help you to break through previous limitations, especially self-imposed ones. Most people can feel their self-confidence rise during this year, enabling them to improve their situation in some way. During personal year 1 people typically begin an important new project, (although they may not realize its significance at the time). The seeds that are warming up and bursting open each contain the blueprint of a future, and so you need to consider carefully what you are setting in motion, yet you ought not to allow fear to prevent you from taking the first step in the direction that feels right.

The research undertaken for this chapter verified that there were more career moves made in personal year 1 than any other year. For example, Ernie Dingo faced his first audience, Sidney Poitier made his film debut, Donna Summer her singing debut, and Barry Humphries launched his first one-man show. Wolfgang Mozart wrote his first symphony in a personal year 1 and Vincent Van Gogh created his first painting. Henry Ford began making cars, and in a later personal year 1, developed the T-Model. Gloria Steinem wrote an insightful report that would launch her public profile and in a later personal year 1 co-founded the Women's Political Caucus. Stephen King began submitting stories, and Tokyo Rose began broadcasting. William Hogarth got his Copyright Act passed, and Alexander Graham Bell his telephone patented. Related to the above, what 'to be' often appeared as a theme associated with year 1. For example, it was in personal year 1 that Leonard Nimoy decided to be an actor, and Mohandas Gandhi a brahmacharya.

The examples amply demonstrate that personal year 1 is the time to *do* something! If you are in a personal year 1, and you are uncertain as to how to begin, this is an ideal time to reflect on the potential encoded within your date path. What steps could you take to become more familiar with the opportunities that it offers? Keep in mind that each successive cycle picks up from where the previous one left off, and that personal year 1 is when you can review the previous cycle in its entirety. What did you begin in your previous personal year 1 (and maybe even the one before that), that you can pick up now and develop? Was there an idea that you have forgotten about? The time is right to re-assess your unfulfilled dreams. A fresh vision is one of the most potent gifts of this year and you will be challenged to enact that vision during the next nine years. Your creativity is needed now. You must stand on your own two feet and rely on your *own* abilities for success. Observe your environment and pay attention. A positive spirit and progressive plans maximize this year's potential.

Personal Year Two

Because you cannot see the seed that is quietly germinating in your subconscious mind, personal year 2 can be a frustrating year. As well as the tree metaphor, another useful image for personal year 2 is that of a bird incubating inside an egg. In other words, personal year 2 can feel quite restrictive! The excitement of year 1 has past and you must now wait patiently, like a pregnant woman, for events to take their course. Just as you cannot crack the egg to see if the bird is hatching or pull up the plant to see if it's growing (without destroying it), you must simply trust whatever is unfolding. Actually, any restriction you may be feeling during this time is coming from a past that you are ready to be free of but from which there are still loose ends. Feelings of rebelliousness typically arise during this year because new dreams are coming in and you want to begin exploring them.

The research findings revealed that more births, deaths and marriages take place in personal year 2 than personal year 1; indeed there were more births in year 2 than any other year. People are less inclined to move in their personal years 2, with nearly every change of residence being work or study related. Career training is more common in year 2 than year 1 and so are changes of name and status (perhaps as a result of actions taken in year 1). Marriages that occur in a personal year 2 (for either partner) have a different quality than those in year 1. The latter seem to last for as long as there is a mutual interest whereas the former tend to be the proverbial 'opposites attract' type of marriages, their success dependant on how well each partner copes with conflicting perspectives and opinions. A special column had to be set up to accommodate one of the findings in personal year 2. Labelled 'competition or tests of resolve', it included the fact that it was in his personal year 2 that Henry Ford first struck competition in the car manufacturing industry, and that Joseph Pulitzer had to begin competing for readers against Hurst. And Napoleon found himself at Waterloo! In all three cases, competition brought out the worst in these people, but it didn't have to be that way. They can serve as a warning when you feel drawn into a conflict situation.

If you are in a personal year 2, the wills of others will predominate much of the time and you may need to exercise diplomacy. Refusing to cooperate and getting emotional will only aggravate the situation. If you are feeling desperately rebellious, slow down, breathe very deeply and try to get things into perspective: this is only a temporary situation. Focusing your energy on the details that you might have overlooked in the excitement of personal year 1 could spare you much stress in the years to come. Think of this time as preparing the nursery for the new arrival; it is soon going to get busy and you must be ready. Money matters tend to loom large in year 2 and you are advised to plan ahead. Check your banking and insurance and read your contracts carefully. Consolidate and review your plans. Number 2 brings into focus the things that you value; everything that you hold dear. Be prepared to stand by those things be they material, personal, intellectual or spiritual. Expect to have your resolve tested. Being well prepared could save you having to fight. Collect and collate information on one project of special interest to you and take a course to update yourself in the field of endeavour that would appear to be opening up. If you are in business, this is also the year to consider the people who are working for you.

Personal Year Three

Whatever has been incubating during the past two years typically emerges during this year, just as our metaphorical tree must at some point strike through the soil and into the air. Then you can see, at last, the form that this cycle might take and the key idea behind it. You may still have trouble actually identifying it, but in most cases its general shape will be apparent. The newly emerging plant may now become an object of interest to other people and this may elicit a facet of your personality that you were previously unaware of. It may bring you new friends and the feeling that comes with being a part of a group with a common interest. Like the emerging tree, you may take on a new role and seek to express it. You might want to strike out in search of new opportunities and experiences. However you could also feel quite vulnerable and afraid. This is still a subjective time, and so the way that you react to your particular circumstances will be vitally important to the success of the overall cycle. Like the new tree you may feel both excited and 'on your own'. If you think of the plant as an emerging idea, then personal year 3 becomes one of ideals, images, and flights of fancy seeking expression. This can set in motion spontaneous shifts in relationships. By year 3, whether personal or worldly, the 9-year cycle is well underway and the way that you handle the flow of energy that comes now will be critical in the years ahead. If it is not channelled in one direction or another, it will simply scatter all over the place.

In the research sample there were actually slightly more firsts in year 3 than year 1. For example, Aldous Huxley secured his first publishing agreement, and Karen Carpenter her first major recording contract. William Butlin opened his first holiday camp, and Henri Matisse celebrated his first one-artist exhibition, each the outcome of much work. Changes of residence also matched year 1 but were of a distinctly different nature. Whereas year 1 moves tended to be very personal happenings, sometimes leaving the person feeling that they had little choice, year 3 moves were more considered. Learning was often the motive; for example Quincy Jones moved his family to Paris so that he could learn from a particular teacher. Occasionally the move was for pleasure, adventure, or to improve one's circumstances, but equally often it was for spiritual or humanitarian reasons. For example it was during her personal year 3 that Audrey Hepburn went to Somalia in support of UNICEF. Another striking feature of personal year 3 was the number of changes in relationships (perhaps as the result of moving, learning, and personal growth). Marriages were more common in year 3 than years 1 or 2 and so were partings, but not necessarily divorces. The best of the year 3 marriages were deep friendships.

If you are in a personal year 3, select something that you would like to learn then do whatever you can to make it happen. This is also the year to cultivate friendships, both old and new, and if friendship can tie in with your new learning, all the better! Your ideas should be allowed to take flight this year, even if only in your personal diary. Number 3 has everything to do with communication and so if you are feeling afraid, vulnerable, or despondent, talk it over with someone. Personal Year 3 is a time to move forward, even to act on a hunch.

Personal Year Four

It is during year 4 that our metaphorical tree strengthens its root system, for if it is to withstand the growth symbolized by number 5, it must stabilize its foundations. In like manner, your personal year 4 is when you need to 'settle down' in some way. Whatever it was that you began in year 1 now needs to be re-examined to ascertain the ground that it stands upon. Only with a strong infrastructure will your project be able to reap fruit that you can enjoy in the years ahead. Like the tree, this means going deeper and seriously questioning the direction you have taken thus far. Is this project going to be able to sustain you and are you going to be able to meet the commitments it entails? Moreover, are you being true to yourself? As the tree must establish its root system so that a strong wind doesn't blow it over, so must you attend to the details of your project so that it can weather the storms that life may bring in the years ahead.

The research revealed that this is the year of career manoeuvres, and the time when people were more likely to follow their heart rather than their head. For example, it was in his personal year 4 that Jerry Springer swapped from law to politics, and John Keats decided to go out on a limb and devote himself to poetry instead of practicing as a doctor, although he had already completed his training. Some turning points were due to circumstances beyond the person's control, such as ill health or war; the person simply had to make the best of things. For example, due to an accident, H. G Wells discovered the joy that reading gave to him and would begin writing his own books. Johannes Kepler was forced by circumstances to defer his training in theology in order to teach mathematics. Although he may not have enjoyed it, he soon realized its implications. It was in his personal year 4 that Peter Falk decided to play Colombo, and Leonard Nimoy, Mr Spock, a substantial career-risk at the time. Each of these decisions would have major implications in the future. There would seem to be no such thing as a lightweight marriage in personal year 4. The successful couples in our survey weathered severe testing together, often of a public nature, growing ever stronger as individuals and soul mates. Indeed there were more enduring relationships formalized in year 4 than any other year and it does not appear to matter which partner was in year 4. Sixty-five percent of these couples mated for life with a further twelve percent riding the storms of life together for more than twenty years before parting.

If you are in a personal year 4 it is time to decide if the way that you have been going is truly the way that you want to continue. If it is not, then now is the time to do something about it. Conversely if what you are doing feels right, you might consider making a deeper commitment to it. If you are able to identify what it was that seeded in year 1 and track its development through years 2 and 3, you are in a position to decide if you want to leave it behind and re-establish yourself, or stick with it. Either way you are going to have to knuckle down, get organized, and persevere. Laying down the foundations of a building may not be terribly exciting, but building your dreams on a weak foundation is asking for trouble. Personal Year 4 has a way of forcing people to be practical. The trick is to have a vision or at least a goal, and to stay loyal to your ideals. If you take one step at a time, you may be surprised at the end of the year by how much you have accomplished.

Personal Year Five

Continuing the plant analogy, this is the year that our little tree will want to branch out and grow in every possible direction. Likewise, in your personal year 5's you are likely to feel the urge to break free from any restrictions you experienced last year, and expand. Year 5 is thus the time to explore the creative potential of the foundations you laid last year. And returning to our other metaphor: if the chicken that was stuck inside the egg in year 2, broke out in year 3, and learned to fend for itself in year 4, it will now attempt to fly over the fence and see what lies beyond. It may be difficult at times to remember that you are in the middle of a nine-year cycle and to stay focused on the goals that you have set. There could even come an urge to escape altogether!

The research findings confirmed that this is a highly creative year. It was in one of his year 5's that Albert Einstein launched the Special Theory of Relativity, and Abraham Lincoln the Proclamation of Emancipation. Edgar Cayce began self-hypnosis to restore his voice. Jean Henri Dunant promoted the first Geneva Convention, and Betty Ford opened her famous clinic. Vincent Van Gogh decided to become an artist, and Michelangelo began work on the Sistine Chapel. Charles Fillmore created a covenant, and Oscar Schindler a list for which he would be both praised and reviled. Even travel tends to be creative in year 5. It was in one of her personal year 5's that Alexandra David-Néel reached Lhasa after the adventure of a lifetime, and Jules Verne sailed to America, also fulfilling a long-term dream. What stood out in the findings related to personal year 5 was the number of significant gains made. Fanny Durack broke the male swimming record and thus became famous in her year 5, Henry Ford sold his first car, and Jacques Cousteau purchased a yacht. James Lynn discovered that the company he had hoped to rise with had decided to sell out, so he took out a risky loan and bought it. Going by the statistics, it would be tempting to call year 5 fortunate but it was also in a personal year 5 that Quincy Jones found himself stranded in Europe, the financial deal he had expected suddenly evaporating. This tells us that the astrological patterns need to support the good fortune that year 5 offers. Interestingly marriages in year 5 seem to have almost exactly a 50:50 chance of success. Some were wonderful partnerships but oddly, one in five lasted less than a year!

Year 5 is naturally a progressive year, although if you are in a personal year 5, you may find that it brings a different direction to what you might have expected, even some fascinating and frustrating twists and turns. If people are showing an interest in your project, make an effort to explain it to them - then be ready for anything! Ideas that do not seem to be working may simply need to be modified. If you are experiencing problems due to nervous exhaustion take heed and slow down. It is your mental attitude that will make all the difference this year, and a flexible one will serve you the best. Personal Year 5 is the ideal time to practice what the Buddhist teachers call mindfulness, which is the ability to remain alert and observe without necessarily feeling the need to get involved. Take a good long look at what life is presenting you, no matter how remote it seems from what you want.

Personal Year Six

Our metaphorical tree is now in flower. Birds are nesting in its branches, their various songs breaking the silence of the day, and a hive of bees or perhaps a nest of wasps may also have taken up residence. Like the tree, you may also have grown 'taller' in some way or at least have a better overview of your situation. And whether your particular environment is buzzing with wasps, bees or humming birds, there is one reoccurring theme in year 6: it is a social year. No matter how you may resist it, personal year 6 will test your creative capacity when it comes to relating to those with whom you share your corner of the world.

The research done for this chapter was not the first to reveal that there is typically much turbulence in the relationship arena in year 6 and that there are significantly more divorces this year. Marriages are common too but no more so than years 3, 7, 8 or 9. What is unusual however is that marriages made in either partner's year 6 are more likely to produce children; childless marriages being more common in the other years. There were more intrigues in personal year 6 too. For example, there were two re-marriages, one working out splendidly but not so the other. And there were two secret engagements, (neither of which resulted in marriage). Tests of character and personal resolve were quite common. For example it was in one of his personal year 6's that Bertrand Russell was put in jail for his beliefs, and a similar story occurred in the life of Yitzhak Rabin. It was also in a year 6 that John Steinbeck travelled to Vietnam to check out for himself what was actually going on there. Common to all the above is an enormous surge of creativity, and this can take practically any form. It was in a year 6 that John Keats wrote his most brilliant poetry, Bill Gates began developing Microsoft, Barry Humphries invented Edna Everage, Vincent Van Gogh completed his first oil painting, HG Wells wrote an immensely popular history of the world, and Johannes Kepler discovered the elliptical orbit of Mars. Often related to the above, there is typically a change in one's domestic environment in Personal Year 6.

Not every project undertaken this year is marked for success, but if you are in a personal year 6 and your activity is based on good will, there will be no regrets. Becoming a part of the solution rather than part of the problem would seem to be one of the major themes of personal year 6. And if you do not *expect* others to honour and admire you for what you do, then any praise that does happen to come your way, will feel like a bonus. Year 6 is likely to be a highly social year with lots of giving-to and receiving-from other people. If you are open to it, there is also likely to be a 'flowering' of significant dreams, vision, insight, and spiritual experiences. Within the cycle of 9 years, something is climaxing this year and therefore needs to be expressed. Can you see what it is? If the cycle has progressed reasonably well, this should be a creative year with plenty of plans made, modified, and remade but you may find it necessary to state your personal needs clearly and assert your personal boundaries. It's a year to be careful in many ways. There will be lots of opportunities for you to give of your time and you will need to decide which such opportunities-cum-responsibilities feel right for you. Managing your various interests so that they can co-exist without upsetting your emotional equilibrium is the task ahead of you. Be aware that running parallel with such outer activity is a substantial shift in your inner world: one flowing into the other and back again.

Personal Year Seven

If personal year 6 symbolizes the tree's flowering and year 8 its fruiting, then year 7 represents the time in between. This suggests that in the life of a tree number 7 encodes the stage at which a plant internalizes its energy and consolidates its forces so that its fruit can be brought to bear. In our personal lives this indicates that during year 7 our inner needs must receive some attention. Through introspection, you can transmute your life experiences into wisdom. Just as you cannot hurry a tree's fruiting without compromising its flavour, nor will forcing issues in a year 7 do you much good in the long term.

Overall, the highest score for launchings, firsts, career advances, decision making and creative activity was a draw between personal years 1 and 7 but the themes that lay behind them were different. In year 1 people typically decide to act but in year 7 they are more inclined to decide *not* to act. Both require courage and presence of mind. The tally in the area of decision making was actually higher in year 7 than any other year, and each and every decision made was carefully measured. For example, it was in one of his personal years 7 that Albert Einstein was offered the Israeli Presidency but he decided not to accept it. Likewise, after careful consideration, Oprah Winfrey decided not to write her autobiography. It was in a year 7 that Mahatma Gandhi undertook the 'salt march' not only in defiance of unjust laws but to change the mind-set of the people. As well as major decisions such as the above, there were more launchings made in year 7, each one being the result of several years of preparation. The themes or titles of works written or published this year have a distinctly 7'ish flavour. For example Edgar Alan Poe published his first detective story, William Cowper a volume of moral satires, and Immanuel Kant his *Critique of Pure Reason*. Bertrand Russell wrote his *Paradox,* and John Bunyan completed his *Pilgrim's Progress*. It proved impossible to categorize the marriages made in year 7 but only about twenty percent fell under the 'brief and turbulent' category. The remainder each bore a unique story.

If you are in a personal year 7 you must make time to rest now, as a busy year 8 is just around the corner. Change is in the air but consider your options carefully. If you are not comfortable with the energy that number 7 bears, this year might be a time of emotional unrest and indecision. It is quite common to feel 'different' in some way during year 7. Let that find its own level within the whirlpool of daily life, bearing in mind that whatever is happening 'out there' is in some way mirroring your own consciousness. Being a year of consolidation, you would benefit from creating time to be alone. During personal year 7 it is vital to delegate excessive responsibility so that you can concentrate on what is important to you. You may find that study or research comes more easily this year. Personal Year 7 is a time of inner growth and discovery and so take a sabbatical or a retreat if you can. This year especially, take time to consider your private and personal needs. This is not the best year for business expansion, yet money may come in its own time and way. Year 7 can bring unexpected surprises.

Personal Year Eight

At this stage in the cycle the tree is bringing forth its fruit in accordance with the laws of nature. in like manner, something that was seeded in year 1 is now bearing results. If the tree is barren, you may need to go back and carefully track each thread in order to understand why. If this is not done, there is a risk that you will repeat this trend in the next cycle. Sometimes there is 'fruit' evident, but not what you expected. Again, you have to reflect back on the cycle in order to understand why. The more honest you are about the role that you have played in the outcome; the more likely you are to set in motion a sweeter cycle next time. Year 8 is always a busy year, especially if there is a bumper crop, but even if there is not, it is the nature of number 8 to try to achieve *something*. Occasionally personal year 8 feels like a race against time - to get something completed before the cycle ends.

Although year 8 brings the impulse to *do* something, statistically it is unremarkable in the area of career decisions and major moves forward. Rather, it would seem to be the year of quiet achievement. Oprah Winfrey ran a marathon in one of her personal year 8's, which just about sums up how this year feels. We seem to just keep on keeping on until the year is done. People are less inclined to change residence in year 8 than in any other year (year 6 being the most popular year for that). And year 8 has a way of raising issues that we hoped would go away. A unique and surprising quality of year 8 is the number of humiliations that people seem to suffer. It was in one of his year 8's that Baruch Spinoza was excommunicated, threatened publicly, and even cursed! Napoleon Bonaparte launched an utterly disastrous invasion on Russia. More recently, Peter Falk decided to try his hand at acting only to receive a devastating review for his efforts, but he pressed on, success following his persistence. And therein lays the key to managing year 8. Changes of status were common in year 8 (second only to year 9), and they swung both ways. For example, in his year 8, Michinomiya Hirohito was enthroned as a 'divine son' and twenty-seven years later, in another Year 8, renounced his divinity. Marriages made in year 8 were mostly long and productive, and in the majority of cases children were born or adopted (there being more adoptions in year 8 than any other year). There were a very few couples who married, quickly realized their mistake and parted, yet even partners that chose not to stay together mostly remained life-long friends.

If you are in a personal year 8 the findings suggest that you will need to deal with whatever issues arise fairly and squarely. Rather than back away, continue to work towards the goals that you have set and find a way around any difficulties that may arise. This is not the year to give up but it would seem that humility might be called for at some point. Even if a big break does come your way, consider the effect that it may have on others and target the best possible outcome for everyone involved. This is a year when stamina will be needed, and resourcefulness. Time management may increase efficiency but don't neglect to slot in time for your personal needs as well as career goals. Wholehearted, consistent, and good-natured effort must be tempered with common sense and so take a break when you need one, and select your confidants carefully. Whatever happens, try to turn it into an advantage, or at least a pearl of wisdom.

Personal Year Nine

Our metaphorical tree is now releasing its unpicked fruit, eventually to be absorbed by the earth. Within this fruit lie the seeds of future cycles and so you cannot simply put the past in the past and forget about it. You must contemplate its significance. Keep in mind that even rotten fruit can enrich the soil and bring forth healthy seeds. Your aim is to be as clean and clear as you can be by the year's end, for the emptier that you are of the last cycle's 'baggage', the more room there will be for fresh inspiration. It's time to examine attitudes and beliefs and their accompanying patterns of behaviour for their worth, and release where necessary. Although it's easy to say "let go," in reality the soul cannot let go of something that it does not understand. The mind will keep churning it over in an effort to make sense of it. Your task in year 9 is thus to figure out how your experiences during the cycle now passing, can benefit the cycle now approaching.

Marriages are more common in years 8 and 9 than other years, yet could not be more different. Year 8 marriages were as likely to be long as year 9 ones short. Naturally there were some wonderful unions made in year 9, particularly where the partners were mutually supportive. An excellent example of a successful year 9 union was that between Elizabeth Bowes-Lyon and Albert Windsor. Notably, if there is a crack in the mental or moral fibre of the person who marries in year 9 or their partner, the union will certainly unravel, even if the couple does try to maintain a public appearance of togetherness. Congruent with the fact that numbers 7 and 9 denote endings; the research showed that deaths were more common in years 7 and 9 than any other year. Changes of status were also more common in year 9, heralding in all cases, the theme of the incoming cycle. It was in his first personal year 9 that Lhamo Thondup was officially proclaimed the 14th Dalai Lama of Tibet. And it was in one of his year 9's that Napoleon Bonaparte crowned himself Emperor, which history would judge as the beginning of the end of his career. Yet it should not be assumed that this year is 'all bad'. Indeed, one of William Butlin's year 9's was described by a biographer as a 'year of triumph'. Samuel Lewis described one of his personal year 9's like this: "Everything has turned around and I think every upset of almost every earlier part of my life has been reversed… My trip so far had been successful far beyond hopes and dreams. It is almost a vindication, but of the softest kind". Despite the constant delays and disappointments that year 9 is notorious for, he received recognition and even ovations for the work he had done, and he witnessed the fulfillment of every project he had undertaken.

If you are in a personal year 9 you may find it useful to imagine that you are perched on top of a fully-grown tree in order to gain a broader view of your life. 'From above' you may be able to gain a clearer perspective of the cycle now passing. This is the year to exercise your imagination, and that takes time. If you deny yourself time to think this year, you will compromise the potential that the incoming cycle offers. Many people experience emotional exhaustion in year 9 or at least tiredness due to the emotional turbulence of the cycle now ending. There will be mixed feelings, which must be dealt with. If the reality of the past is faced rather than denied, the incoming cycle can be created on solid rather than shaky ground. It is time for the wisdom of hindsight, fresh inspiration, wiser ideals and above all, rest. Tolerance, compassion and forgiveness are necessary now and that extends to you. Reward yourself for something you did well.

Some numerologists begin the personal years with the birthday. How that came about is unknown; possibly it was because sensitive people felt a change happening within themselves at around the time of their birthday or a distinct change of energy from that time onwards. Their outer lives could have changed too. This is where a knowledge of astrology is not only handy but essential. There *is* a distinct change on the birthday. Astrologically this is known as the solar return cycle. Every birthday the sun returns to the same place it was in when you were born but other planetary bodies are now in different positions. A planet might have moved away from or shifted closer to one of the Angles (Ascendant, Descendant, IC or MC) and you're surely going to feel that. We are not concerned here with the solar return cycle or any of the other cycles that tick over on the birthday but with a 9-year numerological cycle that is an aspect of much bigger numerological cycles. The personal years are a *personalized* form of the world years, which impact on all of us. In turn, the world years are part of universal laws and cycles none of which are divorced from astrological cycles but which must be interpreted each in their own way. In the next chapter you will learn how the personal years fit into an astrological model that was used in Hellenistic times and probably very much earlier.

Chapter 10

Astronumerology and the Wheel of Life

"All numbers evolved from the circle"

- C. M. Kelland, 'The Mystery and Significance of Number'

Astronumerology is a form of numerology that recognizes the inter-relationship of numerology and astrology. The numerologist does not need to also become an astrologer but will find an understanding of the building blocks of astrology deeply enriching.

The Personal Years within the Wheel of the Zodiac

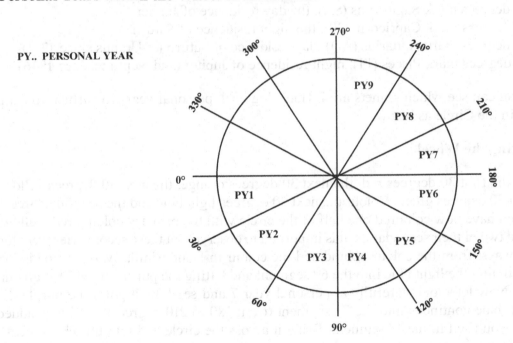

Figure 1: The Personal Years within the Degrees of the Circle

To more fully understand the correspondences presented in this chapter, grab a protractor, some coloured pencils, paper and a ruler and do everything by hand. Begin by drawing a circle and marking off every 30 degrees per the diagram above.

Note how the lines run across the circle: from zero degrees to the left to 180 degrees to the right and from the 90 degrees below to 270 above. From 30 degrees to 210 degrees, from 60 degrees to 240 degrees, from 120 degrees to 300 degrees and from 150 degrees to 330 degrees.

Label the first segment of 30 degrees personal year 1, the second segment personal year 2 etc to personal year 9. You will notice that one-quarter of the circle remains outside of the personal years. This segment of the circle represents the unseen forces that lie behind the personal years. It reminds us that the personal years are a personalized form of a more universal cycle that is linked in with the evolution of humanity as a whole.

The Signs Of The Zodiac and their Rulers

At Zero degrees to the left of the circle, mark Aries (AR): the day residence of Mars
At 30 degrees, mark Taurus (TA): the night residence of Venus
At 60 degrees mark Gemini (GE): the day residence of Mercury
At 90 degrees mark Cancer (CN): the sole residence of the Moon
At 120 degrees mark Leo (LE): the sole residence of the Sun
At 150 degrees mark Virgo (VI): the night residence of Mercury
At 180 degrees mark Libra (LI): the day residence of Venus
At 210 degrees mark Scorpio (SC): night residence of Mars (and Pluto since 1930)
At 240 degrees mark Sagittarius (SA): the day residence of Jupiter
At 270 degrees mark Capricorn (CP): the night residence of Saturn
At 300 degrees mark Aquarius (AQ): day residence of Saturn (& Uranus since 1781)
At 330 degrees mark Pisces (PI): night residence of Jupiter (and Neptune since 1846)

Now you can see which planets are influencing each personal year. To further your insight colour in the Circle as below.

Colouring the Wheel

Colour the first 30 degrees red, the next 30 degrees orange, the next 30 degrees yellow, and the next 30 degrees green. Colour the next 30 degrees light blue and the next 30 degrees dark blue. You have now coloured one half of the circle with the primary colours red, yellow, and blue and two of their secondaries. It is important to observe that these secondaries were formed in two ways: from the colour behind and the colour in front. Similarly, dark blue is formed by continuing the light blue into the 6th segment and letting the purple of the 7th segment mix with it. Now let's look carefully at personal year 7 and see how it got to be purple. Firstly the dark blue continues into the 7th segment (from 180 to 210 degrees). To this is added the red that you used in the 1st segment. Bring it across the circle and into the 7th segment. You now have a mixture of red and dark blue, hence the purple. Let the purple continue into the 8th segment of the Wheel (from 210 to 240 degrees, which covers personal year 8). Then add some orange from the 2nd segment on the opposite side of the Wheel. Various shades of brown will result from this. Move now to the 9th segment of the Wheel (from 240 to 270 degrees =

personal year 9) and let the brown continue into there. To it add a little yellow from the 3rd segment opposite it. Keep darkening your personal year 9 until it is black with glimmers of yellow and brown, like flecks on gold hidden below the soil. Move now to the 10th segment of the Wheel (from 270 to 300 degrees) and let the black move into there, but only gently. To it add white from the 11th segment. This is the grey area of the Wheel. The actual shade of grey depends on the individual state of consciousness but here are the guidelines: number 10 is where the black of absorption meets the white of reflection, creating various shades of grey, like a winter-time landscape. Move to the 11th segment of the Wheel (from 300 degrees to 330 degrees) and imagine some of the grey moving into here like streaks of silver. Now move into the 12th segment and let the silvery-whiteness of the 11th segment mix with the red of the 1st segment and watch those glorious shades of pink fan out.

When the blues from the 5th and 6th segments find their way across the circle, you get sparkles of electric blue in the 11th segment and sublime shades of magenta appearing in the 12th. As you can see, the third and fourth quadrants of the wheel have a wealth of possibilities that the first and second don't.

The centre is pure white. To show this, you can use a splash of whiteout. Most authors acknowledge the rainbow colours in relation to the wheel, but have you ever wondered where brown, black, white, silver, grey and pink fit into the picture? Here you can see that every colour has its place and most importantly, how they interrelate. The relationships across the wheel are becoming increasingly evident. What you do in personal year 1 will underscore personal year 7, what you do in personal year 2 will bear fruit in personal year 8 etc.

See front cover for the full colour wheel.

How the Planets and the Signs Of The Zodiac Interact With the Personal Years

Personal Year 1, Red, Aries and Mars

Reinforcing what research has amply demonstrated, the colour red, planet Mars, and the fiery sign of Aries, tell us that this must be an active year – a time to dare - to move forward, make plans and reach out for new opportunities. To be courageous and take initiative are supported by this dynamic trilogy. Aries/Mars help us to overcome fear, lethargy and resistance, the fieriness that they represent igniting the quest for new adventure. The time for looking back has past. However, as Juno Jordan warns in *Your Right Action Number*, personal year 1 is not time to force issues but rather to act as an inspiration for others; to offer ideas and lead by example. Mars and Aries urge you to exercise your willpower and to act with determination so that you can experience being on a winning team. 'Do not allow others to dampen your enthusiasm", they would say; "believe in yourself and try something new, even if it means going alone. Welcome a fresh challenge and muster the courage to learn as you go along".

Personal Year 2, Orange, Taurus and Venus

As red must blend with yellow to produce orange, so during a personal year 2 we need 'blend' with other people and temper our individuality and wilfulness with thoughtfulness and appreciation. Steadfastness is a keyword for both the earthy sign of Taurus and personal year

2 and patience is another, hence the need for tact, diplomacy and willingness to give and take, share and negotiate. Taurus and Venus would tell people in personal year 2 to try to relax, despite the busyness going on all around them. "Enjoy the simple pleasures of life and try to be at peace with yourself, despite your circumstances", they would say. The presence of Taurus suggests that slow and sure might be the way to go in year 2. The combined influence of number 2 and Venus ensures that partnerships of all kinds feature throughout personal year 2. '2' is the number of polarity and sometimes opposites attract but sometimes they just irritate. Taurus could compound the problem by being stubborn and digging the proverbial heels in. Or, the Taurean influence could help you to find common ground with another person. The choice is yours to make, choice of perspective being an essential part of year 2. The wheel suggests that what you do at this stage will impact on the fruit that appears in personal year 8. The more love you are prepared to put into the cycle the sweeter will be its harvest.

Personal Year 3, Yellow, Gemini and Mercury

With Mercury stimulating movement and the airy sign of Gemini siphoning the energy so generated into the thinking realm, personal year 3 is always a great time to learn something new. During your personal years 3 you are apt to feel vulnerable and nervous at times, yet with the help of these astral influences you can ride it out with confidence. Communication is a keyword for both Gemini and personal year 3 and friends, both new and old, are especially significant in the third year of any cycle. If you communicate your ideas and listen to the ideas of other people, you may be pleasantly surprised to find that some are happy to support your projects when they actually know what they are! The colour yellow stimulates mental activity and so we have here a trilogy that encourages us to expand our thinking, take risks and develop our social skills. If you could hear them, Gemini, Mercury, and number 3 would be telling you to share your ideas in a way that other people can relate to.

Personal Year 4, Green, Cancer and the Moon

In tandem with the number 4, the water-sign of Cancer nurtures the cycle now underway. Both the moon and number 4 have a formative function. As a mother must care for a child by doing all of the mundane chores in a reasonably systematic way, personal year 4 is a time when details need attending to and common sense must prevail. The imagery of the moon sheds light on this year by reminding us that it is our feeling-life that inspires our creativity. As your feelings strengthen, so does the willpower to see your creativity through to completion. The restorative quality of the colour green provides a bridge between the expansive yellow of year 3 and the expansive sky-blue of year 5. Green would remind you to get out in nature often because connecting with the earth and its cycles will help you to appreciate your place within them. If you could hear them, Cancer and the Moon would be telling you that year 4 is the ideal time to ensure that your dreams are materializing with conviction and integrity, because the remainder of the cycle depends on it.

Personal Year 5, Sky Blue, Leo and the Sun

The presence of fiery Leo informs us that in personal year 5 you may feel that the heat is on to get things moving. Your year 5 could thus get quite lively. Suddenly you may be required to adapt to all kinds of unexpected circumstances. With more than half of the cycle gone it is time to act with all the confidence that you can muster. "Advertise", Leo would tell you. "Let people know what you are up to and how they can help. Show enthusiasm for the progress you have made thus far, because how can other people pitch in and help, if they don't know what is happening?" Like the sun, you must radiate outwardly during year 5, touching the hearts of others with the warmth of your best intentions. The astral influences acting upon year 5 prompt you to make the most of any opportunities that come your way. You may find it necessary to select from a variety of exciting options those that will enhance the project that you have chosen to focus upon. The colour sky-blue suggests that it also time to broaden your horizons and adjust to any change that may have occurred in the climate.

Personal Year 6, Dark Blue, Virgo and Mercury

Sorting, analyzing, and making your ideas serviceable to others are the themes that unite earthy Virgo, mercurial Mercury and personal year 6. If you could hear them speak they would be telling you to stick with the task at hand and bring it to a more refined state. The dark blue colour suggests a deeper level of mental activity from Mercury than the bright yellow corresponding to Gemini. In other words what you learned in personal year 3 must now be made coherent. Such depth provides discrimination, which helps you to distinguish between the superficial and the necessary and by so doing you become more efficient. The deep blue symbolizes the oceanic depth of our collective emotions. It takes the intelligence of the soul to navigate a way through the emotional complications that can arise during year 6. Virgo and Mercury would have you channel this psychic energy into activities that are of real benefit to others. The longing to be useful is an ideal based on love. When you keep this in mind you make the most of your personal years 6.

Personal Year 7, Purple, Libra and Venus

Bright red and deep blue must now find their fulcrum. The more one studies the number 7 the more contrary seems its behaviour in the material world. C. M. Kelland (*Figureology, the Science of Number*) described 7 as a 'fighting figure' yet most people today think of 7 as spiritually inclined. In astrology the 7th House governs battles and open enemies and also our most meaningful relationships! And so number 7 can go either way and be active, assertive, and worldly, or contemplative, peaceful, and spiritual – or a juggling act between the two! There was a time when Libra was not thought of as a separate constellation but as the 'claw of the scorpion'. "It is the truth that you are trying to grasp", Venus whispers to us throughout the ages. Taking the time to listen to your soul is the call from the goddess of love, and it is she who will help you to maintain balance in your life. The colours suggest that the wilfulness and courage of Aries must now be internalized and that you need to strike a balance between activity and contemplation, spontaneity and a more measured response. It's time to weigh things up, and sort the gold from the dross. In contrast to year 1, this is where you can look back and reflect upon the decisions that you have made. Libra's airiness will help you to do just that.

Personal Year 8, Brown, Scorpio, Mars and Pluto

The colour brown has the resilience that number 8 is famous for, and dark or light, fertile or polluted, the brown earth will bear fruit according to the laws of nature. Brown is a conglomeration of colours: the red is there to inject vitality along with the yellow to help you explore possibilities. The greens are in there to facilitate growth and the blues to provide a range of consciousness. Thus year 8 represents a time when many facets of life compete for attention. A year without clear, fair, and realistic goals may generate the murky brown of confusion whilst a year based on love promises to generate a deep, rich earthy loam that brings forth a sustaining harvest. Even if it has been an unproductive cycle, common sense and sound judgment may yet save the day because Mars will help you to assert yourself and get things done. The watery sign of Scorpio tends to be reactive, and so you need to bear in mind that pessimism, jealousy, and resentfulness will sour the fruit that is growing, whilst love and respect will sweeten it. Pluto offers a unique treasure to this year: the ability to access personal power sourced at the very depths of your being.

Personal Year 9, Black, Sagittarius and Jupiter

Picking up on the colour black, the imagery of the all-absorbing earth provides the most useful image here. This is the rich 'black earth' from which the word 'kemi' comes. It was an ancient name for the land of Egypt and it means 'field of transformation'. From this source we get the word alchemy. We can also relate Sagittarius as a fire sign to this image if we think of the earth as compost that combusts organic material, purifying and transforming it into useable energy. As black absorbs the other colours, so number 9 tends to encompass the other numbers. Astrologers may initially be surprised to see the buoyant Jupiter and Sagittarius in the realm of the colour black but it is exactly their broad mindedness that are needed during the close of a cycle. They would tell you not to grieve for what might have been but to search for the meaning behind your experience. "What has the cycle taught you?" they would ask. "Where is the wisdom and what lessons do you not wish to repeat in the next cycle?" Personal Year 9 would have you consider such questions and find personal meaning in them so that the up and coming year 1 will set in motion a rich and productive cycle. Jupiter and Sagittarius assist the development of faith in the process of life and a philosophical attitude to whatever it brings.

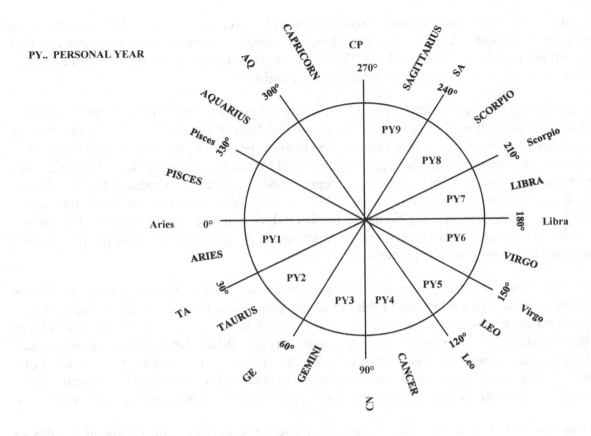

Figure 2: The Personal Years within the Wheel of the Zodiac

When the *Pan's Script* system of correspondences is compared with the tree metaphor presented in chapter 9 and your own experience, the above colours, planets, and signs become useful for understanding the astral forces that influence each personal year.

Potent Partnerships

An offshoot of the correspondences between the planets and the numbers is the awareness that certain number combinations are naturally compatible. You will notice that each of the following pairs adds up to Number 9:

Numbers 1 and 8: the Yang and Yin of Mars, respectively
Numbers 2 and 7: the Yin and Yang of Venus, respectively
Numbers 3 and 6: the Yang and Yin of Mercury, respectively

Numbers 4 and 5: the Moon and Sun, respectively

The astral correspondences of numbers 4 and 5 illustrate that such partnerships can be either harmonious or competitive. If the moon and sun were to fight over who should rule the skies, it would be disastrous for all of us. Precisely because one rules by day and the other by night, life on earth is possible. This can teach us much about partnerships. When each component is recognized as having its unique role to play, the outcome could turn out to be greater than the sum of the parts. The numbers 4 and 5 are often featured in the charts of people who work in the medical profession, and it is their love for humanity (which relates to number 9) that keeps them going despite all of the difficulties. Numbers 4 and 5 can empower you to act for the common good by blending structure and versatility.

On an emotional level, numbers 1 and 8 represent the explosive and implosive sides of Mars. Within a relationship this could spark the proverbial 'war of the roses'. More ideally number 1 represents the principle-centred leader who inspires people to greatness whilst number 8 is the efficient executive with the organizational skill that number 1 often lacks. The difference between these two possible scenarios is represented by number 7 (because $8 - 1 = 7$) and as we know from chapter 7, that means self-honesty. Relating them to number 9, numbers 1 and 8 as a partnership, need to focus their effort (which can be extraordinary), on a common, humanitarian goal. Within a partnership situation the person with the 1 and the person with the 8 need to appreciate each other's contribution.

On an emotional level, numbers 2 and 7 represent the stubborn and indecisive sides of Venus respectively. Within a relationship this could amount to total inertia. More ideally, number 2 represents the team-player who seeks common ground whilst number 7 represents the thinker who discerns the outcome most likely to please everyone. When they exercise versatility, they stimulate each other's ingenuity (that's $7 - 2 = 5$). Both 2 and 7 have an eye for detail and are therefore the ideal research and development team for number 9's humanitarian ideals. Number 2 excels in accumulating and compiling data whilst number 7 analyzes and simplifies.

On an emotional level, numbers 3 and 6 represent the cunning and provocative sides of Mercury. Within a relationship this could 'do your head in' as the saying goes. More ideally, number 3 acts as fact-finder whilst number 6 figures out how to apply such facts in a serviceable way. It is imagination that unites this pair. When they turn their focus to number 9's humanitarian interests and concerns, they are delightful. Number 3 would put on the most stylish fund-raiser in town whilst number 6 would attend to all the details, making sure that everyone was catered for including the disabled, the children and the family pets.

It is easy to see how each of the above partnerships would make an unstoppable team *if* they valued each other's contribution to a goal that had been mutually agreed upon. In chapter 7 you may have noticed that these pairs sometimes appear as challenges. For example, when the big challenge is 4, the small challenge is often 5 (and vice versa). The above interpretations are useful within this context.

Days of the Week

Our 7 Days of the Week match the couplings above:

Sunday – Leo/Sun – Number 5

Monday – Cancer/Moon – Number 4

Tuesday – Aries 1 and Scorpio 8 - the Yang and Yin of Mars (Twis)

Wednesday – Gemini 3 and Virgo 6 – the Yang and Yin of Mercury (Woden)

Thursday – Sagittarius – 9 – Jupiter's day (Thor)

Friday – Taurus 2 and Libra 7 – the Yin and Yang of Venus (Freya)

Saturday belongs to Saturn, Capricorn and the Number 10, which encompasses the first four numbers (1 + 2 + 3 + 4 = 10) and caps off the week.

Yin and Yang

Some images that you may find useful as the theoretical model progresses: Magnetically – yang repels whilst yin attracts. As sound vibrations – yang creates discord whilst yin resolves discord. At the mental level – yang catalyzes change whilst yin resists change. At the heart level – yang gives whilst yin receives. Spiritually yang moves from the centre to the circumference whilst yin moves from the circumference to the centre. Yang is outgoing whereas yin is inward bound. All of the odd numbers are yang whilst all of the even numbers are yin. Astrologically all of the odd numbers are in fire and air signs whilst all of the even numbers are in earth and water signs.

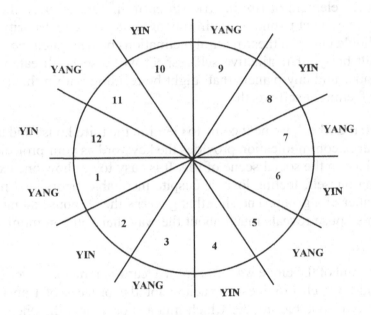

Figure 3: Yin and Yang Numbers

Astrological Houses

In astrology the houses indicate the sphere of daily life through which astral energy patterns unfold and develop in the physical world. And one of the first correlations between numerology and astrology that strikes most people when they begin to compare them is the similarity of the numbers and the astrological houses. There may be as many house systems as there are systems of numerology, but mostly they aim to specify the 'playing field' for the planets. The *Pan's Script* system only works when the houses are kept whole. This is called the Whole Sign House System and it is the oldest astrological system that we have. Vedic astrology has always kept its houses whole, and western astrology is currently learning to value its roots. In a nutshell it means that everything relating to Aries is in one house, everything relating to Taurus is in another house etc.

Ascendant

Beginning again on the left-hand side of the page, we will journey counter-clockwise around the wheel, this time defining the houses in a way that is congruent with our overall model. Their kinship with numerology will thus be emphasized. The first house is the home of the ascendant. It signifies a visible image of Self that you project outwardly. Any planets in this house will affect the way that you appear to other people. The ascendant plus any planets that might be in the first house, influence the manner by which you initiate action in the world around you.

Following on is the second house, which stabilizes this projection with a set of values that justify and sustain it. Because we are in the realm of the planet Venus, we know that these values will be rooted in love (although love can become awfully convoluted at times). We have moved from the element of fire in Aries to earth in Taurus; from the exuberance that comes with being able to act upon our environment to the sense of security that comes from feeling lovable. Should either of these natural inclinations be frustrated, not only will feelings of insecurity result but your instinctive self-respect will also be threatened. The sign that governs the 2nd house and any planets that might be residing within this house reveals how you buttress your feeling of self-worth.

Continuing around the wheel, we next come to Gemini, the third house and the element of air. As in personal year 3, communication provides the keyword as your projected image, secure or not, seeks its place in the social scene of life. It is easy to see how one experience follows the other: asserting oneself, feeling lovable despite inevitable errors, and now being able to function as a member of a group. The sign that governs the 3rd house along with any planets residing within this house reveals much about the way that you communicate your ideas to other people.

Through each quadrant of the circle we move from a 'cardinal' mode, which generates energy, into a 'fixed' mode, which provides a crucible for the process of transmutation. Finally the cycle shifts into a 'mutable' mode, which mutates or adapts the energy to accord with its environment. As well as mutable, the 3rd, 6th, 9th and 12th are also called cadent houses, suggesting a change of rhythm as we spiral into to the next stage of consciousness.

In our symbolic wheel the 90-degree position opens the door to the fourth house. Cancer, the moon and the element water indicate that we are now in the arena of the subconscious. The fourth house represents your roots and parental dynamics; the stuff that nurtures your creativity. Your drive to act, and to feel appreciated by your peers, is now joined by the sense that you are a part of a continuum - a link in a chain - a story that has been unfolding for a very long time. The sign that governs the 4th house along with any planets residing in this house informs the way that you fortify this feeling of connection with your ancestors. Those of you who are able to work with this connection consciously and creatively may discover that this connection can remediate any weakness in the three preceding domains.

In the fifth house your creativity is warmed by the fiery influence of Leo and the Sun. The 5ᵗʰ house provides a place where you can infuse life into your creative projects. The fifth house is associated with your ability to procreate, but you should keep a broad definition in mind here for procreation need not be limited to human children but embraces all creative acts. The sign that governs the 5ᵗʰ house, along with any planets residing in this house, provide clues as what the word 'creativity' means to you.

The life-engendering fire of Leo is followed by the earthy sign of Virgo in the house of refinement. This is where the energy accumulated in the psyche by the previous five houses seeks integration within a purposeful project. The sign that governs the 6ᵗʰ house along with any planets residing therein informs the means by which you will try to 'make a living' and keep your earthly body intact. This is a communal playing field and so it is not simply your personal 'stuff' that you need to deal with here. This is where you attempt to harmonize our own needs with those of everyone else in your family and community.

Descendant

Following on from the sixth house and opposite the ascendant is the descendant, and whilst the ascendant represents what everyone sees, the descendant (DSC) represents a part of you that you find difficult to acknowledge. Whilst you project your ego directly into the environment, you project this shadow-self onto other people so that you come to know it through them. You watch partners and 'enemies' play it out for you. Hence the 7ᵗʰ house is called the house of relationships and the sign that governs the 7ᵗʰ house along with any planets in this house tell you which part of yourself you are most likely to disown and project on to other people.

The 8ᵗʰ house only becomes consciously accessible once you have reclaimed the 7ᵗʰ. When you realize that what you dislike in others are those parts of self that you have rejected, then you are ready to take what you have learned into the eighth house and the oceanic realm of Scorpio and Pluto. True intimacy then becomes a real possibility. The sign that governs the 8ᵗʰ house along with any planets in this house represent the way you interact in your most treasured relationships. This is a powerful place that can reveal how you wield power within intimate relationships.

Completing this series is the mutable 9ᵗʰ house wherein you attempt to extract meaning from the wealth of knowledge you have acquired from the length, breadth and depth of your journey through life. This is where you can integrate your personal experience with universal themes. The sign that governs the 9ᵗʰ house along with any planets within this house inform your 'world myth'.

The meaning that you gave to life in the 9ᵗʰ house seeks materialization in the 10ᵗʰ. The 10ᵗʰ house opens the door to the final quadrant. Here you may discover your super-conscious, transcendent or universal self: your ego internalized as genuine authority. Such authority gives you substance; hence this is an earth house. Through the trials that come with life, you learn how to stand your ground; hence the 10ᵗʰ is traditionally associated with one's authentic vocation. The sign that governs the 10ᵗʰ house along with any planets in therein indicate what your most public work is likely to entail.

In the 11th house you gather around you those people who share your vision of how you would like the world to be. These are your co-workers in the spiritual sense of that term. They can help you to identify with something greater than your personal issues. The sign that governs the 11th house along with any planets in this house inform the vision that you wish to share with others.

The 12th could be called the house of profound realization because it is herein that you recognize that as you do to others, so you do to yourself. This awareness can be as practical as it is life changing. Works of great compassion may emerge from this segment of the wheel, provided that the preceding eleven phases have been tended to satisfactorily. When healthy, the 12th house sign along with any planets in this house represent the way that you regenerate yourself in preparation for the next stage of your development. If unhealthy, they indicate how you can go about restoring yourself.

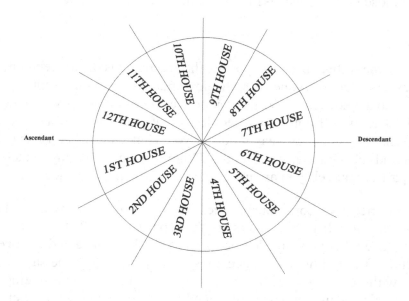

Figure 4: The Astrological Houses

Age Cycle

To add the ages and stages of human life that correspond with the astrological wheel, mark the zero point as 'birth' and then every 30 degree point after that as a multiple of 7. Thus the first segment of the circle indicates the first 7 years of life, the second segment the years from 7 to 14, the third segment from 14 to 21 and so on around to 84. This aligns our human development with the houses as outlined above. What happens beyond 84 you may ask? The answer is rebirth. The 'rebirth cycle' is actually conceived at 63 (mentally) and gestates through the final quadrant, so that whilst one cycle is ending a new one is beginning. Whether an individual is aware of it or not, past, present, and future overlap during the final quadrant. Also worth noting is the fact that 7 years is equivalent to 84 months, making each segment a mini-journey, and every seven years a mini-rebirth.

Aligning our years in this way means that our first seven relate to Aries, Mars and number 1. They will be about exercising your ego or willpower. Ideally, this grants you the confidence that you need throughout the rest of life's journey. During the next seven years in Venus, Taurus and number 2's zone, we modify our approach to accommodate the wills and egos of other people. It is the development of your feeling-life that is most important during the years 7 to 14, and you need healthy role models to accomplish that.

Following on and correlated with Mercury, Gemini and number 3, the years 14 to 21 become a peak time intellectually. Socially active, this is when you learn the art of communicating your wants and desires. If this first quadrant is lived reasonably well, by the time you are 21 you will have gained a level of competence that enables you to act creatively in the world at large and assume responsibility for your own emotional security. But if something has gone wrong along the way (as it often does), then the second quadrant becomes one of remediation. To seek someone who can provide surrogate security while you delve into the depths of your being may be necessary if you do not wish to carry this handicap for the rest of your days.

The second quadrant begins at 21, which may be one of the more subtle reasons why that particular occasion is so significant. True to Cancer and the number 4, the years 21 to 28 are typically spent establishing a home and career.

Then between 28 and 35, with the Sun, Leo and number 5, comes a peak time for creativity within that home and family. Statistics show that nowadays, this is when most couples in Western countries are choosing to create a family but whether this happens or not, does not change the fact that a tremendous amount of energy is generated during this time. To the extent that a family or career allows you to express your creativity, you will experience increased vitality during this time.

The years 35 to 42 (in Mercury-Virgo and number 6's zone) are typically concerned with the community of which you are a part. Your personal health and the health of your offspring to some extent, depend on your 'psychic' health. In other words, the health of your creativity depends on how well you manage to integrate the many facets of your life. However you choose to live these years, the words dynamic and interactive are relevant to the second quadrant of the wheel of life.

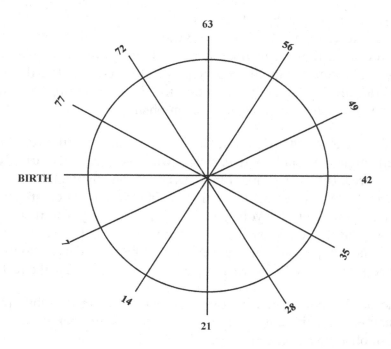

Figure 5: The Age Cycle

One way to continue our journey around the wheel is to relate its 4 quadrants to the 4 phases of life as they were once lived in Ancient India. Called Ashramas, each quadrant would then represent a stage in spiritual development. The first, Brahmacharyashrama, was the student phase when one studied ancient texts with profound meaning. The next was Grahasthashrama, when one was fully engaged as a householder, embracing one's spiritual discipline within a family context. The third stage called Vanaprasthashrama followed naturally as the children one was responsible for become independent. Sometimes called 'the forest stage', it granted the parents or guardians increasing amounts of time for contemplation. Finally came the phase called Sannyasashrama, when one was free from all worldly obligations and could devote one's energies totally to self-realization. Remarkably, this ancient way of life, which so obviously accords with the 4 quadrants, is still practiced by many people to this day. Sadly most lives today are seldom lived so idyllically. People must work to put food on the table until well into their 60's and even 70's in some cases. This corrodes their time for spiritual development and in turn exacerbates any health issues the person may have.

Phases of the Moon

At the time of the new moon the sun and moon rise together in the east. Hence in the *Pan's Script* model the new moon is placed in the east with the rising sun to mark the beginning of the soli-lunar cycle. This accords with the way of the Ancient Egyptians who began their lunar month on the morning when the waning moon could no longer be seen just before sunrise, in the eastern sky. To add the phases of the moon to the wheel of life that you have been constructing you will need your protractor again; this time to mark off 45, 135, 225 and 315 degrees. If you have not already done so, rule across the circle to heighten your awareness of the relationships between the various points. Taking into account the zero, 90, 180, and 270 degrees, which we already have, the lunation cycle divides the circle into eight equal segments:

From Zero to 45 degrees is the New Moon Phase
From 45 to 90 degrees, the Waxing Crescent Phase
From 90 to 135 degrees, the First Quarter Phase
From 135 to 180 degrees, the Waxing Gibbous Phase
From 180 to 225 degrees, the Full Moon Phase
From 225 to 270 degrees, the Disseminating Phase
From 270 to 315 degrees, the Last Quarter Phase
And from 315 to 359 degrees and 59 minutes is the Balsamic Phase.

The magic of manifestation resides in this cycle and if you really want to understand it, begin observing the cycle of the moon in your own area and make notes in your diary. Note especially how you feel at the various phases of the moon. In the Hindu tradition, these 8 points represent Durga: the 8-armed goddess. The astrologer, Dane Rudhyar, pioneered the application of this cycle to human psychology and what follows has been grafted onto his research, taking into account the significance of the numbers involved.

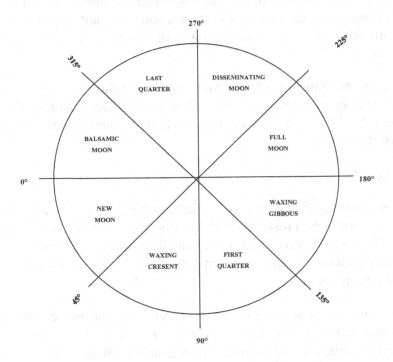

Figure 6: The Phases of the Moon

What is the Progressed Lunation Cycle?

The progressed lunation cycle records the interaction of solar and lunar forces and thus the unfoldment of your needs and desires within a worldly context. Dane Rudhyar emphasized the importance of interpreting this cycle as exemplary of the archetypal cycle of relationships. Because the interaction of sun and moon affects life on earth, this cycle demonstrates the dynamics of this archetypal trinity. Within this trinity, the moon acts as intermediary, modulating the growth potential of the solar force. In the following descriptions, a general account of what each phase means within the overall cycle is offered, followed by a few thoughts on what it might mean to be born during a particular phase of the moon. The examples offered are all musicians; their style perhaps reflecting the phase of the moon in which they were born.

The Moon Phases and What They Symbolize

New Moon Phase

When the moon is between 0 degrees and 44 degrees 59 minutes ahead of the sun it is called a new moon. Beginning in number 1 and progressing to number 2, this new phase relates in part to linguistic intelligence as it is explained in chapter 6.

Born at the beginning of a whole new cycle, you are naturally a self-starter who acts on what feels right at the time. As a small child you were noticeably enthusiastic and energetic, quite often delightful but equally often a handful. The closer the sun and moon are together, the more difficult it will be for you to distinguish between the objective and the subjective self and the more likelihood of mental confusion should you take matters too personally. Typically bubbling over with original ideas, you have a way of getting noticed but you may not always enjoy the attention.

Elvis Presley and his daughter Lisa Marie were both born during a new moon. Maurice and Robin Gibb were also born at the new moon, their brother Barry during the crescent phase, and Andy during the gibbous phase, which means that all four brothers were born during the waxing phases of the moon.

Crescent Moon Phase

When the moon is between 45 degrees and 89 degrees 59 minutes ahead of the sun it is called a waxing crescent moon. The crescent phase begins where the new moon leaves off - in the realm of number 2/Taurus/Venus - and moves steadily towards number 3/Gemini/Mercury. This suggests that relationships and communication are the focus. This phase also relates in part to linguistic intelligence.

Born during the time of the waxing crescent moon, you tend to be naturally curious and outspoken. In some way your life reflects the need to leave the ways of the past, which formerly provided sustenance, and adapt to a new situation. Somehow you must reconcile the 'old shoe' type of comfort that comes from maintaining the status quo with the prompting of new ideas. These will be coming from your reaction to your social setting. You are learning how to cut your own track through the midst of conflicting ideals, whilst acknowledging that your own habitual ways of thinking may be contributing to the situation. A new approach comes when you adjust your perception. To accept what you cannot change and have the wit to change what you can is your guiding light.

John Lennon and his son Sean were both born during a crescent moon, as was Paul McCartney. (Ringo was born during a new moon and George a disseminating moon, making him different in this way to the other Beatles).

First Quarter Phase

When the moon is between 90 degrees and 134 degrees 59 minutes ahead of the sun it is called a first quarter moon but it actually resembles a half-moon in the sky.

The first quarter phase begins in the realm of number 4, Cancer, and the moon and progresses towards number 5, Leo and the Sun. What was previously sub-conscious now surfaces as the motivation to create a saner way of life. There is a strong urge to nurture the Cycle now underway. This phase relates in part to kinesthetic intelligence as it is explained in chapter 6, and accordingly, these dynamic people *do* seem to be constantly trying to move forward.

Born during the time of the first quarter moon phase, you have powerful emotions bubbling just below the surface and spurring you on. Your common sense and perseverance is useful, but it is your dedication and imagination that bring out the best in you. You are probably in the 'thick' of things socially. Actively involved in issues of common concern, you may spend your entire life campaigning for one particular cause. It is natural for you to be constructively creative, and when you offer a unique solution to a social problem, you capture the public imagination. You are learning how to run with opportunities and exercise your talents. To the extent that your projects are based on love, you will find that your energy increases with its active expression rather than decreases.

Barbara Streisand, Faye Tozer, Joan Baez, and Mandy Moore were all born during the first quarter phase of the moon.

Gibbous Moon Phase

When the moon is between 135 degrees and 179 degrees 59 minutes ahead of the sun it is called a gibbous moon. Beginning in the realm of number 5, Leo and the Sun brings the urge to break free from something, and then as the cycle progresses into number 6, Virgo, and Mercury, comes the willingness to act with greater commitment. This phase also relates in part to kinesthetic intelligence.

Born during the time of a waxing gibbous moon, you tend to be passionate about your beliefs, and you have the necessary perseverance to bring your ideas to fulfillment. However your initial enthusiasm may be plagued by worry as your project progresses. Head down, you stick with the task that has caught your imagination until it is brought to the attention of others, whom you hope will also become enthusiastic about it. You can thus be an uplifting combination of exuberance and earthiness (Leo/Virgo). You need to continually check your assumptions and the subtle influences that are acting upon you because these forces serve to maximize the functional value of your ingenuity. You are learning to adjust what does not feel quite right so that it becomes more refined in its purpose. Gradually you become more objective and effective. It is important to image the fulfillment of your project if you want it to actualize at some point.

Billy Ray Cyrus, Bono, Janis Joplin, and Kian Egan were all born during the gibbous phase of the moon.

Full Moon Phase

When the moon is between 180 degrees and 224 degrees 59 minutes ahead of the sun it is called a full moon. Whatever has been going on subconsciously is now fully illuminated for there are fewer places to hide when the moon is full. Revelation is the word that links this phase with the number 7 and power is the word that links it with number 8. Along with the numbers, this phase moves through Libra, which is ruled by Venus, into Scorpio, which is traditionally ruled by Mars. Venus/Mars tells us that this part of the cycle is about relationships of the most dynamic kind. This phase also relates in part to logical-mathematical intelligence as it is explained in chapter 6 and so although we are dealing with relationships, there is some objectivity here. This is not a subconscious phase. The presence of Venus informs us that the motivating power of this phase is love. She would have the cycle sanctified at this point. Progressing towards the number 8, Scorpio, Mars and Pluto, it is a combination of love and intelligence that will bring the fruits of one's labour to bear.

Born at the time of the full moon, you have fiery passions and big ideas. You are learning about relationships and the power of projection and that includes reclaiming whatever you have disowned in yourself and projected onto other people. To the extent that you have been expecting others to live out the hidden sides of your nature, you must now do some honest introspection, (that is if you really want to understand what is going on). Discrimination is vital throughout this phase. As you progress towards the number 8, Scorpio, Mars and Pluto, the fruits of your love and labour will naturally appear in the physical world.

Lady Gaga, Michael Jackson, Paula Abdul and Pink were all born in the light of a full moon.

Disseminating Phase

When the moon is between 225 and 269 degrees 59 minutes ahead of the sun it is called a disseminating moon. And as the name suggests, it is time to share. Beginning in the realm of number 8/Scorpio/Mars and Pluto, this is a busy phase in the cycle. The soul's cup is overflowing and zeal may need to be tempered. With Mars at the helm there's plenty of push here (much like a lava flow). It is certainly not time to wind down, but as the cycle moves into number 9's territory it *is* time to detach oneself from the outcome. Disseminating is a waning phase, which relates in part to logical-mathematical intelligence as it is explained in chapter 6. Together such forces offer the power of hindsight.

Born at the time of the disseminating moon, you are driven by the desire to make a difference, and so you readily share what you have learned. You have powerful, heart-felt ideas that erupt outwardly, scattering 'seeds' that shape our collective future. You are somewhat predisposed to feeling that life is not worth living unless you are contributing to the common good. Relaxation may not be your strongest suit but it *is* something that you must learn because this phase brings a gnawing sense of responsibility to improve the state of the world. It is actually inner transformation that is required, and that takes time to unfold. Commitment to an ideal facilitates this process and educating is likely to be of interest to you.

Cher, Olivia Newton-John, Robbie Williams and Will Young were all born during the disseminating phase of the moon.

Last Quarter Phase

When the moon is between 270 and 314 degrees 59 minutes ahead of the sun it is called a last quarter moon. Beyond the worldly cycle of the personal years and into a less visible realm, it is time to question values and revise goals. In keeping with the cusp of numbers 9 and 10, astrologers have observed that there may be an ideological crisis at this point, which can, in turn, set in motion a shift of social perspective. The progression from Capricorn/10 to Aquarius/11 (both ruled by Saturn), suggests not only the formulation of an ideological principle that can benefit society but its actual embodiment within the person.

Born at the last quarter phase of the moon, you tend to develop inwardly for a very long time, gradually distilling and consolidating your life's experiences. When you do 'come out' it may be quite a dramatic turning point. Metaphorically it will be that critical moment when conservative Capricorn-Saturn yields to innovative Aquarius-Uranus. If you can transmute whatever pain you have suffered in the past into wisdom, you would make an ideal counsellor, advisor and teacher; a veritable pillar on which others can depend – albeit somewhat revolutionary.

K.D. Lang, Michael Hutchence, Mick Jagger and Seal were all born during the last quarter phase of the moon.

Balsamic Moon Phase

When the moon is between 315 and 359 degrees and 59 minutes ahead of the sun it is called a balsamic moon. Uranus, Aquarius and number 11, at the start of this cycle, catalyze fresh inspiration. People can find themselves doing something radically different during this phase. As one's eyes open to more universal themes, Neptune and Jupiter take over. These planetary giants can help people to revise their perspective of life. The expansiveness of such forces enables people to review their past and appreciate their future. The task at this final stage of the journey is to make peace with whatever has transpired so that a new cycle can begin, unimpeded by a wounded ego.

Born at the time of the balsamic moon, you are naturally a social reformer. Disinclined to tear down existing structures, you prefer to improve what is already in place. You have a contemplative side to your nature and as you mature you may develop a profound understanding of life, its cycles, and underlying purpose. Your potential may be apparent at a young age but as you work on your challenges, your thinking undergoes a complete refurbishment. You are perceptive throughout life, gradually gaining awareness into the struggle of humanity – past, present and future – and what it is that underlies that struggle. If you are able to resist self-pity, you may sense a tantalizing new vision that could help to heal our current problems.

Bette Midler, Bob Dylan, Ian Shaw and Stevie Wonder were all born during the balsamic phase of the moon.

Archetypal Space-Time

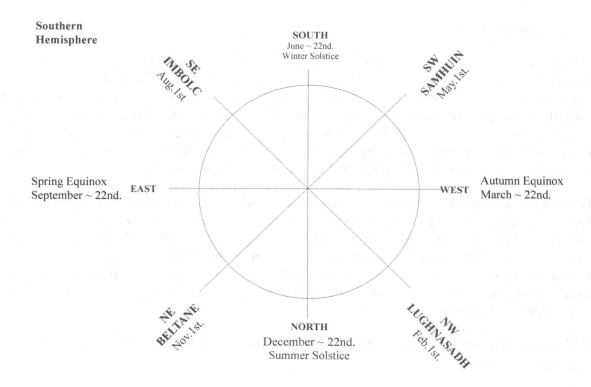

Figure 7: The Counterclockwise Seasonal Cycle

You will have noticed that within this archetypal model of planets, cycles, and signs, everything moves in a counterclockwise direction. What we are looking at is a metaphysical and archetypal reality, symbolized by an archetypal wheel, comprising 12 signs-cum-numbers-cum principles. This is an ideal that is constant regardless of location. Because this archetypal wheel moves in the same direction as the sun in the southern hemisphere (i.e. counterclockwise), we will walk the seasonal wheel as it is experienced in the southern hemisphere and witness the congruency of these correspondences. From time to time we will also refer to an ancient cycle of celebrations to add depth of meaning.

Archetypal Seasons

Beginning in the east, which is always placed to the left-hand side of the traditional horoscope, we place the spring equinox at archetypal 00 Aries. Sunrise can also be placed here. Walking counterclockwise to the northeast, we come to Beltane, which is a traditional celebration held at high spring, when everything is buzzing with life. In the Celtic tradition, twin fires are lit and nature's time of burgeoning fertility is celebrated.

Continuing counterclockwise, we come to the 90° point, which is always north in the traditional horoscope. In the southern hemisphere this is the time of summer solstice and the temperature continues to rise. Age-wise we are 21, physically strong and full of vitality. Astrologically we are at 00 Cancer.

Continuing counterclockwise we come to the traditional celebration of Lughnasadh at the northwest point. We are in archetypal Leo, it is hot, and we are celebrating Lugh, which means light.

Due West are the archetypal autumn equinox, sunset, and 00 Libra, when the harvest runs its course and people begin to restore the balance after the busy season. It's time to reflect on what has transpired and express gratitude.

Continuing counterclockwise we come to the traditional celebration of Samhuin at the southwest point. Samhuin is the most sombre of the eight festivals because it marks the 'time' when we face the reality that winter lays ahead. In contrast to Beltane, fertility is now internalized. Astrologically we are in Scorpio.

At the 270° point, which is 00 Capricorn, we come to the winter solstice. The top of the wheel is always south in traditional astrology and just so, to the south lays Antarctica in the southern hemisphere. This is an ancestral place for people who live in the countries that broke away from it in the distant past.

Finally we come to the traditional celebration of Imbolc and the first signs of spring. The dawn will break in due course and a new cycle will begin.

Thus the southern hemisphere cycle is congruent with the astrological wheel, and yet this is an archetypal journey that is essentially the same for all people regardless of place of birth.

Combining the Solar and Lunar Influences on the Cycle

We are now in a position to combine the solar and lunar cycles and see what they can tell us about each quadrant of the wheel. Beginning again in the east at the spring equinox and passing through the new and crescent moon phases, we see that this is unequivocally a waxing stage, which is exactly what one would expect of a time that corresponds with the years from birth to 21.

At summer solstice the solar force peaks and then begins to gradually wane as it passes through the second quadrant. Meanwhile the lunar force continues to increase. This tells us that although the years 21-42 are spent in the working world, behind the scenes the dynamics of sun and moon are beginning to internalize; a process that stimulates creativity.

At the halfway point (180°) the moon reaches its peak and then wanes throughout the remainder of the cycle. The sun also wanes during the third quadrant until the time of the winter solstice is reached. Our inner life undergoes a profound metamorphosis during the years 42-63.

From the winter solstice to the spring equinox the sun gradually regains strength, days lengthen while nights shorten, but the moon retires completely. One way to interpret this, relevant to the ages 63 and beyond, is to say that as the soul (moon) internalizes all that it has gained from this life cycle, one's authentic individuality (sun) begins to shine from deep within.

When applied to our personal years, the spring equinox adds freshness and focus to personal year 1 while summer solstice suggests long hours in the day-to-day world during our personal years 4. Corresponding to the autumn equinox, personal year **7** then becomes the completion-of-the harvest time and still quite busy. Thus solar forces govern these three cardinal points, and the years 1, 4 and 7 and we note the correlation to the line 1-4-7 of survival intelligence, per chapter 6.

By contrast, lunar forces govern the four midpoints. At 45°, the cusp of the new and crescent moons is in number 2's domain. At 135°, the cusp of the first quarter and waxing gibbous moons is in number 5's territory. And at 225°, at the cusp of the full and disseminating moons, we are in number 8's domain. Thus, lunar forces modulate the line of interpersonal intelligence (2-5-8). Notice also that all 8 cardinal positions: 90, 180, 270 and 360 reduce to the number 9 as so do their midpoints – 45, 135, 225 & 315 and so each fulfils a mini-phase within this universal cycle. While the equinoxes and solstices map the path of the sun, these lunar gateways draw our attention to the dynamic relationship between light and dark as it reflects in our relationships with each other.

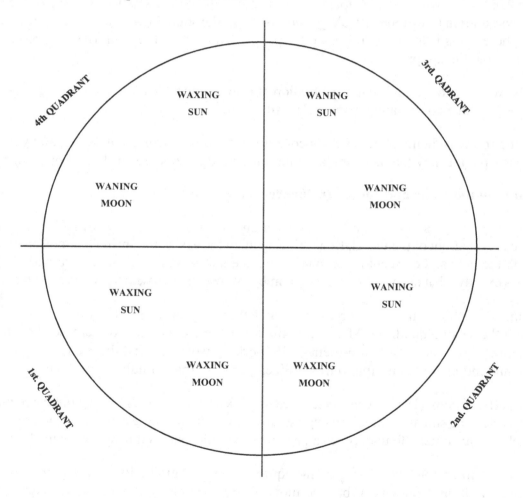

Figure 8: The Combined Solar and Lunar Influences on the Cycle

Chapter 11

The Growth Cycle

Not only the personal years but also the name, cycles to the rhythm of the number 9. In chapter 3 we noted that the first name, as given at birth, encodes the growth number. Now in like manner, we postulate that the original first name catalyzes a cycle of growth that develops throughout life.

Calculating Your Growth Cycle

Lay out your first name only, in cycles of nine, beginning with zero, to represent your birth. It does not matter if you have never used this name. This cycle began operating at birth and will continue until death. There is an intelligence operating here that defies explanation!

For example – the name 'Richard' oscillates in the following way:
The first letter, R, operates from birth to the 9th birthday.
The second letter, I, operates from the 9th birthday to the 18th birthday.
The third letter, C, operates from the 18th birthday to the 27th birthday.
The fourth letter, H, operates from the 27th birthday to the 36th birthday.
The first letter, A, operates from the 36th birthday to the 45th birthday etc.
Another way to illustrate this is:

R	I	C	H	A	R	D	R	I	C	H	A	R
0-	9-	18-	27-	36-	45-	54-	63-	72-	81-	90-	99-	108-

The Growth Cycle Complements the Personal Year Cycle

The growth cycle and the personal year cycle unite inner growth with outer response. However although both have a nine-year duration, the growth cycle operates from birthday to birthday whereas the personal years are aligned to the world years and therefore operate from January 1st to December 31st. And so unless you were born on January 1st or thereabouts, these cycles will not coincide.

Numerologists rarely use the growth cycle yet i have found it to be immensely valuable. Personal research indicates that these twin cycles of nine provide an accurate and informative partnership. Whilst the personal years, being a part of the date of birth, inform the attitude that you need to adopt to your 'outer life', the growth cycle, being a part of the name, suggests the best way to promote your 'inner life'. The first name represents the way your soul will attempt to express itself through your ego but do not try to turn the growth cycle into a worldly cycle like the personal years. Whilst the latter is attitudinal in nature, the growth cycle tells you what is happening within your etheric body, which relates directly to your sense of wellbeing. Hence the following interpretations are weighted in favour of *inner* growth and intended to complement the attitude that you adopt to each personal year.

Interpreting the Letters as Part of a Progressive Cycle

A-Cycles

The letter "A" begins the journey of personal development as symbolized by the alphabet. Its resonance generates ideas, and within the cycle of your name this encourages reliance upon your inner resources. The research shows that you will need to apply your lateral thinking skills during these nine years. Children who experience an A-cycle in their first 9 years tend to be self-motivated and this trend continues throughout the later cycles as well.

Charles Darwin set sail in an a-cycle and returned five years later to a whole new life. He quickly realized that there were adjustments to be made but also fresh opportunities. Within an a-cycle much hinges on your willingness to make decisions that determine the course your life will take. Circumstances may place you in a position where you have to fend for yourself and your survival may depend on how well you cope with other people's egos. Re-locations are common at all ages. Turning your situation to an advantage is important and so is maintaining responsibility for your choices. William Cowper described this period in his life (45-54) as "a second spring". Although the letter A generates energy, it would be wrong to think of an a-cycle as being purely yang or external in nature. Much goes on internally during this time, as exemplified by Gloria Steinem. At 52 she had a cancer scare and had to turn within in order to heal herself, which she did. She then wrote *Revolution from Within*, a title that pinpoints a theme that ought not to be overlooked during an a-cycle. During this time you may actually feel as if you are being turned inside out. These nine years will strengthen your resolve to act decisively and determine your own existence. Expect something altogether different from what you have experienced before.

B-Cycles

The letter "B" and the number 2 have much in common. Both contain the tension of opposition and therein, the potential for growth. Within the cycle of the name, the letter B tends to create nervous tension as dreams and desires push from within for expression in the physical world. These dreams and desires are fertile and highly potent thoughts, partly formed. They can elicit a sense of purposefulness, but also a feeling of frustration held inwardly. Such ambivalent emotions seek clarity and ultimately resolution through real-life experience. If your motivation is uncertain, you will hesitate before acting. You will feel that you need to gather and absorb more data before you can move forward. B is the first of the letters that stimulate transformation through the emotions but unlike such letters later in the cycle, here the process represents an intensely personal dialogue between your ego and soul. The research revealed that children who experience a B-cycle in their first nine years need strong, healthy, and consistent parenting. The impact of both parents was deeply internalized.

Benjamin Franklin was almost given away during his first B-cycle but because of his scholarly ability his father changed his mind and sent him to school instead. During his second b-cycle Benjamin was engaged in a diplomatic mission to France to secure an alliance for the American Revolution. Intermingled with much love-bantering, his mission eventually succeeded. He exemplifies the ability to harness frustration and transmute it into diplomacy. Likewise, the success of your b-cycle depends on how well you are able to strike a balance between self-restraint and self-expression. Throughout this process stamina will need to be actively maintained: physically, mentally and emotionally. These nine years will enrich your feeling life through your relationships with people in general and one person in particular.

C-Cycles

The letter "C" accompanies a feeling of optimism, and that will brighten this nine-year period. Research findings indicate that at all ages this resonance stimulates 'big ideas'. Children who experience a C-cycle in their first nine years tend to enjoy daydreams of what their future could be. These are not to be discouraged for they indicate a healthy, expansive, and creative mind. When they are not lost in wondrous thoughts, such children like to be out and about with the rest of 'the gang'. Companionship is vital to them and friends made during these early years often play a vital role in the fulfillment of dreams later in life. Ample affection and positive role models are also necessary for the healthy unfolding of personal ideals and dream-images.

During his first nine years Calvin Klein would sometimes dream of being a fashion designer. Because he spent much of his time out in the street with the other children in his neighborhood, he developed friendships that would be critical to his success in fulfilling that dream. Even later in life the c-resonance attracts significant liaisons, and new roles to play. C stimulates movement, mostly within the mind but often literally as well. Whether by flights of fancy or actual flights to new landscapes, plenty of nervous excitement is generated by this vibration. Between the ages of 36 and 45, Ehrich (Harry Houdini), travelled to Australia, and there undertook the first flight on record. He also went into movies, creating the entire show himself. Richard Carpenter described his years between 18 and 27 as a "magical time" and this is the potential herein. The letter C will encourage you to exchange ideas and energy with other people. And it will help you to connect ideas. These nine years will stimulate your mental curiosity and encourage you to explore a variety of points of view, which may bring fresh challenges and interesting new projects.

D-Cycles

"D" and the Number 4 are as consistently alike as B and the Number 2. It is the nature of the even numbers to stabilize and none more so than the number 4, yet within the d-cycle of a name, this appears to be anything but true. The research shows that divorces, deaths, and acts of defiance were rift. What is symbolized by the letter D, and captured in its sound, is a crucible in which creative forces interact. Although the end result of this dynamic exchange is life engendering, the process may feel more akin to the upheavals, eruptions, and lightning strikes at the beginning of a world than a harmonic symphony. Yet harmony is precisely the purpose and goal. The d-resonance will help you to endure frustration and develop the determination to create something substantial. It may feel somewhat laborious but if you can accommodate the creative process, gradually you will develop your own style, and by the end of this cycle you may find that you have constructed a foundation upon which a future can be built. D anywhere in a cycle generates deeply creative forces, which feel uncomfortable until they find their place. Clearly then, children who experience a D-cycle within their first nine years would benefit from a stable home-life. They need to know where they stand. They also need to know where they can place their devotion without constantly having to defend the most sacred places within their heart. At any stage in life the letter "d" will deepen your feeling life and draw out of you creative powers that you may have only dared to dream that you had.

Leonar*d* Nimoy began directing movies during his d-cycle, which was certainly a dream come true for him. Likewise, the d-resonance will help you to endure frustration and develop the determination to create something substantial. During these nine years progress may feel somewhat laborious but if you can accommodate the creative process, gradually you will develop your own style, and by the end of the cycle you may find that you have constructed a foundation upon which further inspiration can be built in the future.

E-Cycles

"E" is an *energizing* force but indiscriminate in the experiences that it ushers into the material world. Within the cycle of the name it generates energy and therefore excitement on all planes: physical, mental and emotional. The research revealed that at all ages the letter E accompanied the full array of human experience from poverty to wealth, feelings of exploitation to exultation, mental confusion to brilliant ingenuity. Much related to the evolution of the species, E favours the survival of the most adaptable. Children who have an E-cycle in their first nine years typically experience a change within the home. One of their parents may die, leave, or undergo a change of health, career or status, which often results in a change of residence. For some such as *E*ugene O'Neill, this sets in motion the proverbial rolling stone unable to 'gather moss' or bond with anyone. Yet friendship is vital during an E-Cycle.

The research revealed that a changeable home-life continued through the next nine years but here we are more likely to see children leaving home and making their own way in the world; establishing a career, and perhaps a family, representing attempts to find some sense of security in an ever-changing and seemingly indifferent world. Naturally some people cope with uncertainty better than others do, extroverts being more inclined to enjoy the variety that it offers. Such people are more likely to run with any opportunities that open up. For example, between the years 36 and 45 Walt*e*r Cronkite became a successful news anchor because he was "willing to fly on the seat of his pants". Similarly, if you are able to 'go with the flow' you will find that your body is able to revitalize itself and acclimatize to changing circumstances. Moods may fluctuate but your mind will continually generate solutions to problems. Life itself is the teacher during this time. You can expect it to be eventful.

F-Cycles

"F" facilities the flow of ideas within the mind. Children who experience an F-cycle in their first nine years need an education that caters to both hemispheres of the brain: the facts and figures side and also the more figurative, speculative, and imaginative regions of the mind. Synthesis would seem to be the specific function of this resonance.

Between 27 and 36 Wolfgang Amadeus Mozart tried unsuccessfully he tried to reconcile the difficulties with his father. And the entire aristocracy overlooked him when work that provided status and a secure income became available. Yet his operas were well received and for productivity this period was second to none. Feeling unappreciated by those who hold the purse strings, and even by those you love, is unfortunately common during an f-cycle; but this can be turned on its head. These nine years will test your mettle, integrity, and character. All examples demonstrate progress made but only through persistence, and it may not feel like progress at the time. At any stage in the cycle these nine years necessitate an adjustment of your attitude to life. You may have to sit down and figure out what it is that you actually expect from life and the people that you share yours with. If handled honestly and courageously this period will help you to develop fortitude and increase your capacity for solution finding.

G-Cycles

"G" like "C" is expressive but more grounded. The mining of the gifts within the various stratosphere of the mind is the dominant theme of this cycle. It doesn't seem to matter whether the 'g' is hard or soft, either way this form stimulates the critical faculties of the mind. The function of this resonance is to dig as deeply as possible, bring the ideas to the surface, and then mould them according to your values at the time.

For example, during his first nine years George Lucas grew up in the suburbs and he used this experience as the basis of his film *American Graffiti*. Likewise, your g-cycle will enhance your imagination but also encourage you to keep your creativity 'real' (rather than fanciful). This is a feet-on-the-ground, head-in-the-air resonance. These nine years could magnetize circumstances that elicit righteous indignation, because this resonance has a moral quality about it. Your g-cycles will encourage you to contemplate your values, and stimulate your awareness of the laws of the universe, especially the law of cause and effect. You may find yourself involved in some type of research that ultimately leads to deeper insight into your own nature.

H-Cycles

"H" is an energizing force like "E" but holds onto that energy more than E does. The form of the letter H is more self-contained than the form of the letter E, which symbolizes the ejection of energy in an outward direction. H stimulates change but the emotions that a person's life-experience generates are more likely to be internalized in an h-cycle, where they can smoulder for many years. Erupting periodically, they emerge as 'issues' around the themes of power and justice. Children who have an H-cycle in their first nine years tend to set high standards for themselves and then struggle to reach them. Through no fault of their own, they are vulnerable to feeling powerless, and that can wound them deeply. Any such wounding is internalized where it can cause psychosomatic illness. Such children can spend much of their lives struggling to gain the authority to be heard. Through this process they can become increasingly perceptive. During the years 18 to 27 the research revealed that frustrated plans and dreams generally result in a change of lifestyle.

A dramatic example is Lhamo Dhondup who suffered the invasion of his homeland during his first H-cycle. Although he was the Dalai Lama, he was powerless to prevent the events that occurred. In his next cycle, between 54 and 63, he was awarded the Nobel Peace Prize for non-violent action. Whether it is used for spiritual enlightenment, healing, social justice, or merely self-satisfaction, this resonance offers tenacity and resourcefulness. The opportunity that presents itself during these nine years is to unite the twin powers of your heart and mind. Naturally there will be fears to overcome and decisions to make. Once you've decided what you are prepared to take responsibility for, your creative powers can unite to support it. You will find that these nine years strengthen your resolve to 'make a difference' in some way. H also stands for heat and it will be on during this time. But this is a creative heat that will help you to scale the heights, breadths, and depths of consciousness.

I-Cycles

"I" intensifies the great drama that we know as life. Like A and E, this vowel can generate energy but whilst A is mental and E is physical in nature, I generates energy through the feelings. Children who experience an I-cycle in their first nine years are highly impressionable and may need a calmer and saner environment than others do. Over-stimulation by external sources ought to be avoided whilst the enjoyment of simple pleasures such as caring for animals is encouraged. Learning ways to enjoy their own company such as reading, will help these children to establish independence, and cultivating inspiring role models will give that independence meaning. Naturally inquisitive, older children and adolescents in an "i"-cycle also need their educational environment to be challenging but not stressful. At all ages, ample room for self-expression is vital to health.

In a later I-Cycle, Juliana of Norwich, a 14th Century mystic, began experiencing what she would call 'shewings'. These were revelations or inner illuminations. Her insight included the realization that knowledge of God and knowledge of Self are inseparable and that body and soul render mutual aid. Such awareness resonates with 'I'. Those readers with a more worldly inclination will be pleased to know that during this cycle one's influence generally increases. There is a definite sense of 'rising' during this period, with people such as Amelia Earhart and Billie Jean King going so far as to become icons. But any such increase in your sphere of influence will not be without impact on your emotions, and so if you are in an I-cycle take care of your body, mind *and* soul. These nine years will enhance your ability to generate answers to questions arising from within you. It will attempt to draw out the best in you and stimulate your creative juices so that you can take your place on the stage of life. You can expect it to be *intense*.

J-Cycles

"J" stands for judgment, and judgments are always a mixture of critical thought, feelings, emotions, values, principles, and willpower. Reflecting the fact that so much goes into making judgments, J is a complex vibration. It grants the power to overcome difficulties through **joint** effort. As the 10th letter of our alphabet, and therefore related to number 10, it will help you to stand on your own two feet and find your role in life. Although derived from the letter I, J is actually more like A, because it is mental in nature, but whilst A generates energy, J transforms it. And although intellectual in nature, J works through values that are based on the justice of the heart. Therefore children who experience a J-cycle in their first nine years tend to be self-motivated but in a more complex way than is expressed through the letter A. They are often cherished, but equally often find themselves in a divided household. In hindsight *J*ean Houston would describe her two-culture family as enriching, which is a positive spin on a challenging set of circumstances, the word enrichment describing exactly what children in a J-cycle need.

At all ages J represents a juggling act between willful action and thoughtful cooperation, and so the advice offered is to postpone judgment until you have considered all of the facts, and even then to proceed with the sensitivity of the soul rather than the brutality of the ego. Keep in mind that the decisions you make could boomerang back to you at a later stage. These nine years develop the power to think intuitively and instinctively, and then to act judiciously. Determination will be required to create a path through the maze of human emotions that you will encounter.

K-Cycles

"K" brings partnerships of all kinds into focus: in business and in love and even between children and their parents. Children who experience a K-cycle in their first nine years are generally what can be called 'bright sparks'; however parents need to keep in mind that their mental 'brightness' may take an unusual form. Such children are stimulated by challenge. During the time this letter was active, *K*uppuswami (later Swami Sivananda) described himself as enthusiastic, pushy, and industrious.

Beyond the age of 18 the issue of choice becomes a strong theme associated with the letter 'k'. Friction can arise between the ego and the soul, and similarly between your external life and your internal life. You may have to choose which is of greater importance to you. If they are not in balance, this cycle is an opportunity to correct that. K generates energy through the intuitive faculties. During these nine years you will receive sudden flashes of insight that give you a heightened sense of awareness. But don't let your ego get carried away. Aim to inspire people by who you are rather than your vision of the way things 'should' be in an ideal world.

L-Cycles

"L" like the letters themselves gives form to mental concepts. Within the cycle of the name, its resonance facilitates the ability to perceive cause and effect, which is not as straightforward as it may seem. According the educational theorists this is difficult for young children and so those who experience an l-cycle in their first nine years have a gift that can only be applied with hindsight. The examples revealed that when 'l' is active during the first 18 years, those children and young adults who faired best were the ones that threw themselves into learning something that truly fascinated them. This offset any confusion they may have been feeling. At the same time, it laid the foundation for future success. The problem for people in an l-cycle is that they are dealing with a dynamic that is larger than the personal self. It is for this reason that people who are in an l-cycle typically find themselves in the midst of the 'market place' of life trying to make sense of it all. The more introverted a person is, the more they will feel overwhelmed by this cycle while their more extroverted counterparts relish the excitement. In later cycles it was evident that with age, the majority of people learn how to turn their social environment to their advantage. Those who develop their own style and promote it fair exceptionally well in fact. You will find that this letter will help you to launch your own ideas in a sure and steady sort of way.

Perhaps the finest expression of the letter L is contained within *L*udwig Van Beethoven's flamboyant Ninth Symphony, which was written at the beginning of his second L-cycle. The use of a chorus was a revolutionary idea and through the *Ode to Joy* we can feel the triumph and jubilance of the human spirit. Just so, there is an uplifting aspect to the letter "L." These nine years could precipitate within you, a new way of looking at life.

M-Cycles

"M", our 13th letter, and the number 13, are alike in that both catalyze transformation. Through such change, your subconscious mind will be stirred into action. Naturally such a cataclysmic process strains the nervous system, especially in children. The research indicated that children who experience an M-cycle in their first nine years fair best when they are offered routines upon which they can depend, including longer than usual periods of rest and relaxation. Adults ought not to assume that children know how to relax, but should teach them a technique that suits their temperament. Any bottled up emotions they may be experiencing, can be expressed through drama, drawing, dancing, singing, modelling, or writing. Repressed emotions at any age will affect the body, and a healthy diet is especially important during these nine years. Family upheavals were unfortunately common in the case studies, all the way up to 18. Beyond 18 we witness young adults actively attempting to restore stability in their lives. Thankfully this is not everyone's experience, yet the enhanced ability to stand up for one's convictions is evident in most m-cycles. It would seem to encourage people, from deep within, to participate in bringing about change in the world around them.

For example Tho*m*as Jefferson drafted the US Declaration of Independence during his m-cycle. Similarly your m-cycle will encourage you to share your ideas with other people. If you allow your friends to modify and develop your ideas, you might finish up with something quite 'magical'. In an m-cycle, change occurs gradually, through consistent effort, and by interacting with other people.

N-Cycles

"N" is a mental and transformative. Think of those two frequently used n-words - numbers and names - and how they represent qualities that help us to discern between one thing and another, remember a particular form, and create a network of associations. Such intellectual abilities have obvious social implications and that's the arena in which we are most likely to find the letter "n". Children who experience an N-cycle early in life tend to have a heightened sense of social awareness. Mobility in thinking is often reflected in mobility in life, with plenty of travel or at least a change of residence noted at all ages during an n-cycle. Perhaps related to the word numinous, realizing the significance of one's place, as a 'player' in the bigger picture of life, is also evident. Typically we see people trying to get noticed in response to powerful needs that they barely comprehend. Notoriety turned up now and then in the research. Yet there is a clear correlation between aligning the propensity of this resonance to promote social issues, *long-term* success, and the heart-felt recognition of one's responsibility within the larger body of humanity. "N" facilitates inventiveness.

During her n-Cycle, Sandra Eades went to Bangladesh as an elective in the course of her medical training. Still later this training took her to Canada and the Indian reservations. Gradually within her, the resolve to make a contribution to the well being of her own people was steadily building. She went on to graduate and was awarded Aboriginal of the Year in Western Australia. The details may be specific to one person but this is a typical pattern in a healthy n-cycle. By responding to heart-felt needs a breakthrough in consciousness is possible during these nine years.

O-Cycles

"O" generates energy through the emotions. The research revealed that the letter O has a way of behaving like an emotional pressure-cooker. Yet from this cauldron can emerge some fabulous creativity. The letter "O" will compound any tendency you may have to take on the emotions of other people. Worse, you may feel responsible for them. In young people this can make life uncomfortably complex and confusing. Reflection upon the case studies suggests that the issue of whom to trust with one's deepest feelings is ever present, albeit subconsciously. The positive spin on all of this is that you are learning to see the world through the eyes of friends, family members, and even 'enemies'.

For example, between the years of 27 and 36 Rudolf Steiner lived in the cultural heart of Germany, fulfilling his duties and completing his doctorate. This was a highly social time when he made both friends and enemies. He enjoyed exploring other people's perspectives on life but misunderstandings were unavoidable. The "o"-resonance will help you to feel a part of the collective consciousness. It lends itself to social commentary. Interestingly, it was during an o-cycle that Alphonso (Alan) Alda was offered the Hawkeye role, a character that reveals much about this socially observant letter. "O" will help you to develop insight. It has the power to illuminate the truth. You can expect to oscillate between obsession and objectivity. Use it to enrich your understanding of humanity.

P-Cycles

The letter "P" generates power through rational thinking. This could leave a young child feeling 'different' because they have a certain perceptiveness not shared by their playmates. Fortunately examples of having a secret that makes a person feel *really* different are rare in the first nine years.

Although not a secret, Peter Falk had to have an eye removed when he was three years old, which certainly left him feeling 'different'. Significantly he would learn to use this difference to his advantage, and therein lays the key to a successful p-Cycle. When Peter's next p-cycle appeared, between 45 and 54, he decided to take the role of Colombo into a TV series, becoming thus internationally known as the detective in the raincoat. That subtle, relentless, probing quality demonstrated by the famous detective is typical of the letter "p". At any age, p-cycles are an ideal time to undertake research in any area of life that fascinates you. Specialization is common. Ste*p*hen Hawking did his pioneer research into black holes during his p-cycle. Like him, you too might enjoy studying and then publishing your findings. And if you have a secret that needs airing it may be time to select someone that you can confide in. Anything that is clogging up your thinking will attempt to purge itself during this time. It probably feels like a private matter, but actually there may be many others who are grappling with a similar issue and who would benefit from what you have to say. During these nine years the ability to amalgamate the twin powers of your heart and mind is strong, and it is an ideal time to exercise what the Buddhists call mindfulness. This is the ability to observe without feeling compelled to get involved. You might also need to exercise patience, with yourself as much as with others.

Q-Cycles

"Q" quickens the transformation of soul-power into effective action. The case studies indicate that challenging circumstances in the outer arena catalyze a creative response from within. In the first nine years of life this could be particularly hard on the nervous system! People who experience a q-cycle in their early years are therefore likely to feel tense and uncertain much of the time. In the long run this will deepen their thoughts and feelings, and bear fruit later in life. At all ages q-cycles encourage the soul and ego to work together and present a united front. The soul will attempt to influence the ego while the ego struggles to establish its place within a particular cultural setting. Phonetically, "q" and "c" sound alike but unlike c-cycles, in q-cycles people typically find themselves struggling against the status quo. However, the evidence suggests that when the ego and soul combine their powers to meet such a challenge, anything is possible.

For example when *Q*uincy Jones was five years old his mother suffered a nervous breakdown but by working long hours, his father ensured that the children got what they needed. Interestingly, the second q-cycle (54-63) witnessed a mighty comeback from a nervous breakdown Quincy himself had suffered at 53. By then quite wealthy, he extended his talents to become the executive producer of a comedy show and co-founded a new record label. If you are in a q-cycle these nine years will be full of growth-potential if you can muster your resources: inner *and* outer. The love-power of the soul is seeking expression within your cultural domain and if you are open to exploring the potential of your current situation, you may accomplish more than you thought yourself capable of. There is a role in society that only you can fulfill.

R-Cycles

"R" maximizes the opportunity to take your place on the stage of life. "R" is an extremely intense resonance and unfortunately it must be noted that in a few cases the early years were emotionally guttering, due to circumstances completely beyond personal control. Fortunately however, in the majority this was not the case. R intensifies a person's feeling life and fuels the ambition to overcome any latent feelings of powerlessness. A choice of roles typically ensues, the first often being 'victim', because becoming someone's victim is a challenge that everyone in an r-cycle must face. Once a person finds their way through this, they can choose a more productive role for themselves, and then work determinedly towards actualizing their potential. This choice of role seems to include selfishness or selflessness as a component. Warning: those who chose a socially prominent position at the expense of love did not experience happy endings. The most fascinating observation with later r-cycles is that the role a person chooses for themselves during these nine years is the one that they are most likely to be remembered by. Famous people who die during an r-cycle tend to be remembered as having embodied a mythic or archetypal role. For example Marion Morrison, as John Wayne, became the embodiment of the 'American war hero'.

R-cycles are often political in nature precisely because they tend to objectify the personal and enact the archetypal. Make sure you choose a role that is harmonious with your nature and don't try to be something that you are not. Acknowledge the source of the fabulous creativity that is powering through you, and build into your busy schedule a regular time-slot for rest and relaxation, recreation and rejuvenation. Try to keep what is really important uppermost in your mind. You could travel far, both literally and figuratively, during this cycle.

S-Cycles

"S" stimulates the powers of the mind through the powers of the heart. Once the flow between these two great forces has been established the examples demonstrate not only prodigious achievement but also evidence of self-healing (i.e. Self healing self). Children who experience an S-cycle in their first nine years typically have an experience that becomes significant to the role that they will play later in life. For example, what began as therapy for Shirley MacLaine became her life's passion. Her parents had enrolled her in ballet lessons to strengthen her ankles when, as Shirley describes it, her imagination caught on to the idea of becoming a dancer. By another stroke of 'fate' Sarah Durack would have drowned had she not been saved by a dog. Subsequently she began swimming lessons. Gradually she took hold of the idea of becoming a champion swimmer and went on to break world records.

From age 9 the case studies are loaded with people describing their 'inward turning' in order to heal past wounds, or to restore harmony within their body, mind and soul (which may be the same thing). Aldous Huxley's biographer described the famous author's years between 45 and 54 as a time of "subtle underground transformation", which would ultimately bring him peace of mind. He came to terms with his past and healed his considerable childhood wounds. The fruits of this inner work ripened in the next cycle when the healed became healer and theory became practice. S-cycles are transpersonal in nature. And so those (notably very few examples) who appropriated this essentially spiritual energy for personal aggrandizing did not die happy people because they had not fulfilled the 'love-obligation' that is inherent to being a member of the human race. During the time that the letter "S" is active, your soul will undergo a review of its journey in the material world, attempt to heal its wounded ego, and draw all of its forces into the mind. Take your feelings and the insight that issue from them, seriously.

T-Cycles

"T" transforms our die-hard beliefs into a more universal viewpoint. Naturally this is difficult for children who know nothing about the archetypal forces that seek expression within human

311

life. Yet when the home-life is stable these children fare no worse than any other. The research suggests a significant role for the extended family, particularly grandparents, in the attainment of such a sense of stability. "T" is a heart-felt resonance that indicates a period of soul-searching. During these nine years you will feel the need to succeed at something quite acutely. In accordance with natural law, T tends to bring about a major turning point in a person's life or at least a time of re-evaluation. People who allow themselves to be transformed by love fare best in the long-term, whilst those who resist the transforming power of our common humanity remain stuck somewhere in the past, their attempts to make progress continually thwarted. This resonance will persistently attempt to transmute ego-power into soul-power.

Consistently we find people trying hard, feeling tried, or actually being tried. Anatoly Shcharansky was tried and convicted of treason during his t-cycle and Yitzhak Rabin imprisoned for rescuing illegal immigrants. After a long struggle Katharine Hepburn won her first Academy Award towards the end of her t-cycle. This pattern of reward towards the cycle's end is quite typical. Likewise, later cycles tend to bring recognition for a lifetime's work *provided that* childhood issues have been dealt with. If not, these ghosts of the past will reappear in their quest for integration into the psychic wholeness of the individual. As a counterpart to this inner transition, t-cycles often attract travel. Stay true to your heart during your t-cycle no matter what, and give your inner-warrior a workout. These nine years will challenge you to move beyond the limitations of your physical body and its inherent programming, in order to answer a more sublime calling. You will find that this necessitates the sacrifice of egoism to the integrity of the soul.

U-Cycles

The letter U provides an 'urn' for receiving, holding and transforming thought-forms from the universal mind. In a healthy vessel these thought-forms are congenial with the development of humanity. There is an ancient Egyptian creation story that can serve to explain the way this resonance operates within the growth cycle. A solar deity named Ra lay underwater waiting for the time to rise to the surface. Rather than being idle, he was steadily enclosing himself in a lotus bud that would act like a submarine and support his upward passage. Faithfully the bud supported him as he rose higher and higher, adapting itself to the changes in temperature as it did so. By no means disaffected by the journey, the bud steadily increased its rate of vibration as together they rose to the surface, where the lotus opened completely; revealing its contents for all to see. This story helps to explain why it is that during u-cycles people typically have unusual experiences, indeed often unnerving ones. In many cases these have acted as a catalyst for 'raising one's vibration' until a breakthrough is reached (provided the person doesn't give up). Rarely do names begin with U, but *U*stad Inayat Khan provides us with a handy example. His first nine years were interwoven with the lives of saints, which is an ideal setting for this resonance. Like Ustad, young people who experience a u-cycle in their first eighteen years benefit from studying the lives and ideals of people who have worked towards improving our common humanity.

It was between the years 9 and 18 that L*u*dwig Van Beethoven realized that music could transform people. This made him anxious to break free from classical conventions. What could be called a moral rebirth is quite common during a u-cycle. Between 36 and 45 Aldo*u*s Huxley realized the power of the pen to help people and wrote *The Nobler Hypothesis*. During your own u-cycle you could have a swarm of emotions to deal with and so take one day at a time and keep your sights set on utopian but realizable goals. These nine years are consolidating your intuitive faculties.

V-Cycles

V stands for vision; specifically, the capacity to foresee what needs to be done to enhance your community. Like the similar-sounding "F", this resonance targets the development of intuition but "V" focuses on stabilizing the intuitive faculties rather than transforming them. The letter V resembles U but its point of contact with the earth is more provocative. In tandem with number 22, v, our 22nd letter, catalyzes the realization that co-operation and sensitivity are practical tools that can benefit those around you. And in harmony with number 6 (its Chaldean correspondent) this involves a socially mature response to your environment. Together these numbers stimulate dynamic interaction between you and those with whom you share your community. "Spirit and Nature dancing together" is a song title that encapsulates what is possible in a v-cycle. Your life then becomes a victory-dance. Children who experience a V-cycle in their first nine years thrive on responsibility but should not feel that they have to try to be all things to all people. Too often in a v-cycle we witness young people feeling undervalued.

V encourages people to tunnel deeply into their subconscious strata of humanity. From there, they can create a whole network of ideas. Between the ages of 27 and 36 Clive Staples Lewis (better known as C. S. Lewis) became a Fellow of English and dedicated himself to lecturing and tutoring. Towards the end of the cycle came the spiritual turning point of his life when he switched from being an atheist to a believer, a conversion brought about by imaginative-cum-rational thinking. "V" stimulates this kind of thinking, and the productive work that stems from it, has an inspired edge. Likewise, in your own v-cycle much hinges on how clear and practical your vision is. During these nine years you may be able to give practical expression to your highest ideals.

W-Cycles

W whips up energy generated within the physical body and transforms it into willpower. The most appropriate image is a single cell within a womb dividing and thus multiplying until the physical form encoded in the original cell is ready to emerge. In like manner, "w" vibrates at tremendous speed, creating from within itself a 'substance' generally known as psychic energy. This substantial force heightens the perceptive faculties throughout the entire physical body. It is possible to experience sensations within any part of the body, not just the usual 'nose for smelling, eyes for seeing' etc. Called intuitional feeling, all of the senses can actually operate simultaneously in a deep state of being that has no centre. This enables a person to see through their ears and taste through their skin. Helen Keller gained such sensory awareness when she lost the ability to hear and see and she called it soul-sense. Also called synesthesia or cross-sensing, it may be common to animals. Neurosurgeon and brain researcher Wilder Penfield claimed that, in his opinion, the mind was not lodged in the brain but appeared to be everywhere: in the muscles, tissues, cells, and bones. It is therefore not surprising to find that children who experience a W-cycle in their first nine years are often precocious or at least bright, lively, and impatient. School may bore them because the lessons do not move fast enough and so they tend to be self-taught, learning from life as they go. They typically excel in one particular form of communication. All of this energy can generate wild mood swings in people who are unhappy. When this is not the case, w-cycles attract good fortune because the energy is focused in a positive way. *W*olfgang Amadeus Mozart illustrates much of the above.

During your w-cycle life will become richly textured. You could learn how to heal your own body by entering it with your imagination and seeing it, hearing it, and feeling it from the inside. These nine years will bring a wide variety of experiences that encourage you to become a more versatile and broad-minded human-being.

X-Cycles

"X" excites energy. If the cross stylized by the letter T represents the intersection of spirit and matter as many authors have suggested, then perhaps the x represents past and future intersecting in the present moment. There is something intensely immediate about this symbol. In two swift strokes, the past per the stroke coming from the left, and the future, per the stroke coming from the right, unite. One way to interpret this, which may prove useful to people who are experiencing an x-cycle is to visualize the authority of a previously established order, and the idealism of a future potential, colliding or uniting within you. Children who experience an x-cycle in their first eighteen years are likely to be intensely emotional. If there is any tension between family members, they won't know which way to turn. Adults who can help them to assess their values and focus on those that are worthy of their love and attention, are what these young people need most.

Alexander Graham Bell conceived the idea of the telephone right at the beginning of his x-cycle but he was not given support for the idea until competition forced the issue. One of his financial backers was the father of the woman he loved. Despite opposition on all fronts, Bell persisted with his courtship, perfected the telegraph (which is what his financiers wanted), *and* developed the idea of the telephone. In other words, despite all of the confusion happening at the time, he remained true to his vision. Eventually his quiet persistence paid off, all round. He married the love of his life and his father-in-law patented the telephone idea. The patent was challenged in a long court battle, which Bell eventually won. He became internationally famous for this invention, yet he never lost sight of his primary passion, which was to help the hearing impaired. These nine years may be equally fortunate for you, but they will test your compassion and commitment. A spiritually charged ideal awaits conception and nurturing. X offers you the opportunity make your mark on the time at hand.

Y-Cycles

The letter Y heightens self-awareness. Its form resembles three prongs meeting in the centre, and you could visualize this as three aspects of your life: your past, your future, and your present. This letter prods people to make a moral choice and the question "Whom doth the Grail serve?" comes into focus. Each person's response will accord with his/her consciousness at the time. Y-cycles help people to see possible futures that they could engage in. Children who experience a Y-cycle in their first nine years tend to have a heightened sense of responsibility but unless their home life has provided a clear direction for them, they may feel strangely ambivalent about themselves and life in general. Such children fare best when they have one direction demonstrated by a living example. Yitzhak Rabin was raised in an environment that encouraged a strong sense of duty to his country. And during the return of his y-cycle between 63 and 72, he became engaged in its peace process.

Y-cycles tend to precipitate a crisis that brings people to a point of having to choose between one option and another. Between the years 36 and 45 Harry Truman realized that he was a failure in business but effective as a judge. And between 63 and 72 Mary (Elizabeth) Dole decided *not* to run for Presidency. In some cases there are clearly three irons in the fire: one spiritual or religious, another social or political, and a third that is distinctly personal. During his y-cycle Henry VIII broke with the Catholic Church, annulled his marriage so he could marry someone else, and effectively became Pope of England. Given all of the above, it was not surprising to find that during these nine years most people make a major decision that alters the course of their life. During your y-cycle consider your options carefully, and the likely outcome of each. If you base your choices on the answers that you have received to the most exacting questions that you can think of, it will have been a time well spent.

Z-Cycles

The letter "Z" completes the journey of personal development as symbolized by the letters of the English Alphabet. Like a snowball rolling down a hill, "z" represents the culmination of these vibrations, and this makes its impact considerable. Whatever the particular circumstances, z has energy in abundance. Children who experience a Z-cycle in their first nine years are typically bright and lively. Parents can help them by demonstrating ways by which they can co-operate with others without compromising their personal goals. 'Functional teamwork' is the key phrase here. These children need a comprehensive education because they will want to know and understand *everything*.

In later cycles, your personal life may become subjugated or integrated into your public profile. For example Elizabeth II became Queen of England during her z-cycle, under very different circumstances to Elizabeth I who was already in power by then. Elizabeth, the Queen Mother, was also Queen of England during her z-cycle, as wife to King George VI. And so all three Elizabeth's were queen during their z-cycle. Obviously very few people will experience being Queen of England but these women demonstrate a theme common to all: an increase of power, authority, and responsibility. These nine years will bring you plenty of excitement and opportunities for growth. This could be quite a dramatic time in your life, and you could experience an increased level of prestige. To capitalize on this opportunity, you can spin a web of love that impacts on the lives of those around you (that's number 26 as per the 26th letter of the alphabet). One thing is for certain: you won't go unnoticed. These nine years are building your capacity to meet every situation that you encounter with effective self-discipline.

The Growth Cycle in Action

Richard means wealthy and powerful and we are going to track the life of one very famous 'Richard' who has lived up to the potential of his name.

Richard Charles Nicholas Branson
Born on July 18 1950

= 7. 18. 15 = 40
= 7. 9. 15 = 31
= 7. 9. 6 = 22

   7
  18
<u>1950</u>
<u>1975 = 22 = 4.</u>

Date Path 40/31/22/4, vowel 39/12, consonant 90, name 129/12, birthday 18/9, growth number 43/7, maturity number 169/7. First base 7, birthday base 18/9, home base 15/6; achievement number 25/7 (from birth to 32), attainment 33/6 (from 33 to 41), attainment 58/4 (from 42 to 50) and quest 22/4 (from 51 onwards); 1st challenge 2 (small) and 11 (big), 2nd challenge 3, whole life and polarity challenges 1 (small) and 8 (big), vowel challenge 3, consonant challenge 4, name challenge 1.

<u>The First Nine Years</u>

From his birth in mid-1950 to his 9th birthday on July 18 1959, Richard was in an R-cycle. His first personal year cycle began in a year 4 and therefore ended before his r-cycle was complete:

January 1st – December 31st 1951: personal year 5
January 1st – December 31st 1952: personal year 6
January 1st – December 31st 1953: personal year 7
January 1st – December 31st 1954: personal year 8
January 1st – December 31st 1955: personal year 9

January 1st – December 31st 1956: personal year 1 unites with letter "r" and an important decision was made. Richard was about six when he made the decision as to who his role model would be. That person was his adventurous and entrepreneurial Aunt Clare who flew a bi-plane. She also bred of Welsh Mountain sheep and eventually got them off the endangered list.

January 1st - December 31st 1957: personal year 2 still within an r-cycle
January 1st - December 31st 1958: personal year 3
It was during this year in Richard's first r-cycle that he was separated from his best friend and sent to boarding school where he was lonely and frightened. R can stand for resentment and this is what he felt for his parents at that time. He was dyslexic and assumed to be either stupid or lazy, and beaten for it. Out of a need to survive, he discovered that he excelled in sports.

January 1st – December 31st 1959: personal year 4; half of which culminates the R-cycle while the I-cycle begins. On his 9th birthday on July 18 1959 Richard began his i-cycle.
January 1st – December 31st 1961: personal year 6
It was during that year, when Richard was aged 11, that he suffered a severe blow to his success in sport. He fell badly during a football match and was sent home to recover. January 1st – December 31st 1962: personal year 7. The outcome of his accident was that Richard was sent to a crammer school but he was expelled shortly afterwards.

January 1st – December 31st 1963: personal year 8
His next school was Stowe where he found refuge in the library and made a friend with another lad doing the same thing. Through this friend he became interested in journalism and he wrote a short story that won a prize. His English scores improved rapidly after that but mathematics remained a problem.

January 1st – December 31st 1965: personal year 1 unites with the letter 1 and Richard's entrepreneurial activities begin. His early schemes were not profitable but they helped him realize that he could understand mathematics when it had a practical application.

January 1st – December 31st 1966: personal year 2. Number 15 is Richard's home base number and it was at age 15, during the early months of 1966, that Richard and his friend began discussing ways to change the school rules. And so began *Student - the Magazine for Britain's Youth*. The age equivalent of the home base number is often significant in a person's life.

January 1st – December 31st 1967: Personal Year 3
Richard was sixteen when he received his first cheque for an advertisement in the magazine.

January 1st – December 31st 1968: personal year 4; half of which culminates the i-cycle while the c-cycle begins. The first issue of *Student* was published in January 1968. In October all of the *Student* staff joined Vanessa Redgrave in a protest against the Vietnam War.

January 1st – December 31st 1969: personal year 5
At the end of 1969 Richard was arrested for mentioning the words 'venereal disease' in the magazine.
January 1st – December 31st 1970: personal year 6
In May 1970 the court found him guilty under the strict letter of the law and fined him seven pounds. He had learned not to fear the Establishment. That year he also learned much about conflict resolution as it applies to one's closest friend. That was also the year that the name *Virgin* was born.

January 1st – December 31st 1971: personal year 7
Having decided on a mail order business, it came as a shock when the postal workers went out on strike. As a result, Virgin's first record shop came into being. This was also the year that he ran into trouble with Customs and Excise and had to spend a night in prison. Year 7 is typically the year when we decide *not* to do something and just so, it was the year that Richard decided that he would never again do anything that would cause him to be imprisoned. He met his cousin Simon that year too, and Simon had an ear for promising music.

January 1st – December 31st 1972: Personal Year 8. By Christmas 1972, Virgin had opened fourteen record shops. Richard got married that year as well and although year 8 is generally a good year to marry, this union was not destined to last.

January 1st – December 31st 1973: personal year 9
First base cycle 7 came to a glorious end with *Tubular Bells* topping the charts. Richard was 22 years of age and number 22 is his secondary date path number.

January 1st – December 31st 1974: personal year 1 unites with the letter "c". Dramatically, he and his wife would have died at sea had they not swam the two miles to shore. They survived but their marriage would not. With vowel and name number 12, Richard experienced an energy crisis until age 24 (as explained in chapter 7). It was a significant time in many ways. 1974 was the year that birthday base cycle 18 began and its intense drive would support Richard's next thirty-six years. If you have number 18 in your numbers, Richard's autobiography provides multiple clues for making it work for you.

January 1st – December 31st 1975: personal year 2. A frustrating year, as year 2's often are, in Richard's case it meant coming second with a number of important deals.

January 1st – December 31st 1976: Personal Year 3
A crisis meeting resulted in letting go all of the bands who were not making money and looking for new ways to increase income. It was also in 1976 that Richard met Joan and a magical love affair would begin.

January 1st – December 31st 1977: personal year 4; half of which culminates the c-cycle while the h-cycle begins. It was "hello" to *The Sex Pistols*.

January 1st – December 31st 1978: personal year 5
Richard and Joan fell in love with Necker Island that year and determined to somehow buy it. Virgin Airways was accidently born that year too in response to an airport full of stranded passengers.

January 1st – December 31st 1979: personal year 6
Virgin France began that year, and so did the recession in Britain.

January 1st – December 31st 1980: personal year 7
This chapter of Richard's autobiography is titled "Success can take off without warning" and it covers the final three years of this personal year cycle within his h-cycle. It was a frantic time, a desperate time financially, and a heart-breaking time with the loss of Joan and Richard's first baby.

January 1st – December 31st 1981: personal year 8
Joan and Richard's daughter, Holly, was born. And Virgin Music was finally making a profit.

January 1st – December 31st 1983: personal year 1 unites with the letter "h" and Virgin Vision was born. It produced a film version of George Orwell's *1984*; the budget running out of control and almost bringing the entire Virgin Group down. It won the Best British Film of the Year award but Richard had learned his lesson: making films was a precarious way to make money.

Attainment 33/6 began in the year that Richard turned 33 and would exert its influence until the year he turned 41. The ideal of number 33 is to gather and sort information from diverse sources. Throughout these nine years this theme would prove vital to the success of the business.

January 1st – December 31st 1984: personal year 2
Virgin Atlantic Airways was launched but not without a fall out with a potential partner.

January 1st – December 31st 1985: personal year 3
Virgin won a Business Enterprise Award for company of the year.

January 1st – December 31st 1986: personal year 4; half of which culminates the h-cycle while the a-cycle begins. Growth letter "a" promotes inner growth through self-reliance and original thinking. Significant new beginnings must be expected. Just so, the Virgin Group was floated on the London Stock Exchange in November.

January 1st – December 31st 1988: personal year 6
Richard bought back the shares that he had floated in Year 4 of this Cycle and re-established the Virgin Group as a private company.

January 1st – December 31st 1989: personal year 7. Virgin Vision was sold to an American company, and again we witness people deciding what they *don't* want in a year 7.

January 1st – December 31st 1990: personal year 8.
The first megastore opens in Japan as a result of a fifty-fifty joint venture.

January 1st – December 31st 1991: personal year 9
After a long hard struggle, Virgin Atlantic won the right to operate services out of Heathrow.

January 1st – December 31st 1992: Personal Year 1 unites with the letter
A, which is equivalent to Number 1 and it would herald the beginning of Richard's victory years.

January 1st – December 31st 1993: personal year 2
Virgin Atlantic Airways won an historic libel settlement plus all legal costs from British Airways relating to a dirty-tricks campaign.

January 1st – December 31st 1994: personal year 3
The appendix to Richard's autobiography lists sixteen major developments that year!

January 1st – December 31st 1995: personal year 4; half of which culminates the a-cycle while a new r- cycle begins. Unresolved issues relating to the first r-cycle are likely to have been picked up here and brought to resolution. These would have been intensely personal and not part of an autobiography for the general public.

By the end of this 9-year cycle Virgin had the concept of 'branded venture capital' securely in place and just as well:
January 1st – December 31st 2001: personal year 1 unites with the letter r shortly before the attack on the Twin Towers. Suddenly people didn't want to fly and airlines were going under. Emergency restructuring plans were activated and by the year's end it was clear that Virgin Atlantic would survive.

January 1st – December 31st 2004: personal year 4; half of which culminates the r-cycle while the d-cycle begins. That year Virgin Galactic signed a deal to create the world's first commercial space tourist business.

January 1st – December 31st 2010: personal year 1 unites with the letter d as Richard celebrates 60 years of a deeply fulfilling life.

On his 63rd birthday this great man began a whole new cycle, starting back with R for Richard. This r-cycle will be active until his 71st birthday.

Chapter 12

The Astro-Number Signature

The factor that knits numerology and astrology together is the astro-number signature. This signature is the DNA of astronumerology and typically people are completely unaware of it. Your signature indicates a deep and natural tendency that will be with you throughout your life. Like a subtle dye in water, your signature permeates your entire energy matrix, making it a very important piece of information.

Whole-Sign Horoscope

Your astro-number signature is calculated by combining the information within your horoscope with your numbers in a very specific way. You will therefore need your horoscope in front of you to complete the calculations, and it needs to be a Whole Sign Horoscope. You can either ask an astrologer for help with this or do it yourself per a website such as http://www. horoscopeswithin.com/birthchart.php. While you are there, note your natal moon phase: New, Crescent, First Quarter, Gibbous, Full, Disseminating, Last Quarter, or Balsamic and the exact degree if you can (just in case you need it).

To determine the astro-number signature, the challenge chart has been recycled for ease of comparison. The zero has been removed and so have the karmic numbers. Three rows have been added to accommodate the numbers 10, 11 and 12, which are crucial to calculating the correct signature. A complete astro-number signature worksheet can be found in the worksheets for you to copy and fill in. Please make at least one copy because errors are common even for experienced people.

Treat each number as though it is present and accountable at the time of birth - including attainments and challenges - because at a subtle level, it is. At certain times in your life a particular energy will be more active and accessible than at others, yet always there.

There are two exceptions:

1) The birthday number and birthday base are allotted a single point because they are the same.

2) Each challenge should only be noted once, even if there is a bunch of them focused on a particular number.

Following this chapter, you will also find a worksheet for each of the primary date paths. Completing this first will make filling in the astro-number worksheet easier. You can simply move down the sheet adding each piece of data as you go. The following guidelines have been arranged to accord with these worksheets.

In the top right-hand corner of the worksheet there is sufficient space to draw the 3x3 grid as per chapter 6. Put the date of birth numbers into it for ready reference. Draw a second grid and you can put the letters of the original name into it. You can then note the missing number(s) and intensity number if either exists.

A Checklist for Determining the Astro-Number Signature

The Number Influences

- ❑ Every date chart number must be placed in the signature worksheet even if there are several of the same number
- ❑ The date path number with the 10's, 11's and 12's noted instead of the 1's, 2's and 3's, when the former turn up in the calculation
- ❑ The vowel, consonant, and name numbers of the original name (giving the 10's, 11's and 12's preference when they turn up in the calculation)
- ❑ The intensity number if there is one (adhere carefully to the guidelines in chapter 3)
- ❑ The growth key (giving preference to 10's, 11's and 12's where they turn up)
- ❑ The maturity number (giving preference to 10's, 11's and 12's where they turn up)
- ❑ The first base, birthday base, and home base numbers (giving preference to 10's, 11's and 12's where they turn up in the calculation)
- ❑ The 4 attainments (giving preference to 10's, 11's and 12's where they turn up)
- ❑ The challenges: *mark each number only once* even if it turns up several times in either the date of birth or name challenges. When two different numbers appear in the same spot, count both. If, for example, 4 turns up as the whole life challenge (small) and 5 as the whole life challenge (big), count both. Big challenges 10, 11 and 12 are given preference over small challenges 1, 2 and 3 when they appear together. But do not reduce 13 to 4, 14 to 5, 15 to 6, 16 to 7, 17 to 8, 18 to 9 etc. Ignore all numbers over 12.
- ❑ Include numbers that are missing from both the date chart and the name chart (even if they have already been counted as a challenge)

The Astrological Influences

- ❑ Begin with the ascendant and apply the correspondences per chapter 10: Aries is noted in number 1's row, Taurus in number 2's row, Gemini in number 3's row, Cancer in number 4's row, Leo in number 5's row, Virgo in number 6's row, Libra in number 7's row, Scorpio in number 8's row, Sagittarius in number 9's row, Capricorn in number 10's row, Aquarius in number 11's row, and Pisces in number 12's row.
- ❑ Now note any planets in the first house (the house wherein the ascendant lies). Place any such planets in the same row as the ascendant.

❑ NB: As well the planets Mars, Venus, Mercury, Jupiter, Saturn, Uranus, Neptune and Pluto, we are also including the Sun, Moon, and the Moon's North and South Nodes.

❑ Proceed anti-clockwise to the second house. Place any planets therein in the row corresponding to the sign, as above; (not all houses have planets in them).

❑ mark any planets in the 3rd house in the row corresponding to the sign, as above

❑ mark any planets in the 4th house in the row corresponding to the sign, as above

❑ mark any planets in the 5th house in the row corresponding to the sign, as above

❑ mark any planets in the 6th house in the row corresponding to the sign, as above

❑ mark any planets in the 7th house in the row corresponding to the sign, as above

❑ mark any planets in the 8th house in the row corresponding to the sign, as above

❑ mark any planets in the 9th house in the row corresponding to the sign, as above

❑ mark any planets in the 10th house the row corresponding to the sign, as above

❑ mark any planets in the 11th house the row corresponding to the sign, as above

❑ mark any planets in the 12th house the row corresponding to the sign, as above

❑ Make sure all 4 Angles are included in the count: the Ascendant, Descendant (which is directly opposite the Ascendant), the MC and the IC (directly opposite the MC).

❑ The natal moon phase (covering two segments):

❑ mark the new moon in row numbers 1 and 2

❑ mark the crescent moon in row numbers 2 and 3

❑ mark the first quarter moon in row numbers 4 and 5

❑ mark the gibbous moon in row numbers 5 and 6

❑ mark the full moon in row numbers 7 and 8

❑ mark the disseminating moon in row numbers 8 and 9

❑ mark the last quarter moon in row numbers 10 and 11

❑ mark the balsamic moon in row numbers 11 and 12

The Dominant Element

By applying the correspondences named in chapter 10 the following table can be filled in accordingly. You do not need to 'weight' the components any further.

Air – 3, 7, 11	Earth – 2, 6, 10	Water – 4, 8, 12	Fire – 1, 5, 9
3 –	2 –	4 –	1 –
7 –	6 –	8 –	5 –
11 –	10 –	12 –	9 –
Total =	Total =	Total =	Total =

The Dominant Modality

Cardinal: generates energy	Fixed: stabilizes energy	Mutable: facilitates the flow of energy
1 –	2 –	3 –
4 –	5 –	6 –
7 –	8 –	9 –
10 –	11 –	12 –
Total =	Total =	Total =

NB: the above is a part of the astro-number signature worksheet near the end of the book

The Astro-Number Signature = the Dominant Element + the Dominant Modality

Cardinal Fire = Aries-1
Cardinal Water = Cancer-4
Cardinal Air = Libra-7
Cardinal Earth = Capricorn-10
Fixed Earth = Taurus-2
Fixed Fire = Leo-5
Fixed Water = Scorpio-8
Fixed Air = Aquarius-11
Mutable Air = Gemini-3
Mutable Earth = Virgo-6
Mutual Fire = Sagittarius-9
Mutual Water = Pisces-12

When There Are Multiple Signatures

Occasionally the calculations reveal a multiple signature making further steps necessary. There are 4 steps to follow and they must be followed in this exact order.

1. Check your data: how reliable is it? During the course of the research done to establish the formula, it became painfully obvious that most problems were due to either data or computational errors. Only four percent of people have a twin signature. When you arrive at a multiple signature, check every piece of data meticulously.

2. If you are certain that the date, time, and place of birth are correct and that you have the full name at birth, check your calculations because computational errors are common. If the letter 'y' appears in the name consider that it may be a vowel instead of a consonant or vice-versa. Changing from one to the other can occasionally resolve a signature.

   An example is provided by Oprah Winfrey. When the 'y' at the end of Winfrey is treated as a vowel, the Signature is clearly Libra-7. When it is treated as a consonant it will still resolve to Libra-7 but not without taking a few more steps.

3. If you are satisfied that your source of data is reliable and that your calculations are correct then reduce the moon phase to a single digit. In most cases, this resolves the multiple signatures to a single signature but to do this you need to know the exact degree of the moon phase. In other words, knowing for example that you were born at the new moon phase is not enough when a multiple signature appears. There's a difference between being born at say, one degree of the new moon and 31 degrees of the new moon. Consult the table below to nominate which represents your moon phase number.

   For example, Lisa Marie Presley was born when the new moon was at 39 degrees. Because each number covers 30 degrees of the horoscope, 39 degrees is equivalent to number 2. Including both numbers 1 and 2 as parts of the new moon phase resulted in a twin signature: cardinal fire and earth. Removing number 1 resolved the signature to cardinal earth (Capricorn-10). That said, the tension between these two signatures must be considered as a part of her life-story.

4. If you have applied the above and still have a multiple signature, pencil in the 1's, 2's and 3's that were omitted in favour of the 10's, 11's and 12's. This step should only be taken if it serves to clarify the dominant signature, and if it is applied to one number, then it must be applied to all three. In other words, you cannot be selective about which 1's, 2's and 3's to include.

Exception: October, November, and December birthdays should not be reduced to 1, 2, or 3 unless it is absolutely the only way to resolve the signature. Just one such example turned up in a data pool of one thousand people:

Jane Austen had the twin signature Aries-1 and Sagittarius-9. Her last quarter moon was at 289 degrees, which is in number 10's domain however eliminating number 11 as part of the moon phase made no difference in this case. The 1's, 2's and 3's were added but still did not resolve matters. Jane was born in December, which corresponds to number 12. Usually I would leave this intact and call it a twin signature but in Jane's case, reducing the 12 to a 3 resolved the signature in favour of Sagittarius-9. This made sense given that Jane has the Sun, Mercury and IC in Sagittarius.

When these primary numbers clarify the signature it means that the person is drawing heavily on them. Occasionally the primary numbers introduce a third signature and confuse matters. Treat such cases individually and use common sense as in Jane's case.

In four percent of cases the signature does not resolve. It is then classified as a twin signature and we will be considering such complexities further into the chapter. The rule of thumb is to do everything you can to resolve the Signature *and then* consider the complexities.

The following table should only be consulted if you have a multiple signature.

Moon Phase Degree	Number	Phase
0-29 degrees 59 minutes	1	New Moon
30 degrees – 44 degrees 59 minutes	2	
45 degrees – 59 degrees 59 minutes	2	Crescent Moon
60 degrees – 89 degrees 59 minutes	3	
90 degrees – 119 degrees 59 minutes	4	First Quarter Moon
120 degrees - 134 degrees 59 minutes	5	
135 degrees – 149 degrees 59 minutes	5	Gibbous Moon
150 degrees – 179 degrees 59 minutes	6	
180 degrees – 209 degrees 59 minutes	7	Full Moon
210 degrees – 225 degrees 59 minutes	8	

225 degrees – 239 degrees 59 minutes	8	Disseminating Moon
240 degrees – 269 degrees 59 minutes	9	
270 degrees – 299 degrees 59 minutes	10	Last Quarter Moon
300 degrees – 314 degrees 59 minutes	11	
315 degrees – 329 degrees 59 minutes	11	Balsamic Moon
330 degrees – 359 degrees 59 minutes	12	

Astrologers may be tempted to use this table before circling both numbers. It seems like a logical thing to do but in some cases it creates a multiple signature where one would not exist if both numbers had been applied.

Martina Navratilova provides an example. She was born when the gibbous moon was at 167 degrees. In the above table you will see that this is equivalent to number 6. Yet if number 5 had not also been included, hers would have been a twin signature: cardinal fire and earth. Because number 5 was included, her signature was singularly cardinal fire (Aries-1). This makes sense given that her Ascendant and Moon are in Aries.

Remember that *in all cases, the goal is to try and get a single signature* if it is at all possible. Complexities can be considered as an extra step once this has been established.

What follows is a description of each astro-number signature. Correspondences are considered first for what they can reveal followed by some general indications. Case studies feed into all of this and supply examples to complete each description. A total of ten samples were compared with the random sample below, which formed the basis of all comparisons. For example, one hundred musicians were compared and contrasted with this sample. You can similarly compare your findings with this random sample and the career indicators that stem from it. Musicians, writers, artists, sports careerists, scientists, the spiritually minded and politicians each had their own sample. Male and female actors were given separate samples and the results revealed some big differences between them. There was also a miscellaneous sample for people who did not fit into any of the above.

Sample One: Random (100 People Randomly Selected)		
Aries-1	18	Fire 42%, Water 20%, Earth and Air 16% = 94% + Twin Signatures 6% = 100%
Leo-5	16	Yang 58% and Yin 36%
Capricorn-10	8	1st Quadrant = 26%
Aquarius-11	8	2nd Quadrant = 24%
Pisces-12	8	3rd Quadrant = 20%
Sagittarius-9	8	4th Quadrant = 24%
Taurus-2	6	Eastern Hemisphere (left) = 50%
Cancer-4	6	Western Hemisphere (right) = 44%
Libra-7	6	Northern Hemisphere (lower) = 50%
Scorpio-8	6	Southern Hemisphere (upper) = 44%
Twin Signatures	6	Cardinal = 38%
Gemini-3	2	Fixed = 36%
Virgo-6	2	Mutable = 20%
		No Missing Signs

Astro-Number Signatures

A description of each

Aries-1

In Australia Aries-time (around the spring equinox) is when the joeys emerge from their mother's pouches. The image of the young kangaroo emerging from the pouch reminds us that a person with an Aries-1 signature must move forward from the comfort of being an 'unknown' to the vulnerability of taking their place on the stage of life. Exercising the power to direct one's own life is precisely the aim of the Aries-1 signature.

On the date chart number 1 *initiates* self-intelligence (worldly), linguistic intelligence and survival intelligence, which obviously interrelate.

The spectrum of behaviours that characterize Aries-1 ranges from the proverbial 'lone wolf' to the proverbial 'leader of the pack'. Being a lone-wolf stifles the natural tendency of number 1 to move towards number 2, whilst leading the pack runs with that tendency. If there is one point to be made about the wheel of life, it is that no matter how strong willed you may be, you cannot stop it from turning. It is better to consider yourself a part of, rather than apart from, everything else that is going on. Moving towards number 2 suggests that you will need to exercise patience as well as initiative.

Aries-1 as an embodiment of spring represents a time when underground shoots arise and jostle for a place in the light of day. In human beings, this creates pioneers in all walks of life. It also implies that it is hard for people with this signature to look back, introspect, and learn from their mistakes in a way that is not merely reactionary – unless there are indicators otherwise in their astronumerology.

In an underdeveloped personality, the Aries-1 signature manifests as a 'me-first' attitude; not necessarily 'bad' but naively unaware of other people. As the person with this signature evolves, and the relationship between their ego and soul becomes more evident to them, their energy becomes more focused and consciously directed. At this point, they begin fighting for causes that stretch beyond their personal needs, desires, and opinions. They realize that they are better leaders than followers and they begin to enjoy the excitement of getting something new underway. People with an Aries-1 signature are then inclined to champion others. Being naturally self-willed warriors, who are prepared to fight against any limitation to self-expression, they want to see others taking initiative and performing to the best of *their* ability too.

As a trailblazer, you need room to move. Aries-1 being the most self-motivated of the signatures, you naturally resent anyone curtailing your freedom to act. A mature expression of the Aries-1 signature is the 'spiritual warrior'. At this level you can become a channel for the birth of a truly unique and inspired idea. The word most appropriate for your output would then be 'seminal'. Intuitive, original, and often influential, your ideas germinate within the minds of those that study them, and may then spawn further developments. An Aries-1 signature means being constantly on the go and makes sitting still almost impossible! With willpower second to none, once you set yourself to a task nothing stops you. Whatever obstacles beset your path, you courageously find a way around them. Correlating as it does to the young child, the Aries-1 signature tends to make you guileless; you simply want to get on with life and don't want anyone to stand in your way.

Health-wise you are prone to overworking the body, which can lead to strained muscles, and overworking the mind, which can lead to headaches.

Aries-1 is the most common signature and was well-represented in all of the samples. This signature will support any project you set your mind to but certain career groups were above the random score and others were below it. Actors, sports stars and musicians all scored above the random sample while artists scored slightly below it. Aries-1 was the strongest in the miscellaneous file, which means that people are using its pioneering energy in many different ways. It is also the most frequent signature for self-made millionaires.

In most cases the time of birth is crucial to calculating the signature, but Aries-1 can provide examples that are not time dependent. For example Nat King Coles – regardless of the time he was born - would still have an Aries-1 signature. Born Nathaniel Adams Coles, his name includes intensity number 1 and his date of birth includes challenge 1. He has three personal planets in Aries. In keeping with his signature, Nat was prepared to change his name and lead his band in order to make headway as a musician.

Cricketer, James Antony Brayshaw, does not have a stable signature like Nat, but it is strongly cardinal. There is an intensity number 1 in his name, supporting his signature. His Descendant is in Aries, as is Saturn, and the moon was new when he was born. Jamie, as he is known, represents the many sports stars with an Aries-1 signature and illustrates its competitive side.

James Earl Carter demonstrated competitiveness in the political arena and it got him the top job as US President. His signature is more 'fiery' than 'cardinal'. He has intensity number 1 and birthday number 1 to support this signature. Ambitious and independent, this community leader was quite prepared to butt heads with anyone who stood in his way, which is typical of Aries-1.

Taurus-2

The image to hold in mind here is high spring. There's a riot of colour in the garden and everything in nature is buzzing with life. There is an air of expectancy and a general busyness, much of which relates to the sheer pleasure of being alive. The pleasure and productiveness of nature represent the Taurus-2 signature. Just so the purpose of this signature is to enjoy being alive here and now in the physical world. At the highest level of its expression, Taurus-2 about appreciating the world as a part of ourselves.

The date chart reveals that number 2 sits mid-stream the line of linguistic intelligence where it initiates the line of interpersonal intelligence. Its focus would thus seem to be on using language to interact with other people.

The spectrum of behaviours that characterize Taurus-2 ranges from self-indulgence (that's number 2 slipping backwards to a negative expression of number 1) to indulging another. When this is done mindfully, powerful and productive outcomes are possible. '2' symbolizes polarity. In the process of caring about another person it is possible to experience the extremes of emotion that come with life on earth. However if you work at it, you might be able to locate the central point between such polarities and it is there that you will find what is truly worth holding on to.

People with a Taurus-2 signature typically devote copious amounts of energy to holding on to whatever is of value to them, be it their mate, family, friends, career, home, possessions, creations, or spirituality. Objections and obstacles simply strengthen their resolve. There is powerful binding magic in this brew of emotions, and it provides the natural environment for number 2, which tends to collate, contrast, compare, and combine. Positively this induces an abundance of appreciation, affection, and admiration within the human heart. However if its host is holding on to negative emotions we may witness prejudice, stubborn resistance to change, obsession or jealousy.

Such unresolved emotions could exacerbate latent health issues. Health problems can similarly arise due to overindulgence. You will find that stubbornly refusing to adjust your diet or lifestyle when you need to, works against your otherwise robust constitution. Healthy Taurus-2 people have their feet solidly on the ground but are not unduly obstinate.

As a bridge-builder, you need to develop your people skills and the way that you communicate with other people is a fundamental part of your interpersonal skills. You may find that feeling a part of a group enhances your state of wellbeing. If you are a typical Taurus-2 sort of person, you probably enjoy outdoor activities such as gardening, walking in the bush, or team sports. You have a naturally creative side to your nature, and the kitchen is one place where such creativity is likely to be expressed, but need not be the only place.

Unlike Aries-1, Taurus-2 did not turn up in all of the samples; for example, there were no politicians with this signature. Taurus-2 was most strongly represented by the sciences; indeed no other Signature has as many scientists. Musicians and spiritual people also scored above average.

The strongest example of a Taurus-2 signature came from Sigmund Freud. It wouldn't have mattered what time was on the clock when the famous doctor was born, he was destined to have this signature. Not only does he represent the sciences but he also represents this signature by his interactivity with other people: he created a treatment method through dialogue. Regardless of what you might think of his psychoanalysis, Freud obviously cared about people in distress and his efforts to find a practical solution to the problems that many people face with living in this world represent Taurus-2.

Robert Boyle is another scientist with a strong Taurus-2 signature. In Freud's horoscope Taurus is in the 7th house with his Descendant. This is the place of 'projection' - where we get to sort out the things we disown about ourselves – and this suits Freud's chosen career. In Boyle's horoscope Taurus is in the 11th house, where we gather with associates and talk about our hopes and dreams for the future. Just so, Boyle was part of an 'Invisible College' where scholars gathered to share their (scientific) knowledge. They shared a mutual interest in acquiring knowledge through experimental investigation with the view to profiting from science. This slant towards profit may be one of the distinctions between scientists with a Taurus-2 signature and scientists with other signatures. Boyle was not idealistic but he did make a 'wish list' of possible inventions; most of which have come true by now. Unlike the scientists we will consider with other signatures, Boyle's mind was untroubled by the paradoxes and contradictions of life. He was more 'black and white' in matters of both science and religion.

Representing the musicians with Taurus-2 is Maurice Ernest Gibb, who had intensity number 2 to support his signature, and challenge 2 to spur him along. Maurice was known as the 'quiet one' of the Bee Gees; a mild-mannered, stabilizing influence for his more ambitious brothers. A second example is provided by Igor Stravinsky, who is considered one of the influential composers of the 20th Century. His is a stable signature - one that is not dependent on time of birth - and his impeccable craftsmanship is characteristic of Taurus-2.

Henry Steele Olcott represents the spiritually-minded people with a Taurus-2 signature. In his case, intensity number 2, birthday number 2 and maturity number 2 supported it. Co-founding an organization is indicative of number 2 and Henry co-founded the Theosophical Society with Mrs. Blavatsky. Mars in Taurus in the 8th house indicates the depths he would go to in his spiritual work.

Gemini-3

Gemini-3 corresponds with early summer and invokes an image of gentle breezes laden with seeds. But as anyone who lives in a fire-prone area knows, those early summer winds can be unpredictable. They can catalyze sweeping changes in people's lives.

Mystically the purpose of this signature is to facilitate communication between self and Self. In other words, between your small self that thinks of itself as separate from everything else, and the universal self that knows better. Interaction with other people is necessary for such development, and leads to the capacity to perceive and articulate multiple points of view. Gemini-3 questions the status-quo tendency of Taurus-2 in a bid to gain greater understanding.

Number 3 represents the apogee of linguistic intelligence on the date chart, where it initiates self-intelligence (cultural) by giving voice to one's cultural heritage and ideals, and spatial intelligence through the powers of the imagination and the capacity for abstract thought. Just as number '3' brings one mode of intelligence to a point of culmination whilst simultaneously launching another, so do the mutable signs – Gemini, Virgo, Sagittarius and Pisces – represent the culmination points of a season whilst simultaneously preparing the ground for the cardinal signs: Aries, Cancer, Libra and Capricorn. The third in any series quickens the completion of whatever has been set in motion, by attempting a synthesis.

The spectrum of behaviours that characterize Gemini-3 range from the deliberate polarization of people through the spoken or written word (that's number 3 slipping backwards to a negative expression of number 2) to intentionally uniting like-minded people in informative activities that everyone can enjoy.

The strong imagination inherent to this signature can be both a blessing and a curse. Gemini is known as the sign of communication and this includes communication between who you are on the inside and the face you show to society.

A love of adventure, variety, friends and family accompanies this signature. It comes with a quick wit and an enquiring mind. In love you like to have fun and your imagination seeks variety. You retain a youthful attitude to love throughout life. Communication is vital to you and partners must be able to 'keep up'. You are fascinated by everything, and typically have at least two projects on the go at any one time. Comfortable in the realm of ideas, you are probably a book lover and you could make a good book reviewer. The ability to create fascinating images out of our collective thought patterns is inherent to this signature, and an interest in the 'science' of a topic often accompanies Gemini-3.

Much of your body's vitality is siphoned off into your mind. This could leave your physical body depleted of necessary resilience. That is until you discover the power of your mind to heal; and this is where you can exercise that wonderful imagination of yours. Naturally the above comes with the proviso that all other sensible actions are taken as well such as sufficient time outdoors in the elements: fresh air, clean water, rich soil, and life-enhancing sunshine. Your nervous system is sensitive. Some Gemini-3 people are highly-strung and can become anxious and unwell when things don't go according to plan. You could also experience light more brightly and sound more acutely than other people do, which would further impact on your nervous system.

Gemini-3 is less common than Aries-1 and Taurus-2; in fact with Pisces-12 it is the least common of all of the signatures. Spiritual people hold the majority by far: one in every four Gemini-3 signatures is held by a spiritually-minded person. This is a time-sensitive signature and it was impossible to find someone who held it so strongly that it didn't matter what the time was when they were born. However, Stuart Wilde has a clear Gemini-3 signature. Renowned for his authorship of New Age and self-empowerment books, including the popular series *The Taos Quintet,* and true to his signature, Stuart was versatile in his thinking being at various times a lecturer, teacher, scriptwriter, lyricist, humorist, essayist and music producer.

Apart from 'spiritual', which covers everything from the religious zealot to the individual mystic, the only other category Gemini-3 scored well in was 'miscellaneous', which also permits broad interpretation. Even when a Gemini-3 person could be classified career-wise as a musician, artist, scientist, writer, or actor, there was typically a broad range of interests beyond this. With her highly mutable Signature, Lola Falana demonstrates this. Lola was at various times in her life a dancer, pianist, violinist, recording artist, Broadway and Las Vegas star, film and television actress, commercial spokesperson, author – and spiritual enthusiast, later in life. The latter came about due to a severe bout of multiple sclerosis. MS is a disease that affects the central nervous system. Because it interferes with the transmission of nerve impulses through the brain, spinal cord and optic nerves, it can cause problems with muscle control, vision and balance. Lola attributes her recovery to a spiritual experience.

Representing the entrepreneurs with a Gemini-3 signature is Henry Ford, the initiator of mass produced automobiles. His own tank ran on enthusiasm alone for a long time, enduring several bankruptcies. Enthusiasm for life and learning is a key to understanding this signature. Yet both Lola and Henry became very wealthy and are actually filed under 'self-made millionaires' in the *Pan's Script* data pool.

Cancer-4

Cancer-4 can be imaged as the meeting place of sea and shore. This is the warm water of the tropics on a hot summer's day; there is nothing cold or indifferent about this signature. Cancer-4 people value human warmth and kindness.

Number 4 takes central place in the line of survival intelligence on the date chart and from there it launches the line of kinesthetic intelligence. Directly related to such intelligences are the words 'dynamic', 'dedicated', and 'determined': three vital keys for understanding the Cancer-4 signature.

This is a signature that nurtures a love of old and established things but the person who is working with it in top-form also embraces a fascination with contemporary things (that's number 4 moving up to number 5). Cancer-4 draws our attention to the reality that we are born with a genealogy and die with a legacy, for better or worse. We all have ancestors to learn from and descendants to create a better world for. In relation to the signature that comes before it, Cancer-4 relates to the instinctual urge to move from an idea to a tangible expression of that idea. Furthermore Cancer is a cardinal sign and so there's plenty of initiative here. Cancer-4 people can be enterprising and business-like but in their heart place would always prefer a home-based business to an impersonal one.

Your strongly affectionate nature lends itself to committed relationships. You are generally faithful in love and loyal to your close friends. However your temperament is changeable like the tides. You are very sensitive and can be deeply hurt by criticism. This can make you defensive and hard to reach.

Your well-being depends on your emotional life and suppressing your feelings could lead to stress-related diseases. Worry could make you ill especially when it is associated with the fear of losing someone that you need emotionally. If your security is threatened you could fall prey to depression. This signature is prone to the infiltration of negative thoughts from other people, yet no other signature is more capable of self-healing as well. You may thus find that your constitution strengthens with age, especially if you have worked on yourself personally. Being near water could prove therapeutic when you do succumb to disease.

You may be unpretentious but it is difficult to get anything past you because you are naturally shrewd. You are well aware of the need to work hard and get on with other people. Your family probably means the world to you and you have a knack of extending that family to the stranger who also needs a place to call home. The more turbulent your early home-life, the more you will feel the urge to establish a secure lifestyle. And the more active your feeling-life, the greater the outpouring of fantastically creative and original works. You instinctively know that attitude spells the difference between success and failure and you will find your attitude transforming as your character gains strength.

Cancer-4 is common among male actors but not female ones. It's a popular signature for artists and writers as well. Musicians and politicians also rated above average. Not all were time-sensitive; Leonardo da Vinci for example could have been born at any time on April 14 1452 and still had a Cancer-4 signature. Related to the above, he is hugely famous for his 'fantastically creative and original works', and those d-words - dynamic, dedicated, and determined - were evident throughout his industrious life. Cancer-4 is a common signature across many disciplines and just so, Leonardo was multi-talented although mainly remembered for his art. A subjective signature, Cancer-4 is inclined to universalize from personal experience, and we can assume this was the case with Leonardo. In keeping with this signature, his spiritual inclinations were of the practical, hands-on kind. Cancer-4 tends to be a self-contained signature and there is much about this famous man's private life that we will never know.

Leonardo further provides an example of the significance of the house into which the signature falls in the horoscope - the 8th in this case – the place most concerned with the whole matter of life and death. It's also the place of integration and in Leonardo it is exemplified by the integration and art and science.

Marlon Brando, Ronald Howard, and Danny Kaye are some of the actors with a Cancer-4 signature, and so that any aspiring female actors don't feel disheartened, so did Deborah Jane Trimmer, better known as Deborah Kerr. Danny and Deborah were also dancers, representing the 'sporty' inclinations of this signature. Danny Kaye was a singer, comedian and humanitarian, thus representing the musical and rhythmic side of Cancer-4 as well. Marlon Brando represented its raw passion and emotional honesty. He once refused an Oscar in protest of the treatment of Native American Indians, his emotionally-charged activism touching on the political side of Cancer-4.

Polly Bergen highlights another aspect of this signature. Although she is an actor, singer and author, she is actually filed in the *Pan's Script* 'Rich List' as a self-made millionaire. She founded a successful home-based cosmetic business and 'home' is exactly where Cancer-4 is most comfortable. With her strong and stable signature (four planets in Cancer, including the Ascendant, consonant, name, home base, and challenge 4), Nellie Paulina Burgin (birth name) reminds us of the financially shrewd side of Cancer-4.

Leo-5

Archetypal Leo-time equates with late summer. The undergrowth is lush and dry and the danger of wild fire lingers in the hot dry air, especially when the thunderstorms strike.

The radiant sun rules the sign of Leo and provides the most apt analogy for understanding this signature. Just as the Sun centres the solar system, so number 5 holds central place within the date chart. There, it neither initiates nor culminates but stands at the heart of the lines of interpersonal, kinesthetic, and self-intelligence (worldly and cultural), the purpose of this signature being to enliven creation.

Just as the sun centres the solar system and makes life possible, so can the centeredness of people with a Leo-5 Signature provide stability for those around them. The magnetism of this central location means that people with a Leo-5 signature generally find being the centre of attention the most natural thing in the world, whether they like it or not. The spectrum of behaviours that accompanies this signature ranges from 'tyrant' to 'champion of the defenceless'.

Whether you are the strong, outgoing type of Leo-5 or the more highly-strung type, you tend to get noticed. You shoot from the heart rather than the head and occasionally you bite off more than you can chew. Just as you need to feel special to someone, you know exactly how to make another person feel valued. The dilemma you face is to partake of all of the change and excitement going on in your day to day world, without losing your centeredness as you do so. On the one hand you need to stabilize your life, while on the other you must evolve. Just as the sun 'stabilizes' the solar system by simply being there, its magnetic aura and constant warmth facilitating all forms of evolution, so things tend to simply 'happen' around you. The challenge you face is to be adaptable and focused at the same time. You need to be strong without being dogmatic and confident without being inflexible. Your task is to remain centred within your own circle, which is within you. You may have a tendency to wander off into other people's circles and assume the role of guiding light for them. Then instead of acting as exemplar by simply being yourself, you adopt the mantle of saviour. Should your ego lure you in this direction, you will find a cycle of action and reaction spinning around you, and it could all become too much. Whenever this happens you would do well to remember that the sun generates energy from *within* itself, its external activity a by-product of internal combustion. Likewise, it is from your central core that you are most effective. When you are being true to your naturally sunny disposition, your optimism, enthusiasm and vitality, are contagious. Your joy-de-vive lifts everybody's day.

You are mostly immune to chronic lingering illnesses, except when the sorrows of life get the better of you. The main danger to your health is a careless disregard for your physical body. If you abuse it, you could become accident-prone. You tend to either radiate vitality or collapse in a heap. However your recuperative powers are strong.

The random sample accurately portrays the dominance of Aries-1 and Leo-5. Aries-1 accounts for 17% of all signatures and Leo-5, 16%, and yet their distribution is distinct. Although the artists had the lowest count for Aries-1, there were more artists with Leo-5 than any other signature. The high score for artists reflects the need to be able to showcase their talent if they want to make money. Musicians and writers also scored well and probably for the same reason. 80% of all actors had either an Aries-1 or Leo-5 signature. Actually Leo-5 made a strong appearance in all of the samples and so regardless of your career-choice this is a handy signature to have.

Not all Leo-5 signatures are time sensitive; it is possible to calculate this signature without an accurate birth time, but only in a very few cases. At the other end of the scale, Tracey Emin provides an interesting example. Her birth time was rated AA - it's written on her birth certificate - yet her signature is complex. Originally fixed and mutable, air and fire, when number 6 was removed as part of the moon phase only fixed air and fire remained. However, adding in the 1's, 2's and 3's brought the cardinal mode into play, her outcome twin being cardinal and fixed fire. In this complex mix fixed fire was the only common signature and thus the dominant one. Tracey's Ascendant is in Leo, and her consonant, name and attainment numbers are 5, supporting the conclusion that Leo-5 is her signature. In keeping with the versatility of Leo-5, Tracey's art takes many forms including needlework, sculpture, drawing, video installation, photography and painting. Her Leo-5 signature would have supported her appointment as Professor of Drawing at the Royal Academy: one of the first two female professors since the Academy was founded in 1768. True to this signature, she was either unafraid to take centre stage, or, if she was afraid, she conquered it and took the podium anyway.

Representing acting and related fields are Paul Newman and Steven Spielberg, both highly versatile. Both have intensity number 5 in their names to support their signature, Paul with consonant 50 and Steven with primary date path 5, attainment and quest 5.

Writers with a Leo-5 signature include Maya Angelou, who represents its political inclination as well. Gloria Steinem is another. Henry Kissinger, Jesse Jackson, Karl Marx and Mary Robinson all had a Leo-5 signature to help them shine.

Sporting stars with a Leo-5 signature include Annie Oakley, Greg Chappell, Nadia Comaneci, and Shane Gould.

Virgo-6

The archetypal setting for this signature is the end of summer, when the days and nights are most pleasurable to the senses. To experience such sensations is to know that 'heaven on earth' is possible and this is exactly the ideal behind the Virgo-6 signature.

On the date chart, number 6 culminates the line of kinesthetic intelligence, simultaneously consolidating the development of spatial intelligence. Rhythm and imagination can dance together at this point. In relation to spatial intelligence, Virgo-6 is an observant signature. The pros and cons of an idea can be 'seen' in a sensory sort of way. In other words, how well something is going to work can be sensed. The hard part for the Mercury-ruled Virgo-6 person is to communicate such perception in a way that makes sense to other people. Timing is a part of this, and timing has everything to do with kinesthetic intelligence. If you want your ideas to be well received, you must also consider the shape that your presentation will take, and that takes a particular type of spatial intelligence.

Keywords for Virgo-6 include meticulous, industrious, and reliable. Whatever you do in life, Virgo-6 will attach those qualities to it. Your power to observe and interpret is applied to relationships as much as anything else. You notice everything. You question everything. You try to improve the way that things are done and the way that people behave. You expect perfection of yourself and you expect others to meet your standards (although this may be subconscious). Naturally, this impacts on your relationships with other people. Your challenge is to embrace imperfection. Virgo-6 catalyzes the urge to comprehend the whole strata of the human psyche and although you may resist it, this necessitates including the unruly bits. In keeping with Mercury, you tend to seek security through knowledge, and this applies equally to your relationships and your health. Both in the work-place and socially, you like to be involved in something productive yet it must also engage your imagination. You like to feel a part of an efficient organization in which things tick over as they should.

Worry is your greatest affliction; you can literally worry yourself into an illness: worrying about your relationships, worrying about your work, and worrying about your health! However your concerns about your health generally lead to precautions that prevent most serious diseases. Virgo-6 offers the power of synthesis which means that you can read diverse information about preventative medicine and put it all together in your own way. This could be very effective but in its immature form, synthesis can be simply collecting and hoarding information and doing little with it. If illness does strike, one of the things to do therefore would be to clear the clutter. Then use your Virgo-6 powers to create a whole new chapter in your life.

6% of all signatures are Virgo-6, which is approximately the same as Taurus-2, Libra-7 and Scorpio-8. All of the career-groups studied had representatives with this signature. Art, sport and writing were above average, while acting, music, politics and science were about average.

The most stable Virgo-6 signature came from actress, Helen Hunt. She has accurate birth data yet her signature is so strong that it would not have mattered what time of day she was born. Virgo falls in the 1st house of her horoscope, her Ascendant keeping company with Mars, Neptune and Pluto. Being born in June, Helen's first base is 6, her birthday is also 6, and so are her vowel and name numbers. Her consonant challenge is also 6 and so it would be hard to find a better representative of the Virgo-6 signature than this competent actress. Helen was decisive about her career from an early age and would quickly gain a reputation for being conscientious and industrious. These latter two qualities are vitally important to the overall well-being of Virgo-6 people.

Not quite as stable as Helen's, yet with intensity number 6, growth, maturity and challenge 6 to shape and support it, the basketball star, Michael Jordan, adequately represents the sporting stars with this signature. Whereas Helen's signature is more 'mutable' than 'earthy', Michael's is the other way around.

Acting and sports each require 'artistry' of one kind or another and the arts merit special mention here. Virgo-6 is one of the rarer signatures yet managed to score third in the arts behind Leo-5 and Cancer-4. In Albrecht Durer's art we can witness an amalgamation of Virgo-6 tendencies: his classical motifs reinforced by his theoretical treatises, which involved principles of mathematics, perspective and ideal proportions. Idealism tends to come naturally to Virgo-6 people. Grandma Moses represents its more 'cultural' and 'practical' sides. She became renowned as a folk artist but initially expressed her creative skills through home quilting and embroidery. She only began painting when her fingers became too stiff to use a needle and then her subject matter was country life and American heritage. Her images were later transferred to curtains, dresses and dinner ware. Raoul Dufy similarly painted open-air social events. He developed a colourful, decorative style that became fashionable on ceramics, textiles and public buildings. As well as a Fauvist painter, Dufy was a draftsman, printmaker, book illustrator, designer of furniture, and planner of public spaces. Whether the person involved is the more idealistic or the more practical type of Virgo-6, attention to detail features in all Virgo-6 occupations.

Libra-7

Libra-7 corresponds with the Autumnal Equinox; a time when day and night, light and dark, are in balance. Such forces are also balanced at the Spring Equinox which corresponds with Aries-1 but these two Signatures are poles apart. Like Aries-1, Libra-7 is an assertive and competitive Signature but whereas Aries-1 tends to be pro-active, Libra-7 tends to be re-active. In Aries-1, awareness of self is accentuated, while in Libra-7 it is awareness of other people that dominates. We may resent them at times, but we need other people to act out for us what we think we are and what we believe we are not. There's plenty of room for projection and denial on this side of the Wheel of Life.

There's a delicacy of mental adjustment in Libra-7, which is sometimes interpreted as indecision, but the higher purpose of this Signature is to cultivate a sense of harmony and proportion in all things. Intrinsic to this is a deep sense of justice and the idealism that justice will ultimately prevail.

Within the date chart number 7 culminates survival and self-intelligence (cultural). Concurrently it initiates logical-mathematical intelligence.

Just so, it is the rational side of your nature that keeps you healthy. When your mind is out of kilter you recuperate by withdrawing. Peace and harmony is what you need at such times, and that means copious amount of rest with no emotional discord going on around you.

You probably expend a great deal of energy attempting to balance the seesaw of your mental and emotional dynamics. If you have ever played on a see-saw you will know that there are two ways to balance it. One is to recruit someone to sit on the other end for you and act as your polarity. When the balance is struck a sense of peace and satisfaction prevails, but people being essentially restless; do not sit still for long! Another way to balance the seesaw is to go it alone – to run up it and place your feet squarely each side of the centre. Perhaps you *do* find solo-time pleasurable and *do* need to locate your centre and master the art of balancing your seesawing thoughts and emotions, but if you decide to lock other people out altogether, you miss the greater opportunity of this signature. To make the most of Libra-7 its polarity must be reckoned with, which means being decisive sometimes, like Aries-1, instead of sitting on the proverbial fence.

Libra and Taurus are ruled by Venus and one of the fascinating findings emerging from the case studies was that 24% of female actors had either a Taurus-2 or Libra-7 signature. That means that one in four actresses held a signature that was ruled by the goddess of relationships, beauty, and beautiful things. Within the actresses sample, the Libra-7 signature was twice as high as the random sample. Politicians, writers and the people in the miscellaneous file also scored well here. In keeping with the idea that number 7 initiates the line of logical-mathematical intelligence, the sciences were also well represented by Libra-7.

Oprah Winfrey provides an example of an actress with a Libra-7 signature. And as a talk-show host we have observed that more often than not, she gets the balance right between reflection, which is a Libra-7 characteristic, and action, which is an Aries-1 quality. She thinks things over, weighing up each side carefully, and then decides what she will do about it. She discarded the victim label early in life, '7' being the number that is decisive about what *not* to be or what *no*t to do. Once that decision is secure, the Libra-7 person is then free to explore what to do and what to be. Other Libra-7 actresses include Catherine Deneuve, Jean Harlow, Ida Lupino, Jackie Weaver, Jessica P Lange, Marion Davies, and Miranda July. In a sample size of 50, there was not a single male actor with this signature!

In politics however, the Libra-7 signature generally favours men, and includes US Presidents George Washington, George W Bush, John Calvin Coolidge and John F Kennedy.

Representing the aesthetic side of Libra-7 is the dancer, Suzanne Farrell. Representing its tendency towards 'weighty thinking' is the philosopher, Martin Heidegger. And representing its interest in social justice is High Court Judge, Michael Kirby.

A wide variety of writing styles is represented by Libra-7, some of which embrace the above-mentioned themes and some of which highlight its other tendencies. For example Francesco Petrarch was both a poet and a scholar (and an incidental diplomat). His love of virtue and other such ideals is evident throughout his work. He also idealized love. His biography is full of the paradoxes that typically come with this signature.

Jean-Francois Champollion further highlights the uniqueness of Libra-7. Founder of the science of Egyptology, he wrote *Introduction to Egypt under the Pharaohs* and would eventually crack the Egyptian hieroglyphic code from the Rosetta Stone. A destitute scholar who specialized in the languages of the Orient, he worked as a teacher of history and geography. Libra was in the first house of his horoscope and therefore a visible aspect of his personality. Another unique and scientifically minded man with this placement and signature was Ernst Haeckel, initially a physician but leaving that to focus on biology, he was a naturalist, evolutionist, professor and artist who mapped a genealogical tree relating all life forms; and like so many Libra-7 people, a philosopher at heart. Another fascinating Libra-7 scientist was Nikola Tesla.

Engineer, inventor and discoverer of the rotating magnetic field, he made his first million before he was forty. Then relinquished the royalties on his most profitable invention as a humanitarian gesture; yet he was paradoxically misanthropic.

Scorpio-8

As you contemplate the Scorpio-8 signature you might find it useful to bear this image in mind: winter is approaching and the days are becoming cooler but the earth is still warm and productive.

Within the date chart, number 8 culminates the line of interpersonal intelligence, whilst it consolidates the line of logical-mathematical intelligence.

The figure 8 symbolizes the three-fold nature of this signature. When number 8 enters the astral arena it can go 'upwards' into rapture, or 'downwards' into despair. Either way, it can take a lot of people with it, because intense magnetism accompanies this signature. The third alternative is that it can rest at the centre. If we start at the centre when we draw an 8, we also end at the centre when all of the motion is done. The extremities must be delineated, for we cannot draw an 8 without going up and down, clockwise and anticlockwise and in like manner, people with this signature cannot avoid the highs and lows of life, and the intense feelings that come with it.

There's nothing half-baked or half-hearted here. Like Taurus-2, its opposite and complementary signature, Scorpio-8 is concerned with security, and this applies as much to relationships as it does to the workplace.

The ideal of the Scorpio-8 signature is that wealth and power are managed effectively so that a continual state of plenty prevails. It is how one defines wealth and power that marks the difference between one Scorpio-8 person and another. Those who define it in a purely personal way are not in the right quadrant of the wheel of life, for Scorpio-8 lies within the sector that relates to humanity as a whole.

Health-wise you probably have a strong constitution and you are seldom sick but when you are, it is usually serious. You then need a long rest; and like the earth in winter, a cycle of recuperation is required to fully recover. During this time, you may come to change your attitude to something, which in turn, improves your health. Scorpio-8 is a powerfully emotional signature, and burning resentment exacerbates latent health issues.

Whatever you do, you do it with a passion or not at all. You are intense and focused. Everyone is well aware of your presence, whether you are meaningfully engaged or brooding in the corner. Only with the select few do you share what is really going on deep inside of you. Your sense of justice is strong and personal. It can fuel the drive for revenge or to achieve great things. Your legacy to humanity could be considerable.

As an example of all of the above, it would be hard to beat Emmeline Pankhurst. All of her adult life was devoted to women's rights. As she became more involved with her cause, her methods became more extreme but it was due in large part to her relentless dedication that the UK 'Suffrage Act' was passed in 1918. Not everyone with a Scorpio-8 signature will be as passionate as Emmeline yet passion is one of its keywords. Other politically-minded people with a Scorpio-8 signature include Cecil John Rhodes, Harry S Truman, Jawaharlal Nehru, and John Charles Bannon

Politicians and political activists featured strongly in the case files and right up there with them were the spiritual people. Charles Fillmore represents the 'lighter side' of Scorpio-8 spirituality. Both he and his wife Myrtle suffered health problems and turned to some new ideas that might help. In both cases it did and consequently Charles became an advocate of the premise that god is the principle of love and intelligence, the source of all goodness and available when needed, from within.

Unafraid of the 'darker side' of his Scorpio-8 signature, Austin Osman Spare is renowned as both an artist and occultist. Occult means 'hidden' and refers to the hidden or spiritual side of life. It suits Scorpio-8 people because they typically have a hidden or secretive side to their nature. The relationship between the conscious and the unconscious self was a major theme in Austin's life and work. He placed emphasis on the unconscious part of the mind, believing it to be the source of inspiration and magical power. Austin also believed in what he called 'atavistic resurgence'. This is the idea that the human mind contains atavistic memories that have their origin in earlier species in evolution, and he visually reflected this idea in his art. It would be a mistake to think of Austin as 'otherworldly'; on the contrary, his friends described his as down-to-earth and kind. He loved animals and was a member of the RSPCA. Plumbing the depths of our existence is the hallmark of Scorpio-8.

Austin Spare was productive from his earliest years until his death. If a person is not busily engaged in a personally meaningful project, they are not working with their Scorpio-8 signature but some other part of themselves. Another productive person unafraid to face the darker side of life was Jean Henri Dunant, who founded the International Red Cross organization to care for survivors of war. Representing the self-made millionaires with a Scorpio-8 signature is Jean Paul Getty who made his fortune by mining oil from deep within the ground. Astrology honours the full gamut of human experience, light and dark, rich and poor, and a famous astrologer with a Scorpio-8 signature is Marc Edmund Jones, who wrote *The Sabian Symbols in Astrology.*

Sagittarius-9

The archetypal setting is winter, with its decrease in natural light and increase in cold and damp, which might explain the tendency of people with this Signature to dream of better times ahead.

On the date chart number 9 *culminates* the lines of logical-mathematical, spatial, and self-intelligence (worldly) and the impetus is thus towards the completion of something. Sagittarius-9 aims high and targets the best that life has to offer. A long way from basic survival intelligence, the emphasis here is on the bigger picture. And within the greater schemata of which this signature is a part, the purpose of the Sagittarius-9 Signature is to venture forth into the unknown in order to become more of what we are. There is a sense of urgency about this, as if it must be accomplished before the opportunity is lost.

Like Gemini-3, which is its opposite and complementary signature, people with a Sagittarius-9 signature are continually in motion, but are typically more dramatic about it. If this is your signature, you need a career that enables you to roam either literally, as in the travel business, or vicariously, as in exploring ideas, reading, writing and music. The ideal for your development is both.

Your spirited optimism keeps your life force strong. If you were to be kept confined (as in a prison) where you could not roam all over the place, your health would suffer. Conversely, scattering your energies all over the place would wear you out and cause extreme tiredness. You may even be inclined to lash out and hurt someone.

Similarly your relationships must allow for your need to roam. Yet although there are some outstanding examples of open relationships involving people with this signature, such as Simone de Beauvoir, and George Eliot, and some dramatic multiple marriages such as those of Norman Mailer, and Mickey Spillane, there are equally examples of marriages demonstrating that is possible to feel free within a monogamous relationship.

Futuristic and freedom loving, your imagination roams all over the place. Destined to wander (and wonder), your meandering serves a dual purpose: your own learning and the dissemination of your learning to others. Your mind is exceedingly mobile, as you consider first one point of view then another. From each perspective you extract as much meaning as you can – and pass it along. You get your message across through music and theatrics, song and dance, art and literature, or whatever works best for you. And if you are mystically inclined, your way might also include the subtle communication possible via the inner worlds. Any tendency you may have to make sweeping statements is a challenge that you must face if you decide to set your sights on real spiritual eminence.

Politics may fascinate you but once you are able to appreciate the subtle yet tangible *quality* of truth, you may decide that there are better ways of accomplishing your goals. You are idealistic yet well aware of the passionate side of life. The dual nature of this signature begs the question: which side of life do you wish to focus on, the mortal or the immortal? The potential is there to function effectively in both – to use the intense internal combustion that accompanies this Signature (and is often witnessed as alternating bursts of brilliance and bad-tempered burn-out) - to enhance or enlighten humanity. You could transform the faith that you have in your ideals to faith in humanity and then rather than seeking greatness, it will seek you. The ultimate purpose of this signature is to discover the ideal of ideals, and the myth of all myths.

Scientists featured strongly here, especially those with a bigger-picture perspective. Neil Armstrong, the first person to walk on the moon was one such scientist and his famous words 'one small step for man, one giant leap for mankind' resonate with this signature. Sagittarius is a fire sign with a propensity to go further than others have gone before. Politicians come next in order of frequency. Writers and musicians also scored well.

Representing the politicians is Margaret Chase Smith, whose stable signature comprised five planets in Sagittarius alongside the MC in the 10th house. The moon was in its disseminating phase further supporting it. And her big whole life challenge was 9, adding to the urge to broaden her horizons. She was the first woman to be elected to both houses of Congress in the US and her political career spanned the terms of six presidents.

Before moving into politics Margaret worked on the staff of the *Independent Reporter* as circulation manager: a career that allows for the expansiveness of the Sagittarius-9 mind. Many of the writers with this signature were journalists at some time in their lives. George Eliot is one example and John Updike is another, and interestingly one of his novels is titled *Centaur*, which happens to be a symbol for Sagittarius! 'Huge' is an appropriate word for Margaret Atwood's output; as well as an author in several genre, she is an environmental activist. Many of her poems were inspired by myths, and mythology is quintessentially Sagittarius-9, and so is what she calls 'speculative fiction'.

Equally prodigious, but in the field of music, is Bob Dylan, whose lyrics such as *Blowin in the Wind* and *The Times They Are a-Changing* embrace themes typically associated with this signature. One of the best-selling artists of all time, Bob's lyrics incorporate a variety of political, religious, philosophical and cultural influences. Bob Dylan embraces the infinite sweep of humanity through his music; broad-mindedness being the hallmark of the Sagittarius-9 signature.

Capricorn-10

Archetypally, we are now in the heart of winter when everything slows down externally so that it can quicken internally. Physical growth is curtailed, giving our inner potential the opportunity to consolidate and gain strength.

Within the greater dreaming of the earth-mother, the purpose of the Capricorn-10 signature is to identify our specific role: the contribution that only we can make.

Numbers-wise 10 is the higher octave of 1, and astrology-wise Mars is exalted in Capricorn. In plain English this suggests that the drive represented by Aries-1, (which is ruled by Mars) can be here internalized into rock-solid determination – the sort needed to attain enlightenment (and every other task of real and lasting value). In keeping with its wintry setting, people born with a Capricorn-10 signature seldom expect to attain their goals easily. They are geared up and ready for the long haul of starting at the bottom and gradually making their way to the top.

Like Aries, Cancer and Libra, Capricorn is a cardinal sign, and so there's plenty of initiative here, but it may not be apparent until Saturn has completed its first cycle at around thirty years of age. Like Cancer-4, its opposite sign, there's a tremendous amount of emotion-power here but in Capricorn-10 it is directed inwardly where it becomes fuel for achieving long-term goals. Both signs are family-orientated but Capricorn is inclined to universalize the meaning of family. Cancer is ruled by the moon, which affects a person in a very direct way whereas Saturn, which is more distant, rules Capricorn and so its effect is more subtle. While the moon stimulates the imagination, Saturn works on the conscience. When people work in harmony with the stabilizing force of Saturn, they can create great works that endure throughout time. Such is the purpose of the Capricorn-10 signature.

You may appear to be simply plodding along and paying the bills, but inside your mind there's a plan ticking over. Just as in winter the surface appearance does not give much away yet there is a literal powerhouse of productivity going on beneath it, so you may appear aloof but beneath the surface you are paving the way for a secure and satisfying existence. You are aware of your ability to work your way up into a position of authority. You know how to work methodically to achieve your goals. You probably realize the significance of getting back to the basics and then moving forward via the fundamentals. Capable and ambitious, you firmly but tacitly, take charge of your life.

Childhood may be the most delicate time of your life health-wise; your strength increasing with age along with your resilience to disease. Fear, uncertainty, and pessimism are your greatest enemies. If you can avoid the depression such states of mind can bring, you are more likely to avoid chronic illness and live a good long life. Sunlight, fresh breezes, and laughter will help to restore your health if illness does happen to strike.

The results of the case studies were astonishing. The spiritual sample came out far ahead of all of the others. One in every five of the spiritual people studied had a Capricorn-10 signature. 'Spiritual Mothers' such as Alice Bailey and Mother Meera, and 'Spiritual Fathers' such as the Dalai Lama and Pope Francis, belong here. Indeed you could call them and others like them, Spiritual Elders, and that would be in keeping with the sign of Capricorn. That said, every vocation had representatives with this signature.

Actors and more specifically, actresses, scored higher than average. Some of these people were spiritually inclined while others demonstrate different facets of the Capricorn-10 Signature. Jill Ireland had a stable signature (regardless of her time of birth). Like most actors, she began with bit parts in films and gradually worked her way up. Jill is also remembered for her battle with cancer and as a spokesperson for other sufferers. She wrote a book subtitled *a Personal Story of Survival*, which is a theme most people with this signature can relate to, regardless of their circumstances. Jill testified before Congress about medical costs and was given a Courage Award by the President. Another actress with this signature is Mary Tyler Moore, whose smiling persona masked an inner life of turmoil and denial. She endured years of bit parts and knock backs before gaining a major role in the Dick Van Dyke Show. Then, going it alone in her own series, is Capricorn-10 at its finest. The constant effort required to maintain her success took its toll personally, yet she endured. She wrote an autobiography and was so successful that she could select scripts for lead roles in television movies. Male actors with a Capricorn-10 Signature include Robert Reed and the very successful comedian Jerry Lewis, who, like Jill, became respected within his community as an advocate for those who needed one, in his case, people with muscular dystrophy.

Artists scored around the same as the random sample including Paul Cezanne, who laid the foundations for a completely different mode of painting, and Rosa Bonheur, realist artist and sculptor.

Sporting stars are well represented by this signature, the discipline of learning their sport and becoming one of the best at it, exemplifying Capricorn-10. One such star is Pat Rafter, who began playing tennis with his dad at five years of age. To maintain his place at the top he pursued a rigorous training schedule of three hours a day on the court and another hour in the gym.

Aquarius-11

'Aquarius time' is typically the coldest of all, and so the blooming of the wattles, with their multitude of tiny suns is welcomed with joy and anticipation.

Any interpretation of this signature necessitates keeping in mind that like Capricorn, Aquarius is ruled by Saturn. The specific purpose of the Aquarius-11 signature is to take the individuality established in Capricorn into the collective arena, and maintain it therein, so that one's unique contribution can be experienced by all. By so doing, the person with an Aquarius-11 signature can act as a dispenser of blessings within the greater body of humanity. The struggle to establish one's individuality is therefore more intense in this signature than in Capricorn-10. The double-1 symbolizes this.

To understand the Aquarius-11 signature it is also necessary to understand the nature of its co-ruler, the planet Uranus, which has an orbit uniquely its own. Although it defies the norm, this giant planet is a vital part of the planetary system as a whole. In astrology Uranus is regarded as a higher octave of 'Mercury the Messenger'. Outside the boundaries of traditional astrology, it symbolizes a message from the future. Thus people with this signature tend to think ahead of their time.

Number 11 is the more electrically charged form of number 2, and like people with a Taurus-2 signature, those with an Aquarius-11 Signature possess the magnetic power of attraction, but here we must include the uncanny ability to attract controversy! This is because they break with tradition in order to introduce a new (spiritual) impulse into the mainstream of life.

You are essentially a non-conformist who conforms when you feel like it, patient and accepting when people least expect it, and hot-headed and sanctimonious when we were expecting you to be receptive. Such contradictions steadily resolve as you confront the contradictions going on within you. You then become the motivator who can draw the best out of other people. You do this by establishing rapport between the two wills: yours and theirs. You understand people's craving for freedom because deep within you is the desire to overcome the limitations of mortal existence.

If you are over-active mentally and under-active physically then you leave yourself vulnerable to sudden attacks of illness. Nervous tension and an overactive mind work against your body receiving sufficient rest. When you do finally fall asleep, you may be plagued by weird dreams as your subconscious mind tries to process all of your thoughts. You need lots of fresh air.

As with Capricorn-10, spiritual people featured strongly here, and Padre Pio was the stand-out. Although his birth certificate accurately records his time of birth, he would have had an Aquarius-11 signature at any time of the day. As the first priest to display the stigmata in two thousand years, Padre was unique. Nuns, monks and lay people had experienced the stigmata but never a consecrated priest. The Church didn't know what to do with him but the people adored him. He was relegated to solitary confinement with his hands in tight dressings and sealed with wax and constantly observed to ensure that he wasn't self mutilating. Whilst so confined, people reported seeing him by the bedsides of the sick. He became known as a great healer, visited by multitudes of people, whose donations supported the building of a hospital. I like to think that Padre Pio was ahead of his time, just as his Aquarius-11 signature would indicate, and that one day more people will awaken such latent abilities within themselves.

Because of the maverick nature of Aquarius-11, I looked to the miscellaneous file for further examples. In there I found Juno Jordan, who was a 20th Century numerologist and a real inspiration for me. And that's exactly what people with this signature can be – an inspiration – by simply being themselves and pursuing their passion.

Representing sport are Bruce Lee and Billie Jean King, each an inspiration in their own right as they forged new paths in martial arts and tennis respectively. Billie Jean knew from an early age that she wanted to be a top tennis play and having made up her mind, she was then excited, impatient, enthusiastic and dedicated. She would come to lead the fight for equality in women's tennis and then sport in general. When she was selected the first sportswoman of the year, she became a role model for girls and the women's rights movement in general. Her victory in the 'Battle of the Sexes' made her the patron saint of women struggling to assert themselves; consequently she was nicknamed Mother Freedom. To this day, Billie Jean champions team tennis and believes that boys and girls should work and play together in order to understand one other. Billie Jean is a motivator who helps other to believe in themselves - and all of the above is relevant to this signature.

Representing music is the brilliant Wolfgang Amadeus Mozart and what an inspiration he has been to other musicians! Ludwig van Beethoven, fifteen years younger than Mozart, was deeply influenced by his work. Mozart's secondary date path, consonant number and third attainment were all 11's and he had the Sun, Mercury, Venus and Saturn in Aquarius plus the last quarter moon at 310 degrees (equivalent to number 11). Thus Mozart had a strong Aquarius-11 signature.

Famous writers with this signature include Edith Sitwell, Gertrude Stein, John Steinbeck, Paul Verlaine, and William Butler Yeats. Edith's writing has been described as experimental and eccentric, and difficult to categorize, which is typical of Aquarius-11. Gertrude was similarly described as one of the most colourful and eccentric figures in the post-WW 1 Paris literary scene.

Pisces-12

Pisces-12 correlates with early spring. The wattles are in full bloom along with a strong representation of purples and blues, the deeper shades contrasting with the bright ones. Such contrast is congruent with the symbol of Pisces, which is two fish swimming the circle of life in opposite directions.

Some astrological texts say that once upon a time these two fish swam in the same direction and that the two fish represent the dual paths of spirit and nature. Astrology also informs us that Pisces has two rulers: buoyant Jupiter and watery Neptune, and people with a Pisces-12 signature tend to oscillate between the two. Numerology might interpret the Piscean fish as ego and soul, a duality that can cause tremendous anxiety and confusion for people with a Pisces-12 signature until they allow their ego gains sufficient strength to become a champion of the soul; then life flows, synchronicities increase, and real magic happens! But the mind needs to embrace the possibility first.

The Pisces-12 signature tends to be idealistic with a person focusing on an ideal of personal interest. Once the personal is reconciled with the universal, a workable ideal can be formulated and accomplished. This is important because people with a Pisces-12 signature are naturally social crusaders, their confidence dependent upon their beliefs. Like Virgo-6, its opposite signature, the practical expression of compassion is the goal here. In both cases success hinges on a healthy, cohesive mind. Following on from Aquarius-11, it is now possible to dissolve limitations and create a whole new synthesis.

Pisces is a mutable sign, which implies a flow from one state of consciousness to another. This suggests that your mind will try to embrace the concept of an ongoing process rather than a fixed destiny. Raising public awareness of an issue that you feel passionate about could make you a slave to your ideal, but provided that you are truly devoted to what you believe in, there would be no slave happier. You would then find nothing more fascinating than your chosen occupation. In daring to place your whole life where your ideals lie, you risk being rebuffed by those whose ideals polarize with your own. But if your communication skills are effective, you can help people to see the world in a whole new way. As your ego strengthens, we are likely to find you spearheading a new form of human creativity. You are entranced by a world of the future, a fantasy or genuinely inspired vision, and so you need to keep the soles of your feet firmly connected to the earth-mother, whose dream is flowing through you.

Pisces-12 people are vulnerable to diseases that arise from worry. Health issues can be more difficult to define than other signatures but typically result from depleted nerves or psychic disturbances. Pisces-12 is naturally empathetic and you need to watch out for giving so much of your energy to others that you leave yourself in short supply. Your health is directly impacted by your beliefs, especially self-belief, which tends to be nebulous until the soul and ego stabilize as a single mode of operation. There is a part of you that believes that you could live forever and so you don't bother to look after yourself as much as your physical body needs you to. Your inner resilience is strong though and you instinctively know that you can draw on it at any time. Your sense of humour also helps to ward disease.

Only the artists scored higher than the random sample of signatures. Artists with a Pisces-12 signature include Alex Toth, Diane Arbus, Kathe Kollwitz, Robert Rauschenberg, and Wayne Thiebaud. Of those, Kathe Kollwitz had the strongest signature and most obviously portrays Pisces-12. She became a spokesperson, through her art, for victims of social injustice, war and inhumanity. Pisces was in her 7th house with her south node and Jupiter, and just so, her husband was an important influence on her work. As a doctor to the poor, he put her in contact with working class people, yet she said that it was not compassion or commiseration that initially drew her to represent them but that she saw beauty in them and their way of life. How one perceives life and experiences beauty is fundamental to understanding this signature.

Maybe not an 'artist' in the strictest sense of the word yet Lady Gaga has a Pisces-12 signature and can serve to extend the general theme. Although predominantly known as a singer, songwriter and record producer, Lady Gaga is also a fashion designer and that is definitely an art form. She is also an actress, a business woman, philanthropist and activist and is it typical to find the latter two associated with the Pisces-12 signature.

In Chapter 1 it was noted that number '12' is about believing in your ability to create a change of consciousness by exercising your imagination and expressing your ideas. Just so, it is the might of the pen (or the paintbrush) that interests people with a Pisces-12 signature rather than the sword. When she wrote *Uncle Tom's Cabin*, Harriet Beecher Stowe was wielding the power of the pen to end slavery in the United States. Abraham Lincoln is reputed to have greeted her with the words "so you are the little woman who wrote the book that started the great war". An exaggeration of course but it makes a point. Her Pisces-12 signature fell in her 7th house and just so, her husband was with her all the way on this issue. Similar to the balsamic moon phase, the Pisces-12 signature is inclined to redress social injustice rather than tear down society and start again.

Multiple Signatures

There could be no better place to complete a book on astro-numerology than with the complexities of multiple signatures. Particularly with numerology there is a danger of reductionism: of reducing human experience to a set of characteristics. And we all know that life is not like that; life is complex and people are contrary in their responses to it. With this in mind, let's delve into the world of multiple signatures. It took hundreds of signatures to convince me that the formula was correct and that establishing the dominant signature is valuable to people. If the formula is followed as outlined, you have the best chance of reducing a multiple signature to a single signature. You can then flesh it out its complexities. Some people will identify more with one part of their multiple signature than another. Others will recognize the multiple personalities living with them.

In the case of all signatures – singles and multiples – take a look at all of the person's astronumerology to ascertain *when* a particular signature is likely to turn up in a person's life. Look to the growth cycle (chapter 11) for clues.

For example, Maria Montessori has a twin signature: Cancer-4 and Scorpio-8. The name Maria begins with a letter that resonates with number 4 (13/4 to be exact). We would therefore expect that the Cancer-4 part of her signature would be dominant during her first nine years, and probably throughout her life because M is the head letter (as per chapter 3).

This is just one way of assessing which signature is likely to dominant at any particular time. Astrologers will have many more such as Progressions. For example an astrologer would estimate that Montessori's Progressed Sun would move into Scorpio when she was 54, thus strengthening the Scorpio-8 part of her signature during the latter part of her life.

While some Signatures are changeable, others are rock-solid.

<u>Stable Signatures</u>

A remarkable example of a *Stable Signature* is provided by the inventor Nikola Tesla. His date of birth is recorded as July 10, 1856 at midnight but some astrologers claim that July 9 at 11:59 p.m. is more accurate. Not only does the birth day change but also the date path, home base, the maturity number, and some of the attainments and challenges along with it, and yet one signature remained constant: Libra-7. However the path to that signature was clearer one way than the other. To arrive at Libra-7 via July 10, the 1's, 2's, and 3's had to be called into play because cardinal air and water competed for dominance whereas on July 9 the signature was pure cardinal air. Maturity 74 works much better than Maturity 75 as well, further increasingly the likelihood that Nikola Tesla was born a few moments before midnight.

<u>Complex Signatures</u>

An example of an unusually *Complex Signature* is entrepreneur, Poppy Cybele King, born on May 24, 1972 in Melbourne, Australia. If her mother's memory of the time is correct, she was born at 6:30 a.m. Initially cardinal earth (Capricorn-10) and cardinal water (Cancer-4), removing number 4 as part of the moon phase effectively removed cardinal water but brought mutable earth into the signature (Virgo-6). Adding the 1's, 2's and 3's changed it again, this time to mutable air (Gemini-3) and mutable earth. She has Venus, Mars and the South Node in Cancer plus the North Node and Jupiter in Capricorn. Her *Original Signature* is about them. In Virgo, which is one half of her *Outcome Signature*, she has the IC and Pluto. And in Gemini, the other half of her outcome signature, she has the Sun and Saturn. Virgo-6 would have been strong between ages 9 and 18 per the letter "O" in her name, and at 18 she began her own business. When she was eleven, her Ascendant progressed into Gemini, which would have strengthened the Gemini-3 aspect of her signature. There it united with Saturn, the Sun and Mercury. And seven years later the Progressed Sun joined them. Much more could be written about Poppy's astronumerology but the above amply illustrates the point that some people have very complex signatures and thus very complex lives.

Sometimes the original twin and the outcome twin signature share a common signature between them.

An example is the musician, Quincy Jones. Originally cardinal air and water showed up equally. Removing number 7 as part of the full moon phase effectively removed air but also reduced cardinal and made mutable equal to it. Adding in the 1's, 2's and 3's made no difference and so the outcome was cardinal and mutable water. The common factor is cardinal water and so it is reasonable to say that he has a Cancer-4 Signature. However such signatures should be prefaced with the word 'complex' as a reminder that this is the beginning and not the end of the story.

7 Different Types of Twins

<u>Cardinal Twins</u>: action-orientated, the cardinal twins include Aries-1 and Cancer-4, Aries-1 and Libra-7, Aries-1 and Capricorn-10, Cancer-4 and Libra-7, Cancer-4 and Capricorn-10, Libra-7 and Capricorn-10.

Example: Henri Matisse: Cancer-4 and Capricorn-10 see-sawing between the 6th and 12th houses of his horoscope. This particular pair of signatures knows how to build form from the ground up and nurture it through to completion. Oscillating between the 6th and 12th houses suggests the need to balance the ideal and the real; the beautiful and the ugly aspects of the world in which we live; the mundane reality of working for a living and the belief that greater things are possible.

When one aspect of the twin lies opposite the other, it increases the likelihood that a person will 'own' one part of their signature and 'disown' the other.

Fixed Twins: fixated on something, the fixed twins include Taurus-2 and Leo-5, Taurus-2 and Scorpio-8, Taurus-2 and Aquarius-11, Leo-5 and Scorpio-8, Leo-5 and Aquarius-11, Scorpio-8 and Aquarius-11.

Example: Don Chipp: Leo-5 and Scorpio-8 squaring off between the 1st and 4th houses of his horoscope. There is a strong drive for power between these signatures and lessons to be learned about keeping a steady rein on the ego. The houses indicate that doing something once and then moving onto the next challenge is competing with the need to stay in one place, build emotional security, and nurture one project in particular. Both needs must be considered.

Mutual Twins move energy in a different direction to the way it has gone before. The mutable twins include Gemini-3 and Virgo-6, Gemini-3 and Sagittarius-9, Gemini-3 and Pisces-12, Virgo-6 and Sagittarius-9, Virgo-6 and Pisces-12, Sagittarius-9 and Pisces-12.

Example: Dawn Fraser: Virgo-6 and Sagittarius-9 see-sawing between the 1st and 7th houses of her horoscope. The best-case scenario here is that the perfectionism of Virgo-6 unites with the broad-mindedness of Sagittarius-9 in some form of practical achievement. This will play out between the 1st house of self and the 7th house of partnership. The ongoing challenge is to find a balance between self-will and the will of others.

Fire Twins: warm and spontaneous, the fire twins include Aries-1 and Leo-5, Aries-1 and Sagittarius-9, Leo-5 and Sagittarius-9. Fire twins are excitable; these pairings supporting all forms of enterprise.

Example: Carl Lewis: Aries-1 and Leo-5 fuelling the 1st and 5th houses of his horoscope. This double-whammy of '1 and 5 energy' could easily fill a person with courage, confidence, vitality and joy-de-vie. It's also a recipe for an adrenaline junky that lives life to the max.

Earth Twins: practical and down-to-earth, the earth twins include Taurus-2 and Virgo-6, Taurus-2 and Capricorn-10, Virgo-6 and Capricorn-10. Earth twins are level-headed; these pairings supporting projects that are deemed useful by the person involved.

Example: Albert Einstein: Virgo-6 and Capricorn-10 emanating from the 3rd and 7th houses of his horoscope. Virgo-6 and Capricorn-10 are work-orientated and pragmatic. This combination bears the stamp 'workaholic'. In this case such tendency is working itself out in the relationship arena of the 3rd and 7th houses: between self and colleagues.

<u>Air Twins</u>: bursting with new ideas, the air twins include Gemini-3 and Libra-7, Gemini-3 and Aquarius-11, Libra-7 and Aquarius-11. Air twins are mentally agile; these pairings supporting all forms of correspondence.

Example: Louisa May Alcott: Gemini-3 and Libra-7, mutually supporting her 2nd and 10th houses. Gemini-3 and Libra-7 is a highly social combination, often reflecting genuine interest in people and their ideas. The houses in this case suggest the need for a personal set of values to keep such relationships on track.

<u>Water Twins</u>: deeply imaginative, the water twins include Cancer-4 and Scorpio-8, Cancer-4 and Pisces-12, Scorpio-8 and Pisces-12. Water twins are emotionally sensitive; these pairings supporting all forms of creativity.

Example: Maria Montessori: Cancer-4 and Scorpio-8 moving between her 4th and 12th houses. The double 4 intensifies the need for security but not necessarily or exclusively of the material kind. A person with this combination is also motivated to find security from within.

When the element is the same, it is easier for a person to acknowledge and integrate the twin aspects of their signature.

Career Profiles

What follows are the indications that arose from the case studies. Please bear in mind that they are merely general indicators. You could have a completely different profile to the one described for your field, and be totally brilliant at it. That said the findings are genuine. They are the result of comparing certain career paths with a Random Sample of 100 people. From this 'norms' were established. Results outside of these norms were considered potentially significant and included here.

Musicians

The stand-out quality here was the First Quadrant: there were more musicians in the first quadrant than any other career-path. The first is the most personal quadrant on the wheel of life. Its innate tendency is to impress oneself on one's environment and so the need to be heard is strong here. The first quadrant comprises Aries-1, Taurus-2 and Gemini-3.

Musicians also scored above average in Cancer-4, Leo-5, Virgo-6 and Sagittarius-9. They were strongly represented throughout the entire Northern (lower) Hemisphere of the horoscope, from Aries-1 to Virgo-6. This is the hemisphere wherein personal experience is deeply internalized thus providing fertile ground from which lyrics, melodies, and music in general can flow.

As well as the Taurus-2 signature, musicians were also strongly represented by intensity number 2 (per chapter 3) and missing 2 (per chapter 7). It is the teamwork aspect of number 2 that musicians must pay heed to here. Similarly there were many musicians with either intensity number 6 or missing number 6; it doesn't seem to matter which. Number 6 as the interlocking triangles of sacred geometry, would have the musician draw inspiration equally from their earthly experience and their heavenly ideals. Intensity number 8 and missing number 8 were also strongly represented by musicians. '8' draws attention to the need to integrate the highs and lows of life in one's music.

Comparing the Musician Sample with the numerology of other Samples yielded one potentially significant result: one in five musicians had Growth Number 4. No other career-group came anywhere near that quantity, the average being 13%. Growth Number 4 indicates that personal development comes through giving ideas form, and naturally includes musical form.

As well as comparing their numerology, the birth phases of the moon (per Chapter 10) were also compared between career-samples. It was discovered that 21% of musicians were born at the time of the New Moon, which was more than double the random result. This means that one in five musicians were born at the time of the New Moon and one in five had Growth Number 4.

Artists

There were two stand-outs here: the Second Quadrant of the horoscope and the Element Water. The Second Quadrant covers Cancer-4, Leo-5, and Virgo-6 and all of these signatures scored above the random sample. All of the signatures in the lower hemisphere tend to internalize personal experience, and the Second Quadrant (or second phase in the development of this internalization process) involves comparing oneself with others. Of the three possible signatures in the Second Quadrant, Leo-5 was the strongest. This signature would encourage the artist to find a way to 'stand out' from other people. Leo-5 was more strongly represented by artists than any other vocation.

Cancer-4 is a water sign, and with a strong showing from the other water signs – Scorpio-8 and Pisces-12 – Water as an Element was more strongly represented by the artists than any other career-path.

Artists were strongly represented by intensity numbers 3, 4, 6 and 8 (see chapter 3). The research done for chapter 6 revealed that survival intelligence also seems to help artists. Survival intelligence is represented by the line 1-4-7 in the Date Chart; Number 4 being central to it.

Number 4 was the all-rounder, with artists free to choose signature Cancer-4, intensity number 4, missing number 4, or survival intelligence. Number 4 encourages artists to give form to their ideas.

Sport

There was no stand-out quadrant, element or modality here, but one surprising result was that the planet Mercury seems to favour the sports. The planet Mercury rules Gemini and The 'Virgo-6' Signature is strongly represented by sports people. Mythological Mercury (or Hermes) rules Virgo, and so it might be the cunning side of that archetype that we are witnessing here. Virgo-6 is renowned for perfectionism, and perfecting one's sport is crucial to becoming exemplary at it.

One key difference between the artists and the sports people was that whereas the artists were strong in the element of water, the sports people scored lowest in this element. Their strongest element was fire but they were not as fiery as the actors!

Missing numbers do not aid sporting careers but Intensity number 4 and core number 4 do.

The research done for chapter 6 revealed that self-intelligence (worldly) represented by the line 1, 5, 9 in the date chart, also benefits people who strive to star in the sporting arena.

Writers

The stand-out here was the Western Hemisphere (i.e., the right side) of the horoscope. There were more writers in that hemisphere than any other career-path. What we project onto others and what we attract from others is highlighted within the western hemisphere. It indicates a collective orientation (rather than a personal one). There is typically an element of self-sacrifice on this side of the wheel of life. The western hemisphere covers the second and third quadrants of the wheel and the signs of Cancer, Leo, Virgo, Libra, Scorpio and Sagittarius. In all of the corresponding signatures the writers were above the random sample except Scorpio-8 and only just below average in that case. As per the artists, their strongest signature was Leo-5, which easily surpassed Aries-1.

Intensity numbers 2, 3, 4 and 8 support writers (per chapter 3). Number 2 can help a writer to connect with his/her readers and cooperate with publishers. Number 3 stimulates the imagination while number 4 can help the writer to give such ideas form. Number 8 facilities the integration of the lighter and darker sides of life, which is what a successful writer must be able to do. Missing numbers also seem to aid writers but in a different way. All of the missing numbers from 2 to 9 were strongly represented by writers, facilitating the necessary research and reflection for such work.

Scientists

Rather than a quadrant, hemisphere or element, what stood out here one particular signature: of all of the career samples, science had the greatest representation of the Taurus-2 Signature. It was more than double the random score. Venus, the ruler Taurus, would remind us that 'science' includes the 'people sciences' such as psychiatry, as well as the physical sciences.

Lower than the random sample were Aries-1, Leo-5, Aquarius-11, Pisces-12, and twin signatures but science was not the lowest in any category. Equal to the random sample were Cancer-4, Libra-7, and Capricorn-10. Higher than the random sample were Taurus-2, Gemini-3, Virgo-6, Scorpio-8, and Sagittarius-9.

Missing numbers seem to help scientists to do the research and reflective work necessary to any science and it doesn't seem to matter which missing number it is (see chapter 7). Intensity number 3 and missing number 3 both scored highly suggesting that many of our most famous scientists apply imagination to the scientific process.

A comparison of the Moon Phases at the time of birth revealed that one in five scientists were born at the Balsamic Moon Phase (see Chapter 10). The Random score was only 6%!

Obviously, scientists do much of their work behind the scenes. They study existing research and consider ways to interpret results. This is in keeping with the Balsamic Moon Phase.

Politicians

There were three stand-outs here: a strong Third Quadrant, a weak element earth, and the highest quantity of twin signatures. The Third Quadrant of the wheel of life emphasizes relationships. The Third Quadrant comprises Libra-7, Scorpio-8, and Sagittarius-9 and all were well represented here. Jupiter, as the ruler of Sagittarius, was more strongly represented by the politicians than in another sample.

The research done for chapter 6 revealed that interpersonal intelligence, represented by the line 2-5-8 in the date chart, benefits socially or politically active people, which makes sense. Interpersonal intelligence is essential if an activist is to be effective. Another interesting finding was that the activists scored much higher than other career groups in interpersonal (*introverted*) intelligence, suggesting that many of them mull things over for a long time before acting on their ideas.

It is surely remarkable that politicians scored lowest in the element earth. There were no politicians to represent the earthy Taurus-2; in fact they were the only group with no representative in this signature. Politicians were also lowest in Capricorn-10, which is another earth sign, and although they fared better in Virgo-6, their overall score in earth was only half that of the random sample. Their strongest element was fire, and their strongest signature Leo-5. Twin signatures were more prevalent in politicians than all of the other samples. This suggests that what you see may be only one aspect of a very complex person.

Spiritual People

The stand-out here was the Eastern Hemisphere. The spiritual sample scored higher in this region than any other sample. The Eastern Hemisphere (i.e. the left side of the horoscope), from Capricorn-10 through to Gemini-3, is stronger here than elsewhere. The Eastern Hemisphere is self-orientated, and here represents the quest of spiritual people to better understand themselves. The Eastern Hemisphere comprises the First and Fourth Quadrants, and the Fourth Quadrant comprises Capricorn-10, Aquarius-11 and Pisces-12, but only Capricorn-10 was strongly represented here.

Capricorn and Aquarius are both ruled by the planet Saturn making it the dominant planet in this domain of human interest. The planet Saturn provides structure to people's spiritual pursuits so that their energy does not scatter all over the place.

Capricorn-10 was a surprising stand-out: the spiritual people scored higher in this signature than any other sample. Capricorn-10 helps people to stand tall in the world. It gives them backbone and supports their efforts to stand up for what they believe in.

There was also a stronger representation of Gemini-3 here than elsewhere, which indicates that some of these people are scholars. Number 3 in any form (intensity number, missing number, and signature) supports spiritual development through the stimulation of the imagination and the sharing of ideas.

Three strands of spiritual development are here represented: outer authority (one side of the Capricorn-10 coin), inner authority (the flipside of the same coin), and scholarship, or at least the gathering of information from many sources (Gemini-3).

Actors

Surprisingly there were several differences between the male and female actors in my sample. Male actors scored highest in the northern hemisphere of the wheel of life; the northern hemisphere being the lower sector of the horoscope and covering Aries, Taurus, Gemini, Cancer, Leo and Virgo. This is the hemisphere where self-awareness meets awareness-of-other-people. The score for the female actors in this area was average when compared with the other career samples.

The male actors also scored highest in the element of fire whereas the female actors scored lower than average in this element. Male actors scored lower than all others in the element of air whereas the female actors scored slightly above the random sample.

Interestingly, the planet Venus was more prominent in female actors than any other career sample, and the planet Mars was more prominent in male actors than any other sample. Does that make them more appealing – who knows?

What the male and female actors had in common were the highest scores for the cardinal modality, which means that actors, in general, tend to initiate action. It is unlikely that they would succeed if they weren't self-motivated!

Miscellaneous

This group comprised a chess champion, some journalists, a civil engineer, news presenters and other television personalities, a radio announcer, dancers, lawyers, astrologers, film directors and producers, a historian, an economist, teachers, editors, a sea captain, a managing director, a philosopher, and a couple of entrepreneurs. And there were three features that stood out: they had the strongest representation of the Element Air; they were more Yang than any other Signature, and more Mutable as well. The element air suggests that they think a lot, yang indicates that they act on such thoughts, while mutable suggests that they are capable of switching camps, changing their minds, and considering multiple perspectives. The miscellaneous sample scored higher in Aquarius-11 than any other sample.

The research conducted for *Pan's Script* indicated that there is no single career-indicator in either numerology or astrology; it is the combination of both that is needed. Once you have calculated your astro-number signature and compared it with the above career profiles, place it side by side with your core numbers and type(s) of intelligence so that you can further define and refine the career path that suits you best.

About wealth

The astro-number signatures of 50 self-made millionaires and billionaires were studied as a group to see if any particular signature emerged. It didn't; every signature, element, modality, hemisphere and quadrant was represented. There were no stand-outs and nothing was left out. One's signature is clearly not an indicator of wealth. Put another way this means that (regardless of your signature) you have the potential to create and cultivate wealth in your life, however you define that.

What is notable about the rich-list is the balance between the forces. Not that everyone in the list is a balanced human being (some are, and some are not,) but that the forces behind them are balanced. These are generally not fiery people (although a couple of them are very fiery), with the self-made rich sharing lowest place with the artists in the element of fire. The strongest element was earth but it was only slightly above average. The self-made rich typically have their feet firmly on the ground and some of them are very much in love with our beautiful planet.

Cardinal was the strongest modality but only average when compared with other samples. The fixed modality came in just behind, slightly above average, and then mutable, also a tad above average. This shows flexibility in one's mode of operation, just as there are times to initiate, times to hold fast, and times to move on in business.

As one would expect there was more yang or 'doing energy' than yin or 'receptive energy', but only just. This means that accumulating wealth is not merely about what you do, it almost equally about your receptiveness to other people. Yang is obvious in business; it's about being 'out there' and actively marketing something. It is focused, daring, and enthusiastic. Yang values productivity and success. It seeks to accomplish. Yin on the other hand, is about listening and considering another person's point of view. It is intuitive and inclined to conserve, nurture and protect. Yin values process over product and relationships over goals. It seeks to connect. Creating and cultivating wealth hinges on the art of give and take. Successful negotiation in any walk of life requires a balance of yin and yang. The yang qualities of initiation and task-focus may be vital to wealth creation but they are nothing without a sense of timing, which is a yin quality.

The above findings suggest that as a person becomes more balanced within themselves so is their wealth (on all levels) likely to increase.

LGBTQ: the findings

Because the research undertaken for this chapter revealed a difference between the astronumerology of male and female actors, I decided to divide my research into two groups: those born female and those born male. (Hence there is no intersex representation).

The Moon Phases proved interesting. I had already observed that one in five musicians was born at the time of the New Moon and one in five scientists was born at the time of the Balsamic Moon. To that I can now add that one in four of the LGBTQ Sample born female was born during the Gibbous Moon Phase, a finding that did not apply to those born male. The

Random Sample was 10% and the average was 10.3%, making this a potentially significant finding.

The Signatures were also interesting. Aries-1 was high in both LGBTQ samples, and in the case of those born female, higher than any other sample. Both LGBTQ samples scored lowest in the Gemini-3 Signature. 'Those born male' was the only sample to have no representation of Gemini-3 at all. Between the two LGBTQ samples there was only one representative of the Gemini-3 Signature and that was Chaz Bono: transsexual FTM.

The Cancer-4 Signature was equally fascinating. Female actors scored only 2% for this signature whereas the male actors scored 14%: the lowest and the highest for all of the career samples respectively. Similarly of the LGBTQ samples, those born female scored only 2.8% whereas those born male scored 12.8% for Cancer-4.

Overall there was a distinctly 'yang' quality to those born female within the LGBTQ Sample: The Aries-1 Signature turned up in 28% of cases (compared to the Random 18%), the Planetary Ruler was Mars in approximately one in three cases, the number of Signatures in the First Quadrant was 39%, in Fire Signs 53%, and in Cardinal Houses 67%, all of which are higher than any other sample. All of the Twin Signatures were Cardinal, which was not evident in any other sample, including the LGBTQ sample of those born male. Date Path 1, Consonant 5, and Growth Number 11 all scored at least double that of the Random Sample. All are odd numbers, which are 'yang' (per the correspondences in chapter 10).

The New Millennium Children

These are not 'millennials', sometimes equated with Gen Y or people born between the early 1980's and the early 2000's. This Sample specifically targeted people born from January 1st 2000 onwards. They are of great interest to a numerologist because some of them have Date Chart Patterns that we have not seen for a very long time (see chapter 6). Their astro-number signatures are also interesting.

People born in the twenty-first century had the second lowest score for Aries-1. Artists are still the lowest for Aries-1 but their highest score was for Leo-5, whereas the 'millennium children' scored lower than every other sample in that signature.

Taurus-2 was the stand-out for the millennium children. This is congruent with the first digit of the millennium – 2 – but it would be wrong to think that simply because every child born in this millennium has that number in their year of birth, that this is the reason for this result. The millennium number is merely one of several; typically more than thirty factors are involved in the calculation of the Signature. Their score for Taurus-2 equals that of the scientists, which was higher than all of the other samples. We can therefore expect to see more scientists than we have seen before, including the 'people sciences' because Taurus is ruled by Venus.

The millennium children scored second highest in the Gemini-3 signature (the spiritual people were the highest). Opposite Gemini-3 on the astrological wheel is Sagittarius-9 and the millennium children scored equal lowest in that signature (with the female actors).

The other interesting score was for Aquarius-11. It equalled that of the spiritual and miscellaneous samples; these three scoring higher than all of the other samples. We might therefore see more 'spiritual scientists' in the years ahead, doing things that don't fit neatly into career boxes used by previous generations.

Added together, the three fire-sign signatures (Aries-1, Leo-5 and Sagittarius-9), scored much lower than any other sample. Random was 42% and the range between samples was 32 to 54, compared to only 22% for the millennium children. Generally speaking, they are not as 'fired up' as previous generations.

Added together, the three air-sign signatures (Gemini-3, Libra-7 and Aquarius-11), scored higher than any other sample. Random was 16% and the range between samples was 8 to 24, compared to 26% for the millennium children. Not such a big difference but could indicate that at least a quarter of the millennium children will be 'thinkers'. 24% was scored for the miscellaneous sample and if we can put these two findings together it would suggest that around one in four of the millennium children will be inclined to think outside the square. Whether or not they act on their aspirations remains to be seen.

Dementia: a preliminary study and the enriched understanding of the Numbers that came from it

Dementia is typically defined as the usually progressive deterioration of intellectual functions such as memory that can occur while other brain functions such as those controlling movement and the senses are retained. The word comes from the Latin word dement, which literally means 'mind away'.

On the internet there are several sites dedicated to information about dementia. From the Mayo Clinic site I learned that there are several types of dementia, some classified as progressive and others as conditions known to be reversible with the correct treatment.

On one site I would read the following: "Some of the most common types of dementia are linked with diseases or conditions that have a genetic component…However, it is important to remember that our genes don't cause dementia; they merely increase the risk of developing a dementia-causing condition". Your personal Numbers are similar. They don't cause dementia but certain Numbers seem to increase the risk while others seem to diminish it. Some internet sites mentioned risks, such as alcohol abuse and nutritional deficiencies. Similarly I have identified certain 'threats' encoded in one's numerology.

On one site the word 'protector' was used, and that's the same word that I would come to use in relation to the Numbers. Protectors on the physical plan of life included water, vitamins B 1, B 6, and B 12. My research indicated that there are metaphysical protectors as well.

Because dementia is mental in nature and the Numbers are also mental in nature, this study rests on the premise that they might be related. This preliminary study was based on the numerology of 50 people, who were suffering from dementia when they died. Their core numbers, growth, intensity, missing and challenge numbers, were compared with 50 people who were not suffering from dementia when they died. In a follow-up study, I extended the latter to 100 in order to check my findings.

A summary of 'threats' identified by this study:
Date Path Numbers 2, 9, and 12
Vowel Numbers 2/11, 3, 9, and 33
Consonant Numbers 5/14, 11, and 13
Name Numbers 5, 8, 10, and 11
Birth Day Numbers 2, 6, and 13
Growth Numbers 5, 7, and 11 (all odd numbers)
Intensity Number 3
Date Path Challenges 5, 7, 8, 9, and 11
Name Challenges 5 and 7
Missing Number 8

A summary of 'protectors' identified by this study:
Date Path Numbers 1/10, 4/13/22, 6/33, 7/16, and 8
Vowel Numbers 4/13, 5, 8, and 10
Consonant Numbers 4, 10, and 12
Name Numbers 4/13, 6, and 9
Birth Day Numbers 5, 7, 8, 12, and 22
Growth Numbers 3/12, 8, and 9
Intensity Number 5
Date Path Challenges 4/13, 12, 14, 15, and 16
Name Challenge 2
Missing Numbers 3, 4, and 9

Further Findings:
- Dementia sufferers were ten times more likely to have more threats in their numerology than protectors when compared to those people who did not suffer from dementia. Conversely, the latter were eighteen times more likely to have more protectors than threats in their numerology than dementia sufferers.
- Three 'nons' had no threats at all but none of the dementia sufferers had zero threats. Only dementia sufferers scored zero protectors.

It is important to bear in mind that numbers are neither 'bad' nor 'good'; they have neither 'beneficial' nor 'malign' intent. Within numerology they codify states of consciousness. Some Numbers stabilize creation whilst others de-stabilize it so that 'consciousness' (or 'creativity' if you prefer) can take its next step. Like all of the polarities that govern this world, it's a double-edged sword. For example, lots of 4's in ones' astronumerology may serve to protect the integrity of the mind but could also leave one stuck in the past. Lot's of 11's may stimulate the mind with ideas, hopes, dreams, plans, and visions of how things could be in a more ideal world, and in some cases help humanity to take a step forward in its evolution, but could also leave the individual person unable to relate to the world in the present tense.

Worksheets

Date Path Calculation

By horizontal addition:
Month + day + year of birth
= … … …
= … … … = …
= … … … = …
= … … … = …
= … … … = …
= … … … = …
By vertical addition:
Month =
The Day =
The Year = _

The **Primary** Date Path (PDP)…
The broad band and most important number to know and understand…

The **Secondary** Date Path (SDP)…
The ego's task…

The **Tertiary** Date Path (TDP)…
The theme mediated through the personality…

The **Heart** Date Path (HDP)…
The ideal that manifests as a heart-felt commitment to something…

The **Quintessential** Date Path (QDP)…
The spiritual ideal behind the date path pattern…

DATE PATH =

Are there any numbers missing in the sequence?

Are there any master numbers straining the nervous system?

Are there any karmic numbers?

Are any of the sub-elements repeated?

Vowel, Consonant, and Name Calculation Sheet

The Table of English Letter Correspondences

1	2	3	4	5	6	7	8	9
A	B	C	D	E	F	G	H	I
J	K	L	M	N	O	P	Q	R
S	T	U	V	W	X	Y	Z	

Original Name

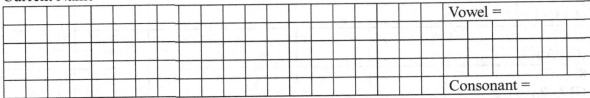

Vowel =

Consonant =

NAME =

Current Name

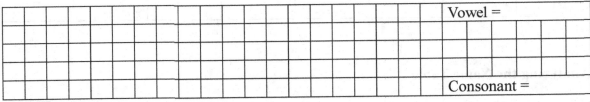

Vowel =

Consonant =

NAME =

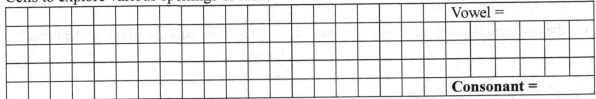

Vowel =

Consonant =

NAME =

Cells to explore various spellings or ideas

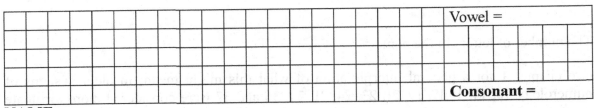

Vowel =

Consonant =

NAME =

Vowel =

Consonant =

NAME =

Name Table

Atop each column write one component of the name. Then separate the letters into their numerical equivalents and total each row:

Letter/ Number	Name:	Name:	Name:	Name:	Name:	Total	Bench mark
1. (A,J,S)							4
2. (B,K,T)							2
3. (C,L,U)							3
4. (D,M,V)							2
5. (E,N,W)							5
6. (F,O,X)							2
7. (G,P,Y)							2
8. (H,Q,Z)							1
9. (I,R)							4

Analyzing the Name Table

Is a link provided for the date path?

Are the numbers that are missing in the date of birth represented somewhere in the name?

Is there an intensity number?

The number of letters in the name =

(see chapter 1 for a general interpretation of what this might mean; in older systems of numerology 10, 14, 15,17, 19, 21, 23, 24, 31, 32, 36 and 37 were considered more fortunate than others)

Challenges Worksheet

<u>The 4 date path challenges</u> (note both big and small, where different)

1. 1st challenge:
2. 2nd challenge:
3. Whole-life challenge:
4. Polarity challenge:

<u>The 3 challenges within the name</u>

1. The vowel challenge, coming from the soul:
2. The consonant challenge, from one's ancestry:
3. The name challenge: the test of one's vitality:

<u>The challenge of missing numbers</u>
comparing the date chart with the name chart:

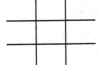   

Sorting and Prioritizing the Challenges

Are there any karmic challenges (13, 14, 16, or 19)?

Challenging Core Numbers: repeated core numbers

Challenged core numbers: is one or more of the core numbers also a challenge?

Are there any numbers missing in both the date chart and name chart?

What is the most frequently occurring number in the challenge chart (below)?

Are there any master numbers straining the nervous system?

Similar groupings and miscellaneous modifiers:

Challenges Chart

Challenge	Where it appears	Totals
0		
1 and 10		
2		
3 and 12		
4		
5		
6		
7		
8		
9		
Karmic Numbers		
Master Numbers		

Life Cycles for Date Path 1

Current Name:
Original Name:
D.O.B:
Date Path:
Place and time of birth:
Current date and age:

Birth/ Personal Yr 1 Year:	Age 9	Age 18	Age27	Age 36	Age 45	Age54	Age 63
Age 1 PY 2	Age 10	Age 19	Age28	Age37	Age46	Age55	Age64
Age2 PY 3	Age11	Age20	Age29	Age38	Age47	Age56	Age65
Age3 PY 4	Age12	Age21	Age30	Age39	Age48	Age57	Age66
Age 4 PY 5	Age13	Age22	Age31	Age40	Age49	Age58	Age67
Age 5 PY 6	Age14	Age23	Age32	Age41	Age50	Age59	Age68
Age6 PY 7	Age15	Age24	Age33	Age42	Age51	Age60	Age69
Age7 PY 8	Age 16	Age 25	Age 34	Age 43	Age 52	Age61	Age70
Age 8 PY 9	Age17	Age26	Age 35	Age 44	Age 53	Age 62	Age 71

Growth Cycle

| 9 | 18 | 27 | 36 | 45 | 54 | 63 | 72 |

Growth Number from first name:

Maturity Number

First Base Cycle
Age: 0-26
Number:

Birthday Base Cycle
Age: 27-53
Number:

Home Base Cycle
Age: 54 onwards
Number:

First Attainment
(Achievement)
0-35
Number:

2nd Att
36-44
Number:

3rd Att.
45-53
Number:

4th Attainment
(Quest)
54 onwards
Number:

1st Challenge: 2nd Challenge: Polarity Challenge:
Whole Life Challenge:
Vowel, Consonant, and Name Challenges:

Astrological Data:
Rising Sign:
Sun Sign:
Progressed Sun:
Moon Sign:
Progressed Moon … … … … … … … 27/28 Emerging … … … … … … … … 54/55 Emerging
Moon Phase at birth:
Lunar Nodes:
Lunar Node Cycle … … … 18.6 … … … … … … … …37.2 … … … … … … … 55.8 …
Saturn Return … … … … … … … … … 29 … … … … … … … … … … … … … … … 59
Uranus … … … … … … … … … … … … … … … … … … … 42 (Opposition)
Jupiter **… …** 12 … … … … … … 24 … … … … …36 … … … … … …47/48 … … … …59/60 …

Life Cycles for Date Path 2

Current Name:
Original Name:
D.O.B:
Date Path:
Place and time of birth:
Current date and age

Birth/ Personal Yr 2 Year:	Age 9	Age 18	Age 27	Age 36	Age 45	Age 54	Age 63
Age 1 PY 3	Age 10	Age 19	Age 28	Age 37	Age 46	Age 55	Age 64
Age 2 PY 4	Age 11	Age 20	Age 29	Age 38	Age 47	Age 56	Age 65
Age 3 PY 5	Age 12	Age 21	Age 30	Age 39	Age 48	Age 57	Age 66
Age 4 PY 6	Age 13	Age 22	Age 31	Age 40	Age 49	Age 58	Age 67
Age 5 PY 7	Age 14	Age 23	Age 32	Age 41	Age 50	Age 59	Age 68
Age 6 PY 8	Age 15	Age 24	Age 33	Age 42	Age 51	Age 60	Age 69
Age 7 PY 9	Age 16	Age 25	Age 34	Age 43	Age 52	Age 61	Age 70
Age 8 PY 1	Age 17	Age 26	Age 35	Age 44	Age 53	Age 62	Age 71

Growth Cycle

        9   18   27   36   45   54   63   72

Growth number from first name:

Maturity Number:

First Base Cycle
Age: 0-25
Number:

Birthday Base Cycle
Age: 26-52
Number:

Home Base Cycle
Age: 53 onwards
Number:

First Attainment
(Achievement)
0-34
Number:

2nd Att
35-43
Number:

3rd Att.
44-52
Number:

4th Attainment
(Quest)
53 onwards
Number:

1st Challenge: 2nd Challenge: Polarity Challenge:
Whole Life Challenge:
Vowel, Consonant and Name Challenges:

Astrological Data:
Rising Sign:
Sun Sign:
Progressed Sun:
Moon Sign:
Progressed Moon … … … … … … … … …. 27/28 Emerging … … … … … … … … … 54/55 Emerging
Moon Phase at birth:
Lunar Nodes:
Lunar Node Cycle … … … 18.6 … … … … … … … … … … 37.2 … … … … … … … … … … 55.8 …
Saturn Return … … … … … … … … …. 29 … … … … … … … … … … … … … … … 59
Uranus … 42 (Opposition) …
Jupiter … … 12 … … … … … … 24 … … … … … … 36 … … … … … … … 47/48 … … … … 59/60 …

365

Life Cycles for Date Path 3

Current Name:
Original Name:
D.O.B:
Date Path:
Place and time of birth:
Current date and age:

Birth/ Personal Yr 3 Year:	Age 9	Age 18	Age 27	Age 36	Age 45	Age 54	Age 63
Age 1 PY 4	Age 10	Age 19	Age 28	Age 37	Age 46	Age 55	Age 64
Age 2 PY 5	Age 11	Age 20	Age 29	Age 38	Age 47	Age 56	Age 65
Age 3 PY 6	Age 12	Age 21	Age 30	Age 39	Age 48	Age 57	Age 66
Age 4 PY 7	Age 13	Age 22	Age 31	Age 40	Age 49	Age 58	Age 67
Age 5 PY 8	Age 14	Age 23	Age 32	Age 41	Age 50	Age 59	Age 68
Age 6 PY 9	Age 15	Age 24	Age 33	Age 42	Age 51	Age 60	Age 69
Age 7 PY 1 *	Age 16	Age 25	Age 34	Age 43	Age 52	Age 61	Age 70
Age 8 PY 2	Age 17	Age 26	Age 35	Age 44	Age 53	Age 62	Age 71

Growth Cycle

	9	18	27	36	45	54	63	72

Growth number from first name:

Maturity Number:

First Base Cycle
Age: 0-24
Number:

Birthday Base Cycle
Age: 25-51
Number:

Home Base Cycle
Age: 52 onwards
Number:

First Attainment
(Achievement)
0-33
Number:

2nd Att
34-42
Number:

3rd Att.
43-51
Number:

4th Attainment
(Quest)
52 onwards
Number:

1st Challenge: 2nd Challenge: Polarity Challenge:
Whole Life Challenge:
Vowel, Consonant and Name Challenges:

Astrological Data:
Rising Sign:
Sun Sign:
Progressed Sun:
Moon Sign:
Progressed Moon … … … … … … … … …. 27/28 Emerging … … … … … … … … … 54/55 Emerging
Moon Phase at birth:
Lunar Nodes:
Lunar Node Cycle … … … 18.6 … … … … … … … … … … 37.2 … … … … … … … … … … … … 55.8 …
Saturn Return … … … … … … … … … … 29 … … … … … … … … … … … … … … … … … … … 59
Uranus … 42 (Opposition) …
Jupiter … … 12 … … … … … … 24 … … … … … … 36 … … … … … … 47/48 … … … … 59/60 …

Life Cycles for Date Path 4

Current Name:
Original Name:
D.O.B:
Date Path:
Place and time of birth:
Current date and age:

Birth/ Personal Yr 4 Year:	Age 9	Age 18	Age 27	Age 36	Age 45	Age 54	Age 63
Age 1 PY 5	Age 10	Age 19	Age 28	Age 37	Age 46	Age 55	Age 64
Age 2 PY 6	Age 11	Age 20	Age 29	Age 38	Age 47	Age 56	Age 65
Age 3 PY 7	Age 12	Age 21	Age 30	Age 39	Age 48	Age 57	Age 66
Age 4 PY 8	Age 13	Age 22	Age 31	Age 40	Age 49	Age 58	Age 67
Age 5 PY 9	Age 14	Age 23	Age 32	Age 41	Age 50	Age 59	Age 68
Age 6 PY 1 *	Age 15	Age 24	Age 33	Age 42	Age 51	Age 60	Age 69
Age 7 PY 2	Age 16	Age 25	Age 34	Age 43	Age 52	Age 61	Age 70
Age 8 PY 3	Age 17	Age 26	Age 35	Age 44	Age 53	Age 62	Age 71

Growth Cycle
9   18   27   36   45   54   63   72
Growth number from first name:

Maturity Number:

First Base Cycle Age: 0-23 Number:	Birthday Base Cycle Age: 24-59 Number:	Home Base Cycle Age: 60 onwards Number:

First Attainment
(Achievement)
0-32
Number:

2nd Att   3rd Att.
33-41   42-50
Number: Number:

4th Attainment
(Quest)
51 onwards
Number:

1st Challenge: 2nd Challenge: Polarity Challenge:
Whole Life Challenge:
Vowel, Consonant and Name Challenges:

<u>Astrological Data:</u>
Rising Sign:
Sun Sign:
Progressed Sun:
Moon Sign:
Progressed Moon … … … … … … … …. 27/28 Emerging … … … … … … … … 54/55 Emerging
Moon Phase at birth:
Lunar Nodes:
Lunar Node Cycle … … … 18.6 … … … … … … … … … 37.2 … … … … … … … … … … … 55.8 …
Saturn Return … … … … … … … … … 29 … … … … … … … … … … … … … … … … … … 59
Uranus … 42 (Opposition) …
Jupiter … … 12 … … … … … … 24 … … … … … … … 36 … … … … … … … 47/48 … … … … … 59/60 …

Life Cycles for Date Path 5

Current Name:
Original Name:
D.O.B:
Date Path:
Place and time of birth:
Current date and age:

Birth/ Personal Yr 5 Year:	Age 9	Age 18	Age 27	Age 36	Age 45	Age 54	Age 63
Age 1 PY 6	Age 10	Age 19	Age 28	Age 37	Age 46	Age 55	Age 64
Age 2 PY 7	Age 11	Age 20	Age 29	Age 38	Age 47	Age 56	Age 65
Age 3 PY 8	Age 12	Age 21	Age 30	Age 39	Age 48	Age 57	Age 66
Age 4 PY 9	Age 13	Age 22	Age 31	Age 40	Age 49	Age 58	Age 67
Age 5 PY 1 *	Age 14	Age 23	Age 32	Age 41	Age 50	Age 59	Age 68
Age 6 PY 2	Age 15	Age 24	Age 33	Age 42	Age 51	Age 60	Age 69
Age 7 PY 3	Age 16	Age 25	Age 34	Age 43	Age 52	Age 61	Age 70
Age 8 PY 4	Age 17	Age 26	Age 35	Age 44	Age 53	Age 62	Age 71

Growth Cycle

| 9 | 18 | 27 | 36 | 45 | 54 | 63 | 72 |

Growth Number from first name:

Maturity Number:

First Base Cycle
Age: 0-31
Number:

Birthday Base Cycle
Age: 32-58
Number:

Home Base Cycle
Age: 59 onwards
Number:

First Attainment
(Achievement)
0-31
Number:

2nd Att
32-40
Number:

3rd Att.
41-49
Number:

4th Attainment
(Quest)
50 onwards
Number:

1st Challenge: 2nd Challenge: Polarity Challenge:
Whole Life Challenge:
Vowel, Consonant and Name Challenges:

Astrological Data:
Rising Sign:
Sun Sign:
Progressed Sun:
Moon Sign:
Progressed Moon … … … … … … … … …. 27/28 Emerging … … … … … … … … … 54/55 Emerging
Moon Phase at birth:
Lunar Nodes:
Lunar Node Cycle … … … 18.6 … … … … … … … … … 37.2 … … … … … … … … … … … 55.8 …
Saturn Return … … … … … … … … … 29 … … … … … … … … … … … … … … … … … … … 59
Uranus … 42 (Opposition) …
Jupiter … … 12 … … … … … … 24 … … … … … … 36 … … … … … … … 47/48 … … … … 59/60 …

368

Life Cycles for Date Path 6

Current Name:
Original Name:
D.O.B:
Date Path:
Place and time of birth:
Current date and age:

Birth/ Personal Yr 6 Year:	Age 9	Age 18	Age 27	Age 36	Age 45	Age 54	Age 63
Age 1 **PY 7**	Age 10	Age 19	Age 28	Age 37	Age 46	Age 55	Age 64
Age 2 **PY 8**	Age 11	Age 20	Age 29	Age 38	Age 47	Age 56	Age 65
Age 3 **PY 9**	Age 12	Age21	Age 30	Age 39	Age 48	Age 57	Age 66
Age 4 **PY 1 ***	Age 13	Age 22	Age 31	Age 40	Age 49	Age 58	Age 67
Age 5 **PY 2**	Age 14	Age 23	Age 32	Age 41	Age 50	Age 59	Age 68
Age 6 **PY 3**	Age 15	Age 24	Age 33	Age 42	Age 51	Age 60	Age 69
Age 7 **PY 4**	Age 16	Age 25	Age 34	Age 43	Age 52	Age 61	Age 70
Age 8 **PY 5**	Age 17	Age 26	Age 35	Age 44	Age 53	Age 62	Age 71

Growth Cycle

    9   18   27   36   45   54   63   72

Growth number from first name:

Maturity Number:

First Base Cycle
Age: 0-30
Number:

Birthday Base Cycle
Age: 31-57
Number:

Home Base Cycle
Age: 58 onwards
Number:

First Attainment
(Achievement)
0-30
Number:

2nd Att
31-39
Number:

3rd Att.
40-48
Number:

4th Attainment
(Quest)
49 onwards
Number:

1st Challenge: 2nd Challenge: Polarity Challenge:
Whole Life Challenge:
Vowel, Consonant and Name Challenges:

Astrological Data:
Rising Sign:
Sun Sign:
Progressed Sun:
Moon Sign:
Progressed Moon … … … … … … … …. 27/28 Emerging … … … … … … …. 54/55 Emerging
Moon Phase at Birth:
Lunar Nodes:
Lunar Node Cycle … … … 18.6 … … … … … … … … … … 37.2 … … … … … … … … … … 55.8 …
Saturn Return … … … … … … … … …. 29 … … … … … … … …, … … … … … … … … 59
Uranus … … … … … … … … … … … … … … … … … … … 42 (Opposition) …
Jupiter … … 12 … … … … … … 24 … … … … … … 36 … … … … … … …, … 47/48 … … … … … 59/60 …

Life Cycles Date Path 7

Current Name:
Original Name:
D.O.B:
Date Path:
Place and time of birth:
Current date and age:

Birth/ Personal Yr 7 Year:	Age 9	Age 18	Age 27	Age 36	Age 45	Age 54	Age 63
Age 1 PY 8	Age 10	Age 19	Age 28	Age 37	Age 46	Age 55	Age 64
Age 2 PY 9	Age 11	Age 20	Age 29	Age 38	Age 47	Age 56	Age 65
Age 3 PY 1 *	Age 12	Age 21	Age 30	Age 39	Age 48	Age 57	Age 66
Age 4 PY 2	Age 13	Age 22	Age 31	Age 40	Age 49	Age 58	Age 67
Age 5 PY 3	Age 14	Age 23	Age 32	Age 41	Age 50	Age 59	Age 68
Age 6 PY 4	Age 15	Age 24	Age 33	Age 42	Age 51	Age 60	Age 69
Age 7 PY 5	Age 16	Age 25	Age 34	Age 43	Age 52	Age 61	Age 70
Age 8 PY 6	Age 17	Age 26	Age 35	Age 44	Age 53	Age 62	Age 71

Growth Cycle

| 9 | 18 | 27 | 36 | 45 | 54 | 63 | 72 |

Growth number from first name:

Maturity Number:

First Base Cycle
Age: 0-29
Number:

Birthday Base Cycle
Age: 30-56
Number:

Home Base Cycle
Age: 57 onwards
Number:

First Attainment
(Achievement)
0-29
Number:

2nd Att
30-38
Number:

3rd Att.
39-47
Number:

4th Attainment
(Quest)
48 onwards
Number:

1st Challenge:

2nd Challenge:

Polarity Challenge:

Whole Life Challenge:
Vowel, Consonant and Name Challenges:

Astrological Data:
Rising Sign:
Sun Sign:
Progressed Sun:
Moon Sign:
Progressed Moon … … … … … … … … …. 27/28 Emerging … … … … … … … … … 54/55 Emerging
Moon Phase at birth:
Lunar Nodes:
Lunar Node Cycle … … … 18.6 … … … … … … … … … 37.2 … … … … … … … … … … … 55.8 …
Saturn Return … … … … … … … … … … 29 … … … … … … … … … … … … … … … … … 59
Uranus … 42 (Opposition) …
Jupiter … … 12 … … … … … … 24 … … … … … … 36 … … … … … … … … 47/48 … … … … … 59/60 …

Life Cycles for Date Path 8

Current Name:
Original Name:
D.O.B:
Date Path:
Place and time of birth:
Current date & age:

Birth/ Personal Yr 8 Year:	Age 9	Age 18	Age 27	Age 36	Age 45	Age 54	Age 63
Age 1 PY 9	Age 10	Age 19	Age 28	Age 37	Age 46	Age 55	Age 64
Age 2 PY 1 *	Age 11	Age 20	Age 29	Age 38	Age 47	Age 56	Age 65
Age 3 PY 2	Age 12	Age 21	Age 30	Age 39	Age 48	Age 57	Age 66
Age 4 PY 3	Age 13	Age 22	Age 31	Age 40	Age 49	Age 58	Age 67
Age 5 PY 4	Age 14	Age 23	Age 32	Age 41	Age 50	Age 59	Age 68
Age 6 PY 5	Age 15	Age 24	Age 33	Age 42	Age 51	Age 60	Age 69
Age 7 PY 6	Age 16	Age 25	Age 34	Age 43	Age 52	Age 61	Age 70
Age 8 PY 7	Age 17	Age 26	Age 35	Age 44	Age 53	Age 62	Age 71

Growth Cycle

9   18   27   36   45   54   63   72

Growth number from first name:

Maturity Number:

First Base Cycle
Age: 0-28
Number:

Birthday Base Cycle
Age: 29-55
Number:

Home Base Cycle
Age: 56 onwards
Number:

First Attainment
(Achievement)
0-28
Number:

2nd Att
29-37
Number:

3rd Att.
38-46
Number:

4th Attainment
(Quest)
47 onwards
Number:

1st Challenge: 2nd Challenge: Polarity Challenge:
Whole Life Challenge:
Vowel, Consonant and Name Challenges:

Astrological Data:
Rising Sign:
Sun Sign:
Progressed Sun:
Moon Sign:
Progressed Moon … … … … … … … … …. 27/28 Emerging … … … … … … … … … 54/55 Emerging
Moon Phase at birth:
Lunar Nodes:
Lunar Node Cycle … … … 18.6 … … … … … … … … … 37.2 … … … … … … … … … … … 55.8 …
Saturn Return … … … … … … … … … … 29 … … … … … … … … … … … … … … … … 59
Uranus … 42 (Opposition) …
Jupiter … … 12 … … … … … … … 24 … … … … … … 36 … … … … … … ,.. 47/48 … … … … … 59/60 …

Life Cycles for Date Path 9

Current Name:
Original Name:
D.O.B:
Date Path:
Place and time of birth:
Current date and age:

Birth/ Personal Yr 9 Year:	Age 9	Age 18	Age 27	Age 36	Age 45	Age 54	Age 63
Age 1 PY 1 *	Age 10	Age 19	Age 28	Age 37	Age 46	Age 55	Age 64
Age 2 PY 2	Age 11	Age 20	Age 29	Age 38	Age 47	Age 56	Age 65
Age 3 PY 3	Age 12	Age 21	Age 30	Age 39	Age 48	Age 57	Age 66
Age 4 PY 4	Age 13	Age 22	Age 31	Age 40	Age 49	Age 58	Age 67
Age 5 PY 5	Age 14	Age 23	Age 32	Age 41	Age 50	Age 59	Age 68
Age 6 PY 6	Age 15	Age 24	Age 33	Age 42	Age 51	Age 60	Age 69
Age 7 PY 7	Age 16	Age 25	Age 34	Age 43	Age 52	Age 61	Age 70
Age 8 PY 8	Age 17	Age 26	Age 35	Age 44	Age 53	Age 62	Age 71

Growth Cycle

9	18	27	36	45	54	63	72

Growth number from first name:

Maturity Number:

First Base Cycle
Age: 0-27
Number:

Birthday Base Cycle
Age: 28-54
Number:

Home Base Cycle
Age: 55 onwards
Number:

First Attainment
(Achievement)
0-27
Number:

2nd Att
28-36
Number:

3rd Att.
37-45
Number:

4th Attainment
(Quest)
46 onwards
Number:

1st Challenge:

2nd Challenge:

Polarity Challenge:

Whole Life Challenge:
Vowel, Consonant and Name
Challenges:

Astrological Data:
Rising Sign:
Sun Sign:
Progressed Sun:
Moon Sign:
Progressed Moon … … … … … … … … …. 27/28 Emerging … … … … … … … … … 54/55 Emerging
Moon Phase at birth:
Lunar Nodes:
Lunar Node Cycle … … … 18.6 … … … … … … … … … … 37.2 … … … … … … … … … … … 55.8 …
Saturn Return … … … … … … … … … 29 … … … … … … … … … … … … … … … … … 59
Uranus … 42 (Opposition) …
Jupiter … … 12 … … … … … … 24 … … … … … … 36 … … … … … … … 47/48 … … … … … … 59/60 …

Over-70's Data Sheet
Current Name:
Original Name:
D.O.B:
Date Path:
Place and time of birth:
Current date and age

Age 72 Personal Year: Year:	Age 81	Age 90	Age 99	Age 108	Age 117	Age 126	Age 135
Age 73 **PY**	Age 82	Age 91	Age 100	Age 109	Age 118	Age 127	Age 136
Age 74 **PY**	Age 83	Age 92	Age 101	Age 110	Age 119	Age 128	Age 137
Age 75 **PY**	Age 84	Age 93	Age 102	Age 111	Age 120	Age 129	Age 138
Age 76 **PY**	Age 85	Age 94	Age 103	Age 112	Age 121	Age 130	Age 139
Age 77 **PY**	Age 86	Age 95	Age 104	Age 113	Age 122	Age 131	Age 140
Age 78 **PY**	Age 87	Age 96	Age 105	Age 114	Age 123	Age 132	Age 141
Age 79 **PY**	Age 88	Age 97	Age 106	Age 115	Age 124	Age 133	Age 142
Age 80 **PY**	Age 89	Age 98	Age 107	Age 116	Age 125	Age 134	Age 143

Growth Cycle
    72   81   90   99   108   117   126   135
Growth Number (first name):
Maturity Number:
Home Base Number:
Quest Number:

Whole Life Challenge:
Polarity Challenge:
Vowel, Consonant and Name Challenges:

<u>Astrological Data:</u>
Rising Sign:
Sun Sign:
Progressed Sun:
Moon Sign:
Progressed Moon:
Moon Phase at birth:
Progressed Moon: 82 … … … … … … … … … … … … … 109 … … … … … … … … … … … … … … … 136
Lunar Nodes:
Lunar Node Cycle: 74.4 … … … 93 … … … … … … … … … … … 111.6 … …, … … … … … … … … 130.2

Saturn Return 88.5 … … … … … … … … … … … … … … … 118 …
Uranus Return 84
Jupiter Cycle ~ 84 … … … … … … 96 … … … … … … 108 … … … … … … 120 … … … … … … 132 … … … … … 144

Astro-Number Signature Worksheet

Number	Where it appears		Totals	
1				
2				
3				
4				
5				
6				
7				
8				
9				
10				
11				
12				

Dominant Element

Air	Earth	Water	Fire
3 –	2 –	4 –	1 –
7 –	6 –	8 –	5 –
11 –	10 –	12 –	9 –
Total =	Total =	Total =	Total =

Dominant Modality

Cardinal	Fixed	Mutable
1 –	2 –	3 –
4 –	5 –	6 –
7 –	8 –	9 –
10 –	11 –	12 –
Total =	Total =	Total =

Source Notes

The author acknowledges with gratitude the work of Lois Rodden and the data system that she established at www.astrodatabank.com, and the astrologers who have maintained the site since her passing. Each has focused on providing accurate date, time, and place information, so that an accurate horoscope can be cast.

However even with AA Rated Data – birth certificate in hand - the name given is not always reliable for the purposes of numerology; for that, Wikipedia has been handy. The author is grateful to all of the persons who have contributed to that Wikipedia with updates about the original name and the story behind changes of name.

In Conclusion

By 2015 I realized that *Pan's Script* had lead me on a dance around the Wheel, step by step:

Aries-1: A whoosh of fabulously enthusiastic energy: what I would call the 'Number Wizardry' phase

Taurus-2: Carefully comparing and contrasting the main two systems of numerology

Gemini-3: Studying biographies and autobiographies and noting trends

Cancer-4: Fleshing out such biographies through real people who had asked me to write reports for them

Leo-5: The first draft of this book, initially called: *Pan's Script, Pyramid Astro-Numerology: A Complete, Easy-To-Use, Model and System,* including esoteric correspondences that relate to the great pyramid of Giza

Virgo-6: A more refined draft, called *Pan's Script for People who Love the Earth.* There was more emphasis on my Celtic heritage in this draft.

Libra-7: Stripping everything back to create a more publishable book, from 600 to 400 pages!

Scorpio-8: Integrating case studies from the past with people currently in the news

Sagittarius-9: *Pan's Script: Your Signature as written in the Stars, Date of Birth and Name* was ready for publication

Capricorn-10: Consolidating the body of statistics

Aquarius-11: Deciding to self-publish with Balboa so that the book was available to people and yet still open to new developments

Pisces-12: Revising earlier research and deciding which to let go and which to contemplate further.

Such is the Creative Cycle of Life!

Index

W

Appendices

The following appendices to Pan's Script are available upon enquiry by email from elkiewhite@gmail.com

Appendix 1: The Date Path: 99 additional examples and detailed bibliography, plus new examples for date paths 1-12.

Appendix 2: Vowels, Consonants, and Names with several examples, a bibliography, and a comparison with Chaldean numerology.

Appendix 3: The Song of the Land and Her Script: an explanation of the letter placements within the circle.

Appendix 4: The Song of the Land and Her Script, part 2: Ogam and Runes

Appendix 5: Personality Types, Decans and Letters, Colours, Crystals and Minerals, some basic palmistry, and a Table of Correspondences.

Appendix 6: The Magic Square and the Cross within the Circle, with a complete list of examples used in the Pan's Script Data Pool.

Appendix 7: The Date Chart, Wheel of Life, Potent Partnerships, and Vedic numerology in comparison with Pan's Script.

Appendix 8: The Great Pyramid of Giza, Sacred Geometry, the Rings of Gaia, the 4 Operations, 4 Functions, and 4 Elements within the 4 Quadrants of the Wheel of Life.

Appendix 9: Starting Every Year on the Right Track: Your Personal Years, Month by Month, and Week by Week.

Appendix 10: Pan's Script and the Tarot, through the stories of the Mabinogion.

Appendix 11: A Guide to filling in the Data Sheet in the Worksheets section of Pan's Script; including the Progressed Lunation and several other astrological cycles.